Debts Unpaid

Power struggles between debtors and creditors about unpaid debts have animated the history of economic transformation from the emergence of capitalist relations to the recent global financial crashes. Illuminating how ordinary people fought for economic justice in Mexico from the eve of independence to the early 2000s, this study argues that conflicts over small-scale debts were a stress test for an emerging economic order that took shape against a backdrop of enormous political and social change. Drawing on nearly 1,500 debt conflicts unearthed from Mexican archives, Louise E. Walker explores rapidly changing ideas and practices about property rights, contract law, and economic information. This combination of richly detailed archival research with big historical and theoretical interpretations raises provocative new questions about the moral economy of the credit relationship and the shifting line between exploitation and opportunity in the world of everyday exchange.

Louise E. Walker is Professor of History at Northeastern University. Her previous publications include the prize-winning *Waking from the Dream: Mexico's Middle Classes After 1968*.

CAMBRIDGE LATIN AMERICAN STUDIES

General Editors
KRIS LANE, Tulane University
MATTHEW RESTALL, Pennsylvania State University

Editor Emeritus
HERBERT S. KLEIN
Gouverneur Morris Emeritus Professor of History, Columbia University and Hoover Research Fellow, Stanford University

Other Books in the Series

139. *Hispanic Technocracy: From Fascism to Catholic Authoritarianism in Spain, Argentina, and Chile, 1945–1991*, Daniel Gunnar Kressel
138. *The Power of Dissent: The Power of Dissent*, Sergio Serulnikov
137. *The Coming of the Kingdom: The Muisca, Catholic Reform, and Spanish Colonialism in the New Kingdom of Granada*, Juan F. Cobo Betancourt
136. *The Shamanism of Eco-Tourism: History and Ontology Among the Makushi in Guyana*, James Andrew Whitaker
135. *Fallen from Heaven: The Enduring Tradition of Europeans as Gods in the Americas*, Nicholas Griffiths
134. *Global Servants of the Spanish King: Mobility and Cosmopolitanism in the Early Modern Spanish Empire*, Adolfo Polo y La Borda
133. *Plebeian Consumers: Global Connections, Local Trade, and Foreign Goods in Nineteenth-Century Colombia*, Ana María Otero-Cleves
132. *Peopling for Profit in Imperial Brazil: Directed Migrations and the Business of Nineteenth-Century Colonization*, José Juan Pérez Meléndez
131. *Being the Heart of the World: The Pacific and the Fashioning of the Self in New Spain, 1513–1641*, Nino Vallen
130. *A Tale of Two Granadas: Custom, Community, and Citizenship in the Spanish Empire, 1568–1668*, Max Deardorff
129. *A Colonial Book Market: Peruvian Print Culture in the Age of Enlightenment*, Agnes Gehbald
128. *Veracruz and the Caribbean in the Seventeenth Century*, Joseph M. H. Clark
127. *We, the King: Creating Royal Legislation in the Sixteenth-Century Spanish New World*, Adrian Masters
126. *A History of Chile 1808–2018*, second edition, William F. Sater and Simon Collier
125. *The Dread Plague and the Cow Killers: The Politics of Animal Disease in Mexico and the World*, Thomas Rath
124. *Islands in the Lake: Environment and Ethnohistory in Xochimilco, New Spain*, Richard M. Conway

(Continued after the Index)

Debts Unpaid

Two Centuries of Trouble and Conflict in Mexico's Economy

LOUISE E. WALKER
Northeastern University

Shaftesbury Road, Cambridge CB2 8EA, United Kingdom

One Liberty Plaza, 20th Floor, New York, NY 10006, USA

477 Williamstown Road, Port Melbourne, VIC 3207, Australia

314–321, 3rd Floor, Plot 3, Splendor Forum, Jasola District Centre,
New Delhi – 110025, India

103 Penang Road, #05-06/07, Visioncrest Commercial, Singapore 238467

Cambridge University Press is part of Cambridge University Press & Assessment,
a department of the University of Cambridge.

We share the University's mission to contribute to society through the pursuit of
education, learning and research at the highest international levels of excellence.

www.cambridge.org
Information on this title: www.cambridge.org/9781009360449

DOI: 10.1017/9781009360425

© Louise E. Walker 2026

This publication is in copyright. Subject to statutory exception and to the provisions
of relevant collective licensing agreements, no reproduction of any part may take
place without the written permission of Cambridge University Press & Assessment.

When citing this work, please include a reference to the DOI 10.1017/9781009360425

First published 2026

A catalogue record for this publication is available from the British Library

*A Cataloging-in-Publication data record for this book is available from the Library
of Congress*

ISBN 978-1-009-36044-9 Hardback
ISBN 978-1-009-36043-2 Paperback

Cambridge University Press & Assessment has no responsibility for the persistence
or accuracy of URLs for external or third-party internet websites referred to in this
publication and does not guarantee that any content on such websites is, or will
remain, accurate or appropriate.

For EU product safety concerns, contact us at Calle de José Abascal,
56, 1°, 28003 Madrid, Spain, or email eugpsr@cambridge.org.

For my father, Charles J. Walker

Contents

List of Figures	*page* ix
List of Tables	xi
Acknowledgements	xiii

	Introduction	1
	Conflicts Between Debtors and Creditors	3
	Chronological Horizons	10
	Sources and Methods	13
	Structure of the Book	17
1	Little Debts: Justice and Citizenship in Small Claims, 1810s–1860s	20
	A Contractual Society	21
	The Judicial City	24
	Mediating Debt Disputes in the *Juicios Verbales*	32
	The Parameters of Economic Justice	39
	Continuity and Change After 1812	46
	The Humdrum as Historic	52
2	Broken Contracts: Precaution and Risk in Litigation and Law, 1860s–1870s	53
	Debt Litigation on the Rise	55
	Trading Information with Friends and Strangers	61
	Risk, Uncertainty, and the *Providencias Precautorias*	71
	Property Seizure and the Politics of Property Rights	76
	Avoiding Obligations and Litigating Trust	82
	Law and Economy: Making Rules for Unpaid Debts	88
	Between Two Worlds	96

Contents

3 Unworthy: Economic Information in Credit Reports,
   1880s–1920s   99
    Credit Reports and the New Horizon of Bureaucratic Trust   100
    Banamex and Financial Exclusion   107
    Evaluating Creditworthiness   111
    Institutional Lending in a Time of Revolution   120
    Defining the Boundaries of Economic Honour   124
    Economic Information from Gossip to Bureaucracy   131

4 Bad Cheques: Property Crime and the Moral Economy of
   Financialisation, 1930s–1980s   134
    The Criminalisation of Uncovered Cheques   135
    Economic Citizenship and Financial Inclusion   141
    Misuse, Malfeasance, and the Growing Pains of
      Financial Modernity   149
    Social Inertia, Friction, and the Latent Coercion
      of Financialisation   153
    From Delinquency to Vulnerability   164

5 Asking for Help: Letters About Fairness and
   Dispossession, 1990s–2000s   168
    From Citizens to Financial Service Users   170
    Institutional Borrowing in an Era of Crisis   176
    Indebtedness and Dehumanisation   180
    Economic Storytelling and the Power of the President   189
    Usury and the New Purgatory   200
    The Credit Bureau and the Black List   206
    Villains and Victims   211

  Conclusion   213

Notes   219
References   275
Index   297

Figures

1.1	Felipe Fernandes v Paulino Olivér for 10 pesos in December 1842	*page* 34
1.2	Juan Arturo Ricardi v Andrés Pando for 100 pesos in May 1856	37
2.1	Questions for witnesses in Ángel Navarro v Antonio Picazo, November 1878	64
2.2	Invoice documenting ownership of furniture, November 1878	85
3.1	Credit report on Manuel León, August 1902	115
3.2	Credit report on E. B. Welch, February 1920	116
4.1	'Elegant' bank teller, ca. 1935–1940	144
4.2	Bank bus on city streets, April 1962	145
5.1	'Without Credit: To the Hanged Man', advertisement in *El Economista*, December 2001	185
5.2	'Pursued by Past Debts', announcement in *La Jornada*, October 2007	208

Tables

1.1	Sample and data universe of *juicios verbales*, 1813–1863	page 24
1.2	Mean amounts and gender of litigants in *juicios verbales*, 1813–1863	26
1.3	Value of a peso in *juicios verbales*, selected examples, 1813–1861	28
1.4	Rate of litigants in *juicios verbales* vis-à-vis the Mexico City population, 1813–1862	31
2.1	Sample of *providencia precautoria* petitions, 1836–1878	58
2.2	Amounts disputed and gender of plaintiffs in *providencias precautorias*, 1836–1878	73
2.3	Amounts disputed and gender of defendants in *providencias precautorias*, 1836–1878	73
2.4	Value of a peso in the 1860s and 1870s	74
3.1	Sample of R. G. Dun credit reports, 1899–1923	106
3.2	Sample of R. G. Dun credit reports, before and after the revolution	106
3.3	Net wealth in R. G. Dun credit reports, 1899–1923	109
3.4	Wealth categories in R. G. Dun credit reports, 1899–1923	110
3.5	Evaluations in R. G. Dun credit reports, 1899–1923	114
3.6	Evaluations and risk variables in R. G. Dun credit reports, 1899–1923	121
4.1	Sample and data universe of *cheques sin fondos*, 1941–1975	140

4.2	Value of *cheques sin fondos* in the arrest records, 1941–1975	148
4.3	Cheque account balances, 1932–1980	148
5.1	Sample and data universe of citizen letters, 2001–2007	172
5.2	Value of amounts in citizen letters, 2001–2007	187
5.3	Explanation frequency in citizen letters, 2001–2007	197
5.4	Multiple explanation combinations in citizen letters (with intersection size), 2001–2007	198

Acknowledgements

I began this book twelve years ago and have received invaluable help and support along the way. I am grateful to the archivists and librarians who guided me through the research, especially the archivists at the Archivo General de la Nación, the Archivo Histórico del Banco de México, the Archivo Histórico del Banco Nacional de México, and the Archivo Histórico de la Ciudad de México 'Carlos de Sigüenza y Góngora', as well as the librarians at the Biblioteca del Banco de México, the Biblioteca Nacional de México, the Fototeca Nacional at the Instituto Nacional de Antropología e Historia, Harvard Business School's Baker Library, the Hemeroteca Nacional de México, and Northeastern University Library's Digital Repository Service and Interlibrary Loan Office. With these professionals in charge, research was productive and enjoyable.

It is a pleasure to acknowledge the enormous intellectual debts I have accrued throughout this process. I had the good fortune of spending time with Linda Arnold as I began this project, and she told me about the archival collections that form the basis of the study. Along the way, she also offered important advice on doing legal history. Jeffery Bortz, Barry Carr, Tom Havens, Pablo Piccato, and the late Linda Hall championed this project in its early stages. I also want to thank the many scholars who have given feedback and advice, in particular: Eva Arceo Gómez, Edward Beatty, Carlos Becerril Hernández, Victoria Cain, Amílcar Challú, Gustavo del Ángel, Aurora Gómez Galvarriato, Luis Jáuregui Frías, Robert Kenzer, Katherine Luongo, Casey Lurtz, Carlos Marichal, Graciela Márquez Colín, Noel Maurer, Pablo Mijangos y González, Sharon Murphy, David Sicilia, and Philip Thai. I thank Christopher Albi, Silvia Arrom, Mary Bridges, Margaret Chowning, Nate Holdren,

Timothy James, Juliette Levy, Daniel Noemi Voionmaa, Tanalís Padilla, Tatiana Seijas, John Tutino, and Kirsten Weld for reading early drafts of chapters and generously offering incisive suggestions. I am also indebted to Alex Lichtenstein, Mark Philip Bradley, and the anonymous reviewers who offered transformative comments on an abridged version of Chapter 1 that was published as a journal article. And I thank Ingrid Bleynat, who read a draft of the book: our transatlantic conversations, held (for me) in the very early mornings, were a great intellectual joy and helped me to think about the underlying arguments. So much of my understanding of historical analysis has come from our conversations over the past twenty years.

This book would not have been possible without the support for research and writing from the Berlin Prize from the American Academy in Berlin, the Charles A. Ryskamp Research Fellowship from the American Council of Learned Societies, and the Frederick Burkhardt Residential Fellowship from the American Council of Learned Societies and the American Antiquarian Society. At Northeastern University, I am grateful for research support from the Offenberg Fund from the History Department; the Research Development Initiative from the College of Social Sciences and Humanities; and the Interdisciplinary Research Sabbatical Fellowship from the Provost's Office, the History Department, and the Center for Emerging Markets at the D'Amore-McKim School of Business. Also at Northeastern, I have depended on my colleagues in the History Department for camaraderie. In particular, I thank my department chairs Heather Salter, Timothy Brown, and Gretchen Heefner for creating a nice environment for our everyday work.

I am grateful to my editor, Cecelia Cancellaro, for supporting the book at Cambridge University Press, as well as to the Latin American Studies Series editors Kris Lane and Matthew Restall. The anonymous peer reviewers offered penetrating insight that guided my revisions of the first draft and they have become, in my mind, models of scholarly spirit and intellectual rigour. The production team, led by Lisa Carter, skilfully guided the manuscript into book form. I am grateful to Judith Forshaw for her careful copyediting, to Meridith Murray for compiling the index, and to Leonard Rosenbaum for proofreading. I also had the great privilege of working with fabulous research assistants who not only helped with the heavy lifting but also shared ideas; it was an honour and pleasure to work with Francisco Javier Beltrán Abarca, Catherine Tracy Goode, Rodrigo Martínez Orozco, Hunter Moskowitz, and Katharina Neissl. And I thank Elena Abbott for her brilliant developmental editing.

Acknowledgements

My debts to my family are boundless. I have dedicated this book to my father, Charles, who has always inspired me to think creatively about economics and who chuckles knowingly every time I tell him that I am writing a book about unpaid debts. My mother, Carol, my sisters Clare and Gillian, and my brother-in-law Nicholas have been by my side, and I thank them for their steady support and good cheer. I have also been lucky to count on the kindness of my aunts, uncles, and cousins in Ireland. Flu and Juan warmly welcomed me into their family in Chile, and I miss Juan. David and Klavdija and their girls, Alisa and Lana, have deepened my world.

To Daniel, thank you for coming on this journey with me. And to our children Santiago and Zoë, now 9 and 8 years old, who have brought so much joy, and who have also helped me understand 'fairness' as a leitmotif in human history. I am looking forward to everything that comes next.

* * *

An abridged version of Chapter 1 was published as 'Everyday Economic Justice: Mediating Small Claims in Mexico City, 1813–1863' in *The American Historical Review* 128, no. 1 (March 2023), 120–143. I am grateful to Oxford University Press for permission to use.

Chapter 5 reprints lyrics from Gloria Trevi's 'Colapso Financiero'. I am grateful to Hal Leonard LLC for permission to use.

Colapso Financiero
Words and Music by Gloria De Los Angeles Trevino Ruiz
Copyright © 1995 by Universal Mus. Publ. MGB Mexico S.A. DE
All Rights in the U.S. Administered by Universal Music – MGB Songs
International Copyright Secured All Rights Reserved
Reprinted by Permission of Hal Leonard LLC

Introduction

Unpaid debts are the core economic problem of the modern world. Power struggles between debtors and creditors have animated the history of economic transformation, from the emergence of capitalist relations in early modern societies to the recent global financial crash, and debt troubles continue to shape the lives of ordinary people around the world.

Debtors and creditors have conflicting, sometimes opposite, interests. They exist in a structurally antagonistic relationship, enmeshed in a perpetual struggle over the value of the debt and the likelihood of repayment. People take chances every time they borrow or loan money and goods. Trouble might emerge from a mistake or a business failure, from bad luck or hardship, or from malicious deception. Debtors risk getting into trouble if they cannot repay. They risk their reputations, their belongings, and sometimes even their liberty. Creditors, meanwhile, risk their money and goods. Sometimes debtors and creditors reap great profits from their agreements; at other times, they lose out. And both creditors and debtors risk falling prey to scams and confidence schemes. Any debt contract, therefore, is an inherently risky enterprise in which good outcomes rely on both parties, and bad outcomes are always a possibility.

This book addresses the power struggle between debtors and creditors in Mexico from the late eighteenth century to the twenty-first. During the two centuries explored in these pages, the capitalist credit economy spread and deepened, creating new opportunities for people to borrow and lend. However, with these new opportunities came plenty of chances to get into trouble. What happened when people could not or did not pay their debts? Of course, ordinary debtors and creditors have always tried to avoid trouble. They use the legal system to defend their property and contract rights; they rely on social and cultural norms about fairness and honour to determine proper behaviour; and they create and use economic information such as gossip and credit reports to inform their sense of risk. These three key strategies, my research shows, have helped debtors and creditors alike shape and navigate interpersonal financial relationships against a backdrop of enormous social and political change.

Nevertheless, unpaid debts have always been a fact of life. Throughout the two centuries studied here, debtors and creditors often fought with each other. When debtors got into trouble, they sometimes landed in jail or on the Credit Bureau's Black List. They also asked for help, pleading with their creditors for flexibility or soliciting leaders such as politicians, priests, and bank managers to advocate on their behalf. The latter tactic was employed in February 2004, for example, by Efrén Romano, a senior citizen who lived in the Coyoacán borough of Mexico City. When pressured to clear a debt with the retail chain store Elektra, he wrote directly to President Vicente Fox for help.[1] Creditors asked for help, too, seeking authorities who would punish debtors who had reneged on their obligations. Such was the case in August 1813, when María Francisca Buseta could not get Victoriano Roa to pay his debt of 80 pesos. She sued him in a small claims case where she sought recourse with one of Mexico City's local elected magistrates.[2] For men and women across the socioeconomic spectrum, these kinds of conflicts were common and familiar, just a normal facet of everyday life.

People like Romano and Buseta play a starring role in the history of debt and credit. The protagonists of *Debts Unpaid* are mostly modest people such as small business owners and office workers. They had some money or assets to lend, and creditors considered them trustworthy enough to borrow. These small-scale debtors and creditors constituted a small but growing group that was fundamental to the expansion of capitalism in the modern world. Capitalism was (and is) an historical process of market relations encompassing more and more aspects of life: from land and labour to production and more.[3] To become entrenched, the capitalist credit market needed to grow bigger, to spread beyond the world of the rich and powerful and to enter deep into the lives of ordinary people. And it did. From the late eighteenth century to the twenty-first, more and more resources flowed into debt and credit market relationships, a wider range of people were included in the growing credit economy, and the obligations that were created formed a greater proportion of household budgets. As market relations spread into the world of small-scale borrowing and lending, the debtor–creditor relationship became increasingly impersonal and characterised by distance and estrangement.

As the credit economy expanded in Mexico over two centuries, people used financial instruments and sought justice when problems arose. For the capitalist credit market to survive, it had to resolve conflicts between debtors and creditors. Many of the agreements forged between debtors and creditors probably began with an opportunity, with people taking a chance because they had a vision of material comfort or prosperity. Debtors started small businesses, studied and trained, and purchased homes. Creditors earned profit on their loans and created a reputation as people of standing in their communities. And, no doubt, many people met their obligations, completing the contract without dispute. This history of unpaid debts, however, examines the conflicts that emerged between debtors and creditors when their agreements soured. While not necessarily a history of crisis or scarcity, this book is about malfunction. It is about what happened when something went wrong.

CONFLICTS BETWEEN DEBTORS AND CREDITORS

Mexico has been a central node in the global economy since the sixteenth century. Spanish America was at the heart of the global shift from mercantilism and feudalism to capitalism in the early modern world, and New Spain and Peru were at the centre of a global revolution in credit. Starting in the 1500s, traders and customs officials innovated new tools for borrowing and lending to facilitate the movement of silver and other goods from the Americas to Europe and Asia. Meanwhile, theologians and jurists responded to emerging practices in debt and credit relations by forging new ideas about the nature of money, what constituted fairness, and how to balance risk and profit.[4]

On the eve of independence from Spain in the early nineteenth century, the market for credit on the streets of Mexico City and in the surrounding viceroyalty was quite different than it was even a century earlier. Over the course of the eighteenth century, as historians Gisela von Wobeser and Matthew O'Hara have shown, ordinary people gained greater access to credit, and lenders could more easily profit from the risks they took with their money and assets. Religious institutions remained the most important creditors, and their records reflect the emergence of new credit instruments such as the *depósito irregular*.[5] Different from older forms of credit such as the *censo*, which had been tied to land and rarely redeemed, the new *depósitos irregulares* were redeemable short-term agreements with flexible collateral.⁶ By the end of the eighteenth century, the *depósito irregular* had become the dominant type of loan in the city and had received official church sanction.⁷ In this environment, new ideas about risk also emerged. In particular, the church pulled back from its censure of usury, which allowed lenders greater compensation for the risks they took on.

As New Spain became Mexico, borrowers and lenders belonged to an emerging contractual society. They were newly constituted individuals 'unshackled', in historian François-Xavier Guerra's words, 'from the older hierarchical and corporative society'.⁸ This new contractual society shifted the parameters of economic freedom and economic citizenship, reflecting a novel articulation of individual rights and the laws concerning property and exchange. While it had its roots in mediaeval Iberia and earlier, this modern contractual society emerged as economic relations became increasingly impersonal in the nineteenth century. Contracts between individuals were the economic and institutional counterpart to political liberalism.⁹ The contractual society encompassed transactions made by major merchants across great distances as well as agreements forged between ordinary individuals in the local economy. This book focuses on the latter: the more prosaic realm where modest individuals got into trouble with each other when debtors fell into arrears and creditors could not collect.

In 1813, when María Francisca Buseta sued Victoriano Roa for 80 pesos, their conflict was part of this history of liberal individualism and the expanding credit economy. Theirs is one of nearly 1,500 conflicts examined in this book, most of which happened in Mexico City. My case studies span different capitalist eras, from 1808 to 2008, although the political history reaches back into the eighteenth century and the legal history into the thirteenth. The conflicts between debtors and creditors are drawn from five main archival collections: the disputes of ordinary people in small claims in the first half of the nineteenth century; legal troubles faced by individuals and small businesses in asset sequestration petitions during the 1860s and 1870s; credit reports on people who were deemed untrustworthy and thus excluded from the credit economy at the turn of the twentieth century; arrest records of people who wrote bad cheques in the mid twentieth century; and the experiences of people who – like the elderly Efrén Romano – were pursued by corporate collections departments at the turn of the millennium. The debt troubles logged in these various archives illuminate the credit market's malfunctions as the frontiers of capitalist accumulation expanded into commercial, industrial, and financial realms. They also demonstrate how people used emerging new credit tools and financial instruments, such as credit reports, post-dated cheques, and credit cards.

Separated by two centuries, María Francisca Buseta and Efrén Romano personified the history of debt trouble. On the surface, their problems were quite different, but there was much continuity at the core of their conflicts. For example, they were both navigating the options available to them according to current laws. The legal backing of debtors' and creditors' agreements changed over time, from the expansion of institutions to resolve disputes (such as small claims hearings) to the articulation of new approaches to property crimes (like the decriminalisation of unpaid civil debts in the colonial twilight and the criminalisation of uncovered cheques in the twentieth century). At any given time, debtors and creditors had to follow the rules of the game as established by the legal framework in which they operated. Buseta hoped that the laws in 1813 gave her the power to seize Victoriano Roa's property in lieu of the 80 pesos he owed her. Romano believed that the rules in 2004 should protect him from Elektra's collection department.

Property rights and property crimes changed considerably during these centuries. In the nineteenth century, political elites transformed colonial-era property rights to spark economic development (and, often, their own enrichment). The most consequential examples include dismantling ecclesiastic and indigenous corporate property. The former, in particular, heralded major changes in the credit economy due to the long-standing importance of religious institutions as lenders.[10] These tectonic changes led to civil war between liberals and conservatives, as well as to rebellion 'from below' in the peasant movements of the Mexican Revolution (1910–1917).[11] Subsequently, the constitutional articles concerning land reform and labour protection made the 1917 Constitution one of the most progressive in the world. In the decades after the revolution, political fights emerged over protecting the rights it enshrined, including property rights, with one of the most well-known struggles emanating from the Mexican government's decades-long process of redistributing land by breaking up large estates.[12]

These histories have been well studied. This book, however, adds an important and distinct dimension to our understanding of the history of property rights and the fights they inspired: the problem of unpaid debts. Debtors and creditors are not as discernible as either the ecclesiastic or the indigenous communities that lost property in the nineteenth century, nor are they as visible as the rural people who received land in the twentieth century. Moreover, much of the historical scholarship on debt and credit has focused on major merchants and lending organisations.[13] There are fewer histories of debt and credit relationships between ordinary people, although research on pawnshops by Marie Francois and on non-bank credit by Juliette Levy shows how questions about trust and risk can be brought to the world of more modest borrowers and lenders.[14] This book builds on existing scholarship by focusing on what happened when problems arose between these individuals of more modest means. The history examined here is not bounded by a community, a location, or a lending institution. Everyday debtors and creditors were a diffuse group: men and women, rich and poor, artisans and office workers, and many others. Those who could (and did) borrow or lend came from many different backgrounds. They were defined as debtors and creditors simply by their position in a contract.

The legal framework for borrowing and lending was an historically constructed power relation. The question of whose interests were better protected – debtors or creditors – was never static. Over time, jurists and legislators acted to alter the power balance between debtors and creditors by redefining property crimes. Some changes benefited debtors by defining unjust terms and protecting them from abuse; others gave creditors more power and created opportunities for them to coerce or pressure debtors. In the scholarship on property rights and property crimes, one major line of enquiry, which exists within a predominantly liberal framework, is concerned with the rights of creditors, investors, and property owners. Another area of research, mainly expressed within a Marxist framework, focuses on the rights of debtors and those dispossessed of property.[15] *Debts Unpaid* draws on both scholarly traditions to explore the relationship between debtors and creditors within a legal framework that was constantly evolving: who had better rights, and how did that change over time?

On the ground, the outcomes of debt conflicts, which are recorded in the archival documents at the heart of this study, suggest that creditors usually prevailed. Yet close readings of the cases show more intricate power dynamics. Some debtors, for example, were adept at avoiding their obligations. Exploratory statistical analysis also suggests that other variables, such as the reason for the conflict (unpaid rent or an outstanding bill with the local butcher, for instance) might have shaped the outcome in favour of one side or the other. Thus, the chapters address both big-picture trends and individual cases to assess how power dynamics between debtors and creditors shifted in relation to the evolving legal landscape and, in turn, how the law affected the everyday world of borrowing and lending.

Ideas about economic justice infused the conflicts that emerged over unpaid debts. Justice for debtors and creditors was, to borrow Plato's word, vulgar. The philosopher distinguished between vulgar justice – everyday acts such as paying one's debts, making recompense for injury, and avoiding unjust acts like theft and embezzlement – and the loftier concept of spiritual justice, which was his central concern and which later commentators described as Platonic justice.[16] Economic justice was different from redistributive justice; it was not about correcting societal ills or constructing a better world. Economic justice was about resolving disputes when someone violated the simple maxim 'render to each their due'. A person's reputation – be it their standing in the local community or their computer-generated credit score – depended on their just acts in daily economic exchange. *Debts Unpaid* addresses a question that has been studied by generations of students of Mexican history, perhaps most emblematically in research on the moral economy of peasant movements: what was considered fair?

The moral economy of debt and credit was about a proper balance between opportunity (to borrow and to lend) and exploitation (how much one party could benefit at the expense of the other).[17] Ideas about what constituted a proper balance were deeply political, forged out of conflict, negotiation, ideology, and self-interest. Ordinary people, cultural elites, and political leaders all had their own views about fair terms and honourable behaviour. Notably, anthropologists have shown how people throughout history have described credit as productive and liberating while characterising debt as unproductive and burdensome. This is a morality axis on which people have strategically positioned themselves across time and place.[18] Debt and credit thus formed a dyadic unit, inseparable and laden with moral tension: vulnerable borrowers and predatory lenders; enduring creditors and delinquent debtors; honourable and dishonourable behaviour. Historians of Latin America have shown how honour was a cornerstone concept in the construction of political legitimacy.[19] This history of debt and credit brings attention to the economic dimension of honour in relationship to fairness and justice. How were fair consequences determined when debtors could not meet their obligations? How did debtors and creditors maintain, lose, or regain their economic honour? The chapters that follow address these critical questions.

Moral tensions had material consequences. For example, jurists outlined the conditions under which debtors and creditors could void contracts, most commonly when the rules relating to just prices and just profits had been violated. These rules were written and rewritten according to prevailing ideological notions, be it a Roman Catholic worldview, a liberal or revolutionary perspective, or a neoliberal standpoint. Leaders, often motivated by their economic interests and personal values, made the rules and attempted to control the narrative. Ordinary people accepted, defied, adapted, and ignored the rules and the narrative, usually in ways that connected to their interests and values.

Whatever the legal rules and moral narrative, economic information was of central importance to debtors and creditors as they angled for advantage. People had to decide whether to borrow or lend in a world full of asymmetric and imperfect information. New Spain was not a trusting place. There was, as historian William Taylor describes, 'a long-prevailing mood in Spanish and colonial Spanish American society of *engaño* [deception] and a wary suspicion that most people, especially in this New World, were not who they appeared to be'.[20] When debtors and creditors struck agreements, a basic question emerged: how did they trust each other? Historians have studied how people, especially wealthy merchants, created structures of trust across cultures and over long distances. Scholars of mediaeval Europe, the early modern Mediterranean, and the nineteenth-century Islamic Indian Ocean have also shown how merchants managed economic information by creating predictable institutions to navigate risk in credit transactions.[21] *Debts Unpaid* brings the research questions about information and trust to bear on petty amounts in local transactions, which were becoming increasingly impersonal through the nineteenth and twentieth centuries.[22] The research presented here suggests how these evolving information systems changed the everyday lives of creditors and debtors and played an important role in the economic transformation to a more impersonal capitalist credit economy dominated by large financial institutions.

The forms that economic information took changed considerably during these years, from gossip in local shops to credit reports written by agents and, finally, credit scores generated by algorithms. New information technologies offered innovative solutions to the trust problem, helping to facilitate borrowing and lending between strangers. The transformation of a person's history into a credit report, a process that took root in the late 1800s, connected the earlier mechanisms of trust among merchants with the commoditisation of personal information that is a hallmark of the recent past. Collecting economic information was and continues to be part of a broader project of inscribing and disciplining ordinary people within the structures of modern nation states and capitalist relations.[23] Information was power, and new technologies changed the dynamics between debtors and creditors. For example, whereas a delinquent debtor might have hidden his mules with a cousin in the 1830s, thus placing the animals out of reach of creditors, by the 2000s it had become more difficult to hide assets. The chapters to come are framed by key questions at the heart of these evolving dynamics: how did the content and form of economic information change over time? And how did debtors and creditors use available information to mitigate risk?

Property rights and contract law, ideas about fairness and justice, and the content and form of economic information mattered greatly in the conflicts between debtors and creditors, and these are principal themes of *Debts Unpaid*. Woven through the chapters are two other topics from the research: the gender of the debtors and creditors, and the amounts owed in their agreements. These latter topics are important for an intriguing – and quite different – reason: they do not appear to have been very important in the conflicts between debtors and creditors. For the most part, gender was not significantly associated with other variables, such as the reason a debt was owed (a personal loan, overdue rent, or unpaid piano lessons, for example) or the outcome of the conflict (such as a court decision specifying terms for repayment). Likewise, the amounts owed were not significantly associated with other variables. For example, the value of the debt was not likely to affect the outcome of a conflict.

On this matter, an important methodological caveat is emphasised throughout: the chapters do not present a single type of conflict across two centuries. The five datasets comprising the archival collections reviewed are entirely different. This caveat notwithstanding, the tension between difference and similarity – different datasets, different contexts, similar results – led to a provocative question: are gender and the amounts owed epiphenomenal in conflicts between debtors and creditors? This history of debt troubles gives a tentative answer: maybe. In the process, it offers a social history of economic relations in Mexico, examining how men and women had similar experiences with unpaid debts, small and large. The analysis of gender and amounts owed is also an invitation for future exploration. With more histories of small-scale economic conflicts in different times and places, historians will be better positioned to contemplate the role of gender and value in the debtor–creditor relationship.[24]

CHRONOLOGICAL HORIZONS

The power struggle between ordinary debtors and creditors was a driving force in modern history. The struggle was intimate and abstract. Standing before the magistrate or sitting down to write a letter to the president, the difficulties and failures of people like María Francisca Buseta and Efrén Romano were on display. The stories contained in this book reflect failures to gauge risk and to budget, as well as to collect and to repay. Each conflict shows the minute complexity of the particular relationships involved. And in the aggregate, as part of a prosopography, the conflicts reveal the debtor–creditor relationship as an abstraction, constituted by both social inertias and changing power dynamics. The *longue durée* illuminates the particular and the abstract.

Bringing case studies together across time and from multiple archives, *Debts Unpaid* presents several temporalities. It traces legal history from mediaeval Iberian legal codes, it presents political history from late colonial liberalism and reform, and it examines economic conflicts between 1808 and 2008. These chronological horizons put the economic world of small unpaid debts on the main historical stage of accumulation and justice.

Everyday conflict over small sums was the stress test for the changing economic order. While this book is mostly about economic relations under expanding capitalism, the power struggle between debtors and creditors transcends capitalist exchange and production. Conflicts between debtors and creditors tested the economic order at any given time, whether it was primarily mercantilist or capitalist or whether the dominant mode of accumulation was commercial, industrial, or financial capitalism. When small-scale agreements soured, the power dynamics between debtors and creditors were exposed and the economic and political order became vulnerable. People needed access to economic justice that was reasonably fair. Without it, they might become less willing to borrow and lend, which would in turn undermine the strength and legitimacy of the economic system and the political authority behind it.

If not smoothly resolved, the unpaid debts of wealthy families, large estates, major merchants, and strategic enterprises could cause economic downturn or even collapse. This was even truer for small debts. Small debts made up the centre of the economic order, and without redress for ordinary debtors and creditors, the economy would fall apart. One small unpaid debt, of course, would not reverberate throughout the economic system. It was constant conflict over small sums that was the test of economic resilience. The almost incessant occurrence of minor disputes between debtors and creditors transformed what might otherwise have been inconsequential quarrels into a main arena of economic expansion.

The *longue durée* captures the relentlessness of small-scale conflict.[25] Indeed, the small scale was fundamental to the economic order throughout the centuries examined here. The values of people's unpaid debts were high enough to matter to individual, household, and business budgets, and the amounts were worthwhile enough to seek recourse if an agreement soured. Even though the disputed amounts, for the most part, were not sufficient to ruin someone or shutter an enterprise, these debts and credits held together the centre of the economy.

The typical protagonists of these conflicts were neither wealthy nor poor. They belonged to a world of petty traders and producers, small shopkeepers and business owners, employees and professionals, and many others. The boundaries of this world were amorphous and changed over time. Therefore, the words I use to describe these debtors and creditors shift and change as well. For the long nineteenth century, I write about individuals, citizens, and ordinary people. For the long twentieth century, my vocabulary expands to the middle classes, consumers, and financial account holders.[26] Many of these people worked for themselves, and their intimate and economic lives blurred in what historian Ingrid Bleynat describes as a proprietary mode of production. Their conflicts, likewise, often mixed the personal and the pecuniary.[27] Their transactions – be they buying, selling, renting, making, growing, producing, providing, or something else – formed the core of the modern economy from which everything else extended. Small debts and credits made it all possible.

Studying the problem of unpaid small debts over the *longue durée* shows the connection between economic transformation and social inertia. The small problems that arose between debtors and creditors were remarkably consistent, not only over time but also across different kinds of conflicts. Different sources – small claims records, property sequestration petitions, credit reports of people deemed worthy and unworthy, arrest records of people who wrote uncovered cheques, and letters written by citizens about their unpaid debts – show people struggling to repay or collect, whether due to hardship, personal mistakes, business failure, or deception. This continuity and consistency has some elements of 'motionless history', a concept pioneered by social historians of the 1970s and employed most famously by Emmanuel Le Roy Ladurie, who showed how slow-changing structures, more than dramatic events, drove historical transformation.[28] The power struggle between debtors and creditors was one such slow-changing structure: conflicts over small unpaid debts, a basic problem in human society, were re-signified in different eras to allow economic expansion over time.

For the capitalist credit market to take root in people's lives, the economic order needed to provide some measure of justice to ordinary people. If debtors and creditors faced similar problems over the *longue durée*, the terms of engagement changed as capitalism expanded. Changing parameters of economic justice, in substantive and procedural terms, gave legitimacy to changing modes of accumulation. Considering matters of substantive justice (the big questions about right and wrong), moral tensions about unpaid debts returned in different eras: most emblematically, perhaps, concerning lending at interest. The rules for usury changed to accommodate the growing credit economy, from Catholic restriction in the sixteenth century to the liberal abolition of restraints in the nineteenth century, and finally to regulation without enforcement after the revolution and well into the twentieth century. Usury remained a trope for moral panic in the twenty-first century, with individuals such as Efrén Romano writing letters to President Fox decrying injustice and pleading for help with their unpaid debts. Political leaders also facilitated the growing credit economy in terms of procedural justice (the practical application and enforcement of rules). They expanded and established legal institutions to address the growing number of disputes over modest amounts, from bolstering municipal small claims hearings in the nineteenth century to creating new categories of property crime for the misuse of financial instruments in the twentieth.

Transformations in economic justice over the *longue durée* buttressed the hegemony of the economic order. Historians of modern Latin America have studied the production of everyday political hegemony derived from a combination of consent from below and coercion from above. Leaders of independent nation states struggled to establish territorial and social control and to forge ideas about the nation that might hold with enough citizens to maintain functional governing structures.[29] The capitalist economy similarly depended on an everyday legitimacy. Legitimacy meant creditors like María Francisca Buseta having enough belief that the local magistrate might help that she appeared before him in 1813, and debtors such as Efrén Romano having enough hope that the president or his staff might help that he wrote a letter in 2004. Buseta's belief and Romano's hope held the capitalist order together.

The link between transformation and inertia presents a methodological challenge in foregrounding economic relationships and allowing the hurly-burly of political history to recede into the background without disappearing. For example, it often did not matter to the outcome of the debt conflicts studied in these pages who was monarch or president, but it was consequential that Carlos III eliminated civil debt imprisonment for artisans in 1786, that Benito Juárez lifted usury prohibitions in 1861, and that post-revolutionary elites criminalised uncovered cheques in 1932. These changes to the rules probably mattered tremendously to people fighting over unpaid debts. At the same time, putting those moments in a longer chronology shows how leaders responded to gradual transformations in the core relationship between debtors and creditors.[30] The driving force of capitalism was not the action of leaders; it was the relentless tide of conflicts between debtors and creditors.

The historical arc between the early nineteenth century and the beginning of the twenty-first was one of freedom and constraint. On the one hand, credit freed up ambition and productivity, allowing people to build lives and businesses. There is a hopeful history of social mobility and enterprise to be found, and, although that is not the focus of this book, the conflicts over unpaid debts offer glimpses into the aspirations that accompanied many of the transactions. Over two centuries, the urban small-scale credit economy shifted from being largely embedded in the personal relationships of a small society to being increasingly organised into more impersonal relationships with new forms of trust mechanisms. On the other hand, as the capitalist credit economy expanded into more and more people's lives, economic citizenship increasingly depended on access to banking and financial services, both public and private. Inclusion and exclusion vis-à-vis the credit economy thus became a fault line not only in individual people's lives but in society more generally. The liberal individual of 1808, unshackled from the disciplinary control of corporative society, became the neoliberal individual of 2008, yoked to a credit score.

SOURCES AND METHODS

Conflicts between debtors and creditors abound in the archives. I concentrated my research in collections that offered fresh and stimulating entries into the world of unpaid debts. The conflicts come from five main archival collections, each forming the basis of a chapter. First are the small claims disputes from the 1810s to the 1860s, the subject of Chapter 1. Chapter 2 addresses precautionary petitions to sequester property when a creditor suspected that a debtor might hide assets. These cases mostly come from the 1860s and 1870s. Credit reports on individuals and businesses deemed worthy and unworthy of trust (the origins of the later credit scores) are addressed in Chapter 3, which focuses on the 1880s to the 1920s. The arrest records of people who wrote bad cheques form the basis of Chapter 4, which covers the decades from the 1930s to the 1980s. And finally, Chapter 5 studies the letters written by citizens such as Efrén Romano to President Fox to explore everyday debt troubles in the 1990s and 2000s.[31] To make sense of it all, I also relied on supplemental archival material and published sources such as legal codes, periodicals, literature, film, song, technical manuals, and diplomatic reports, among others.

While some of these collections had been almost untouched by other historians, these were not small bundles of documents in out-of-the-way repositories. The research was not about detective work, but rather about trying to apprehend what was in front of me. The five main collections consisted of hundreds, thousands, and sometimes tens of thousands of documents.[32] Making sense of that history involved studying both the mountain and the molehill. In broad strokes, my methods were inspired by two traditions: a social science approach that reconstructs economic life by aggregating archival material into original datasets for statistical analysis, and a humanities approach that includes fine-grained analysis of case studies and close readings of a range of historical material.

My methods for research, sampling, analysis, and interpretation involved many challenges and constraints, decisions and compromises.[33] In practical terms, I began by exploring different archive collections about unpaid debts. I read many stories about people who did not pay their debts, considering throughout the process which primary sources might be most productive (and enjoyable) to work with. After deciding on the sources, I developed a sampling strategy for each collection. I started with the small claims. Because I was at the beginning of the research, I spent more time with this collection as I considered the directions in which to take the project. It was fairly speedy work to transcribe the short summaries, and my sample was 1,000 cases, or 2 per cent of the data universe. Thereafter, I aimed for either 100 examples or 10 per cent of the universe, whichever came first. When considering the sample sizes, I settled on these numbers because they suited my intellectual purpose: to explore relationships between variables and use the quantitative results as suggestions for interpretation. The numbers also fit with the practical constraints of in situ research, including the condition of the material. For example, some of the documents were on delicate paper that was tightly bound into ledgers, some collections consisted of hundreds of boxes each with hundreds of files, and some archives did not allow researchers to photocopy or photograph the documents. No doubt, larger samples would improve the analysis; I hope that future researchers will confirm some of my findings and revise others. For ease of context and comprehension, I have described the sampling for each collection in detail within the chapters themselves.

After transcribing the documents, I turned to analysis. The social science and humanities analyses were fused at the beginning. The first step was to read a printout of all the transcriptions and, with a pen and notebook, work out the two most important analytical decisions: what the categories for the datasets would be, and which case studies I would develop. It was at this step that I most closely integrated quantitative and qualitative approaches. Thereafter, the qualitative method was to closely read specific conflicts, analysing along and against the grain to interpret what was included in the archival record and what might have been omitted. The quantitative method involved a few more practical steps: designing the datasets, data coding and entry, data cleaning, and then running statistical tests.

My approach to the statistical analysis was exploratory. I wanted to see as many relationships between variables as possible, and I asked all the questions that my datasets permitted. For example, in comparison with men, were women debtors significantly associated with conflicts that stemmed from unpaid rent? The main tests were bivariate analyses such as t-tests, correlations, chi-squared tests, and Fisher's exact tests.[34] I used the conventional threshold to gauge statistical significance (p-value ≤0.05). For the sake of clarity throughout the book, I only ever use the word 'significant' in this narrow sense. I was interested in results that found significant relationships between variables, and findings of no significant relationship between variables.

It would be unwise, I think, to place too much interpretive weight on either inferential statistics or detailed case studies. Each method has epistemological weaknesses, on which much ink has been spilled. The challenges scholars face begin with collecting the information. At the most basic level, all interpretation is shaped by what makes it into the archive and is thus constrained by the biases of the data universe. Sampling, coding, and data entry are full of imperfect decisions, subjective interpretations, and human error, all of which are compounded when building original historical datasets like those in this book.[35]

Challenges multiply with analysis and interpretation. For quantitative analysis, scholars have expressed concerns about using and interpreting p-values. Some researchers have described how a 'dichotomania' of 'significant' and 'not significant' has harmed the research community through overconfident claims of significance and unwarranted declarations of a lack of significance.[36] Additionally, there exists a danger of fetishising a statistical abstraction, which can become disconnected from the context and contingency of social relationships and institutions. Indeed, an entire tradition of scholars exists that laments the direction of economic history away from historical studies and towards an economics of historical phenomena.[37] Perhaps more famously, qualitative interpretations such as those pioneered by critical theory, subaltern studies, and cultural studies have been pilloried for both content and form.[38] There exists a danger of focusing too narrowly on the particular and idiosyncratic for the joy of uncovering a perspective or experience that is unusual in the historical record. The methodological concern centres on the vulnerability of confirmation bias when argumentation is driven by anecdotal influences.

Put simply, studying the particular and the abstraction involve different challenges. Bringing together social science and humanities approaches to examine an historical problem – in this case, unpaid debts – does not resolve the vexed questions. I neither pretend nor aim to do so. Indeed, my analysis relies on both false dichotomies and anecdotal evidence, and throughout the book I describe the methodological constraints and compromises.[39] Ultimately, I used the two approaches as mismatched frames for seeing the power struggle between debtors and creditors, the difference amplifying the promise and peril of each. The contrast was generative: quantitative results gave clues for what to look for in the qualitative analyses, and vice versa.

The quantitative results yielded by my research provided interpretative suggestions rather than definitive answers. The statistical models revealed relationships between variables that I could not see – or even imagine – during the impressionistic experience of transcribing and reading the documents. For example, the models showed gender fairness in small claims outcomes that would not have been legible to me otherwise. The quantitative analysis also helped put the more tantalising case studies into a broader universe. Statistical results gave an outline, or a sketch, of an abstraction: the underlying workings in the relationship between debtors and creditors. That sketch then provided clues for interpreting the complexity of individual cases: to understand a defendant's strategy in a court case or see how citizens interpreted their experiences; to suss out what was happening between Buseta and Roa in 1813 or between Romano and Elektra in 2004. Likewise, I used qualitative analysis to interpret the statistical results. Close reading of specific documents put the quantitative analysis into context to help me think about whether a statistical significance (or lack thereof) was historically meaningful. In sum, I used social science and humanities approaches to inform and confirm each other and, most fundamentally, to uncover different dimensions of debt trouble.

STRUCTURE OF THE BOOK

Debts Unpaid is organised chronologically to highlight arcs of historical transformation over 200 years. Each chapter moves between reporting the statistical results and recounting specific conflicts, both colourful and prosaic, between debtors and creditors.

Chapter 1 examines how, on the eve of the independence movements in the early nineteenth century, Cádiz liberalism transformed economic justice. After the promulgation of the 1812 Cádiz Constitution, magistrates in Mexico City were elected instead of appointed, transforming the mediation of the *juicios verbales* (small claims under 100 pesos). Tens of thousands of debtors and creditors pressed their claims before magistrates. This chapter shows how economic justice was relatively effective for ordinary people from the 1810s to the 1860s. Cádiz liberalism established a judicial institution to protect property rights, especially for creditors, that enjoyed a broad legitimacy well into Mexican independence.

Chapter 2 analyses the power struggle between debtors and creditors in the 1860s and 1870s, a time when face-to-face economic relationships showed signs of strain as economic life expanded in more impersonal ways. The chapter studies legal conflicts and legal codes to understand the risks that people took when making contractual agreements and how they decided to trust each other. Debtors could evade their obligations in myriad ways, and creditors transmitted their anxieties to the courts by using *providencias precautorias* (precautionary petitions). The precautionary petitions were a preliminary request to sequester goods or people before the initiation of a formal civil suit. Jurists, working in a long tradition, attempted to balance the interests of both parties. And although creditors generally prevailed in legal conflicts, the prospects of debtors were on the rise. This would change.

Chapter 3 continues the analysis of risk and trust by examining a major shift: when the Banco Nacional de México (Banamex) opened its doors in 1884, it hired the American credit-rating agency R. G. Dun to appraise the creditworthiness of people and businesses. Bureaucratic economic information in the form of Dun's credit reports began to replace older face-to-face trust mechanisms. While the debtors named in the *providencia precautoria* petitions or the *juicios verbales* could escape their obligations by hiding goods or simply disappearing, the Dun credit reports inaugurated a new reality where it became more difficult for debtors to hide. Institutional lenders such as modern banks began to expand into the lives of ordinary and middling people, as well as into the firmament of small and medium enterprises. The modern credit economy, with financial exclusion baked in, took root from the 1890s to the 1920s. As this chapter shows, the power struggle between debtors and creditors changed when bankers succeeded in wedging a bureaucratic report between them.

In the aftermath of the Mexican Revolution, bankers thrust the disciplinary power of the state between debtors and creditors. They used their influence to have criminalised as fraud the act of writing an uncovered cheque. From 1932 until 1984, debtors who wrote bad cheques to guarantee loans faced serious consequences, from fines to jail time. By examining arrest records, Chapter 4 uncovers the early history of financialisation, as more people began to use new financial instruments. When people wrote uncovered cheques, some of them experienced first-hand the growing pains that came with participating in financial modernity. Cheques represented the new dynamics of economic citizenship at mid-century, as the government shored up the interests of bankers at the expense of bank account holders. In doing so, political leaders introduced new forms of coercion into the debtor–creditor relationship.

Chapter 5, the final chapter, examines how people explained their debt troubles at the turn of the millennium. The trust problem that the early credit-rating agencies such as R. G. Dun had tried to address – how could creditors trust debtors? – had a new solution: the Credit Bureau, established in 1994. Those who languished on its infamous Black List were excluded from the credit economy and denied new loans. By the end of the twentieth century, forms of economic information had multiplied. Creditors and the companies that served them produced credit scores and foreclosure notices. Debtors fared poorly within the new economic order, as it was more common to discipline delinquent debtors than to police predatory creditors. This chapter shows how the debtor–creditor relationship became one of individual borrowers and institutional lenders. The power dynamics had been transformed, and many debtors faced dispossession through paperwork. Citizens with car loans, home mortgages, and credit cards thus wrote to President Vicente Fox about their economic problems. They explained their situations, attributed blame, and asked for help. Citizens wrote about economic fairness, connecting their lives with long-standing ideas about justice from centuries past.

* * *

María Francisca Buseta and Efrén Romano, who found themselves entangled in difficult debt and credit relationships, are among the protagonists of *Debts Unpaid*. They borrowed and loaned money and goods, and sought justice when problems arose. Their stories show how people understood fairness in their everyday economic lives and illuminate the sophistication of Mexico's expanding credit economy. From the colonial twilight to the turn of the millennium, small conflicts between debtors and creditors made possible the big historical transformations of capital accumulation and economic justice. Taken together, these chapters show how it happened.

I

Little Debts

Justice and Citizenship in Small Claims, 1810s–1860s

On 31 July 1832, Ventura Espinosa sued Luisa Aguilar for repayment of the 6 pesos and 1.5 reales she had owed him for over four months.[1] He clearly expected to win, but Aguilar was ready for a fight. In fact, she turned the tables on him altogether. First, Aguilar argued that she owed Espinosa only 3 pesos and 2 reales. Then, she claimed that Espinosa had attacked her because of her debt. He had, according to her testimony, ripped her clothing and stolen a trunk with some belongings (*trastos*) inside. At the end of the hearing, it was Aguilar who emerged victorious. Not only was her debt forgiven, Espinosa was also required to pay her 4 pesos for the injuries he had caused. Moreover, Mariano Pérez de Castro, one of Mexico City's elected magistrates, ordered Espinosa to return her trunk immediately.[2]

Espinosa had sued Aguilar in a small claims case, a *juicio verbal*. With roots in Roman law, *juicios verbales* were verbal rulings that appeared in late mediaeval and early modern Spanish and Spanish American civil, ecclesiastic, and military law. These verbal rulings constituted justice at the ground level. They were intended, at least in part, to reduce first-instance litigation.[3] Small claims cases (involving under 100 pesos) and crimes such as slander and mistreatment (*injurias leves*) were heard by local magistrates, many of whom had not studied law.

After the promulgation of the 1812 Cádiz Constitution, this tradition of economic justice was reshaped by liberal constitutionalism. Thereafter, the cases were decided by a new class of officials elected by residents: the *alcaldes constitucionales*.[4] Article 312 of the Constitution transferred municipal authority to the people, stating: 'Mayors, councilmen, and city attorneys shall be named by election in the towns, ceasing in function councilmen and others who have perpetual offices in the city council, whatever be their title or attribution.'[5] Articles 313 and 314 outlined the process. Every December, citizens of towns would elect electors in proportion to the size of their neighbourhoods. The electors would then elect mayors (*alcaldes*), councilmen, and city attorneys who would take office in January.

Municipal elections were one of the many changes that transformed millions of people's lives in Spain and its empire after 1812.[6] Notably, the lifespan of the Cádiz Constitution itself was brief. Parliament ratified the Constitution in March 1812, but it was repudiated by Ferdinand VII in May 1814. It then lay dormant for several years until it was reinstated for a three-year period between 1820 and 1823. Cádiz liberalism, by contrast, had a lasting impact in the Americas. Many of the changes it created were left in place when the Constitution itself was abolished. As historian Silvia Escanilla Huerta has shown, for example, indigenous communities in the viceroyalty of Peru 'refused to surrender' the tools of self-government they had been granted. It was, she argues, a 'redistribution of power' that proved 'impossible to undo'.[7]

While scholarship on electoral changes during the nineteenth century has tended to focus on national and gubernatorial theatres, this chapter explores the new world created by municipal elections in the wake of 1812, a change that lasted nearly half a century.[8] In Mexico City, the election of magistrates continued until 1853, when they began to be named by the city government instead.[9] In the pages to come, this chapter describes the world of small claims, analyses fights over property rights, addresses the question of fairness, and, finally, considers change and continuity in the decades following 1812. What it shows is that justice grounded in Cádiz liberalism was both relatively effective and broadly legitimate. The *juicios verbales* mediated everyday life in ways that reflected and sustained the emerging rights of individuals fighting for economic justice.

A CONTRACTUAL SOCIETY

One of the most consequential changes during this era was that justice grounded in Cádiz liberalism shifted away from corporate rights to emphasise individual rights. Article 248 of the Constitution eliminated corporate privileges altogether. 'In ordinary civil and criminal matters,' it read, 'there shall not be more than one single law [*un solo fuero*] for all classes of people.'[10] Article 282 then described the magistrates' role in civil justice: 'The mayor [*alcalde*] in every town shall exercise in it the office of conciliator; and he who has to sue for civil disputes or for injuries, ought to present these to him with this goal.'[11] The people who appeared before elected magistrates were thus newly constituted individuals: 'unshackled', in historian François-Xavier Guerra's words, 'from an older corporative society'. As he puts it, '[A] new contractual society had emerged.'[12]

It was also a more modern society. By the end of the eighteenth century, individuals became 'the normative subject of institutions', a state that Guerra contrasts with the *ancien régime*, in which society was organised into 'a diverse assortment of groups, corporations and political communities … each with its own specific rights and obligations'.[13] Within this contractual society, Guerra suggests, new forms of sociability emerged, especially in the form of voluntary associations such as the *tertulias* or *Amigos de País*.[14] Historians have uncovered emerging individual subjectivities in different realms as well, including Matthew O'Hara's study of pious behaviour in the late colony.[15] Importantly, a generation of revisionist scholarship in the years since Guerra's path-breaking work has shown that the rupture with the past was neither as profound nor as sweeping as Guerra believed, particularly in terms of the arrival of Enlightenment ideology to Latin America via Cádiz and its impact on the emergence of representative government across the continent.[16] Nevertheless, Guerra's emphasis on the emergence of an individual subjectivity is helpful in the context of this chapter's exploration of how contractual society under Cádiz liberalism worked.

A well-known struggle over corporate privileges animated much of the next century in Mexico. The emerging individualism encouraged attacks on corporate rights to community land, which often provoked resistance and conflict, especially in the countryside but also in the city. In his analysis of the dispossession of indigenous people in greater Mexico City, for example, historian Andrés Lira has shown how residents of the former Indian Republics faced and responded to repeated government attacks on their community holdings.[17] The *juicios verbales*, I argue, show another dimension of liberalism in this context: how the courts in Mexico City could, at times, enable mediations that sustained everyday life as individuals fought over how to render each their due in a new era of contractual relationships.

The overall picture that emerges in this story is of a city teeming with petty trade and fairly commonplace conflicts. Indeed, the Archivo Histórico de la Ciudad de México contains over 50,000 *juicios verbales* from 1813 to 1863.[18] While these small claims cases, of course, might involve wealthy litigants, they also included a broad stratum of the middle segments of society: those with enough standing or capital to borrow or lend but who did not necessarily belong among the wealthy. The magistrates' books are full of small-scale producers, vendors, and tradespeople. Most of the people involved were men. In my sample, 80.4 per cent of the plaintiffs were men (742), 15.6 per cent were women (144), and 4.0 per cent were entities such as religious institutions (37). Of the defendants, 85.3 per cent were men (791), 14.6 per cent were women (135), and there was one entity (0.1 per cent).[19] Most of the conflicts were over private matters, as commercial disputes were likely too complex for small claims and went before different courts. Owners of perfume shops, *pulquerías*, ice cream parlours, and one brothel (*casa de trato*) found themselves in small claims hearings as both plaintiffs and defendants. In my sample, 3.3 per cent of cases (28) stemmed from a dispute over a business partnership, and 4.4 per cent (37) were bread-and-butter disputes over salary and labour conditions. Notably, these were individual conflicts; there were no references to collective action.

The *juicios verbales* did not take place in a formal courthouse setting. Magistrates could name the location, including their home, or, more often, just outside their front door.[20] The standard process was for the magistrate to hear from both the plaintiff and the defendant or their representatives. Each party would have a 'good man' (*hombre bueno*) who was not a lawyer but an advocate. On occasion, magistrates allowed written material. Then, after conferring with the *hombres buenos*, the magistrate would pronounce his non-appealable decision. Magistrates evicted tenants, returned stolen goods, sentenced debtors to repayment plans, and urged relatives and neighbours to live in harmony. The scribe (*escribano*) recorded a short summary of the conflict in the magistrate's annual book (*Libro de Juicios Verbales*), which was eventually archived with the city (*Ayuntamiento*).[21]

To reconstruct a history of the everyday economic justice reflected in these cases, my methodology comprises a social history of legal records. The quantitative analysis is based on 934 cases, or approximately 2 per cent of the archive. Because the collection consists of the magistrates' annual books, some of which are tightly bound or have delicate paper, the most careful and efficient strategy was to transcribe every nth case in a book, starting with the first one.[22] Table 1.1 presents my sample and data universe by decade. My original sample was 998 cases, which included 64 cases of *injurias leves* (crimes such as slander or spousal mistreatment).

TABLE 1.1 *Sample and data universe of* juicios verbales, *1813–1863*

Decade	Cases in sample	Data universe	Sample as percentage of universe	Percentage change of universe
1813–1822	45	161	27.9	
1823–1832	370	5,560	6.6	+3,353
1833–1842	173	18,976	0.9	+241
1843–1852	170	17,754	1.0	–6
1853–1863	176	6,700	2.6	–62
Total	934	49,151	1.9	

My decision to omit these cases is connected to my analysis of gender fairness, and I describe the effect of this decision below. The statistical models used include correlations, t-tests, analyses of variances, chi-squared tests, and Fisher's exact tests; the same tests were run for the entire sample and for the sample divided into five-year and decade clusters.[23]

Cádiz liberalism inaugurated a new world in which individuals increasingly entered into contractual agreements as creditors and debtors. As the sheer number of *juicios verbales* from 1813 to 1863 showcases, Mexico City was an urban centre teeming with small-scale conflicts that erupted in the course of everyday commerce. And what did people do when they faced the classic problem of being unable to pay their debts? They pressed their claims before elected magistrates.

THE JUDICIAL CITY

The everyday practices of artisans, small business owners, and employees constituted the urban economy of Mexico City, a cosmopolitan metropolis that was, by some measures, the fifth largest city in the western world at the turn of the nineteenth century. Social historians have unearthed much about the lives of ordinary people in the century's first half.[24] Men and women of modest means – indigenous, creoles, *castas*, immigrants, and others – worked as artisans, as home-based producers, as labourers in textile and other factories, and as domestic servants. They bustled to sell goods and services.[25] They lived together and procreated across racial categories, some more than others, to be sure.[26] And they moved around the city with 'geographic insouciance', to borrow the words of historian Luis Granados describing tributary Indians in 1800.[27]

The demographic history of Mexico City's residents during these years was animated by mobility, by multiple identifications, and by constant change. From the end of the eighteenth century to the middle of the nineteenth century, creoles constituted approximately half of the city's population. Indigenous people were about a quarter, and *castas* were nearly a fifth. Women outnumbered men at around 55 per cent. In terms of occupation, most people worked as artisans, followed closely by domestic and service workers. These groups each comprised between a quarter and a third of the population during the decades under study.[28]

Many of these people appeared before the elected magistrates to denounce others or defend themselves, and this chapter aspires to join the social history tradition by considering what their small-scale economic conflicts show about everyday life in Mexico City. However, the *juicios verbales* records do not, for the most part, provide any demographic information beyond the gender of litigants. There is little information about how individuals earned a living, where they came from, if they used racial or ethnic identifications, if they were married, if they spoke other languages, and so on. Instead, the records offer historians an entry into the judicial and economic lives of ordinary people.

The conflicts in the *juicios verbales* unfolded in the context of macroeconomic crisis. The beginning of the nineteenth century was bleak. The silver boom collapsed, and Mexico City faced rising food prices, bad harvests, epidemics, rapid population growth, underemployment, and rural migration to the city. All these factors combined into what historian Silvia Arrom describes as 'Mexico City's first "urban crisis"' in her study of the Poor House, which was established in 1774 to address the growing problem of mendicity.[29] This macroeconomic decline continued into the mid nineteenth century, with the ongoing economic crisis clearly reflected in the *juicios verbales*.

Over the course of the decades studied in this chapter, individuals fought over smaller and smaller amounts as time went on. Table 1.2 presents the amounts owed in ten-year clusters. It includes the mean, minimum, and maximum, and provides the same information by gender of litigants. The number of observations is included to emphasise that the analysis should be considered suggestive given the low numbers for some years. In terms of frequency distribution for all years, 25 per cent of all cases were disputes concerning 13 pesos or less, 50 per cent were disputes concerning 25 pesos or less, and 75 per cent were disputes concerning 50 pesos or less. The decreasing amounts presented in Table 1.2 fit with the current historiography, which suggests a general deflation of values in the nineteenth century.[30] Clearly, the judicial institution was neither removed from nor destroyed by ongoing macro crises, including

TABLE 1.2 *Mean amounts and gender of litigants in the juicios verbales, 1813–1863*

Year	Mean amounts owed – all litigants		Mean amounts owed – plaintiffs						Mean amounts owed – defendants					
			Male		Female		Entity		Male		Female		Entity	
	Mean	n	Mean	n	Mean	n	Mean	n	Mean	n	Mean	n	Mean	n
1813–1822	56.58	38	60.46	30	45.57	7	17.00	1	60.29	32	36.75	6		
1823–1832	38.35	300	38.54	236	36.89	52	40.88	12	38.63	247	38.03	51	10.00	1
1833–1842	38.45	161	38.60	138	31.94	18	64.13	4	38.23	140	39.98	20		
1843–1852	27.79	153	26.42	121	34.04	19	28.78	9	28.54	128	23.91	25		
1853–1863	28.60	147	28.98	116	20.57	22	44.34	8	30.42	134	9.85	13		
Total	35.42	799	35.56	641	33.15	118	40.52	34	36.05	681	32.05	115	10.00	1

independence, civil war, invasion, and national debt default. In fact, against the backdrop of large-scale turmoil, economic justice carried on working for ordinary people.[31] In the *juicios verbales*, residents continued to show up to defend their property rights and magistrates arbitrated their economic conflicts, thus keeping urban peace in uncertain times.

From unpaid rent and personal loans to money owed for goods sold, Mexico City residents brought a wide range of small claims to elected magistrates. But how small was small? When Ventura Espinosa sued Luisa Aguilar over 6 pesos and 1.5 reales in 1832, for example, what was the value of the money at stake? Table 1.3 provides an overview of the value of various goods during this period, putting the disputed amounts into context.[32] While anecdotal, the information offers a grounded catalogue of the amounts discussed in this chapter.[33] Average monthly rents provide further context for the value of a peso.[34] With 6 pesos and 1.5 reales, Espinosa or Aguilar could have paid for two months' rent and had some money left over. If they were saving to buy an earthenware cup, they would be about halfway there. Meanwhile, for most years during this time, the daily wage for unskilled construction labourers (*peones*) was around 0.4 pesos (or 3.25 reales). Thus, if either Espinosa or Aguilar earned about the same amount as labourers, the debt represented about fifteen days of work. And, as a final reference point for the value of a peso at the time, the peso exchanged at nearly par with the American dollar.[35]

At first glance, small claims conflicts might seem a petty world of negligible amounts and narrow-minded disputes. But, analysed together, they debunk some historiographical assumptions about underdevelopment that date back to the emergence of the Spanish Black Legend. A long-standing interpretation of Spanish imperial economic development that can be traced to sixteenth-century anti-Spanish propaganda produced by the crown's European rivals, the legend suggests that there was excessive regulation and taxation by the state (caricatured as despotic and overweening) and the Catholic Church (depicted as nefarious and totalitarian), and that the result was economic weakness in the viceroyalties and independent republics. The Black Legend has been 'remarkably persistent', as historians Tamás Szmrecsanyi and Steven Topik write.[36] It has, in fact, continued to shape scholarly assumptions about many facets of colonial and postcolonial Mexico, including economic and legal life.

When economic historians describe archaic property rights in colonial and early republican Mexico, the picture they paint is one of arcane courts that were impractical for subjects and, later, citizens. The long-standing interpretation is that an unsatisfactory institutional environment

TABLE 1.3 *Value of a peso in* juicios verbales, *selected examples, 1813–1861*

Year	Item[a]	Value in pesos[a]	Average monthly rent in pesos[b]
1813	1 mule (macho colorado de un cuerpo regular)	15	4.08
1814	1 horse (caballo alasan)	40	4.08
1822	4 cloths (paños)	12	2.67
1822	1 fine duffel cloak (capa de bayeton fino)	18	2.67
1830	2 earthenware cups (tibores de China)	25	2.67
1830	1 barrel of muscatel wine (barril de vino moscatel)	49	2.67
1835	1 horse (caballo)	40	3
1835	1 wardrobe (ropero)	30	3
1840	2 hairnets with 13 pins on each (jaulillas con bolillos)	10	3
1840	18 wicker chairs (sillas encofinadas)	32	3
1842	1 pair trousers (pantalon de dril)	9	3
1842	1 horse (caballo)	7	3
1848	1 chair (silla)	6.5	3
1851	1 sombrero and 1 sarape (shawl), pawned value	2	3
1855	1 cloak (capa)	31.5	3
1855	2 un-upholstered pink armchairs (sillones de rosa sin tapiz)	26.5	3
1861	1 pair English leather boots (botas de cuero ingles)	7	3
1861	5 yards of damask (5 varas de damasco)	8	3

[a] Archive citations for the items in the order that they appear in the table: AHCDMX AJ, vol. 2763, exp. 1, f. 3v, 19 May 1813; AHCDMX AJ, vol. 2765, exp. 2, f. 31v, 13 May 1814; AHCDMX AJ, vol. 2767 VI, exp. 1, f. 64v, 16 December 1822; AHCDMX AJ, vol. 2767 VI, exp. 1, f. 51v, 19 October 1822; AHCDMX AJ, vol. 2852, exp. 1, ff. 46r–46v, 2 June 1830; AHCDMX AJ, vol. 2852, exp. 1, f. 31r, 16 June 1830; AHCDMX AJ, vol. 4372, exp. 1, ff. 16v–17, 6 February 1835; AHCDMX AJ, vol. 4375, exp. 1, ff. 13v–14r, 10 March 1835; AHCDMX AJ, vol. 4443, exp. 1, f. 119v, 7 May 1840; AHCDMX AJ, vol. 4452, exp. 1, f. 2r, 28 April 1840; AHCDMX AJ, vol. 4469, exp. 1, f. 19v, 20 January 1842; AHCDMX AJ, vol. 4469, exp. 1, f. 120r, 11 March 1842; AHCDMX AJ, vol. 4568, exp. 1, f. 2r, 27 April 1848; AHCDMX AJ, vol. 29543, exp. 26, f. 49v, 10 April 1851; AHCDMX AJ, vol. 2947, exp. 1, ff. 12r–13r, 21 May 1855; AHCDMX AJ, vol. 2947, exp. 2 f. 1r, 2 January 1855; AHCDMX AJ, vol. 2954, exp. 1, ff. 1r–1v, 29 January 1861; AHCDMX AJ, vol. 2954, exp. 1, ff. 76v–77r, 16 April 1861.

[b] I am using Calderón's average monthly rents for the years that are closest to my examples: 32.67 reales (4.08 pesos) is for 1810; 21.33 reales (2.67 pesos) is for 1818; and 24 reales (3 pesos) is for 1831. Calderón Fernández, 'Mirando a Nueva España', 184, table 4.2.

forced people to operate, as historian John Coatsworth writes, at 'the margin of the law' in a 'netherworld of semiclandestinity'.[37] In his foundational essay about the causes of Mexico's relative backwardness and macro-level growth divergence vis-à-vis the USA and Britain, Coatsworth invokes the legal netherworld of ordinary people – referring to small enterprises such as petty tradesmen and small-scale producers – to convey the idea of a deficient institutional environment. However, while seeking to challenge Black Legend explanations for underdevelopment, such as Spanish colonial rule or the power of the Catholic Church, Coatsworth in fact recapitulates a Black Legend perspective: that Spanish subjects and Mexican citizens lacked economic legal recourse and that this insufficient institutional environment helps explain Mexico's historical underdevelopment.

Mexico's institutional revolution came later in the nineteenth century, with the Civil Code (1871), the Commercial Code (1854–1855, 1884), and the Mining Code (1884).[38] As Coatsworth outlines, this 'constructive phase' of institutional modernisation built on an earlier, somewhat overlapping, 'destructive phase', which was completed by the 1860s and included the abolition of caste and slave systems, communal property holding, and corporate privileges. Together, he writes, these changes 'redefined property rights and created new legal and social spaces for private enterprise'.[39] In the framework of New Institutional Economics, which has shaped much recent economic history, the property rights of creditors and investors are paramount: when these rights are effective and protected by political authority, they help reduce uncertainty and risk. They also strengthen the incentives to invest, which can deliver private and social gains.[40] (The opposite dynamic, in this framework, is that when property rights are not effective and protected, it can lead to economic weakness and stagnation.) This analytical framework aims to understand macroeconomic questions such as growth divergence, but the (perhaps unintended) consequence is that scholars tend to portray a moribund legal system before the 1870s.

The institutional model of economic history is a compelling narrative and has become an important analytical framework for examining historical underdevelopment around the world.[41] But the institutional deficiency argument breaks down in the daily transactions of ordinary people. The reason why scholars have not seen this breakdown is probably simple: few historians have studied the lowest-level judicial conflicts. In fact, this book offers the first systematic study of Mexico City's small claims cases for all years. To my knowledge, only three other historians have used this collection as a principal archival source.[42] Diego Castillo Hernández and Vanesa Teitelbaum, in separate articles, use cases from the late 1840s and early 1850s to study crime and discipline among the urban poor (*sectores populares*), ideas about honour, and judicial and municipal administration.[43] Graciela Flores Flores's book about judicial institutions includes an analysis of all the *juicios verbales* and *juicios conciliatorios* from the first trimesters of 1830 and 1845, analysing the geographical distribution of magistrates for 1830 to show that they were concentrated in the more central and privileged *cuarteles*.[44] Joining this scholarship by turning to the economic conflicts that were by far the most common dispute in this immense archive, it is notable that the 'institutional deficiency' invoked to explain underdevelopment is simply not found in these mountains of documents.[45] The time has come, this absence suggests, to revise the scope and chronology of the deficiency narrative.[46]

Economic life in late colonial and early republican Mexico City was not a world bereft of judicial recourse. The capital was, indeed, a judicial city, a term that I have borrowed from Graciela Flores Flores's study of judicial institutions during what she terms the 'intermediary period' from the late colony to the 1870s.[47] Starting in the late eighteenth century, the Bourbons reorganised the administrative structure of the city. The Ordenanza de 1782 created eight *cuartels* (boroughs) to bring judicial institutions to 'every corner' of the city and into the 'everyday life' of residents.[48] These reforms created new *alcaldes del barrio*, the unelected precursors to the *alcaldes constitucionales*. They also reorganised first-instance and superior courts, as well as penal and policing institutions. The Bourbon goal, as historian Michael Scardaville has shown, was social control, especially of the lower classes.[49]

In 1812, Cádiz liberalism infused this judicial and administrative structure with constitutionalism, starting at the most basic level with the *juicios verbales*. Although the Cádiz Constitution was repealed in 1814, it belonged to a broader current of liberal ideas that animated Mexico's independence war (1810–1821) and the political struggles in the new republic. A generation of scholars have uncovered a vibrant legal life in the capital city and across the republic in the decades after independence. They have focused, in large part, on judicial institutions and administrative structures, on popular culture and social control, and on legal culture and ideas about liberalism.[50] The *juicios verbales* add a critical dimension to this conversation because they illuminate everyday economic justice and the way in which individuals used the city's judicial and administrative structures to navigate financial imperatives and interpersonal grievances. They were not operating at 'the margin of the law', as Coatsworth put it; they were regularly engaging with the judicial system as they went about the daily business of life and commerce in Mexico City.

TABLE 1.4 *Rate of litigants in* juicios verbales *vis-à-vis the Mexico City population, 1813–1862*

Year	City population estimate (average)[a]	Percentage change of city population (average)	Number of litigants[b] (data universe)	Rate of litigants per 100,000 residents (average population)	Percentage change of litigants per 100,000 residents (average population)
1813	123,907		28	11.3	
1820	165,778	+34	10	3.0	−73
1824	145,695	−12	132	45.3	+1,402
1830	179,545	+23	1,288	358.7	+692
1838	205,430	+14	4,324	1,052.4	+193
1840	207,887	+1	9,928	2,387.8	+127
1842	143,751	−31	4,920	1,711.3	−28
1843	145,000	+1	2,788	961.4	−44
1844	160,000	+10	4,544	1,420.0	+48
1846	187,000	+17	5,932	1,586.1	+12
1850	220,623	+18	1,164	263.8	−83
1852	170,000	−23	7,048	2,072.9	+686
1856	185,000	+9	460	124.3	−94
1857	200,000	+8	640	160.0	+29
1860	228,739	+14	984	215.1	+34
1862	200,000	−13	708	177.0	−18

[a] I analysed the rate of litigants compared with the minimum, maximum, and average population estimates calculated by seven scholars for each year with a population estimate. This column presents the results for the averaged population estimate. Davies, 'Tendencias demográficas', 501; Klein, 'Demographic Structure', 67; Lear, 'Mexico City', 464; McCaa, 'Peopling of 19th Century Mexico', 610; Pérez Toledo, *Hijos del trabajo*, 43–44; Pérez Toledo and Klein, 'Estructura social', 253; Shaw, 'Poverty and Politics', 371.
[b] The number of litigants is a conservative estimate: two litigants per *juicio* and one *juicio* per page of the magistrates' annual books.

Ordinary people had access to economic justice, and they used it. As Table 1.4 shows, more and more residents as a proportion of the city population appeared before the magistrates after 1812.[51] (See also Table 1.1, which presents the data universe by decade, unconnected to city population, and shows growing numbers of litigants.) These findings dovetail with those reached by Graciela Flores Flores, who also finds a substantial increase in the number of litigants when comparing all *juicios verbales* in the first trimester of 1830 with the same period in 1845.[52] According to the data, residents asserted their property rights through the *juicios verbales*, and magistrates protected the property rights of a wide array of residents. Creditors, in particular, did well. Looking at the outcomes of *juicios verbales*, magistrates issued a repayment plan in 74 per cent of cases. Assuming that creditors wanted to be repaid, this was good news.

Mexico City's small claims conflicts reveal not an institutional lack, but a presence. The fight between Ventura Espinosa and Luisa Aguilar shows the institutional strength in Cádiz liberalism: a judicial institution to protect property rights, especially for creditors, that enjoyed broad legitimacy and, as the next section shows, evinced a sense of gender fairness. In a pluralistic legal order that included the notary public's office and the bankruptcy courts, the *juicios verbales* were the ground level of civil disputes, one venue among many in which people could establish and defend their property rights.[53] Together, these legal institutions were the arena of property disputes in the judicial city, and they were regularly used by many.

MEDIATING DEBT DISPUTES IN THE *JUICIOS VERBALES*

While the archival records mostly concern what happened in front of the magistrates, they also reveal details about the transactions that led to the *juicio verbal*, thus illuminating the relationships between acquaintances and strangers that formed the foundation of the urban economy. Some of the fights that made their way before the magistrates were between friends or contacts so close that creditors suspected, for example, where the mules were hidden. Other disputes connected people who were probably strangers. Most fights were simple matters, like rent owed, but there were also more complex disputes involving credit instruments such as promissory notes or IOUs. In each instance, the magistrate's judgement was connected to the nitty-gritty details of the particular case. But, in the aggregate, it seems that magistrates (consciously or not) took into consideration the smooth functioning of the urban economy and tried to keep the peace during uncertain times.

Magistrates usually issued repayment plans (in 74 per cent, or 676, cases), which was surely a win for most creditors. However, magistrates did not side with creditors out of an implicit or explicit alliance. In fact, defendants usually acknowledged their debt, and a repayment plan likely benefited both parties. Contestation, however, complicated the outcomes. In 31.9 per cent (296) of the cases, the defendants disputed the charge. Sometimes defendants declared their innocence; more often they contested specific details, as when Luisa Aguilar admitted to owing about half the amount Ventura Espinosa claimed. While an examination of the conditional percentages shows a significant association between uncontested cases and repayment plans, magistrates were less likely to issue a repayment plan in disputed cases.[54] When magistrates did issue them in the disputed cases, the amortisation period was significantly shorter: defendants who contested the charge had a mean of 179.4 days to clear their debt, while defendants who acknowledged their debts had a mean of 259.4 days.[55] Magistrates might have believed that people who contested the debt were less trustworthy and thus put them on a tighter leash. Or they may simply have worried that in these cases the debtor–creditor relationship was particularly antipathetic and so it was better to discharge it quickly.

Contested cases affected other aspects of the process as well. Magistrates could postpone a case for up to eight days, but they postponed disputed cases significantly more often than uncontested cases.[56] Whether this was better for the defendants or for the plaintiffs, however, depended on whether defendants were right to dispute the accusation. Here, the sources are frustrating, the bare-bones summaries rarely providing enough detail to appraise broader questions about a litigant's intent. On the one hand, delay was helpful to defendants angling for a short-term reprieve to avoid immediate repayment; on the other, it could give creditors the opportunity to regroup. Still, it seems that, in disputed cases, magistrates made careful decisions to keep the peace in potentially volatile situations. Through their actions, they buttressed the smooth functioning of credit transactions in the urban economy.

Webs of debt bound residents to each other, and credit instruments provided elasticity to economic exchanges across the city. In their daily business, residents relied on formal IOUs and other credit documents. This reliance could, perhaps, stem from a low currency supply in Mexico City in New Spain and in the early republic, a phenomenon that has predominated in scholarly interpretation of the Mexican economy.[57] The *juicios verbales* certainly show how the city ran on credit. And in this context, credit documents were essential to urban economic life due to the elasticity of exchange they facilitated. Indeed, historians have uncovered a large amount of lending at other times and in other places before the establishment of modern banks and financial institutions; Mexico is clearly no exception.[58] The *juicios verbales* offer a glimpse into the world of unwritten agreements: a big world of small sums. Exchange would surely have slowed or stopped if residents used cash or goods to transfer value.

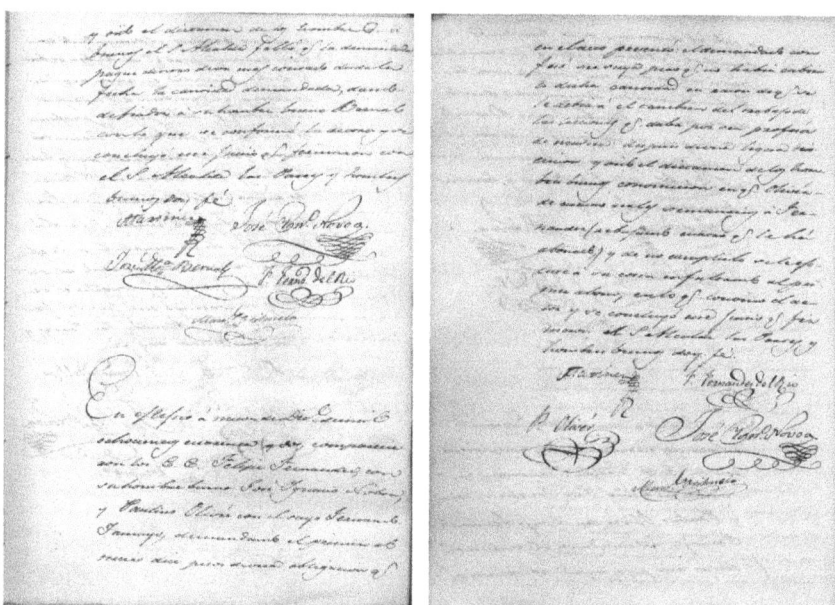

FIGURE 1.1 Felipe Fernandes v Paulino Olivér for 10 pesos in December 1842.
Source: Archivo Histórico de la Ciudad de México 'Carlos de Sigüenza y Góngora'.

Many debtors were also creditors, unable to honour their obligations until they themselves were repaid. This was the case, for example, when Felipe Fernandes sued Paulino Olivér in December 1842 for 10 pesos. Fernandes appeared before Magistrate Martínez with an *obligación*, a document that recognised a debt and sometimes promised its repayment. Such documents could be notarised, but were not always.[59] In this case, Olivér acknowledged his debt and explained that he had not been able to pay because he, too, was owed money. He was a music teacher, and some of his students had yet to pay for their lessons. The case, captured in a short and efficient record in the magistrate's log book, concluded with all parties agreeing to a repayment plan of 4 reales per week (see Figure 1.1).[60] With 140 days to clear his debt, Olivér's schedule was fairly typical: 50 per cent of cases with instalment plans had an amortisation period of 154.2 days or fewer.[61] And because Olivér was given time to collect his own debts, his music lessons could continue apace throughout the city.

The *juicio verbal* was often one part in a chain of such transactions, with magistrates at the centre of negotiating interconnected interests. These interlocking nodes of credit are clearly evident once again in a case from August 1831. In this instance, María Gertrudes Corte sued Luciano Amado for 20 pesos originally owed to her by José María Velasco, to whom, in turn, Amado had been indebted. With a *carta* (a notarised document that outlined a right, often used for borrowing and lending money), Velasco cleared his own debt by transferring Amado's debt to Corte.[62] Corte promptly appeared in front of Magistrate Ignacio Oropeza, demanding payment. Amado acknowledged the debt, explaining that he had been out of work (*sin destino*) for some time and could not repay the debt that day. Instead, Amado suggested, he would pay monthly instalments of 1 peso. Corte refused. In the end, Magistrate Oropeza decided that Amado would pay 2 pesos monthly for four months, by which time he would have cleared a separate debt and his instalments would increase to 4 pesos.[63] Magistrate Oropeza's flexible repayment plan was deliberately designed to give the defendant time to collect from his debtors while honouring the needs of his creditor.

Through credit instruments such as *cartas* and *obligaciones*, people could extend their economic relationships to strangers. Although the record provides no more detail about the relationships between Corte, Velasco, and Amado – Why did Velasco decide to transfer Amado's debt to Corte? Did Corte know Amado? – other cases make it clear that litigants were often several degrees removed from their debtors or creditors. In April 1844, for example, José María Miranda sued Rafael Mendiola for 19 pesos and 6 reales, what remained of an *obligación* of 23 pesos and 6 reales. Mendiola confessed his debt, explained that he was owed money for garments he had already sold, and offered to provide a list of his debtors so that Miranda could demand payment directly from them. Miranda and Magistrate Rafael Cervantes were satisfied with this resolution.[64] Although creditors probably preferred cash payment, they often settled for their debtor's list of debtors, just as Miranda did in this case. And if cash was an abstraction of value, lists of debtors were several steps further removed from material worth. Whether they liked it or not, Mexico City residents were adept at navigating this immaterial world as both debtors and creditors.

While debt and credit could entangle strangers in these complex webs of repayment, the social relationships embodied by credit tools could also be intimate. When Manuel Elisalde sued Josefa Cuellar for 100 pesos in October 1830, Elisalde presented an *obligación* that Cuellar's late first husband, Francisco Builla, had issued in exchange for some merchandise. Accompanied by her second husband, Tomas Girard, Cuellar appeared before the magistrate and replied that she could not fulfil the *obligación* because she was no longer in possession of her first husband's belongings, which had been sequestrated by another court (*embargado*). A question arose about three mules that had belonged to her first husband. According to Cuellar, her second husband had purchased these mules, and she had used the earnings to pay taxes (*alcabalas*) and to cover the cost of judicial proceedings. Elisalde, however, rejected Cuellar's explanation, contending that she had hidden the mules from the *embargo* proceedings and that they were presently in her house. Magistrate Agustín Vicente de Eguia postponed the matter, instructing Elisalde to gather evidence else or Cuellar would be unburdened of the *obligación*. In the meantime, Cuellar and Girard could not transfer ownership or otherwise dispose of the mules.[65] In contrast to the Miranda v Mendiola conflict, in which Miranda accepted a list of debtors (presumably) unknown to him, Elisalde knew enough about Cuellar's life to suspect shady dealings.

Magistrate Agustín Vicente de Eguia's decision to postpone the case was fairly typical in the circumstances. Specifically, magistrates more often postponed proceedings when a conflict involved a credit instrument.[66] It is possible that magistrates were more likely to interpret the relationships embodied in these instruments as too complex for the rather simple resolutions typical of *juicios verbales*. However, there is no evidence that magistrates systematically referred these cases to the higher courts (although plaintiffs could do so on their own initiative). It is also possible that, in contrast to more commonplace cases such as disputes over unpaid rent, magistrates simply felt less pressure to issue a resolution when there was a credit instrument involved.

While it is difficult to do more than speculate about the increased likelihood of magistrates postponing cases with credit instruments, the data does offer useful information about how often such instruments were used and in what situations. Credit instruments appear in 11.2 per cent of the cases, and, within the bounds of this study, they were associated with conflicts over higher amounts.[67] For example, in May 1856, Juan Arturo Ricardi sued Andrés Pando for payment of a 100 peso *pagaré*; this was a simple instrument denoting the amount owed and specifying a payment deadline, much like an IOU.[68] Figure 1.2 shows the archival record of their *juicio verbal*. It is unremarkable within the large volume of conflict records, and, as was typical, the *pagaré* was not included in the record. It does, however, model a fairly typical case in which a credit instrument was used: 100 pesos was the highest amount possible for *juicios verbales*, and this was the amount at stake in the IOU. In this case, Pando agreed to make weekly instalments of 8 pesos, accepting that, at the first missed

Little Debts

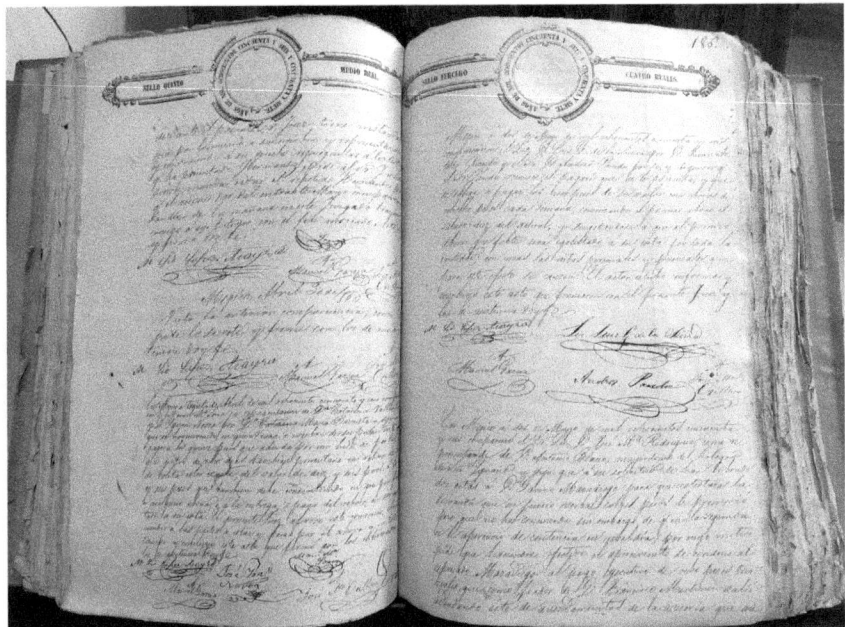

FIGURE 1.2 Juan Arturo Ricardi v Andrés Pando for 100 pesos in May 1856.
Source: Archivo Histórico de la Ciudad de México 'Carlos de Sigüenza y Góngora'.

instalment, he would be subject to embargo proceedings for the full amount.[69]

Disputes over rent were the most common reason that plaintiffs brought small claims, at 26.4 per cent of the sample (or 221 cases).[70] These were straightforward disputes: a tenant owed a precise sum in rent, to be paid in cash. Sometimes a guarantor was required; sometimes eviction was threatened. Tenants usually admitted that they had fallen into arrears. In fact, rent claims were significantly associated with uncontested cases.[71] The complicated disagreements between litigants, attempts to transfer or evade debts, and debates over ownership that appear in other cases – such as Elisalde v Cuellar – do not usually appear in rent cases. Yet magistrates had to get these cases right, because payment or non-payment of rent was one of the most basic transactions of the urban economy. Tenants needed shelter and landlords needed income. In the eighteenth and early nineteenth centuries, as other scholars have shown, tenants struggled to meet their obligations when the cost of foodstuffs and rent rose. They moved frequently in search of cheaper lodgings, they sometimes fled in the middle of the night to escape their debts, and institutional landlords had significant difficulty managing their properties.[72] The *juicios verbales* conflicts show how individual experiences worked in this central part of the urban economy, as well as how economic justice operated on a daily basis. On the one hand, magistrates protected landlords' rights. In comparison to non-rent cases, conflicts over rent were significantly associated with repayment plans.[73] But, on the other hand, magistrates looked out for tenants. The amortisation period was significantly longer in rent cases: defendants were given a mean number of 339.2 days to clear their debts, compared with 187.9 days in non-rent cases.[74] By providing succour to both tenants and landlords, magistrates kept the peace and helped avoid breakdown within the urban rental economy.

Along with many broken agreements, the *juicios verbales* provide illustrative glimpses of other dynamics vexing the relationship between landlords and tenants. When Lieutenant Colonel Estevan Díaz sued Joaquin Guzmán in November 1820, it was not because Guzmán owed him money. Díaz had just purchased the house at 7 San Francisco Street, where Guzmán lived on the mezzanine for a rent of 24 pesos per month. Díaz wanted to raise the rent, and he had found another tenant who could pay more. Guzmán replied that he would not fight the eviction, but he demanded to be compensated for the work that he had recently done repairing the ceiling and painting. The magistrate decided that Guzmán would move out within fifteen days (during which time he would not be charged rent), that the value of the improvement would be assessed by a painter, and that Díaz would pay two-thirds of this amount to Guzmán in instalments. Guzmán would pay, in short order, the rent owed for the current month, prorated to the present day; any remaining debt would be deducted from the reimbursement. In this case, both landlord and tenant did well.[75]

Tenants also sued landlords. Some focused on the quality of the property: for example, Alvina Vallejo sued the convent of San Lorenzo in October 1814 because the water was not working in the Paraíso bathhouse she had rented on a street called Baptisterio de Santa Catalina. The water had been off for nearly four weeks, and Vallejo asked that the convent repair the infrastructure and that rent payment be waved for those weeks. The convent's rent administrator argued that it was Vallejo's responsibility to keep the water running. Magistrate Francisco Azipreste disagreed and ordered the convent to repair the pipes, obliging Vallejo to pay two of the four weeks' rent.[76] The magistrate's decision took into account both the tenant's responsibility to pay the rent and the landlord's responsibility to provide the basic requirement of running water for a bathhouse.

The picture that emerges from these records is that of a dynamic market where magistrates balanced the interests of both parties. For the small claims to have credibility, magistrates considered both a moral economy and the market economy. Rent was among the more basic and practical details of economic life, for both tenants and landlords. And both tenants and landlords had success as they pressed their claims. Gender, however, structured the power dynamics in this area of the urban economy in noticeable ways. Women defendants were significantly associated with rent conflicts, indicating that women tenants were more vulnerable than men to being sued for unpaid rent.[77] In October 1843, for example, Friar Francisco Abecilla sued Doña Guadalupe Cervantes for 86 pesos in unpaid rent on the house where she lived at 5 Calle de Belén. The priest agreed to forgive her debt if she vacated the house within six weeks.[78] Eighty-six pesos was not a trifling amount. Why was Abecilla willing to forsake the sum? Possibly, he was motivated by compassion for Cervantes's circumstances. Alternatively, Abecilla may have been determined to evict Cervantes, even at considerable expense, so that he could secure a more dependable tenant.

If defendants like Cervantes were heads of households, struggling to provide shelter for their dependants (the *juicio verbal* record does not give this detail), an eviction could indicate the feminisation of poverty. While the reasons are not always legible in the records, the overall picture is one in which women tenants were more vulnerable and more likely to be sued by landlords.[79] The *juicios verbales*, in fact, show different gender dynamics in both the urban economy and in economic justice. Within the urban economy, a gender bias clearly structured transactions and relationships between ordinary people. For example, the over-representation of men among plaintiffs shows that women had less access to credit. The conflicts also show that men and women moved in slightly different economic worlds, as women plaintiffs were significantly associated with women defendants.[80] This could suggest several things. First is the possibility that women tended to enter into economic relationships with other women. Or perhaps they were more inclined to sue other women for small claims, believing that they stood a better chance of success than if they went against a male defendant. Whatever the reason, the results show a gendered economic world beyond the legal conflict encapsulated in the *juicios verbales*.

THE PARAMETERS OF ECONOMIC JUSTICE

Did economic justice work? This question is, ultimately, about fairness: whether there was procedural fairness and if there was substantive fairness. Magistrates discharged their duties according to procedure, at least as far as can be gauged from the scribes' summaries. In standardised format and style, scribes recorded an almost daily repetition of prescribed procedure with minimal variation (some of the more striking departures from routine are analysed below). Substantive fairness, however, is more difficult to appraise in historical context. Thus, I take my cue from legal historians who study how non-elites use the legal system: even if courts were not necessarily fair, ordinary people might have believed they held out a chance to improve their position.[81] A good strategy for tackling the question of substantive fairness is thus to consider how the magistrates acted and if they treated some types of litigants differently from others. By this measure, the *juicios verbales* seemed, overall, to work.

Could men and women expect similar treatment? The answer to that question depends on a methodological choice. The full sample consisted of 998 cases, and 64 of these were *injurias leves* (crimes such as slander or mistreatment). I ran every test for the full sample and for a subset that omitted these 64 cases, and found that these 64 cases were skewing my results vis-à-vis the significance of gender in one important way. In the full sample (n=998), gender was significantly associated with specific outcomes. Women, as both plaintiffs and defendants, were associated with resolutions involving no or light penalties.[82] For plaintiffs, if the conflict was over an amount owed, then the outcome was less than ideal: surely the creditor would prefer repayment. For defendants, it was certainly better to be given no penalty or a light penalty. However, if the conflict were personal, then it would probably have been irrelevant for all parties, because, in these cases, magistrates invariably admonished litigants to live in peace and harmony. Importantly, however, gender was not significantly associated with outcomes in the subset omitting the *injurias leves* cases (n=934). Male and female plaintiffs in the remaining 934 cases had the same expectations of outcome, be it repayment, no or light penalties, or postponement.[83] The same was true for defendants.[84]

Because there were no other substantive differences between the full sample and the subset, I omitted the 64 *injurias leves* cases. Thus, all results reported in this chapter pertain to the subset of 934 cases. The methodological decision was imperfect, and there was quite a lot at stake. Simply put, the question of whether gender mattered in the small claims resolutions turned on my decision. Another historian might have included these 64 cases and argued for a more capacious conceptualisation of economic life. But when appraising the significant relationship between gender and outcomes in the full sample, I concluded that the results were an artefact of the *injurias leves* conflicts. The *injurias leves* cases included cases of domestic violence and crimes against honour such as slander. And the peculiarity of the admonishment resolution, typical in the *injurias leves* cases, skewed the analysis of conflicts over small amounts between creditors and debtors. Admonishment might have satisfied plaintiffs if defendants were shamed into mending their ways or if the possibility of further legal action led – at least temporarily – to change. But it could also perpetuate hardship and suffering, such as oppression in marriage.[85]

The decision to omit the 64 cases traded the dimension of personal conflict for a clearer picture of the conflicts between debtors and creditors. It was, I think, worthwhile. In large part, this is because the subset shows an important feature of gender fairness: looking at the 934 cases, gender was not a significant variable in three major categories. First, in terms of outcome, men and women litigants could have the same expectations. Simply put, gender was not significantly associated with resolutions. Second, there was no significant relationship between the gender of litigants and the amount owed, with few exceptions.[86] The absence of a relationship between gender and amount owed holds true across all the various combinations of men and women defendants owing money to men and women plaintiffs. Third, there was no significant relationship between the gender of litigants and the amortisation period for repayment plans. Men and women plaintiffs and defendants could expect similar instalment schedules. Using gender as a gauge, then, these results suggest that the small claims system worked: women and men could expect similar treatment. Moreover, given the gender bias in the broader urban economy and the impact of macroeconomic changes on women residents, the gender fairness reflected in the *juicios verbales* outcomes might have been a judicial response (conscious or not) to keep urban peace in uncertain times.

Could other types of litigants expect similar treatment? Conflicts involving entity plaintiffs were similar to those involving individuals. The only significant result was unsurprising: cases about unpaid rent were significantly associated with entity plaintiffs.[87] This finding fits with the historiography, which shows that religious institutions were the main property owners. For most of the years examined in this chapter, the church was a major landlord in Mexico. This would change when the liberals alienated ecclesiastic property, especially after 1856 when church real estate and capital began to be nationalised and redistributed. Until then, many city residents paid rent or were otherwise indebted to the church.[88] Aside from the connection between entities and unpaid rent, however, there was little meaningful difference between how individuals and entities fared: they could expect similar outcomes from the magistrates.[89] Notably, however, defendants seemed less inclined to dispute a charge when facing an entity plaintiff.[90]

While cases generally seemed to be adjudicated fairly, two conflicts regarding salary disputes shed light on the limitations of the *juicios verbales* records as a gauge for understanding fairness. Most of the records do not offer much detail about the social relationships involved in a particular situation, and interpretative power comes from prosopography (examining the individual cases as part of a group). The result is an abstract analysis of relationships between variables that cannot fully account for the broader social context in Mexico City during these years. The difference between examining the abstract and the particular reflects a core difference between social science and humanities methods, with the limits of the former highlighted by the following two cases, both of which involved foreigners. The archival records for both cases are unusual in that they provide information about the litigants' national origins, including some details about race. Most summaries do not give this sort of information, so there are not enough observations to run tests about origins and racial identification. In the following comparison, then, close reading offers an insight into the range of experiences faced by different people (in this case foreigners) in order to consider the various ways in which the context of broader social relationships might shape outcomes.

In the first case, Zendor Urodani, a black citizen of France, sued Apolinario Darbells, an Englishman, for 10 pesos of back pay in June 1823.[91] According to Urodani, the two had agreed in Manila on a salary of 4 pesos per month, and he had worked for Darbells for the previous ten months. Darbells protested that he had in fact paid Urodani more than the man was owed, despite Urodani's inability to perform his duties because he was always drunk. Urodani's constant inebriation, Darbells claimed, led to several difficult situations, including a robbery of Darbells's property. The scribe recorded Darbells's passionate censure with unusual detail: '[W]ith much ardour and anger, Don Apolinario complained that [Urodani] was a bad man [*hombre malo*].' In the end, Darbells presented accounting books, translated from the English, showing payments to Urodani, and Magistrate José Brito declared that Urodani was owed no further payment.

In the second case, a German woman named Johanna Wilhelmiene Margarita Yahns sued her employer, Federico Huve, in July 1844. She demanded 48 pesos of unpaid salary and the return of her belongings.[92]

The magistrate decided in her favour on both counts. The contract presented to the magistrate had been signed in Hamburg and stipulated that Yahns would work for Huve for five years; that agreement was nullified and the magistrate added that Yahns was free to find other work in Mexico. However, in a separate claim by Yahns in which she accused Huve of having committed a violent act (no further details are given), the magistrate ordered that the case be considered resolved.

Both the Yahns and Urodani cases offer a glimpse of a complex social context full of particular power relations that are largely excluded from most of the *juicios verbales* records. Reading these two cases together raises questions: did the content of the dispute shape the form of the archival record? Did Urodani's and Yahns's origins shape the procedure in their *juicios verbales*, from the scribes' detailed description to the presentation of written evidence? It seems unlikely. After all, historians have used judicial and civil records to document the activities of foreigners – be they from France, England, or Germany – in both New Spain and nineteenth-century Mexico. A wide array of people enlisted bureaucratic machinery, and their origins might not have prompted the scribe to depart from usual practice.[93] Urodani and Yahns were part of a cosmopolitan metropolis, with varying degrees of autonomy in their workaday worlds. Both exercised agency with their lawsuits. So why are their cases such obvious outliers in the *juicios verbales* archive, and what might this reveal about economic justice?

It might have been the atypical nature of the dispute – conflicts over salary and contracts signed abroad – rather than the racial identification or national origins of the litigants that prompted the scribe to record comparatively more detail. Workplace conflicts were unusual in the *juicios verbales*, and they might have challenged what historian Kathryn Burns has described as the notary's role: as a legal 'ventriloquist' who translated and transformed people's wishes and claims into a standardised account.[94] The *juicios verbales* scribes, lower in status than notaries, might have opted to record these unusual disputes more thoroughly.[95] Whatever the reason, the departures from standard practice that resulted in extra details within the archival record offer a glimpse into the broader social world that encapsulated the conflict between debtors and creditors. These cases point to the cosmopolitan nature of Mexico City's urban economy, in which foreigners who might be experiencing economic vulnerability as wage earners could look to the *juicios verbales* in the hopes of economic justice and the chance to have their claims adjudicated fairly.

Nonetheless, the claims brought by Urodani and Yahns also illuminate the parameters – and the limitations – of economic justice, even when there was a general perception of fairness. Much of this chapter examines an analytical abstraction: the relationship between debtors and creditors. The methodological abstraction isolates the economic dimension and helps scholars perceive, for example, the underlying workings of conflicts over unpaid rent. But the abstraction elides the social complexities and particular circumstances that shape each *juicio verbal*. The complex context is thus omitted on two levels: in terms of sources, the unique experiences of people such as Urodani and Yahns are not usually visible in the bare-bones summaries; and in terms of methodology, my decision to focus on an analytical abstraction does not organically show the contextual complexities that may exist. Moreover, the glimpses of race and gender violence in the small claims records highlight the narrow definition of justice under consideration: namely, how the municipal judicial apparatus resolved the economic dimensions of *juicios verbales*. By hinting at the complex social dimensions underlying the short summaries available in the archival record, these two cases indicate that other forms of justice may not always have been served in the process of adjudicating debt cases.

Still, in the economic realm, at least, it does appear that the magistrates acted impartially, and that plaintiffs regarded them as impartial. Although it did not solve all of urban life's problems and conflicts, economic justice did seem to work. Of note was the fact that, even though plaintiffs had the power to choose magistrates, they seem not to have used it. Two caveats are in order. First, although the magistrates were supposed to be distributed across the city, this might not have been achieved in practice. Flores Flores shows that, for the first trimester of 1830, the six magistrates were not located in six *cuartels* but rather concentrated in the four most privileged ones.[96] Some residents, therefore, might have had few convenient choices for a magistrate to hear their claims. The second caveat that relates to residents' power to choose magistrates stems from source and methodology. Because the magistrates changed every year, there were not enough observations for each magistrate in the records to run many models for this study. However, three tests were possible, yielding suggestive information.[97] The mean number of pesos owed by defendants was not significantly different between cases overseen by different magistrates, suggesting that plaintiffs collecting higher amounts did not seek out specific magistrates.[98] Nor did plaintiffs strategise which magistrate might be more sympathetic depending on gender: there was no significant difference in the gender of litigants who appeared before different magistrates.[99] Similarly, if plaintiffs tried to 'shop' for magistrates they believed would require defendants to discharge their debts more quickly, they would have been disappointed: there was no significant difference between the amount of time that different magistrates gave defendants to make payment.[100] The amortisation period likely mattered to everyone, and it was probably better for defendants that plaintiffs could not seek out specific magistrates who required speedy repayment. In short, the magistrates acted in similar ways in the oversight of their cases. And, by this measure, economic justice worked fairly.

Importantly, however, popular impressions of the magistrates were quite different. Historian Vanessa Teitelbaum provides an overview of the 'unfavourable' representation of municipal justice in conservative and liberal periodicals, which depicted negligent magistrates who accepted bribes and created an atmosphere of impunity and corruption.[101] Manuel Payno, a liberal author and politician of the time, penned one of the most colourful condemnations of magistrates in his serial novel *El fistol del diablo* (The Devil's Tiepin), which was published in 1845 and 1846. The protagonist of the novel is Arturo, a 22-year-old from a comfortable family who has just returned to Mexico after studying in England. In *costumbrista* style, Payno presents a mosaic of characters to show the young nation at mid-century, including a corrupt magistrate, Don Caralampio. A *tocinero* (bacon vendor) by trade, Caralampio hears complaints in his *'mala y sucia'* (bad and dirty) butcher's shop. 'Surrounded by a putrid air', he 'administered justice in a fast and easy way, slapping and beating those who were disrespectful to him'.[102]

When Arturo gives Celeste, his love interest, a bejewelled *fistol* (tiepin), her gossipy neighbours denounce her for being a prostitute, a thief, and a hypocrite.[103] Don Caralampio, the magistrate, subsequently tries to pressure Celeste into some sort of sexual payment; when she rejects his advances, he accuses her of stealing the *fistol* and sends her to prison. Later, Caralampio colludes with a *platero* (silversmith), claiming that the jewels are false and thus devaluing the tiepin. The magistrate swaps the genuine *fistol* for costume jewellery that he has purchased in the market. In a final twist, the *platero* murders the magistrate, steals the *fistol*, and absconds into 'the shadows of the night'.[104] Historian Elías Palti describes the episode as part of a 'dialectic of injustice' that runs through the novel, whereby one injustice leads to another outrage.[105]

Payno's text portrays magistrates – and the municipal judicial apparatus more generally – as detestable. While I did not find archival examples of the sort of corruption represented by Payno, historian Timothy James describes the case of one magistrate's son who abused his power by extorting 10 reales from the family of a defendant to have him released from jail.[106] Yet Graciela Flores Flores, while not addressing the matter directly, suggests a general understanding that magistrates, unlike Payno's Don Caralampio, were not all irresponsible and corrupt.[107] How common corruption was among the magistrates thus remains an open question as more researchers explore the vast archive, but the *juicios verbales* records nonetheless suggest a level of fairness, both in perception and adjudication, that is an important part of the conversation.

Of course, fairness is not the same as compliance. A central purpose of the small claims cases was to ensure that residents honoured the agreements that they had struck with one another. And where a debtor's word might not have been enough, magistrates had few options to ensure enforcement. They could issue threats for non-compliance, such as eviction, or they could require collateral or a guarantor (*fiador*).[108] Almost none of the records indicate whether a repayment plan was actually completed. However, it is clear that economic justice failed in at least 10.5 per cent of the cases (98). In these instances, plaintiffs returned to complain that the defendant had not followed the magistrate's instructions in a previous *juicio verbal*.[109] Possibly, defendants in these cases were exercising an informal appeal. After all, when considering the matter of fairness, a basic question remains: how fair could a non-appealable decision be? These 98 cases show how residents might have found strategies of their own to navigate this limitation.

Still, the voluminous piles of dusty archival records suggest that the *juicios verbales* worked for most plaintiffs. Residents had enough faith in the system to try their luck. The small claims hearings were a venue for them to resolve their seemingly minor disputes in a way that felt fair and reasonable. It was a place to air grievances and to seek recompense and resolution. For that, they kept showing up.

CONTINUITY AND CHANGE AFTER 1812

The judicial institution to mediate small-scale conflict was strong, in part because it was both new and old. Although the election of magistrates was an important break from the past, the *juicios verbales* were part of a long legal tradition. To contextualise the *juicios verbales*, then, it is useful to engage with the generations of historians who have tackled the question of change versus continuity around the historical turning point of 1812. Among these historians is a distinguished interpretative tradition encompassing a range of different methodological and ideological approaches that invoke the weight of colonial structures as an explanation for economic and political problems in the nineteenth century. The colonial structures addressed in this tradition include slavery and forced labour systems, rent-seeking accumulation, dependency in global commodity chains, social hierarchies and inequality, and more. While the broader arguments about the impact of deep colonial legacies are accurate, historians within this tradition have grappled with the limitations of an analytical framework in which the past is inescapable or all-explaining. As Matthew O'Hara has written, 'in its most extreme form, such analysis frames the colonial period as a moment of original sin' invoked to explain all subsequent failures. He goes on to propose that the study of how people made historical futures is one way to avoid such a pathologising teleology.[110] Jeremy Adelman, meanwhile, describes how scholarly narratives of weighty colonial legacies create the impression that Latin America is 'shackled to its past'. He proposes 'persistence' as an alternative framework that could allow scholars to consider historical linkages without constructing a 'past is destiny' analysis.[111]

Both persistence and future-making run through the *juicios verbales*. Conflicts such as Ventura Espinosa v Luisa Aguilar belong to a deep history of judicial mediation that persisted across major historical watersheds like 1812. At the same time, Cádiz liberalism created a new future for people like Espinosa and Aguilar. Looking back to the years before 1812, not many scholars have examined ordinary civil justice in late New Spain, especially these ground-level conflicts.[112] But historian Michael Scardaville's analysis of criminal cases provides a good comparison. His sources include the ten extant *Libros de Reos* (Books of Criminals) from the years 1794, 1795, 1796, 1798, 1800, and 1807. His dataset consists of 7,057 arrests and summary judicial hearings, mostly alcohol-related criminal cases but also some *juicios verbales* debt conflicts.[113] He provides a breakdown for 1798, when 45.4 per cent of records were about drinking (with public intoxication at 20.7 per cent, illegal taverns at 18.9 per cent, and tavern violations at 5.5 per cent); these were followed by incontinence at 8.7 per cent, theft at 7.0 per cent, sex crimes at 6.7 per cent, violent crimes at 6.1 per cent, gambling at 6.0 per cent, disorderly conduct at 3.9 per cent, debt at 3.9 per cent, and family offences at 2.8 per cent, while 'other' arrests constituted 9.8 per cent.[114]

Scardaville's inventories contain more biographical data than the *Libros de Juicios Verbales*, which allows for examination of the offender's gender, ethnic identification, age, marital status, and more. Here is a snapshot of his results vis-à-vis the debt cases, for all years: 54 per cent of offenders were identified as Spanish, 23 per cent as Indian, 21 per cent as Mestizo, and 2 per cent as Mulatto; 49 per cent worked as artisans, 36 per cent as low-skilled workers, 9 per cent as merchants, and 6 per cent in other occupations. Offenders were nearly evenly split between those from Mexico City (50 per cent) and those with origins in the provinces (47 per cent). Three per cent hailed from other places. Most were between 20 and 40 years old, and most were married.[115] Comparing Scardaville's dataset with the *juicios verbales*, the gender proportions are different, with women offenders constituting 8 per cent of debt crimes in *Libros de Reos* and 14 per cent of the defendants in my sample. Unless the difference is an artefact of the sources, it could suggest that women had more access to credit or more trouble repaying their debts in the early national period; this question awaits future research. Otherwise, the information gleaned about debt crimes, and ground-level justice more generally, suggests important continuity before and after 1812. Analysing procedures and outcomes, Scardaville finds that magistrates were 'remarkably fair' mediators who generally resolved cases quickly, eschewed harsh sentences, and devised strategies to help defendants pay their fines.[116]

Based on his analysis, Scardaville argues that the cases in the *Libros de Reos* can be seen as combining Bourbon administrative reforms and Hapsburg notions of justice.[117] In the late nineteenth century, the Bourbons reorganised the administrative structure of the city. The municipal reforms substantially expanded the numbers of informal and formal cases by creating a network of neighbourhood tribunals. The volume of criminals apprehended and sentenced increased more than tenfold, from around 1,000 criminals annually before 1783 to more than 10,000 in the early nineteenth century.[118] The growing numbers of litigants in ground-level municipal disputes, therefore, can be traced to Bourbon reforms that created more judicial venues. Yet, Scardaville suggests, the deeper legitimacy and mediating function of the magistrates can be attributed to traditional Hapsburg notions of justice.[119] He describes how the justice system under the Hapsburgs served to enhance the power of the monarch, paternalistic and benevolent, who would mediate injustices on subjects' behalf. The courts were the arena in which to resolve conflicts in a 'fair manner through compromise and concession'.[120] It was certainly a contrast to the more utilitarian and materialistic Bourbon approach of levying fines that would fund law enforcement and increase social control.[121]

While recent historiography adds nuance to this interpretation of law and political authority under the Hapsburgs and Bourbons, the contrast holds.[122] Historians of sixteenth- and seventeenth-century New Spain who examine legal culture to understand everyday life and colonial hegemony have shown that marginalised people, especially indigenous litigants, used the law as a space where they might find justice.[123] And scholars of the late colony have shown that the law and order Bourbon reforms created policing and judicial institutions that had a reputation for being cruel and harsh.[124] Scardaville's magistrates embodied both, illustrating the persistence of Hapsburg justice under Bourbon reforms.

Persistence and change – the combination of old and new – were similarly defining features of everyday economic justice after 1812. Running all models for the entire sample and for five- and ten-year clusters between 1813 and 1863, I found that many relationships (such as between rent cases and repayment plans) were not meaningfully different in different time periods. The degree to which this holds true for the eighteenth century remains an open question awaiting future research, but the results are clear for the decades after 1813. I also ran all models before and after major political events (such as the Parián Riot in December 1828) and legislative changes (like the change from elected to named magistrates in January 1853). Again, I found minimal substantive difference. While the results should be considered suggestive due to low numbers of observations in some of the time periods, it appears that there was important continuity in the workings of economic justice during these decades.[125] Amid macro turbulence, ordinary people continued to show up before the magistrates.

And they came in droves: the numbers of litigants soared between 1813 and 1863. Table 1.4 shows the estimated rate of litigants per 100,000 residents during this period, and Table 1.1 shows the estimated total number of litigants. Both tables show important change over time: the numbers of litigants increased considerably after 1812. As described above, other scholars have found meaningful growth as well. But the increase was not constant. The spikes and drops suggest slow beginnings as the municipal judicial structure emerged and adapted during the decade of the independence war (1810–1820) and the first decade of contested nation-making (1820–1830). The *juicios verbales*, then, enjoyed heavy use and likely strong legitimacy from 1830 to the early 1850s, at which point their use appears to have lessened.

One possibility for the decline after the early 1850s is that magistrates lost some legitimacy when they were no longer elected, which was the case briefly in 1848–1849 and then permanently after 1853.[126] This interpretation would buttress my argument about the importance of municipal elections, but it might be too neat. After all, regardless of whether they were elected, the magistrates seem to have acted in similar ways in their approach to cases. The lower numbers of litigants in the 1850s could also be an artefact of changing administrative procedures for information organisation and preservation. The legislative changes in 1848, 1849, and 1853 eliminated the *Libros de Juicios Verbales*, and the *juicios verbales* cases were henceforth included in books of *juicios diversos*. The reason for the seeming decline of litigants at mid-century thus remains an open question. Future researchers could collect a more robust sample for a clearer picture of the relationship between everyday conflicts and legislative changes. Regardless of the reasons for these spikes and drops, however, the big picture is clear: there was substantial and growing usage from the 1810s to the 1860s.

Litigants and magistrates participated in an institution of economic justice that belonged to the massive transformations of Hispanic liberalism. In Mexico and throughout Latin America, leaders and citizens experimented with different models of constitutionalism as well as new meanings of citizenship and forms of public organisation. New governing structures required new legal and social categories, which generated a fraught and extended process that Jeremy Adelman summarises as 'the invention of something called an electorate ... [and] the invention of a rights-bearing citizen'.[127] The *ancien régime*, with its matrix of social belonging based on overlapping hierarchies with particular privileges and duties, gave way to a new world of individual rights and freedoms. Across the Americas, people began forging new types of subjectivities. The nineteenth century, indeed, might be described as the era of the individual, or, in Ralph Waldo Emerson's words, 'the age of the first person singular'.[128] Historians have shown how liberalism (and its discontents) shaped the conflicts of independence and Spanish American politics and governance. More specifically, a generation of scholars has emphasised the importance of elections for establishing popular sovereignty throughout Latin America, from 1812 to the first half-century of independence (roughly the 1820s to the 1870s for most countries). Much of the focus has been on the national and gubernatorial theatres.[129] But elections also transformed the municipal judicial apparatus, and this is the history of the *juicios verbales*.

The *juicios verbales* show how liberalism worked on the ground. When individuals got into debt trouble, some of them sought help from elected magistrates. This simple, rather boring, municipal hearing evinced the major transformations of liberalism, and particularly of political representation, citizenship, and individual rights. Historians of liberalism have analysed popular politics and political culture to show how ordinary or plebian people engaged with politics, ideology, and the process of state formation across the hemisphere.[130] Ideology manifested itself among elite leaders, to be sure. But it is well established that ordinary people engaged with and produced politics and political culture. Recent scholarship on nineteenth-century liberalism has uncovered, for example, subaltern perspectives and local experiences. Historians of the Spanish colonial world and the early Mexican republic have also examined lower-level, first-instance legal conflicts to address research questions about political culture.[131] Inspired by those studies, this chapter has moved into an even more prosaic realm: bog-standard economic conflicts with almost no mention of ideology or policy.

While there is little evidence that litigants and magistrates made any reference to political ideology (at least as can be gauged from the archival record), the documents reveal the nuts and bolts of a liberal institution functioning at the basic task of governance. The *juicios verbales* thus add a dimension of practical governance to the scholarship on liberalism and political culture. Litigants and magistrates discussed problems and solutions, and, in doing so, they delivered something quite meaningful: a measure of economic justice for ordinary people.

From day to day, the *alcaldes constitucionales* did their job of taking care of municipal business. The economic dimension of citizenship included basic civil responsibilities and rights related to rendering each their due and honouring contracts. These obligations were enshrined in charters, constitutions, and legal codes. Citizenship was also quotidian and active, and the practical meaning of the rules was decided when disputes arose.[132] Part of the success of the *juicios verbales* in mediating disputes probably stemmed from the municipal scale. Scholars of the early modern Spanish world have shown how the parameters of membership and citizenship, and related political and civil rights, were often established at the municipal level (*vecindad*).[133] In this regard, the *juicios verbales* continued a long-standing tradition of local governance: the *alcaldes* may have been elected and the litigants may have been 'unshackled' from many of their colonial corporate identities, but municipal governance had deep roots. The *juicios verbales* illuminate the pragmatic enactment and administration of the rights and responsibilities of people who got into economic trouble in Mexico City. The institution of the *juicios verbales* brought together long-standing Hapsburg traditions, recent Bourbon administrative innovations, and new liberal ideas about sovereignty and citizenship. Herein lay the institution's strength.

THE HUMDRUM AS HISTORIC

The importance of the *juicios verbales* might be, simply, that they happened. The mundane was consequential: by creating a space for the unremarkable everyday need for economic justice, the *juicios verbales* generated stability in a turbulent context. Magistrates mediated small-scale economic conflicts during a time of major political transformations. They delivered everyday economic justice from the colonial twilight to the first decades of the nation state. The chapters that follow show how this sort of ground-level economic justice – these basic civil rights that were enshrined in charters and enacted in conflicts between debtors and creditors – was a bedrock for transformations in the economic and political order that connected New Spain (and, indeed, mediaeval Iberia) with the Mexican state of the nineteenth and twentieth centuries and into the new millennium.

In the *juicios verbales*, both magistrates and litigants embodied new roles and participated in a transformed institution. It was a legal institution with broad legitimacy. It included the election of magistrates while also reflecting an underlying fairness. Cádiz liberalism created institutional strength at the intersection of the urban economy and the municipal judicial apparatus, and the *juicios verbales* provided economic justice for ordinary people. The fight between Ventura Espinosa and Luisa Aguilar, as well as the many other disputes described here, shows people pressing their small claims as newly constituted individuals. Shorn of group identity, for the most part, they appear in the *juicios verbales* as debtors and creditors. In Mexico City, many of these individuals showed up at these hearings to resolve their everyday economic conflicts.

When Ventura Espinosa sued Luisa Aguilar, they participated in a form of judicial mediation with a long history. But it was also a transformed institution grounded by Cádiz liberalism, and one that provided a space for them to negotiate a new future: a resolution that was mediated by an elected magistrate and evinced a fairness. For the growing numbers of litigants, this was enough for them to try their luck. The next chapter, however, explores what happened when more and more people got into trouble with unpaid debts. Tracing how the rules about unpaid debts changed over a *longue durée* that begins in mediaeval Iberia, it examines the different temporalities of economic transformation that shaped the urban economy of Mexico City through the 1860s and 1870s.

2

Broken Contracts

Precaution and Risk in Litigation and Law, 1860s–1870s

When José Nicolás Montes de Oca heard a rumour in January 1865 that the muleteer Hilario Jiménez had returned to Mexico City, he jumped into action. Hoping to repair the damage Jiménez had caused by breaking a contract many years earlier, Montes de Oca rushed to one of Mexico City's first-instance courts and filed a *providencia precautoria* (a precautionary petition). He asked Judge Cristóbal Poulet y Mier to pre-emptively sequester Jiménez's donkeys, which were stabled at a local inn (*mesón*). Montes de Oca presented the judge with a receipt (*recibo*) showing that Jiménez owed him 250 pesos, a debt he had been unable to collect because Jiménez had not returned to the city since 1851. Now, Montes de Oca had good reason to worry that the muleteer might leave again at any moment.

Two witnesses testified to the fact that Jiménez was a flight risk. Gregorio González, a 35-year-old married bacon vendor (*tocinero*) from Mexico City, confirmed that he had heard in a *tocinería* that Jiménez was planning to leave the city imminently. Juan Espinosa, a 77-year-old widowed agent (*corredor*) from San Juan del Río, agreed, adding that he had heard – also in a *tocinería* – that Jiménez was planning to transport four loads of soap when he went. Based on the evidence, Judge Poulet y Mier granted Montes de Oca's request: he temporarily sequestered the donkeys and summoned (*cita*) Jiménez.[1] If, indeed, Jiménez had been planning to depart without paying his debt, his scheme was stymied by gossip at the *tocinería*.

Property sequestration petitions were embedded in daily economic life in the Spanish *ancien régime*, in early modern New Spain, and in republican Mexico. The details changed over time, but the core principle remained the same: creditors could request property sequestration if a debtor fell into arrears or defaulted. Creditors and debtors (and jurists) worried about three categories of problem that could lead to unpaid debts: accidents and unexpected loss, changing market conditions, and malicious intent. In the case of the fourteen-year-old broken contract between Montes de Oca and Jiménez, the former was successfully able to leverage the judicial system to have the latter's donkeys sequestered until a settlement could be reached.

The relationship between creditors and debtors such as Montes de Oca and Jiménez was structurally antagonistic. It was a power struggle over the value of the debt, where one party won and the other lost. And it was not uncommon. When Alfonso X first commissioned the *Siete Partidas* legal code in the thirteenth century, jurists anticipated all sorts of broken contracts between debtors and creditors. After all, as the section on contracts so aptly stated: 'Many inconveniences and serious disputes arise among men on account of contracts and agreements which they enter into with one another.'[2] There was seemingly no way around it: the centrality of contracts to social and economic life had long been established. According to Aristotle's *Rhetoric*, 'most business relations – those, namely, that are voluntary – are regulated by contracts, and if these lose their binding force, human intercourse ceases to exist'.[3]

The rules written by jurists, from the mediaeval Iberian authors of the *Siete Partidas* to the liberal authors of the 1870 Civil Code, regulated the power struggle between creditors and debtors. Their relationship was codified in law and, when something went awry, the conflict played out in the courtroom. Jurists balanced creditors' worries about not being repaid with debtors' concerns over unfair terms. They outlined procedures and punishments for broken contracts that, depending on what had gone wrong, ranged from property sequestration to imprisonment. The smooth functioning of contract disputes was fundamental to economic prosperity and political stability in the territory. Contract law facilitated exchange and legitimised the authority of the monarchy and, later, the republics.

Because many colonial laws remained on the books through most of the nineteenth century, the legal framework governing disputes like the one between Montes de Oca and Jiménez connects mediaeval, early modern, and republican legal codes. Most of the conflicts examined here are from the 1860s and 1870s, and most are precautionary petitions (*providencias precautorias*). However, *tercerías* (claims of third party-ship) and other lawsuits also help map out the conflicts between ordinary debtors and creditors in the capital city. Together, the conflicts and codes explored in this chapter show how individual debtors and creditors angled for advantage, and how jurists working for monarchs and elected leaders tried to balance the interests of each party while considering the greater good.

This chapter first examines legal conflicts and then turns to legal codes. It begins by examining rising litigation rates against a backdrop of increasingly impersonal market relations and an expanding urban population, looking at how creditors used the *providencias precautorias* to allay their anxieties and exploring the many ways in which debtors avoided their obligations. It illuminates how, in the 1860s and 1870s, contract agreements were enmeshed in a social world of gossip and rumour, honour and reputation, and personal relationships. At the same time, contracts were increasingly made between strangers, trust often had to be litigated, and the courts were leveraged to keep things working smoothly. The subsequent examination of legal codes traces how rules for unpaid debts changed over time, suggesting that change and continuity occurred over a long chronology, with neither side enjoying a clear advantage. This formal sense of fairness persisted even as economic subjecthood and long-standing protections from the crown gave way to a new form of economic citizenship designed to encourage trade and economic power. Through both litigation and legal code, traditional economic relations transformed into modern ones within multiple temporalities as the relationship between debtors and creditors shifted to encompass expanding market participation in the nineteenth century.

DEBT LITIGATION ON THE RISE

Small-scale contracts represented the beating heart of the economy. People such as Montes de Oca and Jiménez belonged to a broad and bustling world of proprietary producers, small and medium businesses, petty traders, modest merchants, artisans, domestic servants, and ordinary individuals entering into private agreements with one another. Their economic lives unfolded in butchers' shops and at watchmakers, in boarding houses and in billiards halls, and in factories producing matchsticks, acid, and glass. When they had disputes, they brought them to the civil courts, where they fought over property. Animals such as donkeys and mules, merchandise like religious ornaments and aguardiente (alcohol), equipment including sewing machines and lead-lined chambers, myriad household items from furniture to bird cages and figurines, and much more besides entered the legal record as men and women brought their disputes to court.

The local economy ran on consumption credit for individuals and commercial credit for businesses, all of which flowed through contracts. Contracts, of course, could concern small amounts or great fortunes, and contract law set forth in the *Siete Partidas* and the Commercial Code of 1884 covered long-distance trade by merchants and commercial houses by land and by sea. There exists a robust historiography on wealthy merchants and commercial houses. Scholarship addressing their commercial relations, bankruptcies, and social networks shows their role in economic history. But the world below these big players was, I argue, even more important. This world comprised the firmament of small and medium enterprises.[4] Ordinary people and their businesses, with their contracts and their disputes, formed the bedrock of the economy.

Disputes arose regularly between businesses, between businesses and consumers, and between individuals. The legal backing of contracts was imperative, and the economic power of the realm and nation depended on smoothly resolving small-scale contract disputes. A royal decree from 1786, for example, connected contracts between ordinary debtors and creditors with the commercial prosperity of the empire. Carlos III declared that artisans and labourers would no longer be imprisoned for their unpaid civil debts, an order that changed the power balance between debtors and creditors with the goal of enhancing the realm's economic power.[5] This connection between small-scale relationships and macroeconomic interests went back to mediaeval Iberian legal codes (and, no doubt, earlier), when jurists articulated contract rights in response to the thirteenth-century commercial revolution. Economic power depended on the world of ordinary people like Montes de Oca and Jiménez. While their interpersonal disputes would not reverberate beyond local interests or bring down the economy all on their own, individuals engaging in contractual agreements made up the centre of that economy. Without this entrepreneurial world, the centre would not hold, and the economy would fall apart.

In the nineteenth century, however, something started going wrong for people like Montes de Oca and Jiménez. They were getting into economic trouble more often, and debt litigation was increasing. Such litigiousness was reflected in Chapter 1, which showed growing numbers of ordinary debtors and creditors using the *juicios verbales*. In this chapter, it is indicated by the growing number of disputes in Mexico City's high courts, the records for which are housed in the *Tribunal Superior de*

Justicia del Distrito Federal files at the National Archive. Within these records are heaps of *providencias precautorias*, the petitions used by people like Montes de Oca to safeguard their interests. The *providencia precautoria* was a recourse for individuals before they initiated a formal first-instance lawsuit. It was preliminary, pre-emptive, and temporary.[6] *Providencias precautorias* were an optional first move for plaintiffs with specific worries. People could apply for one before they initiated a civil suit if, for example, they feared that the respondent would disappear (*ausente*) or hide (*oculte*), or that the respondent (or another party) would hide or squander relevant assets (*bienes*).[7]

The process of securing a *providencia precautoria* was complex, but standard. First, the applicant submitted a verbal or written request, demonstrating the necessity of the measure with evidence and witnesses. If the application concerned assets, the applicant described their value. If the application concerned possible flight (*fuga*), the judge would notify the respondent and, if necessary, find and detain them. If the assets involved were money or jewels, these would be deposited with the Monte de Piedad (a charitable institution with various financial roles, including as a pawnshop), furniture would be held in escrow with a custodian named by the judge, and real estate would be safeguarded (*bajo resguardo*) by a custodian. Once the request was accepted (*ejecutado*), the applicant had three days to start civil litigation and, if relevant, *conciliación*. The deadline could be extended if there was distance involved. If the applicant missed the deadline, however, the *providencia precautoria* would be revoked. Likewise, respondents had three days to oppose or appeal (*reclamar u oponerse*). In either case, the judge would summon both parties for a hearing within three days and would receive evidence for an additional six days. Based on evidence heard, the judge would decide to uphold or repeal the *providencia precautoria* within three days of the hearing or six days of receiving evidence. The standard maximum length of time for a *providencia precautoria* was, therefore, three days if uncontested or fifteen days if contested with submitted evidence.[8]

The archive for Mexico City's high courts contains an enormous quantity of these petitions. The collection includes case files from first-, second-, and third-instance jurisdictions, although the specific function of the high courts changed over time along with the considerable changes to Mexico City's judicial structure during the nineteenth century.[9] Put simply, the *Tribunal Superior* courts were below *Suprema Corte de Justicia* but above the magistrates who heard the *juicios verbales*.[10] The archive, as a consequence, holds cases from an array of jurisdictions, which were usually written on the cover or first page of the file. In my sample, there are at least sixteen jurisdictions (several are unknown), and each jurisdiction appears only a few times in the sample. There is a partially functional catalogue that lists the year, case type (*juicio*), jurisdiction (*autoridad*), plaintiff (*actor*), and defendant (*demandado*). Despite some missing or inaccurate information for these fields, the catalogue gives researchers a good sense of litigant names and types of cases over the years. The catalogue, however, does not include box and folder numbers, making it challenging to find specific files. And, for some years, the collection has dozens of boxes with hundreds of files in each.[11]

For the sampling, I collaborated with another historian and we reviewed the boxes from 1836, 1845, 1861, 1865, 1872, and 1878.[12] We researched conflicts over unpaid debts that included *providencias precautorias*, *embargos* (asset sequestration), and *tercerías* (claims of third partyship). This chapter is based on a sample of 137 files. The quantitative statistical analysis is based on a subset of only the *providencia precautoria* cases (97 files). The full sample offers a broader picture of the risks faced by debtors and creditors, with the quantitative analysis more narrowly focused on one type of judicial petition. Table 2.1 presents the subset of *providencia precautoria* cases.

My evidence for rising debt litigation in the Mexico City high courts, though compelling, is preliminary. While the boxes in the archive strongly suggest that there were rising numbers of disputes over unpaid debts in the courts, more precise tabulation of those cases is needed, ideally with an updated catalogue.[13] Because my research was shaped by collaboration, Table 2.1 simply presents the number of *providencias precautorias*

TABLE 2.1 *Sample of* providencia precautoria *petitions, 1836–1878*

Year	Number of *providencia precautoria* cases in sample
1836	2
1845	1
1861	58
1865	11
1872	8
1878	17
Total	97

in my sample; it does not reflect any trends in litigation during these years (such as rising or declining levels of litigation). The total number of *providencias precautorias* in the *Tribunal Superior* collection is difficult to calculate because the catalogue is incomplete and not always accurate.[14] For a rough estimate, I counted the number of *providencias precautorias* in the catalogue, and I did the same for other sorts of cases related to unpaid debts. I focused on the decades from 1850 to 1889. Antonio García Cubas estimated Mexico City's population at 200,000 residents in 1857 and 300,000 residents in 1884.[15] I found that *providencias precautorias* more than tripled during these four decades.[16] Other sorts of debt litigation also rose at a higher rate than the population during the same period. For example, *concursos* more than doubled.[17] *Cesiones* also more than doubled.[18] And *tercerías* increased manyfold.[19] (And, for context, all litigation in the Mexico City high courts increased during these decades, possibly as much as tenfold.[20]) My simple counting of the catalogue entries gives only a very general sense of the files in the archive's boxes, and the information needs to be confirmed by looking at the actual cases.[21] These caveats notwithstanding, the numbers suggest increasing litigation, including debt litigation, during this period.

Notably, economic justice seemed to be working, as people increasingly turned to magistrates and judges for help throughout the century. Moreover, the outcomes of the legal conflicts evinced a strong degree of fairness, as was seen in Chapter 1's *juicios verbales*. The historical question is, therefore: why were people getting into more trouble with little debts? It was not because they lacked effective institutions to protect their property rights, which is a standard scholarly interpretation. It was because the way they did business was becoming outmoded: they assessed trust based on personal relations at a time when economic transactions were becoming more impersonal. In both this chapter and the last, rising debt litigation should be seen as a sign that there were inadequate modes of gauging trustworthiness in a changing urban economy.

When Montes de Oca and Jiménez fought over 250 pesos in 1865, it was an in-between time. Around them, urban economic life was expanding. In retrospect, it is clear that major change was on the horizon. Historian Sandra Kuntz Ficker describes this period as the transition from a traditional to a modern economy. In broad strokes, she suggests, this transition included the structural changes of industrialisation and urbanisation, as well as integration into an international market through railroad construction, foreign investment, and the simple geography of 'being next door to the USA', whose growing economy constituted one of the world's largest markets in 1870.²² The transition to a modern economy occurred within multiple chronological frames, and the inflection point changes depending on the aspect under consideration. Kuntz Ficker traces the structural changes from 1856, but emphasises that the transition really took off in the later 1870s and the 1880s.²³

The 1860s and 1870s offered glimpses of a modern economic future in Mexico City, where most of the conflicts examined in this chapter occurred. But while the future was full of possibilities, getting there was a long and uncertain process. Considering manufacturing, for example, efforts to industrialise in the 1830s and 1840s, especially in textiles, had failed. By mid-century, a new vision of economic modernisation had taken hold. As historian Edward Beatty shows, elites across the ideological spectrum envisioned a future of material progress through the adoption of new technologies to improve agrarian, mining, and manufacturing productivity. Beatty describes how a 'massive wave' of technology imports, from sewing machines to railroads, started around 1870. Within a few decades, it had touched the lives of many ordinary workers and consumers.²⁴

The wave was not yet discernible when Montes de Oca asked the judge to sequester Jiménez's donkeys. The swell was developing, but the old world had not ebbed. Considering national indicators, historian Ernest Sánchez Santiró shows that the Reform War 'truncated' the economic momentum that had originated in the 1830s and 1840s: the economy continued to grow in the 1860s, but at a rate slower than population growth.²⁵ Examining the political economy of market vendors in the capital city, historian Ingrid Bleynat describes the 1870s as a period of 'low stakes' with minimal growth and change.²⁶ Indeed, reviewing the scholarship, Kuntz Ficker summarises the years from 1857 to 1867 as a period with 'few changes' in economic activity.²⁷ She describes how changes were 'interrupted' by political upheaval and highlights how a new institutional framework, and in particular the 1857 Constitution, 'set the conditions' for the later transition to a modern economy divorced from the corporate world of the *ancien régime*. This new framework, she argues, created a private economic sphere distinguished by individual economic action and private property rights.²⁸ These many threads of economic history – industrialisation, technology imports, macroeconomic performance, institutional frameworks – would come together with other modern changes such as urbanisation and railroad construction from the late 1870s until the turn of the century.²⁹ But in the 1860s and 1870s, the modern economic order that ultimately emerged was by no means foretold.

Tensions between macro-level change and the established way of doing things on the ground emerged in Mexico City as the population expanded. Over the course of these years, ordinary people did more business with strangers and transactions became more impersonal. Still, much of economic life for ordinary people was predicated on the social ties of small societies: the judicial system legitimised the anxieties of creditors based on gossip, a person's reputation was paramount in economic transactions, and people could hide from their obligations by physically moving. People such as Montes de Oca and Jiménez lived simultaneously in a world of face-to-face relationships and one of growing impersonal networks. Their conflict in 1865 stemmed from a question that would have been familiar to debtors and creditors centuries earlier: how could they trust each other? Montes de Oca sought the best information he could get, which was gossip at the *tocinería*, and then turned to the courts for recourse. For his part, Jiménez appeared to use distance to avoid his obligation. It was a time when ordinary people might be involved in new sorts of modern economic enterprises, and older modes of establishing trust, based on reputation and face-to-face information, were starting to strain as urban economic life expanded.

TRADING INFORMATION WITH FRIENDS AND STRANGERS

With the city population growing, economic life expanding, and urban society becoming increasingly impersonal in the 1860s and 1870s, debtors and creditors lived in a liminal time. Despite the world changing around them, they continued to make economic agreements and navigate disputes based on the face-to-face relations of small societies, or what sociologist Ferdinand Tönnies terms the *Gemeinschaft*, a community that was 'small-scale, "organic", and close-knit'.[30] Tönnies contrasts this with the larger and more impersonal *Gesellschaft*: a society that was 'large-scale, impersonal, civil and commercial'.[31] Tönnies developed *Gemeinschaft* and *Gesellschaft* as antithetical socio-political concepts. 'In *Gemeinschaft*,' he asserted, '[people] stay together in spite of everything that separates them; in *Gesellschaft* they remain separate in spite of everything that unites them.'[32] Tönnies's sociological constructs are conceptual tools, helpful for highlighting contrasts and examining a general phenomenon in different types of social systems. The concepts are neither evolutionary nor spatial and, in historical terms, elements of both *Gemeinschaft* and *Gesellschaft* can coexist.[33] Tönnies articulated his social theory in the world of Bismarkian Germany, writing that

'*Gemeinschaft* is old, *Gesellschaft* is new, both as an entity and a term'. The newness of the latter perhaps helped him understand the changes around him, including what historian Jose Harris described as Tönnies's coming to terms with 'the psychic anonymity of advanced modernity'.[34]

The *juicios verbales* examined in Chapter 1 likewise represented something new and innovative: individuals shorn of the corporate relations of the *ancien régime* figuring out solutions with elected magistrates when they got into trouble with each other. The *juicios verbales* were a new institutional arrangement that fit with the changing economic possibilities of the nineteenth century. They belonged to a move away from a small society to the more impersonal social relations of a *Gesellschaft*. But the shift from old to new was incomplete, as the *providencias precautorias* show. Disputes between debtors and creditors in the 1860s and 1870s played out simultaneously in the new and the old. The *providencia precautoria* documents show that agreements and disputes between debtors and creditors were enmeshed in the social world of a small society constituted by gossip, reputation, and personal relationships, where the balance between the *Gemeinschaft* and the *Gesellschaft* hinged on information.[35]

Getting good information was one way to address the ever present trust problem, and good information often meant gossip. Gossip, defined simply, is a way in which people transmit or diffuse rumour. Gossip is the mechanism, and rumour is the content.[36] As a category of analysis, gossip and rumours are about transmitting information, and they can certainly transmit important economic information. In fact, a subfield of economics is devoted to the study of rumours, which Abhijit Banerjee defines as 'a class of information transmission processes' used to understand decision-making and optimising behaviour.[37] Gossip and rumours spread information that feeds into a reputation system and can be acted upon. People constantly rely on gathering information through these means to gauge risk and make decisions. The many dimensions of this phenomenon have been engaged by historians. For example, Luise White's scholarship on falsehoods as a source for studying African history has inspired a generation of social and cultural historians to examine rumours and gossip in the archive.[38] And scholars of Latin America have examined gossip and rumour as they relate to political history. However, historians have paid less attention to the economic role of rumours.[39] Analysis of the *providencias precautorias* thus offers an addition to the historiography by examining how creditors and debtors operated in a world of imperfect information.

Gossip shaped individual reputations and helped to establish a debtor's social standing as honourable or dishonourable. In the *providencias precautorias*, economic information was produced within a broader social world, with the economic function of honour becoming more explicit in the later nineteenth century. According to historian Pablo Piccato, intellectual and legal understandings of honour changed from a colonial emphasis on external value based on one's status within social hierarchies to a late nineteenth-century positivist interpretation that honour and reputation had monetary value as a form of private incorporeal property connected to economic development.[40] Reflecting this shift, credit-rating agencies began to measure the commercial value of reputation as a possession in the late nineteenth century (a concept addressed in Chapter 3). Until then, a debtor's good standing could reduce a creditor's uncertainty about their trustworthiness. Because people appraised each other and gauged risk before they entered into economic agreements, their reputation was paramount, and victims could sue in court for damages when they were dishonoured. In the context of imperfect information, then, rumours could be deployed to minimise risk and maximise advantage in an economic transaction. This dynamic of gossip as a reputation mechanism can include, as sociologists suggest, the 'strategic behaviour' of people who spread lies about others or misrepresent themselves.[41]

When a story was crafted, packaged, and spread rapidly, people acted on what they heard. Gossip and rumour were hugely important in the *providencias precautorias*, as borrowers and lenders tried to appraise risk and mitigate loss by putting their ears to the ground. When Ángel Navarro applied for a *providencia precautoria* against Antonio Picazo in November 1878, for example, gossip shaped the economic decisions and legal actions in the case.[42] Picazo owed Navarro 22 pesos and 29 centavos, the remainder of a debt of 65 pesos and 54 centavos related to bacon supplied to Picazo's *carnicería* (butcher) business located on the market plaza. However, Navarro had reason to worry that Picazo might try to get out of paying. It seemed that Picazo's son had been telling people that his father was planning to sell the business in the near future. So, Navarro's representative presented several vouchers documenting the debt and asked for a precautionary ruling to guarantee sufficient assets to cover the debt.

Three witnesses appeared on Navarro's behalf. For most of the cases with witnesses, the archival record includes a page that summarises the questions put to them. Figure 2.1 presents the questions asked in Navarro v Picazo.

The witnesses were asked about the veracity of three statements. The first concerned the debt itself and whether it was true that Antonio Picazo owed Navarro 22 pesos and 29 centavos. The second concerned Picazo's

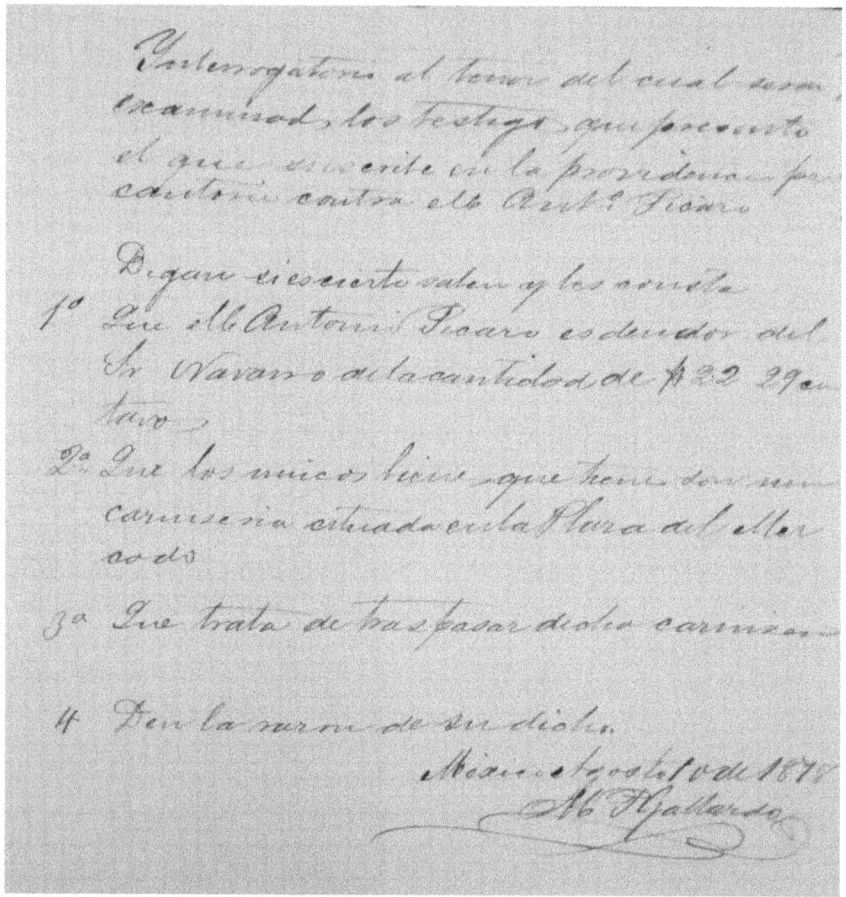

FIGURE 2.1 Questions for witnesses in Ángel Navarro v Antonio Picazo, November 1878. *Source*: Archivo General de la Nación.

resources and whether, indeed, 'his only asset was the *carnicería* on the market plaza'. The third statement concerned Picazo's plans and whether it was true 'that he is trying to transfer [*traspasar*] the *carnicería*'. Finally, witnesses were instructed to 'explain how you came to know this information'.

Félix Ayala was a single 30-year-old bacon vendor from Piedad Michoacán who was a resident of Mexico City and worked for Navarro. He testified in the affirmative to the first three questions. With regard to the fourth, he said that he had seen the debt in Navarro's account books. He also stated that Picazo's son had told him of his father's plans to sell the business when Ayala had visited the shop to sell ham. Indeed, Picazo's son declined to purchase anything because of the plans to sell the shop. León Gómez, a single 22-year-old bacon vender from Morelia and a resident of Mexico City, also answered 'yes' to the first three questions. Apropos the first, he explained that he had been at Picazo's shop to sell meat and lard when the son had told him about his father's plans. The third witness was Manuel Benítez, a married 44-year-old merchant and resident of Mexico City. He also answered affirmatively to the first three questions, claiming that he had seen the vouchers documenting the debt and that, like the others, Picazo's son had revealed his father's plans.

It is tempting to speculate about Picazo's son's motives. Could he have been trying to undermine his father's plans? Or was he gossiping somewhat naïvely? Surely, he must have known he was trading in valuable information when he revealed his father's plans to sell the shop. Unfortunately, the archival record does not give more details and his motive remains unknown. The case record also does not say whether the petition was approved or denied. But what is clear is that the son's information led directly to a creditor applying for a precautionary petition against his father.

Navarro v Picazo shows how economic relationships and conflicts often depended on rumour. Gossip was an important source of information for these cases. Litigants and their witnesses inventoried information about who owed what to whom, as well as who might be selling their businesses or moving out of the city. Gossip depended on personal, sometimes intimate knowledge. And in the absence of formal credit-rating, this information was precious. Notably, gossip did not necessarily provide poorer quality information than the more 'scientific' systems that emerged later. In fact, gossip and rumour had enormous utility in economic transactions and conflicts.

Witnesses represented the face-to-face community in which debtors and creditors operated in the 1860s and 1870s. Witnesses appeared in 41.2 per cent of the cases (40 in total). Most witnesses testified for the plaintiffs as part of their effort to convince the judge that a *providencia precautoria* was warranted. In 35.1 per cent of the 97 cases (34 in total), witnesses appeared for the plaintiffs; in 8.2 per cent of the cases (8 in total), witnesses appeared for the defendant.[43] Men and women both called witnesses, and gender was not a significant variable: there was no significant relationship between plaintiff gender and the presence of a witness, and the same was true for defendant gender and witness presence.[44] It is perhaps unsurprising that witnesses were called in cases with higher financial amounts, as there was more at stake.[45] This connection, however, is particular to witnesses for the plaintiffs. There was no significant relationship between higher amounts and witnesses for the defendants.[46] The presence or absence of witnesses was also not significantly associated with a good outcome (an approved petition). This held true for witnesses in general and regardless of whether the witness appeared on behalf of the plaintiff or defendant.[47] The picture that emerges is that litigants called witnesses as part of routine court procedure, and the presence of witnesses was not significantly associated with the other variables.

The witness testimony brings to life neighbourhood spaces such as *carnicerías* where people socialised while doing business. In the realm of small and medium enterprises, people bought and sold goods and services while trading information that helped them form impressions about trust, risk, and vulnerability. And sometimes that information became evidence in debt litigation. A face-to-face world of relationships and reputations encased the transactions and troubles of ordinary people and their businesses. This was not unique to Mexico City. In his study of early modern England, historian Craig Muldrew describes how socialising created an 'economy of obligation' where people made judgements about the reliability of their neighbours (who might be potential borrowers) through conversations in shops and marketplaces.[48] Because they are about unpaid debts, the *providencias precautorias* and the other petitions studied here do not usually explain how litigants came to their original agreements and on what basis they decided to trust each other. How, for example, had Navarro appraised Picazo's trustworthiness when he advanced the original credit? However, based on the role of gossip in Navarro's decision to file the *providencia precautoria*, it seems probable that gossip at the *carnicería* might also have facilitated these two men's participation in the credit market in the first place.

Trust between debtors and creditors was a social relationship. Indeed, the trust problem was about trusting people, and one of the biggest risks for ordinary debtors and creditors was also the most mundane: personal relationships soured. Perhaps this is what happened, for example, when a man named Juan Castro declared that he would rather throw away the assets in question than pay anything to Mónica Sánchez.[49] The two had operated a boarding house (*comercio de fonda*) together. Sánchez ran the business (*socio industrial*) and Castro was the investor (*socio capitalista*). They had agreed to split the profits. Sánchez requested a *providencia precautoria* in October 1865, claiming that Castro had fired her without paying what she was owed. In fact, he had refused to show her the account book, and he was now trying to sell the business and leave the city. Furthermore, as he himself declared, Castro was threatening to throw away the business assets rather than pay her a peso. She therefore asked the judge to secure (*asegurar*) the boarding house's assets.

Two witnesses testified on Sánchez's behalf: Rufina Reyes, an elderly married woman from Mexico City, and Benito Centeno, a 30-year-old married tailor from Mexico City. They answered three questions:

1. Is it true that Juan Castro is trying to sell so that he can leave the city?
2. Is it true that Castro is trying to sell because Sánchez is demanding payment?
3. Is it true that Castro said he would prefer to throw away the assets (*derrochar los bienes*) rather than pay Sánchez?

Reyes declared that Castro had asked her to tell him if anyone was interested in buying the business because he wanted to leave the city. She added that she had heard Castro say that he preferred to throw away the goods rather than pay Sánchez. Centeno answered in the affirmative as well, explaining that he had heard Castro himself provide all of the information in question. The judge summoned Castro to clarify the amount owed; when both Castro and Sánchez appeared the following day, Castro agreed that he would pay her 14 pesos within fifteen days. He would also cover half the cost of her legal fees. However, it was not an agreement worth trusting. Castro failed to meet the deadline, so Sánchez requested a *providencia precautoria*. Three days later, she accompanied the assessor to the boarding house, where Castro paid the 14 pesos.

Sánchez and Castro had probably started their business with enthusiasm. The boarding house likely represented an opportunity for each to improve their economic condition. Indeed, many of the *providencias precautorias* studied here probably began with an optimistic entrepreneurial plan. But because this book is about what happened when agreements soured, the conflicts – like Sánchez v Castro – do not reveal much of the hopes that led them to take a chance on the partnership. And sometimes plans simply went wrong. When the personal relationships undergirding such arrangements broke down, the economic enterprise could be damaged. The tenor of the Sánchez v Castro conflict stands out for its acrimony and antipathy, particularly the vehemence of Castro's words. Why would he prefer to throw away the goods rather than pay Sánchez? Why would he be willing to destroy his assets? It might be that Castro perceived a transgression by Sánchez that was deeper than a typical business conflict. Whatever the cause of their antagonism, it jeopardised their agreement, their business, and the assets. Small and medium enterprises depended on people trusting people, and Sánchez and Castro had failed.

Personal relationships extended beyond debtors and creditors to include other parties, too. Guarantors also faced trust problems. This was the case for Ángel González, who served as a guarantor (*fiador*) for Florencio Hernández. Hernández was preparing to move from Mexico City to Pachuca. As part of this process, he started disposing of his belongings. This led González to request, through his representative, a *providencia precautoria* on 28 January 1879. González had served as Hernández's guarantor for the rental of his home, and when Hernández fell into arrears, González was on the hook to the landlord for 52 pesos and 80 centavos. He wanted to ensure that enough of Hernández's belongings remained to cover the debt. The day after González made the request, three witnesses supported his claim. Francisco Violante, a 38-year-old married employee from Mexico City, declared that he had heard Hernández describing how he was unable to pay the debt because, since closing his watchmaking business (*relojería*), his only resources were a few pieces of furniture and other objects. A second witness, José Pablo de la Torre, a 28-year-old married employee from Puebla, said the same; he had heard this when he accompanied González's representative in an effort to collect the debt. Finally, José María Violante, a 66-year-old widowed miner from Mexico City, added that, because of his friendship with Hernández, he knew that the man was unable to pay his debts and was planning to move to Pachuca.

On 1 February, the assessor went with González's representative to Hernández's house. Hernández said he was unable to pay the debt, and that his belongings had been embargoed in another court proceeding: three bird cages with canaries, one seamstress's chair, one table, two Apache figurines, two paintings, one mirror, and one book. Three days later, on 4 February, Hernández went to court and opposed the *providencia precautoria*, claiming that González and the witnesses were lying ('*lo dicho ... es falso*'). He also claimed that a procedural technicality had not been followed. The judge summoned all parties for a hearing, which occurred on 10 February after various delays. Hernández (through his representative) alluded to a complex real estate transaction related to the house he was renting, which, he claimed, muddied the waters for the *providencia precautoria*. González disagreed, asserting that the real estate matter was irrelevant because Hernández had already admitted to the debt. The file, unfortunately, does not contain the judge's final decision.[50]

Of course, González's frustration raises the fundamental question: why did he agree to be Hernández's guarantor in the first place? González was certainly not alone in regretting the decision. The archives are replete with examples of guarantors trying to get repaid. At first glance, it seemed a bad risk, as González faced the prospect of losing 52 pesos and 80 centavos. But the file does not give information about the relationship between González and Hernández, and the former might have had a well-defined interest in being a *fiador*. They might have been connected through blood or marriage ties, or perhaps they were entangled commercially. Or they may have been more loosely acquainted, with González serving as guarantor to cultivate or uphold his reputation in the local community.

Serving as a *fiador* could bring a person economic advantage by enhancing their standing. Historian Daniel Vickers has examined the economic function of reputation in early New England, showing how ordinary people balanced collecting debts and getting along with their neighbours. For rural householders, he argues, 'what mattered in this balance was partly that one received roughly what one was owed from all of one's different correspondents considered together and partly that one was perceived around town as a dependable person'.[51] It was the same for people who ran small and medium businesses in Mexico City. They evaluated the trustworthiness of potential debtors and creditors vis-à-vis a person's reputation. If people like González were motivated to advance their pecuniary interests, they might be tempted to risk sums of money to enhance their reputations.

The opposite was also possible, however. *Fiadores* risked damaging their reputations if things went poorly. This is what happened in November 1878 when Francisco Adam requested a *providencia precautoria* against Soledad Montes, to whom he had rented a sewing machine valued at 70 pesos. A company called Fajardo Cabo y Compañía had served as Montes's guarantor in the transaction. According to their contract, Adam would collect (*recoger*) the machine if Montes missed a payment. At this point, Montes had missed a month's payment and, Adam claimed, had disappeared (*se ha ocultado*). Adam therefore requested a *providencia precautoria* to secure the machine, which he believed was in the possession of Fajardo Cabo y Compañía.

The first witness, Miguel Esnaurrizar, a 19-year-old employee (*dependiente*) from Mexico City, declared that the circumstances outlined by Adam were accurate, that he did not know Montes, and that the *fiador* had had a butcher's shop on the Segunda Calle de Plateros. However, he stated that, the shop was now closed. The second witness, Agustín Ramírez, a 25-year-old married metalsmith (*latonero*) from Mexico City, said the same, except that he noted that Montes's *fiador* owned a matchstick factory on the Calle del Niño Perdido. Finally, the third witness, Nabor Chávez, a 42-year-old merchant from Mexico City, affirmed the events as described by Adam, but shared that he knew neither Montes nor her *fiador*. No doubt Adam was keen to secure either the sewing machine or enough assets from Fajardo Cabo y Compañía to cover the debt, but the case highlights the difficulty of debtor–creditor relationships in an increasingly impersonal environment.

In the end, the judge ordered the *providencia precautoria*. However, neither Montes nor her *fiador* could be located. Eight days later, Adam's representative returned to report that the *providencia precautoria* had not worked (*no dio resultado*). He requested that the judge return all the paperwork so that he might pursue the matter in another court.[52] In this example, it seems possible that both Montes and her *fiador* had engaged in dishonourable behaviour, and both risked damaging their reputations.

This was the liminal world of the 1860s and 1870s. New economic possibilities were emerging, such as renting a sewing machine. The machine was emblematic of a nascent industrial capitalism and represented a mechanisation of production that both alienated people from their labour and interposed an estrangement between ordinary people in face-to-face economic relationships. As Edward Beatty shows, the adoption of new technologies embodied in machines, in occupations ranging from sewing to glass blowing, started around 1870. He describes how 'their adoption altered both production and people's lives by substituting mechanical methods for what had previously been homemade, handmade, and locally made'. He continues to suggest that, 'by 1910, many Mexicans found work in the new industries, consumed the products of new factories, and saw their lives affected in powerful ways'.[53] Soledad Montes and her guarantors belonged to that new world. But, in 1878, they could still disappear, leaving creditors such as Francisco Adam high and dry, because they operated simultaneously in an impersonal world and a face-to-face one.

While impersonal and personal modes of economic life existed simultaneously for the two centuries covered by this book – as they did at many other times and in many other places – the balance between them was changing.[54] The sewing machine conflict shows a new world of the machine and the economic relationships it represented encased in an older world where a debtor and her guarantors could simply vanish. And as the broader economic possibilities for ordinary people started to expand, older modes of establishing trust failed more frequently. It is perhaps no surprise, therefore, that debt litigation was on the rise.

RISK, UNCERTAINTY, AND THE *PROVIDENCIAS PRECAUTORIAS*

Creditors and debtors clearly took risks when they struck agreements. Creditors knew that it was possible the debtor would not repay, and debtors knew they risked legal and financial penalties if they were unable to meet their obligations. Risk meant that the possibility of an undesirable outcome existed for both sides. Related to uncertainty but with nuanced differences, risk generally concerned probabilities that could be foreseen, like a debtor falling into arrears because of a change in employment or personal circumstances. Uncertainty, by contrast, was more related to the unforeseeable future, like a debtor being trampled to death by a horse.[55]

Creditors tended to operate in the world of practical risk calculation. They tried to anticipate what their debtors might do, knowing that, if misfortune befell them, some debtors would endeavour to discharge their obligations while others could be expected to evade and abscond. Creditors thus usually tried to get their hands on the debtor's property – Jiménez's donkeys, for instance – to secure the debt. If the original debt had not been secured by collateral, a creditor could subsequently attempt to seize property if a debtor fell into arrears. For creditors who found themselves in such a predicament, they had a powerful legal tool at their disposal: the *providencia precautoria*.

The archival record of the *providencias precautorias* gives quite a bit of information about the relationships existing between debtors and creditors. When compared with the *juicios verbales* studied in Chapter 1, the more extended record is a function of the fact that these conflicts unfolded as a different type of legal case in a different jurisdiction. The *providencias precautorias* were presented in first-instance courts with formally trained judges; the *juicios verbales*, which were heard by magistrates who often had no legal training, were intended to keep disputes out of the first-instance courts. Whereas records of the *juicios verbales* consisted of short descriptions of quick resolutions, the *providencia precautoria* petitions show how debtors and creditors tried to minimise risk, from gathering information to jostling for their interests in the courtroom. The *providencias precautorias* were not used exclusively to resolve economic disputes, but most of them were about broken contracts, and most of these petitions were submitted by creditors. And because the *providencias precautorias* gave creditors the power to pre-emptively seize property or detain debtors, there was much at stake.

For the quantitative analysis of the *providencia precautoria* cases, the main variables can be grouped into two categories: people and their problems; and the judicial proceedings themselves. The first set of variables encompasses the litigants' economic lives: litigants' gender, the financial amount involved, and the reason behind the problem (non-payment of rent, for example). The second set of variables reflects issues of economic justice: the witness testimony, the evidence given, the circumstances presented (such as if the applicant claimed that the respondent was about to return or to leave the city), the resolution, and the length of time a case lasted.[56] The tests run included t-tests, correlations, Fisher's exact tests, and chi-squared tests.[57]

These petitions show how people used the courts to repair the damage from a broken contract. As with the *juicios verbales* cases, most litigants were men. Of the plaintiffs, 87.6 per cent (n=85 cases) were men and 9.3 per cent (9) were women.[58] Of the defendants, 90.7 per cent (88) were men and 5.2 per cent (5) were women.[59] Unlike the *juicios verbales*, the most common reason for the conflict was commercial, with 30.9 per cent (30) of the *providencias precautorias* relating to a debt connected to a business, followed closely by unspecified debts at 28.9 per cent (28). The only other reasons that appear in more than 10 per cent of the petitions are rental conflicts and conflicts over goods or assets (*bienes*), such as furniture or machinery, each at 11.3 per cent (11 cases).[60] The financial value of disputes in the *providencias precautorias* are higher than in the *juicios verbales* (which concerned amounts under 100 pesos) but still relate to the world of ordinary people. The minimum amount disputed in any petition is 7 pesos, with the maximum being 4,500 pesos.[61] Tables 2.2 and 2.3 present the financial amounts at stake by gender of both the defendants and the plaintiffs.

Finally, Table 2.4 offers context for the value of the amounts described in this chapter by sketching the value of the peso in the 1860s and 1870s. Section A presents four examples of assets valued over 100 pesos that appear in the *providencias precautorias*.[62] In my sample, not many petitions clearly described the assets at stake or their full value (unlike the data in the *juicios verbales*). There are many reasons for this omission in the individual records: the *providencias precautorias* often involved a combination of assets and services; the dispute concerned only a portion of the original debt; the disputed amount represented only a portion of the

TABLE 2.2 *Amounts disputed and gender of plaintiffs in* providencias precautorias, *1836–1878*

	Total amounts					
	Male plaintiffs			Female plaintiffs		
Year	Mean	Minimum	Maximum	Mean	Minimum	Maximum
1836	1,185	1,185	1,185			
1845	352	352	352			
1861	340	7	4,500	128	52	205
1865	562	32	3,000			
1872	386	140	520	539	20	1,167
1878	225	22	1,000	339	339	339
Total	367	7	4,500	393	20	1,167

TABLE 2.3 *Amounts disputed and gender of defendants in* providencias precautorias, *1836–1878*

	Total amounts					
	Male defendants			Female defendants		
Year	Mean	Minimum	Maximum	Mean	Minimum	Maximum
1836	1,185	1,185	1,185			
1845	352	352	352			
1861	326	7	4,500	90	90	90
1865	507	32	3,000	1,000	1,000	1,000
1872	549	28	1,167	20	20	20
1878	224	22	1,000	285	70	500
Total	365	7	4,500	336	20	1,000

asset's value, and so on. For example, the highest disputed amount in the sample was 4,500 pesos in a conflict that transpired in 1861 between two business partners over the transfer of a spinning mill (*fábrica de hilados*) in Tacubaya. The archival record, however, does not indicate whether the disputed amount represented the full or partial value of the mill.[63] Table 2.4 presents, instead, the valuation of a different business: a *zapatería* worth 14,722 pesos in 1877, which featured in a dispute over some equipment and furniture (the value of which was unspecified).[64] Even when the archival record gives the full value of an asset, it can be difficult to interpret the information: what, for example, was the condition of the horse or the scale of the *zapatería*?

TABLE 2.4 *Value of a peso in the 1860s and 1870s*

Section A: Value of assets[a]

Year	Value (pesos)	Asset	Valuation detail
1861	719	Sugar, ca. 4,500 kg (410 arrobas, 21 *libras*). No further details given.	Value determined at sale in May 1861, with full amount to be paid within two months.
1872	499	Equipment for hair salon (*peluquería*). Includes furniture and tools.	Value initially determined at beginning of business partnership (no date given).
1877	14,722	Shoe factory (*zapatería*) 'Botín Español' at 5 Calle de Vergara. Includes stock, furniture, and equipment.	Value determined at time of sale in July 1877, with 5,000 to be paid in cash at sale and remainder in *pagarés* of six and twelve months.
1878	110	Horse, with saddle and bridle. No further details given.	Value determined at sale in November 1878, with the full amount to be paid within two months.

Section B: Salaries in Mexico City Poor House, 1870[b]

Annual salary (pesos)	Employee position
600	Director
360	Top positions (assistant directors, girls' teacher, boys' teacher, doctor, clerk, master tailor, laundress)
288	Artisan masters (master carpenter, master shoemaker)
240	Supervisor (boys' department)
96	Nurse (male and female), assistant laundress, gatekeeper
48	Water carrier
36	Firewood steward
15	Supervisor (baths)

Section C: Cost advertised for stagecoach travel (*viajes en diligencia*), 1869[c]

Cost (pesos)	Trip
45	Mexico City to Guadalajara
41	Mexico City to Zacatecas
38	Mexico City to Aguascalientes
25	Mexico City to Guanajuato
15	Mexico City to Querétaro
6	Mexico City to Cuernavaca

[a] All examples from the *providencia precautorias* records. For sugar in 1861: 'Providencia Provisional y Precautoria contra Don Juan de las Cuevas, Pedida por Don José María Bustamante', 18 September 1861, AGN, TSJDF, c. 351. For *peluquería* in 1872: 'Peredo Eduardo Demanda a Blancas José María Sobre Providencia Precautoria', 20 May 1872, AGN, TSJDF, c. 523. For *zapatería* in 1877: 'Providencia Precautoria Pedida por Don Pedro Berruecos contra Don Nicanor y Don Julián Samarriba y Gómez', 20 July 1878, AGN, TSJDF, c. 651. For horse in 1878: 'Alegría Mariano contra Pablo Samaniego. Providencia Precautoria', 28 January 1879, AGN, TSJDF, c. 645.
[b] All salary data from Arrom, *Containing the Poor*, 269, table 31.
[c] *La Iberia*, 20 November 1869, 4.

Section B of Table 2.4 presents annual salaries earned by employees of the Mexico City Poor House in 1870, drawn from Silvia Arrom's *Containing the Poor*, as another framework for interpreting the amounts discussed in this chapter.[65] The director earned 600 pesos (although this would be increased to 1,200 in 1872, when the city council raised her salary to what the previous director, a man, had received).[66] Employees in top positions earned 360 pesos, and women held six of these ten positions. Given that 360 pesos is very close to the median value of all the disputed amounts in the *providencias precautorias* dataset (363 pesos), the salaries help explain what was at stake in these petitions: a year's income for fairly high-level professional work. Arrom's research further contextualises the distribution of the amounts disputed in the sample of *providencias precautorias*: 25 per cent of the disputes concerned amounts lower or equal to 44 pesos, less than the annual salary of the Poor House's water carrier (48 pesos) but higher than that of the firewood steward (36 pesos). Along with the baths supervisor (who earned 15 pesos per annum), these were the three lowest-paid employees at the Poor House. Next, 50 per cent of the disputes concerned amounts lower or equal to 92 pesos, a little lower than a nurse's annual salary (96 pesos). Seventy-five per cent of the *providencias precautorias* concerned amounts lower or equal to 250 pesos, an amount that represented more than the annual salary earned by the supervisor of the boy's department (240 pesos) but meaningfully less than that earned by the master carpenter and the master shoemaker (288 pesos). Put simply, most of the amounts disputed in the sample of *providencias precautorias* fall within the range of annual salaries at the Poor House in 1870.

Section C gives examples of the cost of stagecoach travel in 1869, as announced in the newspaper *La Iberia* on 20 November 1869. The lowest amount disputed in my sample of the *providencias precautorias* (7 pesos) is just higher than the cost of travel from Mexico City to Cuernavaca (6 pesos). In its totality, therefore, Table 2.4 presents some anecdotal context for the amounts discussed in this chapter. Another shorthand strategy for interpreting the amounts converts the pesos to American dollars, which exchanged at nearly par during the 1860s and 1870s.[67]

Providencias precautorias were a large part of legal life in New Spain and Mexico. The merits of the 'precautionary principle' are debated in international legal systems today, with scholarship focusing on the principle's recent origins.[68] However, it has a deep history in Mexico and New Spain.[69] One of the many legal options available in debt litigation, the precautionary nature of these petitions sheds light on when people felt vulnerable and how they anticipated problems. Precaution, as a concept, gave a very particular right to act pre-emptively, which illuminates the power dynamic between debtor and creditors. Overall, the financial amounts at stake in these petitions relate to the modest and middling world of working labourers, artisans, and professionals. For these people, the amounts would have been important and consequential but also relatable and, for some, attainable. The 97 *providencia precautoria* files, together, paint a picture of the firmament of small and medium enterprises: most litigants were men who found themselves in trouble because something had gone wrong in their business dealings.

PROPERTY SEIZURE AND THE POLITICS OF PROPERTY RIGHTS

Creditors used the courts, with success, to get their hands on the property of delinquent debtors. Tallying the outcomes, creditors did well: 83.5 per cent (81) of the *providencias precautorias* were approved, 6.2 per cent (6) were denied, and the resolution was unknown in 10.3 per cent (10) cases. Creditors tended to 'win'. Thus, in practical terms, the *providencias precautorias* gave creditors substantial power over debtors to seize property or detain persons. Montes de Oca, for example, transmitted his concerns to the court, and the judge acted.

Within a context that benefited creditors, different types of people could expect a similar process and similar outcomes in the *providencias precautorias*. The resolutions were not significantly related to other variables in the dataset, which suggests that the resolutions were random. For example, tests found no statistically significant relationship between gender and outcome: the gender of the plaintiff was not significantly associated with a petition being approved or not. The same was true for the defendant.[70] The amount in question also did not matter vis-à-vis outcomes: the mean amounts owed in approved petitions and denied petitions were not statistically different from each other.[71] And finally, the reason behind the financial conflict, such as unpaid rent, did not matter either: there is no statistically significant relationship between the reason for the conflict and whether a petition was approved or denied.[72] Looking at the relationships – and the lack of them – between these variables and outcomes, the overall picture is therefore similar to the findings of Chapter 1: the courts, which were the main arena for settling property disputes, appeared to have worked fairly. Different people and different sorts of problems were not treated differently in legal proceedings.[73]

Insofar as the *providencias precautorias* generally favoured the creditor's petition, what circumstances led to denial? Judges denied six *providencias precautorias* because of improper procedure, insufficient evidence, or incorrect jurisdiction. For example, in January 1878, Agustín Heeser, through his representative José Rufino Azuceno, sued Peraire y Compañía for 159 pesos, the remaining debt for merchandise (*efectos*) that Heeser had sold them. The debt was documented in a *carta*. In recent days, however, the señores Peraire had closed their billiards hall in the Hotel Nacional. Thus, Heeser requested a *providencia precautoria* to prohibit the removal of any assets from the business until the debt was settled.

Heeser presented three witnesses. Enrique Biron, a 49-year-old single artisan originally from France and resident of Mexico City, testified that the señores Peraire owed Heeser 159 pesos (he had seen the *carta*), that their billiards hall had been closed (he had seen it from the street), and that the business's assets were still in the location (this was public and well known). The other two witnesses corroborated Biron's account. Pedro Lanon, a 30-year-old merchant, also a resident of Mexico City, originally from France, presented similar information: he had seen the *carta*, had frequented the billiards hall often; he knew it was closed, and knew that its goods were under lock and key at the hotel because he had heard it from Juan Labasque, who had been the one to lock the door. Finally, Enrique Casuerregui, a 34-year-old married employee (*dependiente*), again from France and also a resident of Mexico City, testified that he knew of the debt because he worked for Heeser. He had seen the billiards hall closed, and the owner of the building had told him that he had confiscated the business's assets.

The judge denied Heeser's request, however, arguing that the witnesses did not present sufficient evidence to support their statements. They had assured the court that they had seen the *carta*, but, the judge asserted, it did 'not prove anything'. The judge also said that, although Heeser had argued that Peraire y Compañía had goods being held by the building's owner, he did not claim that they had no other assets.[74] The first point raises a question: did the judge dismiss the witnesses' testimony because they were foreigners? After all, the witnesses in the Montes de Oca v Jiménez case had also testified based on gossip, as was common for witnesses who appeared in the *providencia precautoria* hearings. However, there are not enough cases with foreigners to run tests, so the question remains open. In an archival record suffuse with examples of court proceedings relying on eyewitness accounts based on gossip, rumour, and personal relationships, the case certainly stands out.

In other respects, the six denied cases were not especially remarkable: as in Heeser v Peraire, all people involved were men. The 159 pesos at stake in Heeser v Peraire were at the lower end of amounts disputed, with the other denied cases concerning 14 pesos, 200 pesos, 520 pesos, 1,000 pesos, and an amount not specified. The business conflict at the root of Heeser v Peraire was fairly typical as well: two of the other denied petitions stemmed from business conflicts. The remaining denied petitions concerned an unspecified debt, a previous sequestration (*embargo*), and unpaid rent. Overall, aside from the prominence of Frenchmen in Heeser v Peraire, the denied cases were unexceptional.

Prevailing in court, however, might not always have been the goal of a petition. Creditors sometimes initiated a judicial proceeding as a strategy to leverage a private arrangement, as filing a petition could be a form of pressure.[75] This was probably what happened when Carlota Luna applied for a *providencia precautoria* against Francisco E. Trejo in May 1878. She petitioned the court, she claimed, because he had failed to make payment on a *libranza* (payment order) for 200 pesos.[76] The *libranza* was dated 10 January 1876, and Trejo had promised to pay within six months but failed to do so. Interest began accumulating on 10 July 1876 at a rate of 3 pesos per month; it totalled 139 pesos by the time Luna appeared before the court. Luna thus demanded payment of 339 pesos, but because Trejo was currently in Colima, Luna was unable to recover her debt. She claimed instead that Trejo was owed money by one Francisco Berti, and she requested that the court order Berti to subtract 339 pesos from the amount he owed to Trejo and hold the funds until the matter could be investigated further. She also asked the judge how she should proceed with a suit against Trejo, given the distance between Mexico City and Colima.

Luna presented three witnesses for her case: José Luis Morali, a married 58-year-old merchant and resident of Mexico City; Agustín Barrete, a married 48-year-old merchant who was from Colima but had become a Mexico City resident; and Juan Lozano, a married 56-year-old merchant from Morelia and also a Mexico City resident. Each witness was asked three questions. 'What assets does Trejo possess?' They all answered that, to their knowledge, Trejo did not have assets. 'Does Berti owe Trejo money?' Two of the witnesses answered yes; the third professed ignorance. 'How do you know about Berti's debt to Trejo?' They replied that they were friends of both Luna and Trejo, and one of the witnesses described how it was well known that Berti owed Trejo 900 pesos. As a result of this testimony, the judge ordered Trejo to appear in court in Mexico City within forty days. But, less than two weeks later, Luna withdrew her complaint, explaining that she had reached a private arrangement with Trejo's representative. No doubt, the threat of a court appearance eased the process.

Luna was not the only applicant to pursue a strategy of leveraging the precautionary ruling to force a debtor into a satisfactory agreement. Sometimes merely filing a petition was sufficient. Of the 97 *providencia precautoria* cases, 14.4 per cent were withdrawn (14 cases). The withdrawn petitions were not significantly related to variables such as the gender of litigants or the amount involved.[77] In these cases, the plaintiffs may indeed have been angling for private resolution, using the preliminary filing as a threat of future legal action. And many of the withdrawn petitions might have achieved their purpose. As Luna v Trejo shows, creditors used the courts in ways that were not always what the system intended. People were infinitely creative in their uses (and abuses) of legal petitions.

The existence of legal recourse, from these preliminary petitions to extended civil suits, helped creditors trust debtors. But because the *providencias precautorias* gave creditors tremendous power, the petition had its critics. A December 1869 editorial in the liberal newspaper *El Siglo Diez y Nueve* excoriated the 'diabolic' precautionary rationale that stripped citizens of their property before a suit got underway. It described how 'innumerable families have been ruined by having had this petition filed against them'.[78] A May 1877 editorial in the liberal *El Monitor Constitucional* further argued that, without better pay, the judiciary was vulnerable to corruption, especially through petitions such as *providencias precautorias*. '*Las diligencias de embargo, las providencias precautorias,*' it read, '*se efectúa á merced de la influencia pecuniaria de los interesdos*' (implying that the judges who oversee the embargo and precautionary petition proceedings often expect some pecuniary reward from the interested parties).[79] Public fears about corrupt judges, however, might have been overstated. Insofar as can be appraised from the variables and quantitative tests, the judges who heard *providencias precautorias* seem to have acted fairly. Men and women could expect similar outcomes, disputes of small and large sums were treated in a similar way, and so on. But regardless of whether or not some judges accepted bribes, the fear itself was a critique of a petition that gave creditors so much power.

Conflicts such as Luna v Trejo belonged to two historical temporalities: the political history of the nineteenth century, a time of massive and rapid change in the property rights that structured much of economic life; and the legal history of contract law, which also changed but on a more extended chronology. Property rights were the rules pertaining to the ownership and use of 'things', including land (private, communal, and public holdings) and intellectual material (such as patents or artistic works). A capacious category that covered many kinds of things, property rights could also encompass a contract as something that could be exchanged (such as through debt transfer). At the most basic level, property rights were rules governing the relationship between a person and a thing, such as the nature of a person's dominion over a thing and a person's right to use, profit from, or alienate a thing.[80] Contract law, by contrast, was about relationships between people. People came together to make contracts, which were mutually binding agreements or promises that might or might not be written down. Contract law governed these relationships, such as who could contract with whom and on what terms.

While property rights and contract law were different – the former was anonymous; the latter was intimate – the interface between them was large and consequential.[81] Property sequestration penalties for broken contracts, for example, were part of that interface. When Judge Poulet y Mier granted Montes de Oca's *providencia precautoria*, the opposing parties entered the interface: Montes de Oca and the contract versus Jiménez and the donkeys. Property rights and contract law, together, were the rules of the game when people struck economic agreements with each other. And these rules were fundamental to economic exchange.

At the interface of property rights and contract law, the *providencias precautorias* add nuance to a major theme in Mexican history: the politics of property rights. Property rights changed massively in nineteenth-century Mexico, especially those pertaining to corporate land ownership. The consequent upheaval of social structures – and people's lives – was one component of the civil wars between liberals and conservatives in Mexico and, indeed, across Latin America.[82] Liberal elites in Mexico worked to privatise corporately owned land with the aim of encouraging investment, increasing access to credit, and sparking economic growth. The outline of this history is well known. The period of liberal reform (1855–1857) included the *Ley Lerdo*, which forced the sale of communal lands, especially ecclesiastic and indigenous holdings. It also included the *Ley Juárez*, which reduced the legal privileges of the military and the clergy. Both were part of the 1857 Constitution, which proclaimed Mexico a liberal, secular republic. These changes led to violent conservative dissent and several years of civil war. When the liberals triumphed briefly in 1861, they passed a new legal code, the *Código de la Reforma*, which expanded the 1857 rules. Several more years of civil war ensued, however, until the liberals emerged victorious in 1867.

There is a robust scholarship on this history, analysing the effects on indigenous communities and ecclesiastic institutions, the gaps between constitutional ideals and on-the-ground realities, political turmoil at the local, national, and regional levels, and the liberal and conservative worldviews.[83] When the liberals returned to power during the Restored Republic (1867–1876) and under Porfirio Díaz (1876–1880 and 1884–1911), they began a wave of codification that has come to be called the 'institutional revolution'. Among other legislation, the Civil Code was passed in 1870, and both the Commercial Code and the Mining Code were passed in 1884. Generations of historians have explored the dislocations and opportunities created by the changing property rights regimes in the later nineteenth century, particularly vis-à-vis land ownership.[84]

Contract law – the rules for debtors and creditors – also changed during the nineteenth century. By the late nineteenth century, for example, both debt imprisonment and usury restrictions were gone. The first was a victory for debtors; the second for creditors. Both of these changes, however, began centuries before in mediaeval Iberia, as discussed later in the chapter, and extended beyond the conflicts between liberals and conservatives over property rights. Amidst the enormous and violent disagreement between liberals and conservatives, there was some common ground when it came to contract law. Both liberals and conservatives wanted people to establish enterprises, and they supported economic freedom for debtors and creditors, including freedom from the older constraints of debt imprisonment and usury prohibition. Shifting the chronological perspective and examining the *longue durée* of legal history thus illuminates some correspondence between liberal and conservative worldviews.

The *providencias precautorias* add nuance to the parameters of scholarly debate about property rights and power struggles. Debtors' rights exist in opposition to creditors' rights, and vice versa. Yet there exists something of a bifurcation in the scholarship: some scholars highlight the experience of debtors, while others focus on creditors. Within the social history tradition, on the one hand, there exists a tendency to emphasise the weak property rights of debtors, which scholars examine in chronologies of exploitation and resistance.[85] Within the institutional model of economic history, on the other hand, the main historical research questions concern the rights of creditors, and scholars connect the weak property rights of creditors and investors to poor macroeconomic performance.[86] Focusing mostly on the rights of one side can lead to problems for historical interpretation: it can overstate the vulnerability of either debtors or creditors because it misses the primary tension, which is the power struggle between the two.

Debtors and creditors were defined by their dyadic relationship in a contract, inseparable from the moment they entered into an economic agreement with one another. One goal of this book is to expand the scholarly conversation so that analyses of property rights begin with a consideration of both parties. The debtor/creditor dyad illuminates a key power struggle in the history of exploitation and opportunity, with their mutual dependence clear to jurists from mediaeval Iberia to nineteenth-century Mexico.

In the final analysis, *providencias precautorias* helped both creditors and debtors. Creditors enjoyed considerable power to sequester property. The numerous *providencia precautoria* files in the archive show that a legal institution with stable and predictable rules to protect the rights of creditors existed throughout the nineteenth century. Creditors were likely reassured that they had legal recourse if their debtors fell into arrears or defaulted, whether they used the petition to litigate or used it simply as a strategy to leverage a private resolution. Indeed, as the next section shows, creditors had many reasons to worry about being repaid. But the existence of a legal tool for creditors was probably also good for debtors. Hesitant lenders, assured by the legal backing of contracts, might have been more willing to enter into economic agreements, thus creating more opportunities for people to borrow. In a risky world of imperfect information, the relationship between debtors and creditors functioned, in large part, through litigated trust.

AVOIDING OBLIGATIONS AND LITIGATING TRUST

Of course, both parties had good reason to be concerned. Creditors and debtors alike were vulnerable to deliberate deception, defined here as when one person intentionally causes another to believe something untrue, with the goal of achieving economic advantage.[87] This definition fits with the legal category of fraud in the 1871 Penal Code, which is examined in greater detail in the final section.[88] While most of the *providencias precautorias* did not involve fraud, deception was not negligible. Debtors and creditors deceived each other in 24.7 per cent (24) of the cases. The quantitative results show that men and women were both involved in deception: the tests did not find a significant association between the gender of litigants and scams.[89] Likewise, I did not find a significant association between the amount disputed and fraud: the mean amounts owed in cases that involved deceit and cases that did not were not significantly different from each other.[90] And I also did not find a significant association between scams and the other main variables, such as the reasons for the case and the resolution.[91] Of course, the distinction between avoiding obligations and deliberate deception was sometimes a matter of perspective, meaning that the coding of this variable was especially subjective. In some instances, cases were coded as involving a scam when a litigant accused the other party of deceit, such as hiding goods or giving false information. In other cases, it was the historian's judgement, centuries later, that something fishy was going on.

Although creditors were more likely to be concerned about changing circumstances or conditions than were debtors, both were vulnerable to deception. Creditors, for example, could avoid receiving payment in order to extend the economic arrangement or increase the penalty for non-payment. This seems to have happened to debtor Vicente Arnaiz in October 1861, when he requested a *providencia precautoria* against his landlord, Manuel Carrera. Arnaiz had rented lodgings from Carrera, but he had moved out on 13 October and wanted to end his tenancy (and therefore stop paying rent). He had tried, on several occasions, to return the key to Carrera, but the landlord refused to accept it, using 'false pretexts [*vanos pretextos*] and only because he wanted to continue receiving the rent payments'. Nearly two weeks later, on 26 October, Arnaiz asked to deposit the key with the judge, who agreed and also issued a summons for Carrera. While Arnaiz and Carrera eventually reached a private agreement, their case offers insight into one of the ways in which creditors might avoid their obligations.[92]

Debtors, meanwhile, could avoid their obligations in myriad ways. They hid. They stashed their belongings. They extracted themselves from judicial proceedings by claiming to be a different person. They used the distance between towns and cities to their advantage. Creditors had to worry about a huge number of scenarios, but, broadly speaking, they fitted into three categories (with considerable overlap): accidents and unexpected loss, such as from illness or fire; changing financial or economic conditions, such as business failure or changing prices; and malicious intent, such as deliberate deception at either the initial agreement or later during the repayment period.

There was, put simply, a trust problem. Disputes between debtors and creditors were like an elaborate game of hide-and-seek, played throughout history in relation to evolving identification technology. As historian Valentin Groebner has shown, new identification technologies were met with new forms of disguise over the *longue durée* of European history from the twelfth to the seventeenth century.[93] Both the dynamic of hide-and-seek and the trust problem at the root of it changed when modern credit reports and ratings created new structures of surveillance. These made it harder (though not impossible) for debtors to hide.[94] Previously, however, there were many ways for debtors to make themselves invisible (or 'unseen' by the courts) and thus avoid their obligations.

One of the simplest ways to get out of paying a debt was to claim to be another person, and *tercerías* could serve this purpose. A *tercería* was a petition submitted by a third party into ongoing legal proceedings. They were intended to help people protect their property from mistakes made by relations, acquaintances, and strangers, be it an innocent case of mistaken identity or a matter of malicious misrepresentation. Someone might use a *tercería* to protect their property from being wrongfully sequestered (*embargado*), for example in the case of a mix-up between common surnames.[95] This may have been what happened when Carmen and Francisca Vicente requested a *tercería* quite urgently on 8 January 1878. Manuel de Vicente's furniture was scheduled to be auctioned off (*rematar*) that very day, likely as the result of bankruptcy proceedings, although the record does not give information about what led to the auction. Carmen and Francisca insisted that they owned the furniture in question. The judge denied their petition, stating that it was too late for a last-minute appeal.[96]

There are many ways to read this case. It could be that Carmen, Francisca, and Manuel were allied: if they were related and working together, Carmen and Francisca's claim might have been a last-minute effort to protect their family's belongings. If this were the situation, it would showcase how people worked together to evade their obligations. Or it could have been that, while the three were related, Manuel was a feckless relative and Carmen and Francisca were trying to protect their property. Alternatively, it might simply be a case of mistaken identity resulting from a common surname. Because the documentation does not include the nature of the relationship between Carmen, Francisca, and Manuel – including whether they even knew each other – the motive in this case remains a point of speculation.

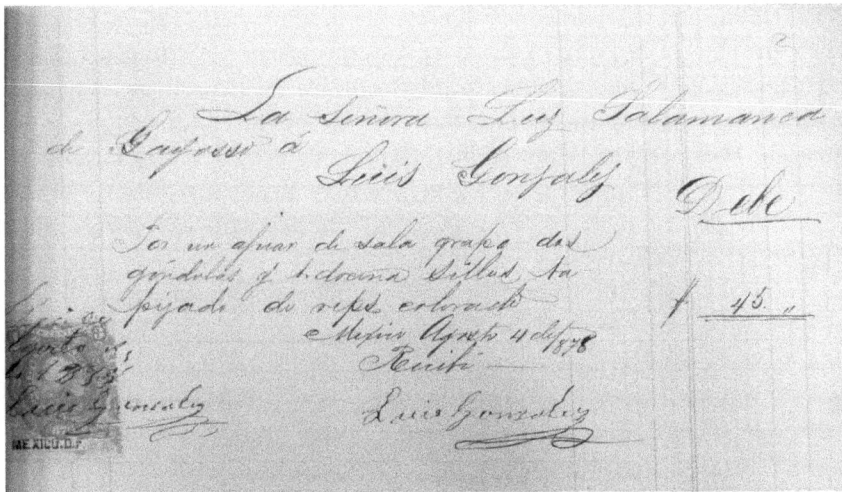

FIGURE 2.2 Invoice documenting ownership of furniture, November 1878.
Source: Archivo General de la Nación.

Notably, the possibility of collusion runs throughout the *tercería* petitions, especially where the lines of relationship are more legible. This scenario was more explicit in Luz Salamanca de Gayosso's *tercería*, for example, in which furniture was once again the concern. A creditor named Alejandro Gaytán had embargoed the furniture of Luz's son, Antonio Gayosso, to secure an unpaid debt amounting to 63 pesos. On 25 November 1878, however, Luz asserted that she – and not her son – owned the living-room furniture in question. To prove her ownership, Luz presented an invoice (*factura*) dated 4 August 1878 showing that she owed 45 pesos to someone named Luis González for a furniture set and a dozen chairs (see Figure 2.2).

While the outcome is unknown (the file ends), several possible interpretations emerge: as Antonio's mother, was Luz protecting his interests? Was Antonio in such dire economic trouble that his creditors tried to embargo the furniture only weeks after it had been purchased? Or was Luz protecting her own interests from getting mixed up with those of her (perhaps prodigal) son? The invoice suggests that Luz did indeed own the furniture and that the *tercería* was not collusion, but it is nearly impossible to know for sure.[97] Of the seven *tercerías* examined in this chapter, three were initiated by women. Future researchers with a bigger sample could investigate whether women were significantly associated with submitting these petitions.[98] If they were, it might indicate that women bore an extra burden when it came to defending their property rights, and that their property was more likely to be misappropriated by others. In fact, the legislation on *tercerías* specifically mentions their use by women as a tool to protect dowries, noting that 'the opponents were usually poor women'.[99] If a relative had staked a woman's property to guarantee a debt without permission or authority, as may have been the case in the Gayosso proceedings, a *tercería* could protect the property from wrongful sequestration.

While *tercerías* offered one way debtors might get out of paying, it was not the only strategy available. Duplicitous debtors could also put their assets out of reach with a disingenuous legal petition, such as a fraudulent sequestration (*embargo*). This is exactly what Emiliano Duviard suspected his debtor, Florimundo Ferrary, of orchestrating in 1861. Ferrary owed Duviard approximately 3,000 pesos for the sale of merchandise, mostly religious ornaments. Duviard filed a *providencia precautoria* in June 1861 when he learned that Ferrary had invested 2,080 pesos in a glass factory called Fábrica de Vidrios in Texcoco. More to the point, Duviard had learned that another person was endeavouring to extract Ferrary's funds from the glass factory: one Señor Tortolis had embargoed 1,700 of Ferrary's 2,080 pesos. Duviard contended that the Tortolis *embargo* was a sham (*simulado*), deviously devised (*imaginado maliciosamente*) to isolate Ferrary's funds out of reach of Ferrary's legitimate creditors. Duviard therefore requested a *providencia precautoria* to ask that the factory owners retain the 2,080 pesos. The outcome is unknown, because the file does not include the judge's decision.[100]

In lieu of orchestrating a legal sham, however, debtors could avoid obligations by simply hiding assets. For example, Maximino Río de la Loza requested a *providencia precautoria* against Florencia Delmotte (widow of Gustavo Reijmolen) in October 1865 because he believed that she was hiding goods rather than paying her debt. Delmotte owned an acid factory (*fábrica de ácidos*), which she had used to guarantee a debt of 11,207 pesos plus interest. She had originally owed this sum to one Fridolin Rubli, who had transferred it to Río de la Loza; the file does not provide more detail about the original debt. The factory and its machinery, tools, lead-lined chambers, and ovens all fell within the scope of the mortgage (*hipoteca*). The debt was to be paid within a year of Río de la Loza's request for repayment, which he had issued, and interest was to be paid regularly (the file does not specify when he had requested payment or the interest rate). In this case, Río de la Loza requested the *providencia precautoria* to secure the factory (*aseguramiento*) because

Delmotte had not paid the interest, which was 'now considerable'. Further, Río de la Loza said that Delmotte was violating the terms of the loan, which stipulated that the equipment should not be moved or sold and that any profits were to be used to service the loan. He brought three witnesses to support his claims.

Delmotte, through her representative, opposed the *providencia precautoria*, on the grounds that the information Río de la Loza provided was false. She claimed that some items had simply been moved during the inventory of her late husband's estate. Nevertheless, the judge issued the *providencia precautoria*, and eleven days later Río de la Loza accompanied the assessor (*ministro ejecutor*) to compile the inventory, with a hearing with both litigants scheduled five days later. In the end, Delmotte sent a note to the judge on the day of the hearing that she would be unable to attend; the archival record does not give the outcome.[101] Whether Delmotte had indeed hidden the equipment, Río de la Loza's suspicion was a common one. The malicious hiding of assets, as the final section in the chapter will show, was a central preoccupation for jurists writing rules about unpaid debts.

In the world of debt avoidance, geography was also power: debtors could eschew their obligations by moving or fleeing. *Providencias precautorias* could be handy, therefore, if a creditor suspected that a debtor might be about to leave or return to the city. Of the 97 *providencia precautoria* petitions, 18.6 per cent (18) involved the defendant either leaving or arriving in Mexico City. This variable was not significantly connected to the other main variables: tests found no significant relationship between the debtor leaving or returning to the city and the plaintiff's gender. Similarly, tests found no significant relationship with the defendant's gender, the amount owed, the reason for the debt, or the resolution.[102] Men and women alike might come and go from the city and thereby avoid their obligations, regardless of the amount in question or the reason for the debt. Likewise, judges were no more or less likely to approve a petition based on flight risk.

Rumours circulated when a debtor was about to leave or return to the city. This was what happened when José Nicolás Montes de Oca requested a *providencia precautoria* against the muleteer Hilario Jiménez (related at the beginning of this chapter). It was also the case when Francisco Reyna requested a *providencia precautoria* against Cesario Medina in December 1861. Reyna had given Medina 14 pesos to purchase barley seeds, with the apparent understanding that Medina would repay the capital and that they would divide the profits. Reyna had received neither the repayment nor his half of the profits. When Reyna heard that Medina, who lived outside the city, was expected to visit in two days' time, he requested a *providencia precautoria* asking that the judge seize Medina's donkeys. Two witnesses supported Reyna's version of events: Guadalupe Peláez, a married 32-year-old domestic servant (*doméstico*) from Toluca, and José María Torres, a single 32-year-old domestic servant from Taxco. Although the judge granted the *providencia precautoria*, the file ends with no information about whether Medina responded to the judge's ruling.[103]

This dynamic of hide-and-seek is a main theme in the court cases. Most debtors who avoided their obligations did so through some sort of disappearing act, hiding assets or themselves. It was quite straightforward in cases like Francisco Reyna v Cesario Medina over the barley seed debt or Maximino Río de la Loza v Florencia Delmotte regarding the equipment in an acid factory. But even the *tercerías* could be conceived as the erasure of a juridical person. The modern system of surveillance – be it 'seeing like a state' or the financial surveillance of credit-rating – had not yet emerged.[104] In the 1860s and 1870s, people could be unseen in a number of different legal and extra-legal ways. And for creditors, that constituted the core of the trust problem.

Indeed, the possibility of a breach cast a shadow over almost every economic transaction. In the context of imperfect information – gossip and rumours could be untrue, and reputations could be faked – creditors and debtors worried about deception.[105] Other scholars have examined the history of imposters and charlatans in early modern Europe and its dominions and have shown how suspicion and deception were part of daily life.[106] Writing about two well-known fraudsters in the second half of the eighteenth century, for example, historian William Taylor suggests that, in Spain and Spanish America, 'the default was at least as much toward suspicion and *engaño* as presumption of truth'.[107] The mundane ruses of debtors and creditors studied here were part of this longer history that seems to have continued until information technologies meaningfully limited the possibilities for economic simulation and dissimulation. Until then, the possibility of breach of trust, from cheating and mischief to confidence schemes, formed the backdrop to all economic transactions.

LAW AND ECONOMY: MAKING RULES FOR UNPAID DEBTS

The rules regarding unpaid debts in the nineteenth century belonged to a deep legal history. Jurists working for monarchs and elected politicians wrote laws reacting to the problems they witnessed between debtors and creditors. In turn, the laws on the books set the parameters for prosaic legal conflicts such as Montes de Oca v Jiménez with the sequestered donkeys and Adam v Montes with the rented sewing machine. For centuries, major themes including debt imprisonment, property sequestration, fraud, just prices, and usury had structured the legal framework for conflicts between debtors and creditors, and they continued to do so in the 1860s and 1870s.

Colonial and mediaeval contract and property law shaped the legal framework for unpaid debts in the nineteenth century. The rules discussed here come from the Spanish *ancien régime*, the colonial twilight, and the liberal codification, and the main texts examined are the *Siete Partidas* (1256–1265), the *Novísima Recopilación* (1805), and the *Código Civil* (1870).[108] The rules governing economic life had been innovative from the start. According to historian Robert Burns, they were urgently needed to address the 'desperate' business needs created by the commercial revolution that had transformed European economic life by the thirteenth century.[109] The *Partidas*, a comprehensive legal code written by a commission of jurists under the direction of Alfonso X, remained particularly relevant in nineteenth-century Latin America. The *Código Civil*, written six centuries later by a commission of liberal jurists, was influenced by French and other continental codes of the time, with some vestiges of the *Partidas* and earlier texts.[110] Part of a wave of codification in the later nineteenth century, the *Código Civil* was as comprehensive as the *Partidas*, with the commission providing what it considered particularly important solutions to the pressing problems it highlighted.[111] The *Novísima Recopilación*, however, was a different sort of legal text. It was a compilation of royal laws on the books in 1805. Ordered by Carlos IV, it was an update of the earlier *Nueva Recopilación* (1567).[112] It included a range of rules from the *Siete Partidas* and the Bourbon reforms of the eighteenth century.[113]

Together, these legal texts encompassed, in broad strokes, the rules governing debtors and creditors in the nineteenth century. While the corpus analysed here is representative, it is not exhaustive. My approach is historical rather than jurisprudential, and the guiding questions are as follows. When did the rules protect the interests of debtors and when did they protect creditors? What did the jurists consider fair or just terms when something went wrong? And how did that change over time?

Contracts were mutual promises, verbal or written, that bound people to one another. Laws and legal theory defined the nature of these promises by outlining who could enter into contracts, under what terms, and what happened when people did not comply. And jurists who were engaged in drafting such matters into law anticipated all sorts of problems. Some of the specific procedural details changed over time, certainly, but the main elements of debt litigation from the 1590s would remain familiar to debtors and creditors in New Spain and Mexico until the 1890s and beyond. Debtors could request an *espera* (a stay of payment or respite). Creditors could request that a debtor's assets be frozen in various ways, including through a *cesión de bienes* (giving up property), *sequestración* or *embargo de bienes* (seizure of property), or a preliminary *providencia precautoria* petition like those examined in this chapter. Repayment plans could be ordered by a variety of jurisdictions, from the municipal authorities studied in Chapter 1 to higher royal courts, as well as by ecclesiastic, military, and merchant jurisdictions. As part of a repayment plan, authorities might order the debtor to secure the debt with a *garantía* (collateral) or provide a *fiador* (guarantor). A debtor could declare *quiebra* (bankruptcy). When a debtor owed several people, creditors could request a *concurso de acreedores* (contest for creditors) to determine who should receive priority.[114]

Penalties for breaking a promise depended on the terms of the contract, the circumstances of what went wrong, and the intent of the parties involved. However, one important element of civil litigation began to shift by the end of the eighteenth century: debt imprisonment. Debt imprisonment had long been the most severe punishment for unpaid debts, as late mediaeval and early modern Spanish law gave judges the power to imprison delinquent debtors at the request of their creditors. 'Where a decision has been rendered against anyone, ordering him to pay the debt which he owes to another party; and he refuses to do so,' read the *Partidas*, 'the judge of the district should put him in prison on the demand of him who is entitled to payment, until he pays what he owes, or surrenders his property.'[115] Debt detention's various forms, from servitude to arrest to prison, all fell under the broad concept of *privación de libertad* (deprivation of liberty).[116] Debtors could be imprisoned or detained while a civil suit proceeded, for example. A royal decree (*real pragmática*) from 1590 collected in the *Novísima Recompilación* described how debtors could be kept in jail during a process of transferring assets even if they participated in good faith in the proceedings (by not hiding assets and so on).[117] In practical terms, a debtor could be detained for several years as a civil suit unfolded.[118]

But debt imprisonment was amended in meaningful ways starting in the late eighteenth century, and prospects for debtors improved. Jurists changed the law in piecemeal fashion, with different laws protecting debtors in specific corporate groups. As described at the beginning of this chapter, for example, Carlos III decreed in 1786 that it was prohibited to imprison artisans and labourers for civil debts or minor infractions, 'no matter the amount of debt or nature of infraction'.[119] Exceptions were made for matters involving fraud or when the debt was owed to the royal treasury (*fisco*). Reflecting the legal pluralism of the time, new reforms introduced protections for different groups against debt imprisonment as well.[120]

These restrictions on debt imprisonment directly connected small-scale conflicts and macroeconomic concerns: improving the circumstances of ordinary people by decriminalising unpaid debts was intended to promote trade and wealth. Moreover, loosening restrictions fitted with the broader Bourbon attempts to support economic freedom without weakening royal authority.[121] As a result, the end of debt imprisonment altogether was nigh by the mid nineteenth century. In 1854, the liberal intellectual José Hilarión Romero Gil characterised debt imprisonment as a relic of the past.[122] This was a big change, and good for debtors.

Most of the rules in civil litigation, however, were not about debt imprisonment; rather, they concerned property sequestration. The third *Partida*, addressing property, outlined the reasons for allowing pre-emptive sequestration. It focused on cases where plaintiffs suspected that the defendant would 'waste, conceal, or transfer' the property; the plaintiffs would thus ask the authorities to confiscate the property 'before they present their claims'.[123] In these scenarios, the property in dispute could be placed in trust while the civil suit proceeded.[124] Creditors in the thirteenth century, when the *Siete Partidas* was drafted, were just like creditors who filed *providencias precautorias* in the nineteenth century: they feared that debtors might squander or hide assets before a civil suit got underway. Meanwhile, the fifth *Partida*, addressing contracts, described what would happen if a debtor succeeded in 'maliciously dispos[ing] of their property with the desire to cause their creditors to lose the debts which they owe them'.[125] Such malicious alienation might occur through selling, bequeathing, giving away, exchanging, bestowing as dowry, or pledging property, as well as by releasing their own debtors from payment. In these instances, creditors had one year to request that such transfers be voided and that they be compensated for lost rents or profits.[126] Notably, late mediaeval and early modern laws protected some groups from property sequestration by limiting what could be seized. Most of these rules concerned agricultural work, by prohibiting, for example, the sequestration of beasts of burden, or by limiting the number of livestock that could be seized.[127] Safeguarding agricultural tools and the like from sequestration was yet another way in which the treatment of ordinary people's petty debts connected with (and preserved) broader macroeconomic interests.

Jurists from the thirteenth century to the nineteenth also addressed what would happen if a debtor disappeared. The *Partidas*, for example, described consequences for a debtor who promised to make payment in a certain place but 'maliciously absents himself to avoid complying'. The *Partidas* also included instructions on procedures to follow when a debtor 'flees from the country because he is unable to pay what he owes'. In the first case, the local judge could order the debtor to return to the agreed-upon place.[128] But if the debtor absconded to a place without a judge or a magistrate, then the creditor was empowered to detain the debtor or to ask the local authorities to do so.[129] In the *Exposición del Código Civil* (1870), jurists also expressed concern about debtors who 'maliciously' moved away because creditors might have to spend additional money trying to locate them.[130] Article 1637 of the *Código Civil* therefore specifically describes how debtors should compensate creditors for such costs.[131]

Jurists also anticipated creditors disappearing. There were instances, for example, when creditors might hide in order to avoid receiving payment, thus engineering a scenario whereby the debtor would incur fees or penalties for failure to repay. Mediaeval jurists had anticipated this problem in the *Partidas* by allowing debtors to place the payment in trust of a 'reliable person' or in the sacristy of a church and thus be released from the debt.[132] The *Código Civil* gave debtors another option when faced with the '*resistencia infundada*' of a creditor: to deposit their payment with the court.[133] In broad strokes, the concerns about debtors and creditors hiding persisted across centuries, and jurists worked to balance the interests of both parties.

Overall, considering the rules, creditors and debtors both gained and both lost, depending on the circumstances. The liberal jurists in the exposition of the *Código Civil* described how they weighed conflicting interests in specific situations. When considering penalties for unpaid debts, for example, they worked to protect creditors. 'The fundamental goal [*objecto esencial*] of the penalty,' they wrote, 'is to compensate [*indemnizar*] the creditor for the damages provoked by the non-compliance of the obligation.'[134] Article 1430 specified that the penalty should not exceed the value of the original contract.[135] The penalty, however, should be just. They described as 'notorious' the damage caused by the unequal status between some debtors and creditors, as well as the high penalties for default specified in many contracts. High penalties could function, they argued, as a 'very powerful incentive for the creditor to put obstacles for the debtor to comply or, at least, for the debtor to fall into arrears'. Creditors could then demand a high penalty for an unpaid debt, thus banking a 'considerable gain'.[136] Debtors, the jurists wrote, 'many times, forced by necessity, accept the imposition of excessive penalties'.[137] Article 1432 thus gave judges the power to reduce the penalty 'in an equitable manner, considering the terms and other circumstances of the obligation'.[138] Fairness, in this context, introduced better protections for debtors while privileging compensation for creditors.

The legal framework changed when debtors or creditors defrauded or swindled one another. In the *Partidas*, contract fraud had belonged to the criminal world. The seventh *Partida* distinguished between major deceit crimes and comparatively minor swindles.[139] The latter category was defined as *dolus malus*: 'deception which men practice against one another by false, evasive, and insincere words, which they utter with the intention of cheating and deceiving them'. This sort of 'wicked' deception could be committed by deceitful words or by disingenuously keeping silent.[140] In this category of rather routine fraud, the economic troubles of ordinary debtors and creditors were addressed as contract fraud, which occurred 'with respect to a sale, a purchase, all exchange, or any other contract or agreement which men enter into with one another'.[141] Victims of contract fraud, or their heirs, could bring suit for reparation, and the agreements based on false information would be set aside.[142] Beyond contract fraud, the mediaeval jurists wrote about 'knavery which has no specific name' because 'it is impossible to explain by examples how many kinds of fraud men commit against one another'. In these cases, they did not prescribe a definitive punishment but instead left it to the discretion of judges.[143]

Liberal jurists in the nineteenth century, by contrast, advanced a more general definition of fraud, moving away from the tradition of definition by example. By the time of nineteenth-century codification, most of the rules about contract fraud could be found in the Penal Code rather than the Civil Code. Previous codes, from the *Partidas* and earlier, had enumerated examples of fraud without offering a broader definition or framework, and consequently many deceptive acts fell outside the parameters. In 1871, the *Código Penal* emerged as part of an international trend to articulate a more general concept of fraud, an effort that dated back to the 1791 French Penal Code.¹⁴⁴ Fraud was thus defined in broad terms in Article 413 of the 1871 *Código Penal*: 'There is fraud, whenever a person deceives or takes advantage of another's mistake, with an unlawful act, or achieves an undue profit, to the detriment of the latter.'¹⁴⁵ Notably, a downside of the more general conceptualisation of fraud was that it was so broad that customary economic exchanges between ordinary people could be criminalised. This would happen, for example, with uncovered cheques after the revolution, as discussed in Chapter 4.

This new, general conceptualisation of fraud signalled a major change in legislative history. With Article 413, the authors of the *Código Penal* articulated a broad category of property crimes involving deception, giving authorities the framework to punish myriad forms of deceit. Article 414 of the *Código Penal* emphasised the commission's definition of deception:

Fraud is deception [*estafa*]: when the person who wants to obtain money in cash, in paper bills, or in bank bills, or in the form of a document that implies an obligation, release, or transfer of rights or assets that do not belong to him, gets it [the money] by means of machinations or tricks [*maquinaciones o artificios*] that do not constitute a crime of *falsedad* [counterfeiting or perjury].¹⁴⁶

Article 415 then asserted that the penalties would be similar to those given for non-violent robbery, as outlined in Article 376.¹⁴⁷ The remaining articles in the Penal Code chapter on property fraud had more in common with earlier laws. They listed examples of fraudulent acts ranging from quackery, bait and switch, and padding (or shorting) weights and measures to signing over uncovered *libranzas* and *letras de cambio*. Exploiting superstitions by conjuring spirits or presaging events was also listed as fraud.¹⁴⁸

If laws concerning fraud provided general context for determining good and bad behaviour, those concerning just prices and just profits were very precise. When jurists wrote these rules, they quantified fairness. From the *Partidas* to codification, jurists prescribed calculations for determining fair terms in contracts. These rules were about information, as jurists addressed problems that arose from deliberate deception and from imperfect information. Just prices were mostly about sale contracts. When a sale incurred a debt – when purchasers and venders became debtors and creditors – rules about prices could be applied to their conflicts. According to the *Partidas*, valid purchase and sale contracts should have a clearly indicated price, and if the fairness of the price were questioned as being 'unreasonably' high or low, the just price would be 'settled by the judgement of reliable men'.[149] Purchasers could demand that a contract be set aside if they could prove that they had paid more than 1.5 times the just price; vendors, likewise, could demand the same if they sold for less than half the just price.[150] The same ratio appears in the *Novísima Recompilación* to determine when deception (*engaño*) was involved in a sale.

However, unlike their predecessors, liberal jurists were keen to eliminate reasons for voiding contracts. In the interests of economic freedom and citizen responsibility, as well as to minimise litigation, they argued that citizens should take some responsibility for fair terms. Everyone should know the rules, wrote the authors of the 1870 *Código Civil*, 'because the general and particular rules of the contracts have been established, and the *Código* should be known by every citizen'.[151] Citizens' responsibility replaced old protections from the crown and the early nation state: economic subjecthood was giving way to economic citizenship. But the authors did not manage to eliminate every reason for voiding contracts. In the 1870 *Código Civil*, they allowed one exception: when a purchase and sale contract violated the just price. They set the ratio at paying more than double or receiving less than two-thirds, and determined that the just value would be decided by an adjuster.[152] No matter how keen they might have been to move beyond old protections and thrust citizens into new roles as modern economic actors who took responsibility for their contracts, the liberal jurists provided a formula for fairness in 1870 that looked quite similar to older calculations.

Writ large, just profits – and especially rules about usury – are perhaps the most well known topic in the history of economic fairness. Through the publication of the *Partidas*, as historian Richard Burns shows, the legal framework for usury had moved from prohibition to regulation, which helped keep the credit system flexible during a time of commercial expansion.[153] In New Spain and Mexico, the allowable interest rate varied by jurisdiction and according to the type of contract involved. It was often around 5 or 6 per cent, although sometimes 12.5 per cent was permitted for specific contracts.[154] The broad goal of usury regulations was to protect vulnerable debtors, and this was expressed clearly in instructions to municipal judges in 1543. As articulated in the *Novísima Recompilación*, judges should not favour creditors and they should 'castigate those merchants and usurers' who scheme to fraudulently bury usury in the terms of a loan and thereby 'destroy the poor'.[155]

This state of affairs changed in 1861 when Benito Juárez repealed the usury restraints as part of the liberal reforms in the *Código de la Reforma*. Suddenly, the rate of interest could be agreed upon by the concerned parties.[156] The repeal was a benefit for creditors, who, at the most basic level, were no longer vulnerable to penalties for charging high interest rates. It was a sea change in ideas about fairness.[157] When Juárez lifted usury restrictions, according to historian Juliette Levy, 'he eliminated the concept of unjustified gain'. She continued, '[I]n the modern Mexico Juárez fashioned, the notion that pecuniary gain implied guilt was a throwback to a colonial, premodern Mexico, and his decree effectively ushered in a new chapter in Mexico's financial history.'[158] Indeed, Juárez's abrogation of usury restrictions was part of a broader vision for economic freedom later upheld by Maximilian. And, in the end, Juárez's repeal of usury restrictions was not undone by nineteenth-century conservatives but by the revolution.[159]

As these rules for debtors and creditors show, change and continuity occurred over a long chronology, with neither side enjoying a clear advantage. By the late nineteenth century, creditors had made important gains, especially regarding usury. So had debtors when it came to imprisonment. But with the thorny questions of property seizure, absentee debtors, and fraud, there was meaningful continuity over time as jurists attempted to balance the opposing interests of debtors and creditors.

From the beginning, jurists expected trouble over unpaid debts from accidents and unexpected loss, from changing conditions, and from malicious intent: notably, the exact same types of problem that creditors worried about as well. But jurists anticipated bad faith on both sides. From the thirteenth century to the nineteenth, jurists saw both rapacious creditors and delinquent debtors, and they wrote laws that considered the vulnerability of both. Jurists – and the political authorities they worked for – sought to strengthen the economy by creating rules for debtors and creditors that balanced opportunity and exploitation against a backdrop of expanding market participation.

BETWEEN TWO WORLDS

The rules for unpaid debts in the nineteenth century worked on the ground to enhance the legitimacy of the political system within the context of promoting macroeconomic freedom, trade, and expansion. Jurists were keenly aware that the problems of ordinary people were connected to the economic power of the territory. Indeed, the firmament of small and medium enterprises was the core of the economic order. Transactions and disputes between ordinary people and their enterprises mattered to the economic power of the realm and the nation, whether the broader mode of accumulation was feudalism, mercantilism, commercial capitalism, or industrial capitalism.

Changes to contract law and property rights were intended to enhance the wealth of the territory and the legitimacy of its rulers. That is why Alfonso X commissioned a legal code that articulated rules for contracts, why Carlos III eliminated debt imprisonment for many ordinary people, and why Benito Juárez removed usury prohibitions for everyone. It is also why jurists worked to balance the interests of debtors and creditors within customary understandings of fairness. Monarchs and elected leaders, as well as their jurists, adjusted the rules to reflect the changes in economic life they saw around them and to advance their vision for wealth and prosperity.

When José Nicolás Montes de Oca fought with Hilario Jiménez over donkeys in 1865, or when Francisco Adam fought with Soledad Montes over a sewing machine in 1878, they reflected the complexities of economic decision-making in an in-between time. Historical change was gathering on two temporalities. The long arc of legal history was bending towards economic freedom for ordinary debtors and creditors; the shackles of punishment for unpaid debts and unjust profits were loosening. At the same time, a nascent industrial capitalism was developing. From around 1870 until the outbreak of the revolution in 1910, new relations of production would touch the lives of many Mexicans as workers and consumers. The world around them was beginning to change, and quickly. In fact, the relationship between Montes de Oca and Jiménez and between Adam and Montes would have been more familiar to their counterparts in mediaeval Iberia or early modern New Spain than to their peers just a few decades later. They were still planted in an old world of face-to-face economic relationships, even if they played an occasional role in a new, more impersonal one. It was an awkward fit.

Debt litigation was an effect of this strain between two worlds. The *juicios verbales* studied in Chapter 1 provided a new avenue for the speedy and fair resolution of unpaid debts under 100 pesos. The growing numbers of litigants who appeared before magistrates from 1813 to 1863 showed how debt litigation in the *juicios verbales* was increasing at a staggering rate. The boxes from the *Tribunal Superior de Justicia del Distrito Federal* suggest that the same was true in the first-instance courts concerning debts valued both under and over 100 pesos. There was, simply put, a growing demand for dispute resolution throughout the nineteenth century. And what this rising litigiousness shows is that the older modes of establishing trust were fraying in a world where the economic lives of the non-wealthy were expanding. Macroeconomic change was manifesting in debt trouble for ordinary people, and they were addressing it through civil litigation.

Relief would come, however. With credit-rating agencies emerging at the end of the nineteenth century, the relationship between debtors and creditors would be transformed once again. But it would not be transformed by the social relations of mechanised production or by new legal codes. Rather, it was a new information technology that would catalyse change – the credit report – which would accompany the modernisation of banking and the institutionalisation of capital.

3

Unworthy

Economic Information in Credit Reports, 1880s–1920s

In 1884, American consuls across Mexico were asked to report on attitudes towards debt among wealthy merchants, low-level employees, and farm hands. The State Department asked, 'Are people adverse to contracting debts?' The answers were unequivocal. 'This question may be answered by a comprehensive negative,' stated David H. Strother, the Consul-General in Mexico City. 'All classes of people who desire or need anything seem ready to go in debt to gratify their wishes or supply their necessities.'[1]

Consuls across the country echoed Strother's assessment. Consul Louis H. Scott answered that people in Chihuahua 'are decidedly in favor' of contracting debt. Consul Louis H. Ayme agreed, writing: 'Yucatan is preeminently a "credit" country, cash transactions being extremely rare.'[2] Indeed, the consuls' descriptions of Chihuahua and the Yucatán could describe, with some variation, the whole country: residents regularly navigated debt and credit transactions in their businesses and in their personal lives. Across the Republic, local urban economies ran on small and medium debts and credits, a facet of everyday life legible in the archives when these relationships soured. While some formal lending organisations appeared as litigants before judges and magistrates, most conflicts were between people. Financial institutions had not yet rooted themselves in the world below the wealthy.[3]

Thus, when the Banco Nacional de México (Banamex) opened its doors in 1884, it had a substantial potential market for clients – people and businesses alike – to whom it could lend money. And it used an innovative new strategy to find its potential debtors: it engaged an American credit-rating agency to appraise the creditworthiness of people and businesses. With this move, Banamex began a transformation in the creditor–debtor relationship and ushered in a new era in the history of information and surveillance. It introduced an intermediary – the credit-rating agency – that came between debtors and creditors with a new information technology: the credit report. The credit report helped institutional lenders such as Banamex trust ordinary or middling people by transforming the way they acquired and acted on economic information. The reports, which reflected Banamex's vision for the financial future, enabled the bank to vet and assess potential clients based on their own criteria for creditworthiness at the turn of the twentieth century.

It was a new solution to the trust problem, and it facilitated the expansion of modern financial institutions. Religious institutions had been displaced as major creditors from the mid nineteenth century, with the nationalisation of ecclesiastic property and capital.[4] Financial institutions like banks stepped into their place. Unlike religious institutions, which were embedded in the local social world, banks such as Banamex did not have access to the sort of economic information that came from personal ties. They had to seek other sources of intel on their clients. As Banamex endeavoured to appraise risk through the novel use of credit reports, there was much at stake: people and businesses deemed unworthy were excluded from the credit economy based on a matrix of capital, character, and capacity. Over time, moreover, the process for determining creditworthiness became increasingly opaque. In the two decades preceding the emergence of Banamex and its credit report system, everyday debtors and creditors had been experiencing the tension between an expanding population and traditional trust mechanisms structured around face-to-face relationships. Now, as institutional lenders expanded into this small-scale economic world, people became alienated from the economic information circulating about them that determined their eligibility for getting a loan.

CREDIT REPORTS AND THE NEW HORIZON OF BUREAUCRATIC TRUST

R. G. Dun & Company offered a new kind of financial service in Mexico. The agency touted its modern method for appraising creditworthiness, claiming to move beyond the entrenched practices of relying on gossip and rumour to gauge reputation and risk. Their credit reports represented a shift from damage control to risk calculation in the credit economy. When a creditor filed a *providencia precautoria*, it was damage control:

they had already entered into a relationship with the debtor and were acting on their suspicion that something was going wrong. Dun's reports, in contrast, helped creditors take better risks in the first place by allaying their anxieties before they entered into an agreement. Dun agents investigated a person's moral rectitude, business acumen, and financial standing, and then packaged the information into a formal report for subscribers. Aiming to change the risky world of borrowing and lending, the agency began a revolution that transformed the role of honour in economic transactions. Put simply, they offered a modern mechanism to address the increasing breakdowns in trust described in Chapters 1 and 2.

Banamex subscribed to Dun's services for a simple reason: it wanted credit reports in order to expand its client base by extending credit to those promising individuals and businesses predetermined by Dun agents to be a good bet. The credit reports thus represented the bank's imagined community of clients. The best borrowers, in Banamex's vision, were wealthy men. For many middling people and modest enterprises, the changing financial landscape brought new and different challenges and opportunities. The financial exclusion of women, however, was baked into these banking and credit-rating institutions from the outset. There was only one credit report on a woman in my sample of 123 reports.

The establishment of Banamex was the financial watershed in the modernisation underway during Porfirio Díaz's rule in 1876–80 and 1884–1911. Under the slogan 'Order and Progress', Díaz presided over the modernisation of infrastructure and communications; this included constructing railroads and stringing telegraph cables, as well as creating export zones for plantation crops and mines. Historians have done much to uncover the history of economic modernisation, the history of social displacement, resistance, and repression, and the history of society and culture during the Porfiriato.[5] Noel Maurer has shown, for example, how Díaz faced the challenge of credibly convincing investors, and especially foreign investors, that Mexico was a good bet after decades of political instability. Because Díaz created Banamex to assure creditors that the government would repay its debts, Maurer describes Banamex as a 'semiofficial superbank'. It had a monopoly on federal lending and it controlled federal spending through tax collection and payments, an arrangement that put important constraints on the government's ability to default with one lender and turn to another.[6] Along similar lines, scholars have analysed the formal banking and credit institutions that managed the domestic and international capital flows of Díaz's economic modernisation.[7]

This chapter turns to the relationship between Banamex and its potential customers in the local urban economy to understand how the emerging modern financial capitalism and its new information technologies changed the relationship between debtors and creditors. The chapter focuses on the world of small and medium enterprises, such as modest milliners, but the sample also includes credit reports on wealthy individuals and companies that were deemed desirable clients. The wealthy, presumably, had many connections with Banamex and other banks. Indeed, some of the country's richest people appear in the reports, although Banamex hardly relied on the Dun reports for intel on millionaires. In general, the credit reports were an important contact zone between the bank and middling people.

The Mercantile Agency, the precursor to R. G. Dun & Company, was founded by Lewis Tappan in 1841 in New York City. Through it, Tappan offered a new information service to his subscribers. With a network of correspondents in the field gathering details on specific enterprises and people, as well as teams of clerks organising the information in the central office, Tappan's company was the first credit-rating agency in the world. The mid nineteenth century was an opportune moment for innovation in finance and credit. Merchants in the USA, as in Mexico, had previously relied on personal ties and experience or on the opinions of other merchants for credit information. But this method of information collection was becoming more and more unfeasible as the American population grew. The sheer volume of trade conducted across a vast geography and growing business landscape made traditional methods of establishing trust more tenuous.

In this environment, historian Bertram Wyatt-Brown writes, 'the opportunity to improve the conditions of finance and credit was there for anybody to seize'.[8] Indeed, Tappan knew the risks of selling on credit to buyers from far-flung places. As a partner in a dry goods house, he had suffered losses himself because he did not have good enough information about his customers. When the Panic of 1837 hit, he had difficulty collecting. It was just a few years later that he founded the Mercantile Agency, which promised to provide reliable and detailed credit information about businesses and individuals across the USA.

Tappan opened his office in July 1841 across from the Merchants' Exchange and set out to enlist subscribers. Depending on their annual trade, clients paid between 50 and 300 American dollars a year for access to Tappan's ledgers: the famous – and infamous – red books. He recruited correspondents in towns across the country who reported on the character, capacity, and capital of local entrepreneurs. Correspondents submitted reports to the central office, where subscribers enquired about potential buyers and clerks read them the relevant reports. While the original purpose of the Mercantile Agency was to serve the needs of New York sellers, Tappan's subscriber base grew quickly. To meet the growing need, he and his successors improved internal procedures: the low-paid, part-time correspondents who were often accused of relying on gossip were replaced by trained professionals who requested signed financial statements from their subjects. They corroborated these signed statements with bank officials and through public records. Clerks also began to relay information via telephone. Typewriters were introduced. Before long, local branches opened.[9]

The credit reports offered subscribers information to appraise risk over long distances and also provided information for local lenders. However, as the Mercantile Agency grew, it faced legal suits from outraged businessmen who asserted that the agency had unfairly smeared their reputations, as well as from subscribers who attributed their losses to bad information. To counter such legal challenges, the agency relied on strategies such as venue-shopping, pressuring witnesses, and drawing out proceedings to increase the cost of a lawsuit.[10] Within a few decades, the company, now with important competitors, operated across the USA and in Canada. Eventually, in 1859, it was renamed by Robert Graham Dun; in 1933, it merged with the J. M. Bradstreet & Son Company to form the Dun & Bradstreet Company.[11]

R. G. Dun & Company led a shift from personal networks of trust to the quantification and commodification of risk. It was a process that would not be complete until later in the twentieth century.[12] Communications scholar Josh Lauer describes Dun's credit-reporting as a technology of risk. 'The underlying aim of this new business institution,' he maintains, 'was to make credit risk calculable.' It was a new approach, as calculating risk was different from risk spreading, which was the function of insurance.[13] Unlike the empirical accuracy of emerging actuarial mathematics, early credit-reporting offered subscribers a 'comparative yardstick' to gauge risk.[14] Lauer goes on to describe how early credit professionals, like the agents studied here, admired the quantitative classification of insurance actuaries. As he puts it, '[T]hey looked to the insurance industry for inspiration and dreamt of the day when creditworthiness, like mortality, could be calculated using actuarial methods.'[15] However, the mathematical techniques for quantifying credit risks were not developed until the late 1930s, and they were not generally used until the late 1950s. Until then, credit-reporting of the sort provided by Dun simply offered an information package that purported to be researched, objective, and streamlined.

As the new unit of analysis in the calculation of risk, the credit report began to influence how people behaved because they changed the parameters of economic surveillance.[16] Indeed, Tappan, an ardent evangelical Congregationalist, had been partly motivated by the possibility of reforming behaviour.[17] While the people named in the *providencia precautoria* petitions could escape their obligations by hiding assets or disappearing, the Dun credit reports were part of a new world where it was more difficult to make oneself 'unseen'. In his history of personal information in America, Dan Bouk examines how individual people came to be represented by 'data doubles' in nineteenth-century bureaucratic systems: 'Data doubles stand in for [people] in bureaucracies. They represent [people] on paper or in computer systems.'[18] The credit report – a data double *par excellence* – represented a person's character in the Mercantile Agency's filing system. When information brokers such as Tappan commoditised the reports, a cycle emerged: a field agent created a data double that represented, for example, a local haberdasher; the agency sold access to the credit reports; and a subscriber used the information to make strategic decisions about whether to extend or deny credit to the haberdasher.[19] Because a bad credit report could have devastating consequences, small- and medium-sized business owners necessarily shifted their behaviour to ensure their creditworthiness in this new information landscape.

Credit-rating agencies thus created a new social reality as well. New technologies of economic information heralded the beginnings of new forms of surveillance, and credit-rating became 'one of the most totalizing and invasive systems of surveillance to emerge anywhere in the nineteenth-century world'.[20] By reducing a person to a credit report, Josh Lauer argues, companies such as R. G. Dun actually invented a novel identity: the disembodied financial identity. In Mexico, the commoditised data double began to emerge near the end of the nineteenth century before becoming more fully realised in the late twentieth and early twenty-first centuries (see Chapter 5).

The Banamex archive has six books of Dun reports, covering the years 1899–1923. Five of these books contain reports mostly about people and businesses in Mexico City; the sixth book is mostly focused on Zamora, Michoacán. The Banamex collection is unusual because most of Dun's historical credit reports are archived at Harvard University's Baker

Library. The reports in the Banamex archive are authentic Dun credit reports, but the six books were probably assembled by Banamex employees. It is likely that, as a subscriber, Banamex requested hundreds of individual credit reports, and then bank employees glued them into the six large red books as an information library. Perhaps, then, Banamex's books are best described as scrapbooks. The Banamex books look similar to the official ledgers – also large red books – that Dun used in its New York headquarters.[21] The verisimilitude could easily reflect a bank bureaucrat's desire to imitate or reproduce the aura of financial modernity symbolised by the famous ledgers. Whatever the explanation for the red scrapbooks, the credit reports themselves are genuine and reflect the venerable tradition of Dun's credit reports in business history.[22] Moreover, the simple fact that these reports exist outside the Baker collection offers an important and unique perspective: it sheds light on how one subscriber used Dun's service to construct a vision for its future.

The reports in Banamex's archive offer historians a valuable entry point into economic life in Mexico in the late nineteenth and early twentieth centuries. This chapter discusses the five scrapbooks that focus mostly on Mexico City.[23] I did not analyse the book about Zamora because the economic context and social relations there were quite different, as Gladys Lizama Silva demonstrates in her article about the Zamora book.[24] The most efficient and careful sampling strategy for the remaining five scrapbooks, each tightly bound with delicate carbon copy paper, was to transcribe reports on every nth person, starting with the first. The five books contain reports on approximately 1,395 companies and individuals in total for the years 1899–1923. My sample consists of the reports on every tenth person or business (approximately 10 per cent of the universe). I read and coded 210 unique reports. Of these, 17 reports were dropped for different reasons. For example, nine people were not found at the address, 4 reports were illegible, and so on. Of the 193 remaining reports, many were multiple reports about the same person; some gave updated information, while others confirmed the original report.

After merging the multiples, the final dataset consisted of reports on 123 distinct individuals or companies; this is the basis for the quantitative analysis. The data universe of 1,395 distinct companies or individuals was calculated by counting the names in the index of each book. This data is not included in the following tables, as the years for each report are not listed in the index. Moreover, the books are not strictly chronological, and there is overlap. Table 3.1 presents the sample for all years. Table 3.2

TABLE 3.1 *Sample of R. G. Dun credit reports, 1899–1923*

Year	Reports in sample	Percentage of sample
1899	1	0.8
1900	2	1.6
1902	6	4.9
1903	15	12.2
1904	14	11.4
1905	6	4.9
1916	1	0.8
1918	2	1.6
1919	11	8.9
1920	13	10.6
1921	29	23.6
1922	21	17.1
1923	2	1.6
Total	123	100.0

TABLE 3.2 *Sample of R. G. Dun credit reports, before and after the revolution*

Time period	Reports in sample	Percentage of sample
Before 1910	44	36.1
1917 and after	78	64.0
Total	122	100.0

presents the same for before and after the Mexican Revolution (1910–1917). The report from 1916 is excluded.

The variables reflect the information compiled by Dun agents: gender, age, marital status, net wealth, business category (agriculture, mining, commerce, agent/commissions, finance, manufacturing, other), business reach (international, national, Mexico City), whether the business was insured, and the agent's evaluation.[25] These reports belong to the early phase of Dun's credit-rating, when the agency had not yet developed a numerical evaluation. Following other researchers, I coded the agents' evaluations based on a qualitative analysis of the collection: desirable credit connections, good credit connections, fair credit risks, fair risks with a guarantee, and not creditworthy. My quantitative analysis explored descriptive statistics and tested for relationships between variables. Tests included t-tests, univariate analyses of variance, correlations, Fisher's exact tests, and chi-squared tests.[26]

The credit reports provide intimate financial and social details about a wide array of people and businesses. The guiding questions in the following pages are: who was deemed worthy? And why?

BANAMEX AND FINANCIAL EXCLUSION

When Banamex requested credit reports, the bank was trying to determine which people and businesses might make good clients and which they should leave off their client roster. The Banamex Dun books represent the bank's strategic, ideological, and socially constructed vision for its future community. Banamex's imagined clients were men, who were generally wealthy, middle-aged, and engaged in commerce. Many people and groups were therefore excluded from the bank's vision for itself and for Mexico's financial future. The economics scholarship on financial exclusion examines some of the reasons that people were left out, focusing on both the supply side (such as a lack of bank branches in some areas or a lack of access to financial products) and the demand side (such as the underuse of existing services, which was a phenomenon often connected to broader dynamics of social exclusion).[27] In Mexico, financial exclusion was a part of modern banking from the start.

Of the 123 reports in my sample, there was only one woman.[28] Rosa Pérez was a milliner. She started her own business when she was 28 years old with a loan of 3,000 pesos from a friend, the widow of a 'rich Spanish capitalist'. Two years later, on 14 September 1903, Dun Agent 6 investigated her creditworthiness. Before starting her millinery business, Pérez had been an employee of the Telefonica Mexicana Company in Tacubaya. She was now based at 9 San José Real in Mexico City. She told Agent 6 that the original loan had been interest-free and that she was not obliged to repay at a specific time. Agent 6 judged her statement to have been made in good faith. Further investigation found that Pérez had bought most of her supplies in the local market, and her purchases ranged from 10 to 200 pesos, for which she paid in instalments. Once or twice, she had bought supplies from Europe through a local agent. Overall, her suppliers were satisfied with her payment record. Agent 6 described her business as 'small but fairly prosperous' and described Pérez herself as 'favorably spoken of'. She was 'said to attend closely to her business, to be careful and well intentioned'. However, Agent 6 concluded, because she did not have capital of her own, Pérez was not 'in a position to seek credit for more than very limited amounts'.

A second report, this one from 18 October 1904, confirmed the information but added that Pérez had been late making some payments. Although, in the end, she had cleared her debts, the evaluation added that any credit issued should be for short periods ('*a cortos plazos*'). The second report was likely compiled by a different Dun agent, as there were different agent numbers assigned to the files, and while the first was in English, the second was in Spanish.[29] According to Dun, Pérez was considered a fair credit risk.

How did Pérez compare to the men? No statistical tests were possible, of course, but a simple description shows that she was different in three important ways. First, she was among the more modest potential clients, as only six people or businesses in the sample had a lower net wealth than her.[30] Second, the reports cover only three years of her history; overall, the average length of time for reports was 8.5 years.[31] And third, at 30 years old, she was younger than the average man, who was 42.5 years old (although this might not have been as consequential as the other two factors).[32] By other measures, however, Pérez was not very different from the men. She was engaged in commercial activities, which was common.[33] In terms of business ability, she was described favourably, which was also typical for the men.[34] Neither her marital status nor where she was from is mentioned in the report, which was not unusual.[35] Based on these similarities and differences, it is difficult to understand why this rather modest milliner was the one woman among Dun's potential clients. If my interpretation is correct – that Banamex requested reports as part of an effort to expand its clientele – why did it request a report on Pérez? Surely her friend, the wealthy widow, would have been a more likely candidate.

Regardless, the wild gender imbalance is strikingly different from the economic worlds seen in the *juicios verbales* and the *providencia precautoria* petitions. In those cases, men outnumbered women as litigants, suggesting that men had more access to credit than women, but the imbalance was not so extreme. Why are these reports different? I have two interpretations. Gender might not have mattered as much in the shops, in the markets, and in people's homes as they bought and sold goods or borrowed and loaned money and assets on a face-to-face basis. But if women debtors were actively discriminated against by new financial institutions such as Banamex, it would indicate that the maleness of Mexico's burgeoning banking world was not a reflection of the broader social world; it was a deliberate creation. Banamex, in this interpretation, simply did not envision women as clients.

Alternatively, the gender imbalance might be an effect of the structure of the credit report, which reduced a social network into a brief bureaucratic assessment. Most of the reports indicate whether the subject was married, but they do not generally include much information about the spouse. Marriage networks were hugely relevant on the ground when appraising a person's creditworthiness in terms of capital and character.[36] These early credit reports might simply have inadequately communicated those social networks of wealth.[37] Exclusion, in this interpretation, was not Banamex's intent per se. Rather, the bureaucratic erasure of women was a deeply embedded exclusion that Dun agents and Banamex employees might not even have been aware of. Whatever the reason for the imbalance, however, some sort of gendered exclusion was at play.

Besides being overwhelmingly male, Banamex's imagined community was wealthy. The average net wealth was 516,462 pesos, with a minimum of 0 (the second lowest was 1,000) and a maximum of 10,000,000 pesos. In terms of frequency distribution, 25 per cent of people had a net wealth of 20,000 pesos or less; 50 per cent had 50,000 pesos or less; and 75 per cent had 150,000 pesos or less. Table 3.3 presents the net wealth reflected in the reports; Table 3.4 aggregates the net wealth into categories. Both tables present the distribution for the entire sample, as well as divided into two subsets: before and after the revolution (omitting the report from 1916).[38]

Wealth clearly mattered in the evaluation of creditworthiness. There is a statistically significant relationship between wealth size and the outcome of the evaluation. The best evaluation that a person or business could receive was to be deemed a 'desirable' credit connection. People in the highest wealth category, Group A, were over-represented in the 'desirable' evaluations. An examination of the conditional percentages shows

TABLE 3.3 *Net wealth in R. G. Dun credit reports, 1899–1923*

Measurement of net wealth	Entire sample (n=102)	Before 1910 (n=34)	1917 and after (n=67)
Minimum	0	0	0
Minimum after 0	1,000	2,000	1,000
Maximum	10,000,000	10,000,000	10,000,000
Mean	516,462	756,323	401,704
25th percentile	20,000	14,000	23,750
50th percentile	50,000	41,250	51,000
75th percentile	150,000	500,000	144,327

TABLE 3.4 *Wealth categories in R. G. Dun credit reports, 1899–1923*

Wealth category	Entire sample		Before 1910		1917 and after	
	Count	Percentage	Count	Percentage	Count	Percentage
Group A (over 150,000 pesos)	28	27.5	11	32.4	17	25.4
Group B (50,000–149,999 pesos)	24	23.5	5	14.7	18	26.9
Group C (20,000–49,000 pesos)	25	24.5	7	20.6	18	26.9
Group D (under 19,999 pesos)	25	24.5	11	32.4	14	20.9
Total	102	100.0	34	100.0	67	100.0

that a higher proportion of reports involving individuals with a net wealth in Group A were considered desirable (17.6 per cent) than reports involving the other wealth groups (1.4 per cent).[39] And people or businesses with the lowest wealth category, Group D, were over-represented in the 'not creditworthy' evaluation: a higher proportion of reports involving individuals with a net wealth in Group D were considered not creditworthy (25.9 per cent) than the proportion of reports involving net wealth in other groups (6.3 per cent).[40] Similar results emerge when looking at individual net wealth rather than wealth size groupings. People with higher net wealth were significantly associated with better evaluations: the mean net wealth for reports in the category 'desirable' is significantly different from the mean net wealth for reports in the category 'fair', as well as from the mean net wealth in the categories 'guarantee required' and 'not creditworthy'.[41]

The connection between net wealth and positive evaluations fits with Dun's evolving modus operandi of isolating wealth from its context. Wealth was important to the evaluation, but it was not meaningfully connected to the other variables. Overall, very little significance emerged between net wealth and variables such as age, marital status, and whether the business had international or national reach or was based solely in Mexico City.[42] There was also no significant connection between net wealth and business sector (with the exception of people working in the financial sector, who had significantly higher net wealth than people in other sectors).[43] Dun agents, gathering intel on the ground, had begun to isolate wealth from its social context, reducing people and businesses to their financial value. This missing context likely included wealth's embeddedness in marriage networks, which could help explain the gender imbalance in the credit reports as well.

As leaders at Dun headquarters worked to hone their evaluation system, they created two different ratings: a numerical system for capital and an alphabetical system that combined character and capacity. Historians have shown how the numerical/alphabetical organisation was a key step in the creation of a more scientific credit information system.[44] While this system was not used in the reports in the Banamex archive, it was becoming the standard in the USA by the end of the nineteenth century and reflects the growing trend towards isolating wealth from other criteria. Put simply, rich men were deemed worthier of credit, a conclusion that is neither surprising nor particularly important.

EVALUATING CREDITWORTHINESS

Overall, the reports show how new financial institutions such as Banamex and Dun idealised a certain type of borrower. But a handful of male millionaires did not make an economy. The Dun reports on middling economic actors were far more consequential to the arc of economic history. The modernisation of a trust mechanism and, thus, of the credit economy happened at the interface between Dun agents and the people in the lower wealth groups. The innovation was not to give the very wealthy desirable ratings; it was about the parameters of 'fair' evaluations.

The Dun reports provide an entry into the world of middling people engaged in small and medium enterprises. When Charles Winslow, the American vice-consul in Guerrero, responded to the State Department's survey regarding whether people were amenable to credit contracts, he described different classes of people and ranked them according to their ability to repay their debts in a timely manner. The most reliable debtors, he believed, were *rancheros*, first-class merchants, and retail dealers in groceries and miscellanea. They were followed by an in-between group of army officers, custom house guards, master craftsmen, owners of saloons and bar rooms, and salaried clerks, all of whom Winslow suggested might be reliable debtors. For Winslow, day labourers and artisans made unreliable debtors because their pay was bad and they were 'naturally lazy'. Winslow further advised against lending to the idle and vagrant population, the 'loafers, beggars, common gamblers, "dead beats"'. He warned, moreover, about genteel loafers who 'go about well dressed, and put on airs ... for this class of customers the tradesmen keep a sharp lookout, though they sometimes succeed in deceiving, as they are very sharp'.[45] Winslow's descriptions were the sort of rudimentary business intel the Dun agency aimed to improve. The Dun reports helped institutional lenders to better 'see' the people in Winslow's in-between group. Their goal was a more systemised ability to discern these people's capital, character, and capacity. With that perspective, lending institutions could more confidently expand into people's economic lives.

In the course of writing their reports, agents were expected to edit out any reference to themselves. As the 1918 instruction manual emphasised in italics (italics were used only twice in the whole manual), *'the word "We" must ... never be used in any report'*.[46] Agents were unnamed; they were usually represented by a number that kept their identities confidential and enhanced the report's appearance of objectivity. Agent subjectivity, however, was one of the only variables significantly associated with the evaluations.[47] Some agents were more generous in their appraisals while others had more exacting standards. Analysing the six agents who wrote at least 9 reports, for example, Agents 11 and 82 stand out.[48] Together, they wrote 15.4 per cent of the reports in the sample (19 reports combined).[49] Agent 11 was more generous, giving a higher proportion of 'good' evaluations than other agents.[50] Agent 82, by contrast, was tougher. Compared to reports written by other agents, a higher proportion of Agent 82's reports recommended that the potential borrower get a guarantee.[51] Considering other variables, such as the net wealth of the people and businesses evaluated, the reports by Agents 11 and 82 are not significantly different from those by other agents.[52] A tendency to be forgiving or fastidious could be explained by the agent's personality or idiosyncratic network of informants. Regardless, while the reports that Dun sold were produced, collected, and interpreted by people in conversation with other people, this fundamentally subjective facet of the documents was given a veneer of objectivity through the erasure of the agents' names.

However, the company manuals hint at what some of the interactions between agent and potential client might have been like on the ground: awkward and tense. While the reports themselves purposely do not include details about these interactions, the manuals provided clear instructions to agents on how to behave. When asking for financial statements – information that was of utmost importance to the company – agents needed 'perseverance, tact, and diplomacy'. The manuals were rife with examples:

A reporter, when calling on a merchant for a statement, should not be obtrusive if the man he seeks to interview is otherwise engaged. When a favorable chance offers, present your card and ask if it is convenient for him to see you. Many reporters are known to have a crude manner of introducing themselves ... Endeavor to show a proper deference ... Many men resent being made a target of direct and continuous interrogations.[53]

The company acknowledged that people had good reason to avoid giving statements. If the statement might reveal financial stress, ambiguity could be an advantage. 'There is a difference between the man who makes a statement and one who does not,' the manuals state. 'If anything, the man who does not gets a little the best of it.'[54] Agents visiting a business to elicit information were also encouraged to look around and 'size it up' by observing if the stock was well presented, if the location was desirable, and what class of clientele it attracted.[55] No doubt, such intelligence gathering would not go unobserved by most business owners. More generally, whether asking for statements from individuals or information from those in the know, the company advised agents that they should make themselves interesting by following current events: 'You will meet many men who will take very little interest in you or your business unless you are able to make yourself a little bit interesting to them by knowing something of current topics.'[56] These instructions suggest that agents faced a rather unpleasant and difficult task in establishing the creditworthiness of people who Banamex might want as new clients.

Most people and businesses in the Dun scrapbooks were deemed fair credit risks and thus potential clients for Banamex. They were deemed creditworthy for moderate amounts to be used in the normal course of business. They were described as having good personal character and business capacity. Those assessed to be fair credit risks make up 55 per cent of the sample (60 individuals and businesses). Leopoldo Andino, for example, was a 45-year-old married man who owned a hat shop (*sombrerería*).[57] Originally from Spain, Andino was one of 62 foreigners in the sample (50 per cent), and foreigners were not significantly associated with negative or positive evaluations.[58] Agent 52 evaluated Andino's creditworthiness in August 1922, noting that people spoke well of Andino in terms of personal character and business capacity. He had a net worth of 20,000 pesos, which put him in the 26.5th percentile in the sample. He was doing a satisfactory trade, albeit with a drop in sales because of the country's unsettled political context ('*la situación poco bonancible por la que atraviesa el país*'). He was deemed a fair credit risk for a moderate amount to be used in the regular course of business ('*un riesgo*

TABLE 3.5 *Evaluations in R. G. Dun credit reports, 1899–1923*

Evaluation	Frequency	Percentage
Desirable	5	4.6
Good	16	14.7
Fair	60	55.0
With guarantee	14	12.8
Not creditworthy	14	12.8
Total	109	100

regular a crédito, por las cantidades moderadas que solicite durante la marcha normal de sus negocios').

The agents who wrote the reports in Banamex's archive did not assign a number to a person's creditworthiness; the numerical and alphabetical systems used in the USA, as described above, were not yet practised in Mexico. Instead, these reports belong to a moment of transition, with agents packaging information into a report following general guidelines, but with much idiosyncrasy as they determined whether potential clients were desirable, good, fair, fair with a guarantee, or not creditworthy.[59] Table 3.5 presents a snapshot of the evaluations.

Which factors mattered when agents decided a person's creditworthiness? As discussed above, rich people were considered less risky than those of more modest means.[60] People deemed 'desirable' were those who Dun agents enthusiastically described with words such as *desirable* and *ideal*, conveying the impression that Banamex would be fortunate to have them as clients. Agents gave this evaluation to 4.6 per cent (five) of the people or businesses in the sample. Among them was the famous Madero family of Coahuila, covered in reports from 1901 to 1903. The septuagenarian patriarch of the family, Evaristo, had an estimated net wealth of 6 million pesos, which put him in the 98th percentile in the sample. Agent 11 wrote of Evaristo: 'His credit is unquestioned ... he seems to be considered in all respects a desirable credit connection.'[61] Interestingly, Francisco I. Madero, who was Evaristo Madero's grandson and later became one of the leaders of the revolution, was not mentioned in these reports. He would have been nearly 30 years old at the time.

Agents also sometimes recommended that creditors require a guarantee to make the borrower more desirable, which happened in 12.8 per cent of the reports (14 individuals and businesses). In August 1902, for example, when appraising the creditworthiness of Manuel León – a young, single man engaged in commissions who was well regarded in

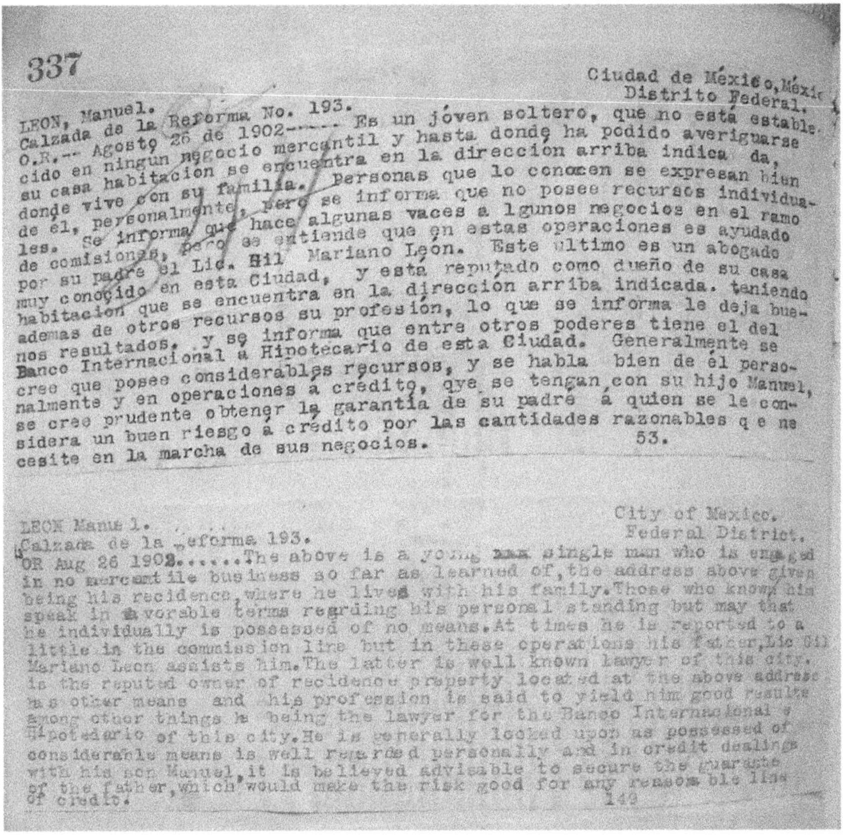

337

Ciudad de México, México,
Distrito Federal.

LEON, Manuel.
Calzada de la Reforma No. 193.
O.R.-- Agosto 26 de 1902------ Es un jóven soltero, que no está establecido en ningun negocio mercantil y hasta donde ha podido averiguarse su casa habitacion se encuentra en la direccion arriba indicada, donde vive con su familia. Personas que lo conocen se expresan bien de él, personalmente, pero se informa que no posee recursos individuales. Se informa que hace algunas vaces algunos negocios en el ramo de comisiones, pero se entiende que en estas operaciones es ayudado por su padre el Lic. Gil Mariano León. Este ultimo es un abogado muy conocido en esta Ciudad, y está reputado como dueño de su casa habitacion que se encuentra en la dirección arriba indicada. teniendo ademas de otros recursos su profesión, lo que se informa le deja buenos resultados, y se informa que entre otros poderes tiene el del Banco Internacional é Hipotecario de esta Ciudad. Generalmente se cree que posee considerables recursos, y se habla bien de él personalmente y en operaciones á crédito, que se tengan con su hijo Manuel, se cree prudente obtener la garantía de su padre á quien se le considera un buen riesgo á crédito por las cantidades razonables q e necesite en la marcha de sus negocios.
53.

City of Mexico.
Federal District.

LEON Manuel.
Calzada de la Reforma 193.
OR Aug 26 1902......The above is a young single man who is engaged in no mercantile business so far as learned of, the address above given being his recidence, where he lives with his family. Those who know him speak in favorable terms regarding his personal standing but may that he individually is possessed of no means. At times he is reported to a little in the commission line but in these operations his father, Lic Gil Mariano Leon assists him. The latter is well known lawyer of this city. is the reputed owner of recidence property located at the above address has other means and his profession is said to yield him good results among other things he being the lawyer for the Banco Internacional e Hipotecario of this city. He is generally looked upon as possessed of considerable means is well regarded personally and in credit dealings with his son Manuel, it is believed advisable to secure the guarante of the father, which would make the risk good for any reasonable line of credit.
149

FIGURE 3.1 Credit report on Manuel León, August 1902. *Source*: Archivo Histórico del Banco Nacional de México.

personal terms but who had no means of his own – the Dun agent advised that creditors should seek a guarantee. Figure 3.1 shows the report, which is one of many that were in English. In particular, the agent suggested a guarantee from León's father, Lic. Gil Mariano León, a well-known lawyer whose clients included the Banco Internacional e Hipotecario.[62] When Dun agents advised a guarantee, it indicated that the person or business might still be a potential client for Banamex, just not on their own standing.

People deemed 'good' risks were also described positively. There were no conditions placed on their creditworthiness, such as the conditions placed on those deemed fair or needing a guarantee. But the reports do not read as glowing endorsements. The tone is different from reports on desirable credit connections such as Evaristo Madero. Agents gave good

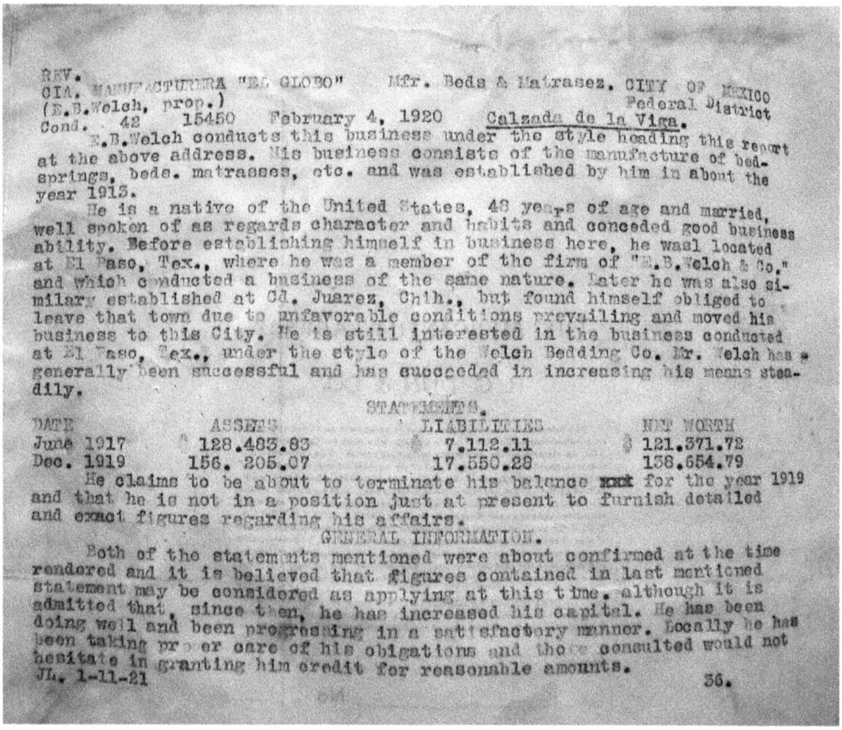

REV.
CIA. MANUFACTURERA "EL GLOBO" Mfr. Beds & Matrasez. CITY OF MEXICO
(E.B.Welch, prop.) Federal District
Cond. 42 15450 February 4, 1920 Calzada de la Viga.

E.B.Welch conducts this business under the style heading this report at the above address. His business consists of the manufacture of bed-springs, beds. matrasses, etc. and was established by him in about the year 1913.

He is a native of the United States, 48 years of age and married, well spoken of as regards character and habits and conceded good business ability. Before establishing himself in business here, he wasl located at El Paso, Tex., where he was a member of the firm of "E.B.Welch & Co." and which conducted a business of the same nature. Later he was also similary established at Cd. Juarez, Chih., but found himself obliged to leave that town due to unfavorable conditions prevailing and moved his business to this City. He is still interested in the business conducted at El Paso, Tex., under the style of the Welch Bedding Co. Mr. Welch has generally been successful and has succeded in increasing his means steadily.

STATEMENTS.

DATE	ASSETS	LIABILITIES	NET WORTH
June 1917	128.483.83	7.112.11	$ 121.371.72
Dec. 1919	156. 205.07	17.550.28	138.654.79

He claims to be about to terminate his balance xxx for the year 1919 and that he is not in a position just at present to furnish detailed and exact figures regarding his affairs.

GENERAL INFORMATION.

Both of the statements mentioned were about confirmed at the time rendered and it is believed that figures contained in last mentioned statement may be considered as applying at this time. although it is admitted that, since then, he has increased his capital. He has been doing well and been progressing in a satisfactory manner. Locally he has been taking proper care of his obigations and those consulted would not hesitate in granting him credit for reasonable amounts.

JL. 1-11-21 36.

FIGURE 3.2 Credit report on E. B. Welch, February 1920. *Source*: Archivo Histórico del Banco Nacional de México.

evaluations in 14.7 per cent of reports (16 individuals and businesses). Two examples show the range of different potential clients classed as 'good' credit risks. The first was E. B. Welch, a 48-year-old married manufacturer of beds and mattresses. Agent 42 reported in February 1920 that Welch was originally from the USA, having worked in the same line of business in El Paso, Texas, where he retained an interest in that operation. Welch first established himself in Mexico in Ciudad Juárez, but, in 1913, he moved to Mexico City because of the revolution and 'the unfavorable conditions prevailing'. He had an estimated net wealth of 138,655 pesos (which put him in the 72.5th percentile of the sample) and was a 'good' credit risk. Figure 3.2 presents the report, which includes a financial statement (these are given in 35 of the reports, mostly in the post-revolutionary years). As Agent 42 reported, '[L]ocally he has been taking proper care of his obligations and those consulted would not hesitate in granting him credit for reasonable amounts.'[63] Still, while the report does not impose the sort of conditions recommended for Leopoldo

Andino, the hat shop owner, it lacks the enthusiastic tone used for Madero.

The second example of a 'good' evaluation comes from the reports on the well-known capitalist Eusebio González, which were put together in January 1920 and February 1923. González was a 52-year-old married landowner. He was originally from Spain, but his family had been based in Celaya for a long time, where they made their fortune. González was prominent in the commercial, banking, and industrial sectors, and his net wealth was estimated at 10 million pesos. His wealth put him in the 100th percentile of the sample, where there was only one other person with an equally high net wealth. The first report concluded that González would meet his obligations, but it lacked the glowing language of the Madero report. The second report cautioned that 'his affairs are not in the same satisfactory terms as stated in the previous report'. The tepidness of this response to an unusually wealthy man stemmed from the fact that, in the previous year, González had been obliged to sell some properties. He also had sizeable liabilities and owed a large sum to a local bank. 'Nevertheless,' wrote Agent 42, 'he is considered to be very solvent [ambliamente solvente].' González, like Welch, was a 'good' credit risk.[64]

The Eusebio González case, however, illuminates the subjective nature of the data coding. Another historian might have put González in the 'desirable' category; during the coding, I considered both. Ultimately, I decided that the information given was meaningfully different from that in the reports on the Madero family. Although González was still wealthy and powerful, Agent 42 indicated that he had a somewhat rockier year, which would be key information for potential creditors. Indeed, in its 1918 instruction manual, R. G. Dun advised agents that unfavourable information 'must be promptly handled', and such information would include bills of sale and new liabilities.[65] Comparing Welch and González within the 'good' category illustrates the boundaries of the world created by the Dun reports. Banamex most certainly did not rely on the Dun report as it made decisions about its relationship with rich capitalists like González, but a similarly lacklustre (or negative) report could have serious consequences for medium or small business owners.

In my sample, 12.8 per cent (14) of people or businesses were deemed not creditworthy. Those who fell into this category were often reported as having professional and personal shortcomings. For example, the Cheban brothers, who owned a shop in Mexico City and a factory in the city of Puebla, among other enterprises, were appraised and deemed unworthy of credit in June 1920. The brothers – Luís, Amín, and Antonio – were natives of Syria and had a net worth of 10,000 pesos (which put them in the 15.7th percentile of the sample). The agent described them as delinquent in repayment, difficult to deal with, of limited business aptitude, and prone to squabbling among themselves.[66]

Just above this 'not creditworthy' category, however, sat the crucial section of the population deemed 'fair' risks, like Leopoldo Andino, the hat shop owner. As financial institutions sought to expand beyond the wealthy, these 'fair' evaluations opened up the world of potential clients by giving a stamp of approval to a broad range of people and enterprises. Having a known history or reputation was a key factor in the 'fair' evaluations. The length of a person's known history was significantly connected to the evaluations. The average length of known history was 8.25 years, with a minimum of zero years (the next lowest was one year) and a maximum of 57 years. Generally, Dun agents gave more positive evaluations when they had information about a longer history: people who received 'fair' evaluations generally had longer known histories.[67] Relatedly, the people who were deemed creditworthy 'with a guarantee' had shorter known histories.[68]

History clearly mattered. Knowing more about someone's history made them seem less risky. Indeed, in its 1902 instruction manual to field agents, the company emphasised that the year an enterprise started was of 'much importance'.[69] Of course, knowing more about a person's history indicated only a longer stretch of time; it was not necessarily indicative of more detailed or better information. By contrast, two other variables that might help gauge risk – if a business had fire insurance and if the net wealth was unknown – did not appear to impact the evaluations much at all. Only 9.8 per cent of reports (12) concern businesses with insurance, and having fire insurance was not significantly associated with the evaluation.[70] This might be because insurance was relatively new, as historian Anna Alexander shows, with private insurance companies replacing mutual aid societies in the late nineteenth century.[71] Most of those with insurance used it to cover their merchandise, which, as Alexander outlines, was a central benefit of the service. Dun agents reported on businesses insuring their stocks of furniture, automobiles, hardware, drugs, wine, liquor, fancy groceries, and so on.[72] While insurance is not significantly related to a person's age, net wealth, or wealth size, it is clearly related to commerce: there is a statistically significant relationship between insurance and the commerce sector.[73]

Dun agents also did not necessarily consider it a risk to have an unknown net wealth, as was the case in 17.1 per cent of the reports

(21). Unknown net wealth was not significantly connected to the evaluation.[74] A person's net worth could be unknown for myriad reasons. Ángel Aguirre, for example, was a well-regarded *corredor de cambios* (exchange broker) who was robbed in 1904. A few months later, in September 1904, the Dun agent did not provide an estimate of his net wealth, likely because the amount was in flux following the 'audacious robbery'. Aguirre was a 30-year-old Spaniard who had come to Mexico at age 18. He was married and had access to capital: the agent reported that his wife was expecting an inheritance, that various relatives had helped him out after the robbery, and that a local *casa financiera* was willing to lend him money. (And with this, the report gives a glimpse into the role of marriage and social networks, which tend to be left out of the reports.) The agent thus deemed Aguirre a 'good' credit risk despite not having a clear sense of his current wealth status.[75]

Not all instances of unknown wealth stemmed from extraordinary circumstances such as robberies. Bernardo Cornejo, a 34-year-old married notary public from Mexico City, was also deemed a 'good' credit risk in 1904 despite the agent not knowing his current net wealth. He owned several properties, some of which were encumbered, the agent reported, and 'it cannot be learned that he possesses any means beyond these properties'. He continued, 'But, he is believed to be receiving a good income from his profession.'[76] Manuel Sánchez, meanwhile, a 64-year-old married lawyer originally from Tabasco, was deemed a 'fair' credit risk that same year. He had moved to Mexico City several years earlier and worked for the federal government and the congress. Although his net worth was unknown, he was 'known to own some capital'. The agent reported:

[I]t has not been possible to determine the amount; he has the reputation of paying his debts usually on time; competent people that have been asked, think that if Sr. [Sánchez] asks for a loan, for important sums or for a long term, he must demonstrate his right to it [*mostrar su derecho a ello*].[77]

Notably, these examples belong to a liminal moment in financial history, when unknown or uncertain net wealth was not crucial to an evaluation of creditworthiness. Despite Dun's *raison d'être*, local information or gossip remained key. Economic transactions were still embedded in personal and even intimate knowledge. The unavailability of information about one's net wealth was not significantly related to any of the other variables: not to the age of individuals, not to the business sector, not to a business's reach.[78] It simply did not matter much, which, at face value, did not fit with the Dun business plan and model. According to the 1918 manual, acquiring information about a person's capital was one of the most important tasks with which an agent was charged, and when such information was unavailable, the evaluations '*should be relatively not so high*'.[79] This advice was the only other time that italics were used for emphasis in the manual, suggesting its importance. But perhaps Dun's instructions were taken as aspirational; clearly, agents on the ground did not always follow the guidelines.

All of the Dun agents' careful efforts to categorise potential creditors were in the service of helping Banamex (and Dun's other subscribers) make better decisions about who to trust. Table 3.6 presents a snapshot of the different evaluations and the risk variables relating to net wealth, length of known history, and fire insurance. Banamex's ultimate goal was to make money, and, as the table shows, the 'fair' category represented Banamex's best bet for future growth. This was a world of people and enterprises with enough capital and with sufficiently established track records to constitute good risks. It was by far the biggest world of potential debtors, and it propelled the bank's expansion. However, also reflected in Table 3.6 is the impact of what might be considered the biggest risk to doing business in the early twentieth century: the Mexican Revolution.

INSTITUTIONAL LENDING IN A TIME OF REVOLUTION

The revolution began in 1910 as a struggle for justice by different groups: by peasants and workers who fought for land and labour rights, and by liberal elites who wanted greater political representation. By 1920, the latter triumphed, but the liberal elites nonetheless included many of the peasants' and workers' land and labour demands in the 1917 Constitution and other state-building projects.[80] From the perspective of risk analysis, the revolution meant staggering rates of death by unnatural causes. At a time when the most advanced risk calculations came from actuarial science, it speaks volumes that contemporaneous insurance policies had war exclusion clauses.[81] Historian Robert McCaa estimates the human losses of the revolution at 1.5 million 'excess deaths', which would make it the ninth deadliest international conflict of the past two centuries (tied with the Spanish Civil War).[82]

Death and destruction were not good for business. For banks, the revolution brought chaos. As Noel Maurer describes, 'The hyperinflation, confiscations, and erratic economic policies of the various revolutionary

TABLE 3.6 Evaluations and risk variables in R. G. Dun credit reports, 1899–1923

Evaluation	Mean net wealth (pesos)	Mean length of time (years)	Before 1910 (n)	1917 and after (n)	Originally not from Mexico (n)	Unknown net wealth (n)	Insurance (n)
Desirable	2,458,157	3.6	4	1	0	1	0
Good	984,629	7.8	10	6	11	4	3
Fair	238,089	10.2	15	45	35	7	9
Not creditworthy	27,136	9.8	4	10	10	3	0
Guarantee mentioned	27,930	3.6	5	9	3	4	0
Total	387,164	8.6	38	71	59	19	12

and counterrevolutionary regimes thoroughly traumatized Mexico's financial institutions.'[83] Violations of property rights, he continues, 'turned Mexico's economic life upside down'.[84] Beyond wartime expropriations, the 1917 Constitution changed the rules of the game as well. Article 27 reserved all subsoil rights for the state. It also gave the state the power to expropriate large estates, which led, in the 1930s, to major land redistribution. Maurer argues that the greatest challenge for the immediate post-revolutionary governments was to convince bankers and investors that their property rights would be protected.[85]

The Dun reports help to determine the impact of the revolution on how creditors appraised risk. Dun seems to have largely suspended its credit-reporting activities during the revolution. Of the 123 reports in the sample, 44 were from before 1910 and 79 were from 1918 to 1923. Only one report was written during the revolution. Dated March 1916, the report was conducted by Agent 41 on the American-owned Yaqui Delta Land & Water Company. Agent 41 does not give a direct evaluation. 'It is said that hefty sums [*fuertes cantidades*] of money had been invested for development,' the agent reported, 'but at that time, the revolution broke out in Mexico, and there has not been any activity in those properties.' It was unclear, as yet, how things would go for the Yaqui Delta Land & Water Company. Agent 41 continued, 'The Compañia represents being in a position of not being able to accept credits, and, in general, it is considered a strong corporation; however, currently, the value of their properties in Mexico is of a speculative nature.'[86] The conclusion that no evaluation could be made illustrates why it made sense for Dun to stop its work during the revolution.

The reports do show, however, the differences in how Dun – and by extension Banamex – acted before and after the revolution.[87] The two main changes are unsurprising. First, Dun agents were more cautious in their appraisals after the revolution. Reports with positive evaluations were over-represented in the years before 1910 when compared with the years after 1917. Before the revolution, agents gave a higher proportion of 'desirable' and 'good' evaluations; the difference is statistically significant.[88] In contrast, people or businesses with the 'fair' evaluation were over-represented after the revolution.[89] There is no significant difference in the proportions of the 'not creditworthy' or 'guarantee recommended' evaluations in reports from before and after the revolution.[90] All of this suggests that agents were more cautious after the revolution. The second change after the revolution was that Banamex was specifically less interested in potential clients from the agricultural sector: there was a higher proportion of reports on the agricultural sector before the revolution than after, while no other sectors had significantly different proportions before 1910 and after 1917.[91] Given the massive upheaval of the revolution, especially in the countryside, this change is easy to understand.

Not everything changed with the revolution, however. With the exception of its diminished interest in the agricultural sector, the bank's imagined clientele remained the same: Banamex wanted rich clients. The mean net wealth in reports before 1910 is not significantly different from the mean net wealth in reports after 1917.[92] Likewise, the cumulative frequency distribution of net wealth is not significantly different before and after the revolution.[93] Finally, there was no significant relationship between the four wealth size categories and the time period.[94] Banamex's vision was, clearly, consistent.

The Dun collection in the Banamex archive gives the impression that the revolution was an aberration. There is only one example of the Mexican Revolution having a positive impact on the person's business: Federico G. Dávalos did well during the conflict. In a September 1920 report, Agent 52 described Dávalos as a 35-year-old married wholesale grocer who was originally from Mexico City. He had studied in a military school in France and entered the Mexican army upon his return. He had been a member of President Francisco León de la Barra's general staff and later worked as a teacher at the military college in Mexico City. He married a wealthy woman. In 1915, he signed a contract with the government to provide drugs and medicines, and the Dun agent reported that 'it is believed to have rendered him satisfactory results'.[95] Then, in June 1918, he entered a partnership to conduct a large wholesale and retail grocery business in Mexico City called Las Bodegas Universales, which he subsequently retired from in order to establish his own wholesale grocery business in March 1920. His net wealth by that point was estimated at 51,000 pesos. With all factors considered, the Dun agent thus deemed him a 'good' credit risk. In contrast, the other reports that reference the Mexican Revolution describe economic difficulties caused by what Dun agents usually described as 'abnormal conditions'.

Agents seem to have followed the same modus operandi before and after the revolution. When evaluating creditworthiness, agents focused on how much money a person had. Dividing the sample into pre-1910 and post-1917 subsets, both time periods show richer people receiving better evaluations than poorer people.[96] Despite some differences, the overall picture stays the same: the evaluations changed somewhat after the revolution, but not when it came to a person's wealth. Banamex's imagined community showed little change against a backdrop of a revolution that fundamentally redrew the economic and political relations of the country.

DEFINING THE BOUNDARIES OF ECONOMIC HONOUR

In 1884, the same year that Banamex opened its doors, American Consul-General David H. Strother described the disciplinary function of honour in debt and credit relationships:

> [T]he proverbial Spanish sentiment of honor in regard to debts contracted, or pecuniary engagements undertaken, is well understood and maintained in Mexico among merchants and traders, as among the steadier individuals of all classes, and as a rule credit is more readily given and less frequently abused than it is usually in more enterprising and speculating communities.[97]

In Strother's assessment, creditors and debtors in Mexico compared favourably with their counterparts elsewhere: they were more willing to extend loans and more careful to avoid default. The premium placed on honour and reputation generated an economic advantage.

The Dun reports help elucidate the definition and parameters of economic honour as the modern banking system emerged. Those deemed unworthy of credit were generally found wanting in capital, capacity, or character. However, there were discrepancies in the Dun reports, such as when a person with poor capacity was deemed creditworthy. These outliers illuminate the nuances of economic honour in an increasingly de-personalised system of assessments and reports, as well as how one's honour might be tarnished or saved. Scholars generally agree that honour was one of the organising principles of social and cultural relations in Mexico and Latin America, and there exists a substantial scholarship exploring its myriad facets (especially honour vis-à-vis gender and sexuality).[98] Honour and reputation were also important to economic transactions, as Chapter 2 examined.

Dun agents did not deem all people with poor character or capacity unworthy, just as they did not consider all people with high net wealth worthy. The Dun 1918 instruction manual addressed the matter in the section on 'discrepancies between report and rating', which was mostly about when the information provided in a financial statement did not square with the opinions of locals: in other words, when capital did not square with capacity and character. The manual advised agents that they 'should not inject into a report arbitrary and unauthorized estimates merely for the purpose of making the figures correspond to what they conceive to be the proper rating'. Instead, agents should indicate if a financial statement was considered correct, generally correct, or nominally correct.⁹⁹ On the ground, agents were tasked with appraising creditworthiness by triangulating considerations of capital, capacity, and character. The final evaluation, in sum, was a judgement on a person's economic honour.

Agents described, in formulaic language, people's 'morals and habits' and their 'business ability'. Most were described favourably. Agents conceded positive personal character to 77.2 per cent of people (95); they described the negative or neutral character of 8.1 per cent of people (10); and 14.6 per cent of the reports (18) included no reference to character at all. Meanwhile, agents considered 65.9 per cent of people (81) to have good business acumen and 17.1 per cent (21) to be lacking in capacity, while 17.1 per cent of reports (21) did not reference capacity at all.

While a person's moral character was most likely derived from gossip among local traders, the company encouraged agents to appraise the presentation of a person or business as a gauge of ability: 'If a reporter finds a man careless and slovenly in his store management, in the keeping of his stock of goods and in the general conduct of his business, he should state these facts as he finds them instead of saying "Reported of limited ability."'[100] Neither character nor capacity were precisely defined, and these terms could have been proxies for other criteria or judgements.[101] Indeed, these terms may have been mutually reinforcing proxies for one another. It is especially difficult to separate character and capacity from each other because these variables went together. There is a positive correlation in the reports between good character and good capacity, and a positive correlation between poor character and poor capacity.[102] Negative appraisals of character and capacity were connected to negative evaluations, with those deemed unworthy of credit being significantly associated with poor character and poor capacity.[103]

Just like the connection between high net wealth and positive evaluations, it is hardly surprising that negative appraisals of character and capacity were associated with negative evaluations. The boundary between economic honour and dishonour, in the statistical analysis, was quite straightforward. Only four reports described people as having a poor character, and two of these reports had a 'not creditworthy' evaluation. The first such report concerned the Cheban brothers, who, as described above, the agent deemed unworthy in part because of their disagreeable personalities. The second example comes from the report on Luciano Marx. In July 1921, Agent 81 reported on Marx's questionable morals and business practices. 'Regarding his morals, customs and business methods,' the agent wrote, 'there are some reservations.' A 50-year-old married Frenchman who had lived in Mexico for several decades, Marx worked as a representative for several French wine and liquor houses. He had an estimated net wealth of 11,000 pesos, which put him in the 19.6th percentile of the sample. Agent 81 does not provide any more detail about why Marx had questionable morals and business practices, and simply advised prudence: 'according to the people consulted ... he must be considered a cash only client and one should act with some caution in any dealings with him.'[104] Marx was deemed not creditworthy.

In the other two reports that described moral failings, creditworthiness was appraised somewhat more sympathetically, suggesting that agents sometimes gauged economic honour with nuance and generosity. Bernardo Rivadeneyra, a landowner from Puebla (Atlixtac), was reported to be addicted to gambling. In February 1902, Agent 15 noted that Rivadeneyra, who was over 70 years old, had an estimated net wealth of 30,000 pesos, putting him in the 36.3rd percentile of the sample. His hacienda, Tlacoxcalco, was managed by one of his sons, 'who is reported to be rather loose in his habits, [the] same being said of the father, who has the reputation of being addicted to gambling'. Agent 15 added, though, that 'aside from his gambling propensities', the father was 'well thought of'. The agent recommended, therefore, that creditors should obtain a guarantee from his son-in-law.[105]

The second example of a more sympathetic approach to character flaws comes from the report on Rufin Martin, a businessman in Mexico City who was reported to have a difficult personality. In January 1921, Agent 81 reported that Martin, who was a married 58-year-old owner of a dry goods store and a hat factory, had an estimated net wealth of 62,500 pesos, which put him in the 56.9th percentile of the sample. However, Agent 81 reported that Martin was known to creditors in the city, who described him as 'hard to deal with'. He was 'reported as somewhat slow, at times, in the discharge of his obligations'. These creditors (all local finance houses) nonetheless continued to sell him bills of 'some importance', but they were careful to define the terms clearly. Martin was thus deemed a 'fair' credit risk.[106] Agents 15 and 81 might have deemed Rivadeneyra and Martin poor credit risks based on their personal characters and business capacities. Instead, the agents outlined the risk by explaining how locals appraised the economic honour of these men and how people described the circumstances under which they might extend credit to them. Examining individual reports of this sort, then, offers intriguing nuance as to how the Dun agents gauged economic honour.

Only twelve people were described as lacking business capacity. Of these, seven were deemed not creditworthy. A typical example was Antonio Bizet, a Mexican of French extraction, who was 48 years old when a Dun agent evaluated his creditworthiness in April 1903. Bizet had failed at a music store, a flour mill, and a hat business. The first two enterprises had been funded by his brother-in-law, who consequently suffered considerable losses. The Dun agent described the first venture as disastrous, the second as having equally poor results, and the third as not providing the desired results. Despite describing Bizet and his wife as 'economical and hardworking people, who try to comply with their obligations', the Dun agent reported that 'he is rather slow and unsatisfactory in his paying methods'. Furthermore, Bizet's net wealth was unknown. Were Bizet's failures the result of bad luck or incompetence? There is not enough information about the businesses to determine. Yet the agent was quite damning, albeit in bureaucratese: 'Bizet appears to have been unfortunate, in his several enterprises.'[107] With this new language of objectivity, Bizet was relegated to the pile of the unworthy.

Three of the people found to have questionable business ability, however, were nonetheless deemed 'fair' credit risks. First, in May 1903, Agent 24 reported on Luis Rocha, a 38-year-old from Mexico who worked in commissions. Rocha had been a musician until 1899, when he went to New York to attend business college. At the time of the report, he was representing various American business houses, including Yale & Town Lock Co. Rocha was well regarded in terms of character. Agent 42 reported that he 'is believed a man of good habits'. He had an estimated net wealth of 20,000 pesos, which put him in the 26.5th percentile of the sample. Yet Agent 24's appraisal stands out for its caveat about Rocha's capacity: 'a man of ... fair business ability, but lacking, a trifle, in energy'. Rocha, simply put, was lazy. Still, based on all he had going for him, he was considered a 'fair' risk.[108]

The other two examples of people classified as 'fair' risks, despite their iffy business acumen, were a glazier who was too old to compete in his line of work and a spendthrift jeweller. Rafael González was a 57-year-old married businessman who had worked in various enterprises, especially glassworks, for several decades. When a Dun agent reported on him in August 1901, he was found to be well regarded in terms of character, and his capital was estimated at 37,500 pesos, putting him in the 43.1st percentile of the sample. The agent, however, noted that his age was becoming a problem. 'It is said,' the agent wrote, 'that, due to his old age, he is not active in business matters, and he can't compete with other similar cases advantageously.' Still, he was deemed a 'fair' credit risk.[109]

Twenty years later, in November 1921, Agent 81 reached a similar conclusion about Francisco González. He was 44 years old, married, and originally from Guadalajara. He had worked in the jewellery and watch business in Mexico City since 1917. He was well considered in terms of character, and he had an estimated net wealth of 80,000 pesos (the 61.8th percentile of the sample). Agent 81 reported, however, that 'his abilities for his line of work are just regular [*solo . . . regulares*]. He is rather liberal regarding his spending for personal expenses.' González was therefore deemed a 'fair' credit risk.[110]

The reports on these three men suggest that, perhaps, capacity was not the most important criterion. With good capital and character, some laziness, incompetence, or poor judgement might be overlooked. It is perhaps unsurprising, then, that most of those deemed unworthy had little or limited capital.[111] Eugenio Model, a 65-year-old Frenchman who had lived in Mexico for more than 20 years, was typical. He had worked as a representative of French business houses. Although he had done well in this work and had married a wealthy woman, he lost everything in mining speculation and his net wealth was zero.[112] He was deemed not creditworthy in April 1921. Given his disastrous speculation and his lack of capital, Model's negative evaluation fits with the broader picture that higher net wealth was related to better evaluations.

Where they exist, discrepancies between wealth and evaluation show how economic honour could be complicated. Juan Dupont was the person with the highest net wealth who was deemed unworthy. Originally from France, Dupont had lived most of his life in Mexico. When Agent 11 reported on Dupont's creditworthiness in August 1903, he did not give the man's age or marital status, but noted that Dupont had several sons. Although Dupont's estimated net wealth had reached 100,000 pesos, which put him in the 69.6th percentile of the sample, he was deemed unworthy of credit because of several business failures that involved considerable losses and demonstrated poor judgement. Originally employed by a local dry goods firm, he had worked for 20 years in glassware and crockery. He had owned an unsuccessful glassware factory in Tlaxcala, 'which is said to have been a serious loss to him'. After selling this factory, he continued to manufacture glassware and crockery for a time in Tlaxcala. By 1903, however, he primarily manufactured his wares from his private residence in Mexico City, helped by three or four of his young sons.

This was only the beginning of his business ventures. In 1903, he owned two stores in the city, run by him and his brother. Five years earlier, in 1898, he had also entered into the hotel business, opening a hotel and restaurant in Mexico City. This was in partnership with three others; Dupont furnished all the capital and left the management to his partners. And if his glassware factory had been a 'serious loss', the hotel and restaurant were a failure: 'the enterprise has proven a disastrous one for him'. The venture had required most of his surplus capital, and most of what he put in was lost. The partnership was dissolved and Dupont, at the time of Agent 11's report, was the sole owner of the failing business. By then, he was trying to sell the hotel and one of his shops, but to no avail.

In the end, Dupont was deemed unworthy. The agent reported:

Several local banks and business firms who have had dealings with him and who are disposed to regard him as a thoroughly honest and well-meaning man claim to prefer not to extend him any further credit on account of the difficulties they have had in collecting bills from him. Some of the real estate which he is said to own here is reported to be heavily encumbered.

Despite his still considerable net wealth, Dupont's lack of business acumen threatened to further diminish his capital. 'Mr. Dupont's friends are disposed to criticize his having embarked in the hotel business which he did not understand and could not give his personal attention to,' the agent wrote. 'He is also criticised at times in other respects for the lack of business judgment he displays.' In terms of Dun's criteria – capital, capacity, character – Dupont passed muster only on the third because local creditors referenced his honesty.[113]

At the other end of the wealth spectrum, people with low net wealth who were deemed worthy show the value placed on capacity and character. Rafael Llanos had the best evaluation of those in the lowest 10th percentile.[114] He had a net worth of only 2,000 pesos, putting him in the 5.9th percentile, yet he was deemed a 'good' credit risk in July 1903. Llanos was from Spain, single, over 50 years old, and worked in commissions. He arrived in Mexico in 1893 and worked for eight years as a travelling salesman until settling in Mexico City. For his first six months in the city, he worked as the manager of the saloon at the Grand Hotel. Since then, he had been working as a salesman for local firms and as an agent for various commission and brokerage businesses. The agent wrote that Llanos promptly met his obligations and that he 'bears a good reputation in every respect, as being honest and conscientious'. As the agent noted, 'Authorities agree in pronouncing him worthy of [the] trust and confidence usually placed in an agent.'

Based on the detail included in the report, I coded this evaluation as 'good'. Following the taxonomy outlined above, some historians might contend that Llanos is better classed as a 'fair' credit risk by interpreting the Dun agent's language as more cautious or reserved than I have done. During the coding, I went back and forth between the 'good' and 'fair' designations. (This example clearly highlights some of the challenges of historical data entry and underscores, I think, why quantitative results must be read as suggestive in the same way that qualitative interpretation should be.) I ultimately decided that my hesitation stemmed mostly from Llanos's low net worth: surely he would not receive the same evaluation as the capitalist Eusebio González, described above? Classing Llanos as 'good' better captures the intent of these Dun reports. No doubt, if Banamex were to extend credit to Llanos or González, it would do so for very different amounts, and the contracts would look very different. The challenge of interpreting the agent's evaluation of Llanos illuminates the historical transformation underway, whereby concepts of honour were being translated into bureaucratic reports.

The three other people from the lowest net wealth category who still managed to receive an evaluation of fair or better were more straightforward cases. First was Rosa Pérez, the lone woman from the sample described at the start of the chapter; she had a net wealth of 3,000 pesos and received an evaluation of 'fair' in 1903. Next was Juan Castillo, who, with a net wealth of 4,250 pesos (8.8th percentile), received a 'fair' evaluation in 1918. Castillo was a 40-year-old married mechanic who owned his own workshop. Previously, he had worked as a mechanic for an important print and lithography shop. He was well regarded in terms of personal character and in his capacity as a mechanic. Agent 82 deemed Castillo a 'fair' risk for moderate amounts to be used in the normal course of his business.[115] And, finally, there was Francisco Montes de Oca. With 5,000 pesos, which put him in the 9.8th percentile of the sample, Montes de Oca received a 'fair' evaluation in 1921. He was a 59-year-old from Mexico City who had worked in various sectors. He had, for example, worked as a government employee and had owned both a children's ware shop and a toy factory. After selling the shop and factory, his net worth was estimated at 5,000 pesos, which came almost entirely from the sale. At the time of the report, he was about to open a small stand in one of the local market halls where he planned to sell cheap native dry goods. In terms of character and capacity, Agent 42 wrote, Montes de Oca was 'well spoken of as regards character and habits', but was considered to have only a 'moderate business ability'. Montes de Oca was thus deemed a 'fair' risk for moderate amounts from local sources.[116]

The reports on Pérez, Castillo, and Montes de Oca show how people with moderate or limited net wealth could be considered creditworthy when local sources appraised them as economically honourable. Although none of these individuals fit neatly within Banamex's vision for its ideal community, they were considered reasonable candidates for lending, even when Montes de Oca's moderate ability and Pérez's occasional late payment were taken into account. Such discrepancies arising between anticipated classification based on net wealth and actual classification based on the more amorphous categories of character and capacity show how Dun agents stretched the boundaries of economic honour. Agents gave many of the less straightforward cases 'fair' evaluations. These evaluations, in turn, were hugely important to the expansion of the credit economy. The marginal cases show the nuances of appraising economic honour and weighing risk when the subjects of the reports represented, for Banamex, a world of potential clients. As the credit economy expanded and institutional lenders sought to establish credit relationships with more people, they turned to the world of small and medium enterprises. People like Montes de Oca with his toy shop and Rufin Martin with his dry goods shop and hat factory represented the future.

ECONOMIC INFORMATION FROM GOSSIP TO BUREAUCRACY

The bureaucratic report came between debtors and creditors at the end of the nineteenth century and the beginning of the twentieth, and it signalled an enormously consequential change in their relationship. It was not, however, a comprehensive change. Dun purported to offer its subscribers better information than gossip or rumour, but agents could not escape the long-standing practice of gathering this kind of personal perspective.

The appeal of bureaucratic economic information was clear: creditors hoped that there would be less misinformation. Gossip, after all, was strategic behaviour that people often used to spread lies about others, manipulate their own image, or advance their own interests.[117] Local gossip nevertheless remained an important source of information for determining a person's economic honour. Agents relied on gossip, on the sort of intimate information that had been so critical for the precautionary petitions explored in Chapter 2. This would change later in the twentieth century when computers calculated credit scores, but, in these early years, Dun operated a network of agents and clerks to package and transmit local gossip under the guise of impersonal, objective economic information.

In other words, the company transformed the form but not necessarily the content of the economic information they passed on to their clients. This tension between gossip and 'objective' research is evident in the instructions that Dun issued its agents. In a section of the 1897 instruction manual titled 'Regarding Unfavorable Rumor', the company described how Dun relied on local gossip for information but got into hot water because of it. 'We often get into trouble,' the manual explained, when agents rely on unfavourable rumours, especially in small places: 'If the rumor is not true, the people are very apt to hear about it and then write us to know who it was that circulated such and such a report.'[118] Dun advised agents who heard unfavourable rumours to pursue the matter discreetly. The 1897 manual suggested that agents should begin their investigation not by enquiring about the individuals involved directly, but instead by asking about what items had recently been recorded, such as judgements or bills of sale. Agents could then check the list for individual names.[119]

Notably, Dun did get into trouble and faced lawsuits in the USA when subscribers complained of receiving poor-quality information or when people claimed that their report was inaccurate.[120] Still, in the 1897 manual, the company did not prohibit agents from relying on unfavourable rumours: 'No absolute rule can be laid down for handling such cases, but wiring in regard to all rumors of that description should be very carefully done.'[121] The early Dun reports such as those in the Banamex archive are snapshots into a liminal world where new techniques such as verifying company details in public records blended with a long-standing tradition of relying on gossip for credit information.[122] At least during the early years of the twentieth century, creditworthiness continued to depend on rumour.

By 1918, however, the instructions began to change. Instead of clinging to the admission that 'no rule can be laid down', the rule became that agents needed the approval of managers to investigate rumours.[123] Over time, the manuals show a slow, though ultimately still incomplete, move away from rumour. As part of the process, the company instructed its agents to adopt more bureaucratic phrasing. The 1897 manual told agents to use the passive voice: agents should write 'caution is deemed advisable' instead of 'we advise'.[124] By 1918, however, the manual asserted that agents should avoid the word 'advise' altogether, stating that 'the words "advise" or "recommend" are objectionable'.[125] Instead, the head office instructed agents to emphasise that any unfavourable comments came from local sources: '[I]t is proper to say that the "trade", or "those consulted do not consider the account desirable".'[126] The immediate objective was probably to protect the agency from lawsuits by disgruntled creditors who might blame Dun if a well-reviewed debtor defaulted. But bureaucratic language also created or enhanced the impression that these reports were objective evaluations.

Through its evolving efforts to translate personal information and financial history into objective reports, Dun offered a new solution to the trust problem: an information package presented as a credit report. First offered in the form of an appraisal written in bureaucratese rife with the passive voice, then later represented by a number indicating a credit score, the process for determining creditworthiness was becoming increasingly opaque. Moreover, the early history of credit-rating and formal banking, which evinced notable bias and exclusion, became the foundation for later systems. The Dun reports fed right into the twenty-first century's algorithmic reputational societies, which are examined in Chapter 5.[127] And with each step of this process, people became alienated from the economic information that circulated about them.

For institutional lenders, the new information system helped them appraise the prospects of middling people and of small and medium enterprises. The credit report helped them expand into a world that, as Chapter 2 showed, had been structured around face-to-face economic relationships. Bureaucratic economic information became a tool for institutional lenders wanting to enter that credit market and make a profit from debt. Although the 'new' trust mechanism had much in common with earlier information systems, the credit report facilitated a broad shift from person-to-person lending to institutional lending. And if bankers had successfully wedged the bureaucratic report into the relationship between debtors and creditors, the next step in the consolidation of Mexico's modern financial industry was for bankers to thrust the disciplinary power of the post-revolutionary state between them.

4

Bad Cheques

Property Crime and the Moral Economy of Financialisation, 1930s–1980s

In the 1970 comedic film *La hermana trinquete*, superstar actress Silvia Pinal plays a thief with a good heart who steals for both pleasure and profit. She carries out non-violent robberies in a range of disguises, from playing a nun to masquerading as an airline stewardess. In one escapade, she steals from a pair of grifters, a man-and-woman team who are defrauding an art collector in a hotel in Acapulco. The art collector, who appears to be American, wants to buy paintings owned by a third person, who is refusing to sell. The grifters offer to sell the collector some uncovered cheques written by the paintings' owner. The collector could use them, the grifters suggest, to pressure the owner to sell the art. As the con man explains, 'the paintings' owner knows that the cheques are a crime big enough for the authorities to lock him up for a long time'. With the uncovered cheques in his possession, the collector would have considerable leverage over the owner. Unsurprisingly, the unethical art collector agrees to the scam, buying the cheques for 30,000 American dollars.

Pinal's character, meanwhile, has been watching and listening in using hidden recording devices. Incognito as the heavily pregnant 'Señora Estrada', she executes an elaborate plan that includes a blackface disguise and a cameo by iconic comedian Roberto Gómez Bolaños, all to outsmart the grifters at their own game. In the end, Pinal gets the cash and the con man is arrested. But, in a gesture of gender solidarity, Pinal's character orchestrates events so that the female grifter remains free. Pinal gives the woman what would have been her cut, a measly 5,000 dollars, and advises her to consider working alone in the future. Pinal then walks out of the hotel 25,000 dollars richer. The film, emblematic of contemporaneous Mexican cinema, offers a clear message: writing an uncovered cheque was a big risk.[1]

For about five decades of the twentieth century, it was a serious crime to write an uncovered cheque in Mexico. The act was defined as fraud from 1932 to 1984. During these decades, a cheque-writer (the drawer, or *librador*) with insufficient funds in their account gave the cheque-receiver (the payee, or *beneficiario*) tremendous power. They also risked going to jail, as the grifters in *La hermana trinquete* made clear. Of course, most people arrested for uncovered cheques were not involved in elaborate schemes to swindle foreign art collectors, but the files of people arrested in Mexico City for writing uncovered cheques chronicle the trouble that individuals regularly got into with these financial instruments. *Libradores* wrote cheques for all sorts of reasons, such as rent payments or to purchase goods. And when those cheques bounced, *libradores* were arrested, charged, and arraigned. They gave declarations, the prosecutor submitted evidence, and then the judge decided their fate.

The history of bad cheques is the story of how everyday financial habits and customs were criminalised to promote consumption and advance financial modernisation. This chapter examines what happened to people who wrote uncovered cheques from the 1930s to the 1980s. It analyses economic citizenship during Mexico's mid-century boom, shows who was included in this world, and explores the tension between transformations of financial capitalism and continuities in the debtor–creditor relationship. It then turns to the power dynamic between *libradores* and *beneficiarios* and shows how coercion shaped the history of financialisation. Tracing these dynamics across five decades through the lens of the uncovered cheque reflects pivotal changes in the financial and moral economy of the twentieth century. Lawmakers, jurists, and everyday economic actors negotiated in theory and practice whether the cheque was a payment tool or a credit instrument, in the process transforming traditional ideas about economic honour and legal justice within the increasingly impersonal modern economic landscape. By the time celebrities like Silvia Pinal and Roberto Gómez Bolaños enacted the consequences of writing bad cheques in *La hermana trinquete*, a new financial framework had become mainstream.

THE CRIMINALISATION OF UNCOVERED CHEQUES

In the years following the revolution, the government established high penalties for uncovered cheques. It was keen to promote consumption and financial modernisation, and cheques were a symbol of both. As one congressman put it when debating the regulation of credit instruments, 'the cheque is a product of an advanced civilisation'.[2] The modern cheque emerged in the nineteenth century. It might be traced to 1851, when City Bank of New York introduced the chequebook at the Great Exhibition. Before their more contemporary iteration, cheques had a longer history that scholars trace to the first millennium.[3] But it was nineteenth-century legislation that created the modern juridical basis for these tools.

In Mexico, cheques were first regulated in 1884, and then again in 1932 with the *Ley General de Títulos y Operaciones de Crédito*, which was part of a series of modern banking laws passed in the 1920s and 1930s.[4] These banking laws were part of a broader effort by the post-revolutionary government to move towards financial modernisation after the tumult of the revolution.[5] Leaders at the time wanted to signal stability and to convince investors – both domestic and foreign – that Mexico was a good bet. The government's finance policy officials thus gave bankers considerable influence. As historian Noel Maurer has shown, the government invited bankers to 'steer legislation' and 'allow[ed] bankers to write a new and favorable banking law'.[6] According to Maurer, the resulting legislation was unsurprising, having been 'tailor-made to protect the interests of the existing banks'.[7] By mandating harsh penalties for uncovered cheques in the *Ley General de Títulos y Operaciones de Crédito*, political elites acted to protect bankers' interests.[8]

Cheques were an instrument of financial capitalism that middle-class people could hold in their hands. Modern financial capitalism, defined simply as accumulation and profit through financial transactions, began with the banks and financial institutions of the late nineteenth century. Banking and financial institutions such as the Banco Nacional de México and credit-rating agencies, as Chapter 3 showed, inaugurated a new history of inclusion and exclusion. In the mid twentieth century, people, households, and small businesses participated in this world by writing cheques, which were an early example of the modern financial and credit instruments that included credit cards and other sorts of products later in the twentieth century (see Chapter 5). Scholars have described this sort of participation as the financialisation of everyday life: how ordinary people interact with financial products.[9]

Much of the financialisation scholarship focuses on mortgages and stocks at the end of the twentieth century – historian Per Hansen dates the shift to financialisation to around 1980 – and emphasises new forms of discipline and new financial identities.[10] My conceptual framework draws on these approaches, especially via-à-vis discipline, but keeps the focus on the relationship between debtors and creditors. The coercion and exploitation in that relationship belong to a deep history that connects to the anxieties of creditors in the nineteenth century and the concerns of jurists in the thirteenth century. The novelty of financial products such as cheques and credit cards represented another chapter in the relationship between debtors and creditors, who were locked into a power struggle over the value of the debt.

Cheques were a liminal sort of financial instrument, and their in-betweenness exposed clashing moral economies. Cheques were instruments of payment, but people often used them as if they were credit instruments. Legal scholar José Gómez Gordoa describes cheques as 'almost cash', as the *librador* was supposed to have funds in the bank account at the time of writing to cover the amount. But cheques were not quite cash (hence, 'almost' cash), because the *beneficiario* might discover while standing in front of the bank teller that the *librador* had insufficient funds or that the bank account had been cancelled. In other words, cheques were not quite cash because they depended, in Gómez Gordoa's words, 'on the honour of the *librador*'.[11]

Honourable behaviour, however, was understood differently by bankers and by bank account holders. Bankers defined writing an uncovered cheque as dishonourable, thus conceptualising cheques as being as close as possible to cash. But people who used banks understood ethical economic behaviour differently and commonly gave and received uncovered cheques as guarantees or promises of future payment. This usage thus stretched the 'almost cash' dimension of these instruments into the realm of credit. Understandably, bankers wanted to stop these practices, as bounced cheques were costly for financial institutions. It was a clash of moral economies, of what historian E. P. Thompson described as the way in which people understood 'the proper economic functions of several parties within the community'.[12]

Luckily for bankers, they had considerable influence on the crafting of banking laws. Political elites and legislators acted to protect bankers' interests using law as a hegemonic tool to change the behaviour of *libradores* and *beneficiarios*. The criminalisation of uncovered cheques, a financial tool on the threshold of cash and credit, shows just how much bankers and creditors enjoyed *de jure* power. They could land *libradores* who misused cheques in jail by denouncing them to the authorities. Moreover, criminalisation allowed some creditors to transform their *de jure* into de facto power: *beneficiarios* could leverage the threat of denunciation to other ends, as the grifters in *La hermana trinquete* suggested the art collector might.[13]

Political elites did not act to protect bankers out of any sort of alliance, as the relationship between the two groups was quite acrimonious.[14] Rather, when it came to uncovered cheques, the broader policy goal of criminalisation was to stimulate consumption, which was key to the mid-century developmental model: import substitution through domestic production and industrialisation. The one-party state was thus motivated to secure new and powerful property rights for bankers. In 1932, this was what legislators achieved by formulating uncovered cheques as a property crime. As a result, they facilitated the economic transformation of finance capitalism and financialisation in post-revolutionary Mexico.

Cheques were now regulated by the 1932 *Ley General de Títulos y Operaciones de Crédito*, and writing an uncovered cheque was fraud, punishable with jail time and fines.[15] Articles 175 to 207 of the legal code's fourth chapter address the topic. The second paragraph of Article 193 concerns bounced cheques. 'The *librador* will be committing fraud,' it states, 'if the cheque is not cashed because the *librador* lacked funds when the cheque was written, [or] if the *librador* used the funds he might have had before the term expired, or if the *librador* lacked authorisation to write cheques.'[16] In short, it was considered fraud for a *librador* to write a cheque if they had insufficient funds in their account at any time during the period reserved for the *beneficiario* to cash it (in most instances, this was fifteen days). It was also considered fraud to write a cheque without authorisation, for example if the account had been cancelled.

Articles 386 to 390 of the *Código Penal Federal*, which was passed in 1931 and remained in force with modifications in the intervening years, outlined the penalties for fraud. Article 386 established that jail time ranged from six months to six years, with fines ranging from 50 to 1,000 pesos. Subsequent changes included the introduction of gradations. A revision to Article 386 in 1946 set the following penalties: for up to 50 pesos defrauded, jail time was from three days to six months, with fines from 5 to 50 pesos; for 50 to 3,000 pesos defrauded, jail time was listed at six months to three years, with fines ranging from 50 to 500 pesos; and for over 3,000 pesos defrauded, *libradores* faced three to twelve years in jail and fines up to 12,000 pesos.[17] A *librador* who wrote an uncovered cheque for any reason – be it hardship, business failure, personal mistake, financial illiteracy, or deliberate deception – thus broke the law and faced serious consequences. In fact, all manner of everyday economic arrangements and agreements were classed as white-collar crimes. And within this legal framework, the *beneficiario* had substantially more power than the *librador*.

When *libradores* and *beneficiarios* used cheques, they became, for a period of time, debtors and creditors. In a shop, for example, when a consumer paid a shopkeeper with a cheque, they were, in essence, promising to pay at a future time. It might be a matter of minutes, days, or weeks, but the cheque remained a promise of payment until the shopkeeper took it to the bank counter (and then, depending on the circumstances, until the cheque cleared). It was during this time lag that *libradores* and *beneficiarios* entered into a debtor–creditor relationship, and, if something went awry, they became frozen in it. Thus, economists have examined the *cui bono* question: who benefited? *Libradores*, after all, might still use the funds or earn interest on them prior to the *beneficiario*'s deposit.[18]

People also wrote postdated cheques or gave cheques as guarantees.[19] When they did so, they tried – intentionally or not – to transform the cheque into a credit instrument. Credit instruments including *letras de cambio* (bills of exchange) or *pagarés* (IOUs) were obligations to make payment at a certain future date. Notably, *libradores* would have been better off writing a *pagaré* than an uncovered cheque, even if they ultimately defaulted on their obligation. The consequences for writing a bad cheque were much harsher during these decades.

The criminalisation of uncovered cheques signalled a big historical change. Since the late eighteenth century, legal codes and legislation had been moving away from harsh penalties for unpaid debts (such as in IOUs or bills of exchange). Debt imprisonment, as Chapter 2 showed, had been eliminated by the mid nineteenth century in a top-down effort to encourage trade and support the region's economic power. The introduction of jail time for uncovered cheques reversed that historical trend, which, very likely, was why creditors wanted cheques as guarantees in the first place.

The arrest records chronicle the troubles of people who wrote bad cheques. The collection, housed at the Mexico City Archive, has approximately 2,300 files on people arrested for '*cheques sin fondos*' (uncovered cheques) from 1941 to 1975. The records are from Mexico City's Lecumberri prison, where the *libradores* were processed. The files cover the period from the initial arrest until the judge's decision, during which time most of the *libradores* were released on bail. The files are not, therefore, what scholars usually consider 'prison files'. (Presumably there exists an administrative record for those who were either denied bail or

TABLE 4.1 *Sample and data universe of* cheques sin fondos, *1941–1975*

Year	Cases in sample	Universe	Sample as percentage of data universe
1941–1950	7	140	5
1951–1960	30	600	5
1961–1970	55	1,100	5
1971–1975	23	460	5
Total	115	2,300	5

ultimately found guilty and jailed, which would have information about their time in the correctional institution, such as medical treatment and mail logs.) These records are also different from the court records studied in previous chapters. While the *juicios verbales* and the *providencias precautorias* might be considered the fullest archival record of the judicial action in play, these documents include only partial information about the actual court case. For example, some of the *cheques sin fondos* files reference but do not include witness statements; in contrast, witness statements are part of the *providencia precautoria* files. As the *cheques sin fondos* files offer only a glimpse into the legal history, the source is thus best considered as a start rather than a complete picture. There likely exists a judicial archive with the complete court records for these conflicts that might, in the future, be open for historical research.

The digital catalogue was searchable, but the archive did not allow for photographing or photocopying the documents themselves.[20] The quantitative analysis presented here is based on a sample of 115 files (approximately 5 per cent of the data universe). For the sampling, I transcribed every twentieth *cheques sin fondos* file, starting with the first one in the catalogue. This yielded 122 files, of which 7 were dropped because they were not about bad cheques (they were probably misfiled). Table 4.1 presents the sample and the estimated data universe.

The files give information about the people arrested, why they wrote a bad cheque, and their subsequent legal problems. Most of the people were middle-aged, middle-class men from Mexico City. Most got into trouble because they had insufficient funds in their accounts. And most were found guilty and fined rather than jailed. The main variables analysed can be grouped as follows: details pertaining to people (with demographic data such as gender, age, income, prior arrests, and so on); details pertaining to the precipitating problem (with information about the reasons for writing the cheque, the amount in question, and what went wrong, such as whether an account was cancelled or there were insufficient funds); and details pertaining to the judicial process (including whether the *librador* admitted wrongdoing and if they were found guilty or innocent).

The statistical analysis was exploratory, testing for all possible relationships between variables to look for connections or a lack thereof. The main tests were correlations, t-tests, chi-squared tests, and Fisher's exact tests.[21] Overall, the variables help reconstruct a picture of the people who got into trouble with cheques, the sorts of problems these people had, and what they experienced in the legal process. For the specific conflicts described below, I provide all known information, including the profession or religion of the people involved.[22]

The conflicts in the *cheques sin fondos* files show changing ideas about fairness. The moral economy of the *librador–beneficiario* relationship centred on the proper functioning of both parties within a contract bound by an acceptable amount of exploitation. The guiding historical questions, then, are: how much exploitation or coercion would be allowed or accepted by *libradores* and *beneficiarios*? And how much would be allowed by the political authority? The boundaries of acceptable exploitation were political and ideological, and they changed over time. In this era of mid-century financialisation, the boundaries shifted meaningfully as citizens faced harsh penalties for misuse and were vulnerable to latent coercion.

ECONOMIC CITIZENSHIP AND FINANCIAL INCLUSION

Most people who wrote uncovered cheques in the mid to late twentieth century were middle-class citizens who had been included in the new financial institutions. Political citizenship, in broad terms, is about defining who belongs to a nation and outlining their rights and responsibilities. Economic citizenship, in post-revolutionary Mexico, was also about the terms of inclusion: membership and participation in the nation's economic institutions and macroeconomic growth. Historians of economic citizenship in Latin America have focused on mass consumption and populism, examining, for example, state programmes to integrate citizens into a modern consumer society and to limit social stratification.[23] The uncovered cheques show a related dimension: integration into economic and financial institutions, or what has come to be called 'financial inclusion'.[24] The chequebook was a symbol. People became economic citizens when they opened bank accounts, wrote cheques, and accepted the regulatory and disciplinary power of the state. In the twentieth century, economic citizenship was increasingly about participating in banking and financial institutions. And the terms of economic citizenship benefited the banks rather than the account holders.

Cheques were part of the growing consumer economy, used by small business owners and their customers to facilitate exchange, and legislators aimed to instil broad societal confidence in the financial instrument to encourage growth.[25] Financial modernisation from the 1930s to the 1980s was, therefore, a tool to support consumption within the mid-century developmental model of import substitution industrialisation. (Later, finance itself became the goal, as examined in Chapter 5.) Legislators promoted financial modernisation to buttress the consumer economy and facilitate entrepreneurial initiative, and consumers and business owners alike used cheques to buy and sell goods that were made in Mexico.[26]

The use of cheques grew during the middle decades of the twentieth century, a period of economic boom often called the Mexican miracle.[27] It was a time of relative stability and prosperity for some citizens. The revolution ended in 1920, and a new political elite emerged among the leaders of the forces that had triumphed during the armed conflict. After nearly a decade of political intrigue, elites consolidated and founded a new political party in 1929. Thus began seventy-one years of one-party rule. Originally called the Partido Nacional Revolucionario (PNR), it became the Partido de la Revolución Mexicana (PRM) in 1938, and finally the Partido Revolucionario Institucional (PRI) in 1946.[28] The party promised to deliver on the achievements of the revolution and to create a stable nation state after the country had been nearly torn apart during the fighting.

Among the party's goals were the protection and expansion of its political power and social control. Ostensibly democratic, elections were held like clockwork, and the PRI's candidate was declared winner of every presidential contest until 2000. Limited spaces were allowed for opposition parties at the state and local levels.[29] The party functioned as a negotiation table, attempting to balance the interests of almost all sectors of Mexican society: workers, peasants, the urban poor, the middle classes, business leaders, the church, and more.[30] The party allowed some space for dissent, but it resorted to violence against citizens – including detention, torture, assassination, and massacre – when it perceived threats to its hegemony.[31] Against this backdrop of one-party politics, the PRI managed and benefited from a mid-century economic boom with average annual growth rates of over 6 per cent from 1940 to 1970.

The Mexican miracle brought material comfort to growing numbers of citizens. The PRI channelled resources into hospitals and schools, public transportation and highways, modern apartment complexes and suburban neighbourhoods, public markets and shopping centres, and universities and technical training institutes. On the cultural front, the government built museums, funded archaeological excavations, and subsidised the film industry. It was the golden age of Mexican cinema and the literary scene was thriving.

Only some groups of citizens enjoyed the prosperity, however. These citizens lived mostly in the capital and other major cities, and they loosely formed the middle classes. The middle classes were growing as a proportion of the population: by some measures, from approximately 20 per cent in 1950 to 30 per cent in 1970.[32] It was a protean group that included technicians and professionals, entrepreneurs and employees.[33] Writing in 1970, Octavio Paz described how the boom had produced 'two Mexicos, one modern and the other underdeveloped'. As he put it, '[H]alf of Mexico – poorly clothed, illiterate, and underfed – has watched the progress of the other half.'[34]

In Paz's 'modern' half, citizens participated in the financial world with their chequebooks. Citizens with bank accounts started to use these financial and credit instruments in the middle of the twentieth century as banks encouraged ordinary people to join the modern financial world. As the Banco Industrial y Agrícola advertised in the newspaper *El Siglo de Torreón* in August 1942, cheques offered people a safe and easy way to make payments. Moreover, it touted, 'THERE ARE NO small or large accounts, we offer the same SERVICE TO EVERYONE.'[35] Indeed, for financial capitalism to spread and deepen, more people needed to get banked and use their chequebooks.

During this time, financial institutions redesigned their spaces to reach more customers. The teller's counter had once been an austere and imposing place, as Figure 4.1 shows. Surrounded by heavy wood panelling, the bank teller stands beside his counter at a Mexico City bank sometime between 1935 and 1940, only a few years after the 1932 law regulating cheques had passed.[36] Everything about the space, it seems, was designed to intimidate. A few decades later, banks looked quite different. By 1962, as Figure 4.2 shows, citizens could do their banking at mobile units. The Banco de Pequeño Comercio rolled up in a bus and opened its window on the streets of Mexico City, reaching account holders in a far more welcoming atmosphere as they went about their daily lives.[37]

FIGURE 4.1 'Elegant' bank teller, ca. 1935–1940. *Source*: Instituto Nacional de Antropología e Historia.

Bounced cheques were part of the Mexican miracle's prosperous new economic reality.[38] *Libradores* and *beneficiarios* used cheques in their personal lives and working lives throughout the era. In their personal lives, they consumed the modern goods and services offered by the miraculous boom. As long-standing financial instruments, cheques facilitated exchange in a rather broad world of bustling enterprise, just as they had throughout history. Historian Marco Spallanzani, for example, has shown that cheques in Renaissance Florence were used by 'men of very modest commercial status' as a convenient way to pay small sums in routine transactions, for example when a Florentine haberdasher paid someone else less than half a florin to empty a cess pit in 1477.[39] Economists Stephen Quinn and William Roberds have also described how, in early modern Europe, cheques served the needs of 'ordinary businessmen' in local commerce. They note that, by contrast, bills of exchange served 'prominent merchants' and could be used across localities.[40] Clearly, cheques have a long history of easing the friction of exchange among small and medium proprietors.

At mid-century, a particular conflict perfectly captures how the economic boom was supported by these kinds of financial exchanges and the instruments enabling them. The conflict broke out, fittingly, between

FIGURE 4.2 Bank bus on city streets, April 1962. *Source*: Instituto Nacional de Antropología e Historia.

libradores and *beneficiarios* connected to the film industry in the midst of cinema's golden age. Diego Palomino was a 29-year-old single journalist from Mexico City who lived in the Santa María la Ribera neighbourhood in 1955. He was unemployed at the time, but the previous year he had worked for a magazine that focused on the film industry, *Constelación Fílmica*. His exact role at the magazine is unclear, but while there, he wrote two cheques totalling 4,092 pesos on the company account, both made out to Rotograbados (presumably a printing service). After the cheques bounced, Dolores Castaño filed a claim with the *Procuraduría General de la República* (attorney general) on behalf of Rotograbados. Palomino was arrested in January 1955.

Palomino admitted to writing the cheques, but gave a rather convoluted explanation. He blamed his colleague Adela Céspedes, an accountant and treasurer at *Constelación Fílmica*, for the issue. He claimed that Céspedes had assured him that there was enough in the account to cover the cheques. Furthermore, he accused Céspedes of stealing from the company. While Palomino's explanation is difficult to follow, the details of his story suggest a tangled series of events. He stated that a lawyer had showed up at his house on behalf of Dolores Castaño (of Rotograbados), counselling him to write the cheques on the company account so that Céspedes – and not Palomino – would be responsible for the outstanding invoice at the heart of the conflict. It is unclear how this might have worked, if it was indeed true. And, in the end, it was Palomino rather than Céspedes who was found at fault. Palomino was detained at his arraignment and, after a series of appeals, was found guilty. He was released on probation with a fine of 4,000 pesos and was ordered to pay additional damages for the amount involved: 4,092 pesos.[41]

In some ways, Palomino's case was fairly typical. Like Palomino, most *libradores* were found guilty. *Libradores* were found guilty and sentenced to pay a fine in 36.5 per cent (38) of the files; they were found guilty and sentenced to prison in 18.3 per cent (19) of the files. *Libradores* were found not guilty in 34.6 per cent (36) of the files.[42] And, like most *libradores*, Palomino was a man. Among the *libradores*, 8.7 per cent (10) were women and 91.3 per cent (105) were men. In contrast, Palomino's case was unusual because the *beneficiario* was represented by a woman (Dolores Castaño). Among *beneficiarios*, 8.6 per cent (8) were women, 83.9 per cent (78) were men, and 7.5 per cent (7) were entities.[43] Put simply, there was nothing particularly remarkable about Palomino's case.

The Rotograbados v Palomino conflict conjures up the new world. The case was connected to the secondary industries surrounding the golden age of cinema, a world created by the post-revolutionary state in the context of macroeconomic growth. But it was also a very old sort of economic conflict, mixing economic trouble, personal grievance, and deliberate deception. The old relationship between debtors and creditors that the previous chapters traced from mediaeval Iberia up to the nineteenth century was re-signified in conflicts between *libradores* and *beneficiarios* during the Mexican miracle.

A bounced cheque, however, was as much a symbol of prosperity as it was of hardship. Most people who wrote uncovered cheques during these years were middle-class citizens who had been included in the modern financial institutions. The sorts of small and medium businesses that were somehow caught up in the economic troubles showcased in the *cheques sin fondos* records buttress this interpretation. Film magazines, printing businesses, sports arenas, and casinos all fell within the world of middle-class people engaged in small and medium enterprises as consumers, workers, and proprietors. And the incomes of those arrested further suggest how modern financial institutions were reaching into the lower range of the middle classes. In the sample, 27 files give information about the *librador*'s daily income (*utilidad diaria*): the minimum daily income was 30 pesos, the maximum was 300 pesos, and the average was 104 pesos. These figures correspond to estimates for a middle-class income range. For the year 1950, for example, historian Howard Cline estimated that the middle-class income ranged from 15 to 500 pesos daily; for 1960, sociologist Arturo González Cosío estimated 135 pesos daily.[44] Consider the following example from the *cheques sin fondos* files: in 1961, Morris Slowitz ran a printing business earning 100 pesos daily (his troubles with uncovered cheques are described in the following section). This daily income put him below González Cosío's narrow estimate of 135 daily pesos for a middle-class income in 1960, but within the range given by Howard Cline for 1950 (regardless of whether it was adjusted for 5 per cent annual inflation). Thus, while the estimates are quite rough, this example supports the general impression that the *libradores* in the *cheques sin fondos* files earned what could be described as middle-class incomes.

Furthermore, the amounts that the cheques were written for suggest a middle-class world.[45] Table 4.2 presents the monetary amounts that uncovered cheques were written for by decade, and also gives the value in historical American dollars. The sums involved were relatively unremarkable: important enough to pursue legal redress, but probably not enough to derail the plans of most of the people who appeared before the judges.

The history of cheque accounts shows how elites – legislators and bankers alike – attempted to create an inclusive institution to incorporate more and more people into the credit economy. And it worked. During the mid-century decades, cheques became widely available. National historical statistics measure the cheque account balances from 1890 to the present. Table 4.3 shows that the proportion of cheques vis-à-vis total liquid financial aggregates (total bank notes, metal currency, and bank accounts held by residents) increased from approximately 30 to 60 per cent during the years under study. In other words, as cheque account balances grew, the importance of cheques ballooned.

Clearly, citizens were keen to participate in a growing consumer society: they eagerly opened bank accounts and wrote cheques. The people who were arrested for writing uncovered cheques, however, experienced

TABLE 4.2 *Value of cheques sin fondos in the arrest records, 1941–1975*

Years	Value of cheque in nominal pesos (minimum amount)	Value of cheque in nominal pesos (maximum amount)	Value of cheque in nominal pesos (mean)	Value in historical American dollars (mean)[a]
1941–1950 (n=2)	2,000	9,100	5,550	1,140
1951–1960 (n=18)	190	27,653	5,275	443
1961–1970 (n=47)	160	22,130	4,456	357
1971–1975 (n=21)	240	28,960	10,983	879

[a] The amount of each cheque was converted to American dollars and then averaged for the decade. Conversion calculated using Lawrence H. Officer, 'Exchange Rates Between the United States Dollar and Forty-one Currencies', MeasuringWorth, 2024.

TABLE 4.3 *Cheque account balances, 1932–1980*

Year	Cheque account balances in pesos (billions)	Value of total liquid aggregates in pesos (billions) (M1)	Cheques as a percentage of M1
1932	0.1	0.3	33.3
1940	0.4	1.1	36.4
1950	3.3	6.2	53.2
1960	10	18	55.6
1970	31	51	60.8
1980	297	492	60.4

Source: INEGI, *Estadísticas Históricas II* (1999 edition), 867–868, table 20.1.

the growing pains of financial capitalism first-hand. Financial inclusion could liberate: it freed up credit and opened new opportunities. But inclusion also constrained: when something went wrong, *libradores* got into quite a lot of trouble.

Although the world of uncovered cheques was largely a middle-class one, newspaper accounts chronicled, with colourful detail, when the rich and famous were caught in the act. Artists, in particular, attracted newspaper attention. As one reporter explained in a convoluted 1975 case involving musician Tito Bauche (who had apparently been paid with an uncovered cheque): 'As usual when artists are involved in police matters the situation is theatrical.'⁴⁶ At other times the coverage was about political intrigue, such as when violinist Elias Breeskin was arrested in 1945 for writing an uncovered cheque. The case was generally regarded as politically motivated because Breeskin was sent to the penal island of Islas Marías as punishment.⁴⁷ Yet even within these reports on the famous, journalists often referenced the growing numbers of ordinary people caught up in legal trouble because of uncovered cheques. It was a society-wide epidemic. As an article from April 1952 about the arrest of a Mexico City businessman concluded, 'Now there are so many cases.'⁴⁸

MISUSE, MALFEASANCE, AND THE GROWING PAINS OF FINANCIAL MODERNITY

From a bank's perspective, there are three main things that might go wrong with a cheque: there are insufficient funds in the account, the account has been cancelled, or the *librador* does not have an account. Within the *cheques sin fondos* files, these concerns are borne out. There were insufficient funds in the account in 77.7 per cent of the files (73); the account had been cancelled in 13.8 per cent (13); and instances where the *librador* did not even have an account occurred in 8.5 per cent (8) of cases.⁴⁹ Statistically, these three problems were not significantly related to the other variables (an exception regarding age is considered later in the chapter): for example, they were not significantly associated with variables such as gender or outcome.

While writing an uncovered cheque for any of these reasons was against the law, these were substantively different problems. The qualitative distinction between insufficient funds, cancelled accounts, and non-existent accounts therefore helps puzzle out the difficult research question of whether a person's debt trouble stemmed from a mistake or from malfeasance. When did citizens make mistakes due to not understanding the juridical nature of the cheque, for example? When did a *librador* write an uncovered cheque because of personal hardship or business failure? And when did *libradores* deliberately misuse or abuse the financial instrument?

Lack of funds could have been due to financial illiteracy or something shadier. It was suspect behaviour, however, when individuals wrote cheques on cancelled accounts or non-existent accounts. This is what Emilia Stein did. A 29-year-old housewife originally from Veracruz who lived in Mexico City (in the Condesa neighbourhood), she was arrested in September 1962. In a departure from the typical summary of circumstances in the archival record, Stein gave a fair amount of information about her lifestyle in her declaration: she enjoyed going to the movies and the theatre, reading romantic novels, and swimming. She did not take drugs or drink alcohol or play games of chance. She smoked. She had never had a contagious disease. She did not have a nickname. Her mother was alive; her father was dead. She found herself in her current legal predicament because, in March 1961, she had written an uncovered cheque for 500 pesos to the company Playeras Parker. (The time lag between the transaction and the arrest, which was eighteen months in Stein's case, varied quite a bit in the sample.) The company's representative added that Stein had purchased merchandise for her business, which might have been a small-scale informal activity, since she listed her profession as housewife. However, the cheque bounced because she had cancelled her bank account prior to giving Playeras Parker the cheque for 500 pesos. Although Stein disputed the charge, it was, all things considered, a fairly straightforward case of malfeasance.[50]

Most commonly, however, *libradores* ran into trouble when cheques bounced because there was not enough money in the account to cover the promise. Older *libradores*, in particular, had a problem with insufficient funds. The youngest *librador* in the sample was 19 years old, the oldest was 63, and the average age was 39.[51] The mean age of *libradores* in files with the problem of 'insufficient funds' was significantly higher than the mean age of *libradores* with other problems.[52] Morris Slowitz was the oldest *librador* with insufficient funds in his account to cover his cheque. He was a 63-year-old printer who had no prior arrests. He had some high school education, and he earned 100 pesos daily to support himself and his wife. Slowitz was originally from Poland and was likely holding American citizenship (the file is unclear on this point). He was thus among the 10.8 per cent (8) of *libradores* whose origins lay abroad.[53]

In April 1961, Slowitz bought a machine on instalment from A. B. Dick of Mexico; this was likely a copy machine, a mimeograph, or a small duplicator press, as the company was a leading manufacturer. Slowitz paid the deposit with a cheque for 4,799 pesos. When the cheque bounced because Slowitz had insufficient funds in his account, the company filed a claim with the *Procuraduría General de la República*. Slowitz was then arrested in June 1962. Like Stein, he disputed the charge, saying he had given the cheque as a guarantee. He had used the machine for about a month, but it was too expensive to run. He tried to return it, but could not because of a workers' strike. He said that he was ready to return the machine at any time. A. B. Dick's representative, however, said that

Slowitz had given the cheque as first payment, and that Slowitz had also given several *pagarés* to cover future instalments. The judge found Slowitz guilty in November 1962 and sentenced him to probation with a fine of 5,000 pesos.[54]

Might older *libradores* like Slowitz have been more financially illiterate? When compared with the precipitating problems in other cases – like the account having been cancelled – not having enough money could be construed as a mistake, thus indicating illiteracy instead of deception. But, of course, scholars can only speculate about whether Slowitz made an innocent mistake. After all, the historical record is incomplete. The explanations given are what *libradores* presented to the authorities. Nobody wants to go to jail, so presumably there was some strategy involved in what they shared. Perhaps Morris Slowitz truly did not understand that cheques could not be given as guarantees, or perhaps he did not understand the fine print of his consignment purchase and mistakenly thought he could return the machine. Perhaps he was an easy target for an unscrupulous salesperson who deliberately gave him the wrong impression. Or maybe Morris Slowitz was lying. Perhaps he knew that the cheque would bounce. Perhaps he wanted to use the machine for only one month or for a particular job, and he thought that A. B. Dick, a large international company, would absorb the loss.

In the middle of the twentieth century, *libradores* certainly had opportunities to misuse cheques as a financial instrument. Newspaper reporting recounted, often with relish, scams and swindles perpetrated using uncovered cheques.[55] While most of their reporting was about major graft, some of the coverage focused on small-scale grift, such as when Salvador Rizo defrauded three Mexico City butchers' shops in 1976 by purchasing animal fat with '*cheques "de hule"*' (or 'rubber cheques').[56] But, for the most part, such cases did not make for splashy news fodder, and the intent is difficult to assess.

Morris Slowitz, like Diego Palomino and Emilia Stein, was emblematic of the mid-century economic boom. All three belonged to a Mexico City that buzzed with entrepreneurial activity. They participated in finance capitalism. They opened bank accounts and used modern instruments, navigating an increasingly sophisticated financial world. And all three were arrested and found guilty for writing uncovered cheques. Examining what went wrong suggests that *libradores* with insufficient funds might have been more likely to have made a mistake than those who had cancelled their accounts, but historians cannot know for sure. Whatever the explanation, financial illiteracy was clearly a growing pain of financial capitalism.

As more and more citizens used cheques, they faced a steep learning curve, and the stakes were high. The PRI's political elite did not establish financial literacy programmes to protect citizens until the 1970s; until then, the focus was on punishing citizens. It seems, however, that judges gave *libradores* with lower incomes a break. Lower incomes were connected to better outcomes: the mean daily income in files with the outcome of 'not guilty' was significantly different from the mean daily income in files with other outcomes.[57] Felipe Rivera, whose case is examined later in this chapter due to the unusual violence involved in his conflict with León Solís, had the lowest income among *libradores* who were found not guilty. The troubles of another *librador* in this group, Isaías García, serve as a more mundane example.

García was a 34-year-old married man who had a primary school education. He worked as an employee and earned 64 pesos per day. He was arrested in August 1975 for writing an uncovered cheque for 2,000 pesos. While García admitted to writing the cheque, he said that he had given it to José Falcón to guarantee a debt, and that Falcón had promised to return the cheque when the debt was paid. Falcón said that García had given him the cheque as a salary payment, with no further details provided in the record. García disagreed. In fact, García presented a witness to testify that not only had he given the cheque as a guarantee, but that he subsequently cleared the debt. The judge found García not guilty.[58]

The connection between low incomes and good case outcomes stands out. Tests did not find significant associations between income and the other major variables. Why, then, did people with low incomes more frequently receive a 'not guilty' outcome? Might judges have considered a person's low income when providing a better resolution? Judges might have been advancing an ethical critique that, despite the universality of cheques as financial products available to different people from a wide range of circumstances, it was fairer to distinguish between two types of *libradores*: citizens with higher incomes who had been included in the economic boom, and citizens with lower incomes who were, if not excluded, certainly not the main beneficiaries of economic growth. It could be that judges, consciously or not, held some *libradores* more responsible for their actions than others. Whatever the reason, the results show that lower income was significantly associated with better outcomes, suggesting that it might have been a good strategy for *libradores* to downplay their resources. Moreover, as financial institutions reached into the lives of more and more citizens, judges might have had greater sympathy for the more modest *libradores* who struggled on the learning curve of financial modernity.

The risk of mishap and malfeasance grew apace with the use of cheques in Mexican society, and banks at the time could only do so much. *Libradores* received chequebooks when they opened bank accounts, and their signatures were recorded on a signature card that was distributed to many branches within a city or region. While bank tellers were supposed to confirm the *librador*'s signature, in practice this could prove more difficult than it sounded. They did not always have time to verify the signature, or they might not be able to distinguish false signatures. It could also be that they lacked a signature card for verification. Historian Bernardo Bátiz-Lazo describes how, in Britain, banks simply assumed the cost of cheques with false signatures; it was only with the development of ATMs and PIN numbers that banks were able to push the responsibility for misuse or for fraudulently using PIN numbers onto customers.[59] In Mexico, tellers confirmed the *beneficiario*'s identity with an identification card, such as a workplace credential or a social security card, which usually did not have a photograph. As a result, underhand dealings were not uncommon.

An internal work plan from the Banco de México offers a glimpse into the central bank's perspective on the challenges they faced with bad cheques in the middle of the century. The plan outlined suggestions for tellers to make a 'real effort' to reduce the improper (*indebido*) use of cheques in the Mexico City area. The first point concerned signatures. The report urged branches to confirm a prospective client's references and signature, even when the client deposited cash upon opening the account. The directive suggests that branches sometimes skipped this step. Most of the other recommendations came down to information sharing: the names of *libradores* who had written bad cheques or were otherwise 'dangerous or undesirable' should be circulated between branches and between institutions, and the local clearing house should provide a daily report. 'It is of utmost interest for all Banks that they work together to achieve the general acceptance of cheques,' the work plan asserted.[60] Banks clearly needed better information about their clients, which suggests that the credit reports examined in Chapter 3 were not yet common (they would become more important at the turn of the millennium, as Chapter 5 shows).

SOCIAL INERTIA, FRICTION, AND THE LATENT COERCION OF FINANCIALISATION

Despite the novelty of the mid-century consumer society with its modern financial instruments, there was meaningful continuity in the mundane debt troubles of ordinary people. Just as they had before, many honest people struggled to repay and collect because of personal hardship and failed business ventures. And just as mediaeval jurists had anticipated that some debtors would act in bad faith, it is clear from the *cheques sin fondos* files that some of the citizens included in the financial institutions of the mid twentieth century did just that. Other evidence of more continuity than change exists in the data on gender and the overarching relationship between debtors and creditors.

The gender ratio of *libradores* and *beneficiarios* in the *cheques sin fondos* files is closer to the ratio found in the archives of *juicios verbales* and *providencias precautorias* than it is to the gender ratio reflected in the Dun credit reports. Of the 123 credit reports in the Dun sample, there was only one woman (0.8 per cent). As examined in Chapter 3, this radical over-representation of men suggests the beginnings of exclusion in the modern financial institutions.[61] With uncovered cheques, in contrast, 8.7 per cent of *libradores* were women; among *beneficiarios*, 8.6 per cent were women.[62] In the *juicios verbales* sample, 14.6 per cent of the defendants were women, while 15.6 per cent of the plaintiffs were women.[63] In the *providencias precautorias* sample, 5.2 per cent of the defendants were women, and 9.3 per cent (9) of the plaintiffs were women.[64] These sources, of course, are very different – different types of evidence, different data universes, different sampling strategies, and so on – so, placing the ratios together is not a formal comparison. But it is notable that, even though the Dun reports showed how new financial institutions such as Banamex envisioned an overwhelmingly male clientele, women were not fully excluded.

Continuity also came in the economic troubles of men and women. As with the testing detailed in previous chapters, the statistical analysis of uncovered cheques found little substantial difference in the experiences of men and women. Gender was not significantly associated with the other variables, with few exceptions.[65] Tests did not find significant relationships between the *beneficiario*'s gender and the *librador*'s demographic variables (such as age, prior arrests, and income), for example.[66] In terms of economic justice – the legal proceedings, as can be gleamed from the files – tests did not find a significant connection between gender and the different case outcomes. For example, tests found no statistically significant relationship between *libradores*' gender and a 'not guilty' outcome.[67] And in terms of how long the legal drama lasted, the average duration was 661.2 days (the duration was calculated by counting the days between the first and last documents in the file, which usually corresponded to the initial arrest and the judge's decision).[68] Tests found no significant difference between men and women regarding prolongation.[69]

These results suggest that men and women got into similar trouble with uncovered cheques and had similar experiences with the legal system, a finding that held just as true here as it did with the *juicios verbales* and the *providencias precautorias*. However, as with the statistical analysis in previous chapters, the 'not significant' results show only that the test did not uncover a significant connection. There may well exist a statistically significant relationship between gender and the other variables, but the tests are not finding one for myriad reasons, such as sample size, coding decisions, dataset design, and so on.[70] Interpretation of the quantitative results, just like the qualitative reading of a case study (like trying to puzzle out Emilia Stein's intent when she wrote a bad cheque), is exploratory. With that caveat, the results suggest that gender was not a key factor in the troubles that people had with uncovered cheques.

The cheque amounts add to the picture that different kinds of people had similar kinds of problems with these instruments. The statistical tests did not find a significant association between the amounts the uncovered cheques had been written for and the other variables. Considering the demographic variables, tests found no statistically significant correlation between the amounts and variables such as gender, age, prior arrests, and so on.[71] Similarly, the cheque amounts also were not associated with the different case outcomes. For example, tests found no significant difference between the mean cheque amount in files with a 'not guilty' outcome and the mean cheque amount in cases with other outcomes.[72] And in terms of duration of the legal drama, tests did not find a significant correlation between the cheque amount and how long the proceedings lasted.[73] The overall picture is that people had similar experiences whether they were fighting over large amounts or small sums.

The social life of small-scale debts endured over the *longue durée* despite the economic transformation underway. The mode of accumulation and the development model changed greatly after the revolution. So, too, did the material culture of capitalism with the proliferation of consumer goods such as film magazines and the growing use of chequebooks as a financial instrument by the people who published them. But the relationship between debtors and creditors remained, at its core, similar across different historical eras of capitalism. That gender and cheque amounts were not hugely important in the conflicts between *libradores* and *beneficiarios* suggests important continuity with the earlier conflicts over unpaid debts examined in previous chapters. And people continued to get into trouble for similar reasons, from changing personal and business circumstances to mistake, misdeed, and malfeasance. The seemingly fast-paced economic transformation at mid-century belied important historical continuities in the debtor–creditor relationship. And it is that very coexistence of the new and the old that led to problems between *libradores* and *beneficiarios*, especially when they gave cheques as guarantees.

Scholars have described the increasing immateriality of economic exchange in the twentieth and twenty-first centuries, with some parts of the world moving towards frictionless exchange (from cash to cheques to credit cards, and so on).[74] Frictionless in this context simply indicates the efficient transfer of value with rapid verification.[75] Cheques, when compared with cash, met the first criterion but not the second. Cash was heavy, dirty, expensive to move, easy to lose or steal, and, as anthropologist Bill Maurer writes, the realness of cash went beyond its physicality: '[P]eople feel cash, and when they hand it over, they feel its loss.'[76] Cash was weighted with physical and emotional friction. Like cash, cheques generated a form of emotional friction that came from the promise and the threat. The *librador* promised that the account had enough funds to cover the cheque, and they faced the threat of jail time if their promise was broken.

As the main alternative to banknotes and coins in the mid twentieth century, cheques solved some of the problems of cash. But, like cash, cheques were laden with expensive friction: banks sorted, routed, and delivered the actual cheque, and they floated costs until the settlement was received. In terms of the transaction costs of different transfer mechanisms – with 'frictionless' considered an ideal – cheques were still full of friction.[77] The growing number of cheques to be cleared in the middle of the twentieth century, and the costs associated with these transactions, motivated banks to move towards automation, as Bátiz-Lazo explains in his history of the ATM.[78] Indeed, the costs of clearing cheques led bankers in the 1950s and 1960s to hope for both a cashless and cheque-less world, pinning their futuristic visions on emerging financial technologies.[79] Computerisation heralded the decline of cheques by the 1990s. But until then, cheques were an early financial product in the move away from the materiality of cash and were a symbol of financial modernisation.[80] Notably, the colloquial phrase in English for writing an uncovered cheque reflects some of this dematerialisation: cheque kiting. This refers to the period between the point when the *librador* gives the *beneficiario* the cheque and when the funds clear, an in-between time when the promised amount is immaterial. It is, in effect, up in the air, or 'in flight'.[81]

Much of the learning curve of financial modernity hinged on the tension between materiality and immateriality. The *cheques sin fondos* files are full of people using cheques as guarantees, in the same way debtors might have staked a piece of furniture or a mule as collateral in the previous century. Nearly half of the *libradores* – 46.1 per cent (53) – said that they had given the cheque as a guarantee. When *libradores* like Morris Slowitz gave cheques as guarantees, however, they misused the financial product. They encumbered what was supposed to be an almost immaterial mode of exchange (a cheque weighed about 2 grams) with the heavy friction of a mule (weighing, on average, 400 kilograms). The social lives of unpaid debts persisted much as they always had, greying the divide between the materiality of a mule and the immateriality of a cheque.

The consequences, however, had changed: *libradores* who gave cheques as guarantees could be sent to prison. Economic transformation did not come from the growing use of new financial products, but from the disciplinary power of the state. The balance of power between *libradores* and *beneficiarios* at mid-century was very different from the conflicts between debtors and creditors examined in the previous chapters. In 1932, when bankers and legislators invented a new kind of crime – the fraudulent act of writing an uncovered cheque – they did so to fit the needs of the post-revolutionary economic world. Political leaders saw the beginnings of modern financial capitalism around them, and they wanted to encourage financialisation. Thus, as they wrote down the new banking laws, they sided with creditors and created a legal framework that had the coercion of debtors baked in. The new regime of latent coercion was a testament to bankers' remarkable power and influence.

Historian Orsi Husz's study of cheques in Sweden offers an illuminating point of comparison that underscores just how much power the Mexican bankers enjoyed. According to Husz, cheques became widespread in Sweden in the 1950s because banks took over payroll functions for companies. Workers were given cheque accounts en masse. From the outset, writing an uncovered cheque was no more than a civil infraction. Swedish bankers had recourse to the fraud law only if the cheque-writer acted with fraudulent intent. By the 1960s, Swedish bankers were pushing for a legislative change that would criminalise writing uncovered cheques. They wanted to increase penalties and exact more severe consequences on people who wrote uncovered cheques. But their lobbying failed, and the act remained a civil infraction.[82] Swedish bankers – if they knew about the Mexican legal framework – would probably have envied their Mexican counterparts who had no such difficulty setting the rules to their benefit.

Bankers and political leaders had created a new kind of white-collar crime with serious consequences. When *libradores* wrote uncovered cheques, they faced harsh penalties for misuse, became vulnerable to latent coercion, and risked their personal freedom because either the *beneficiario* or the bank could press charges, and those charges could result in jail time. The authorities, no doubt, intended to push citizens into 'proper' behaviour by creating a structure of intimidation and coercion. Financial modernisation thus depended on a modernisation of violence. And, as a result, when a *librador* wrote an uncovered cheque, the *beneficiario* could wield it as a form of extra-legal pressure. Authorities, intentionally or not, created a modern sort of violence that was different from physical force. Brandishing uncovered cheques, *beneficiarios* could compel *libradores* to do their bidding.

Why would *libradores* give *beneficiarios* such power? Despite the high stakes involved, the stories behind the bad cheques in the *cheques sin fondos* files were largely unexceptional. The most common reason why the risk was taken in the original transaction was to pay for goods or services (34.4 per cent, or 22 cases), followed by paying for loans (26.6 per cent, or 17 cases), business transactions (20.3 per cent, or 13 cases), rent payments (14.1 per cent, or 9 cases), and salary payments (4.7 per cent, or 3 cases).[83] The prosaic quality of these transactions shows how latent coercion infused everyday exchange.

Many *libradores* wrote bad cheques because, quite simply, they did not have enough money for the transaction. Their stories were often about everyday economic woes. While some of the *cheques sin fondos* files were about financial illiteracy and financial fraud, financial hardship was a major reason why people gave others such power over them. Take, for example, Raquel Robledo. Robledo had originally trained as a surgeon but worked as a shopkeeper. She earned 150 pesos per day. She was 46 years old, married, and evangelical. She had no prior arrests. She was originally from San Luis Potosí but lived in Mexico City, in the Vértiz Narvarte neighbourhood where she rented a house from Bertha Fernández. On 12 July 1963, Robledo gave Fernández a cheque for 750 pesos, a partial payment of the 1,400 pesos that she owed in rent.

When Fernández tried to cash the cheque the next morning at 9.30 a.m., it bounced. As the investigation later discovered, Robledo had only 292 pesos in her account when Fernández deposited the cheque. But the investigation also showed that Robledo made two deposits later that same day. By the end of the day her account balance was thus 4,308 pesos, plenty for her rent payment. Although Robledo claimed that she had given the cheque on the understanding that Fernández would cash it after 11 o'clock on 13 July, the judge rejected Robledo's explanation. According to the court, she was responsible for the cheque the moment it left her hands. He found her guilty and sentenced her to six months in prison or probation with a bail of 2,500 pesos.

Needless to say, Robledo appealed. In her second declaration, she described the events in greater detail. According to Robledo, Fernández came to her business on the afternoon of 12 July to collect the rent. Robledo told Fernández that she could pay the following day. Fernández said that her husband was sick, and that she was taking him for medical treatment. Robledo promised to pull together as much cash as she could. However, at that moment, another creditor appeared in Robledo's business: a man with the surname Rojas. He had arrived to collect a different debt (no more details are given). When Robledo explained that she could not pay him for a few days, Rojas suggested that she give him a cheque, which he would cash on the 15th; Robledo agreed. Fernández overheard this exchange and proposed a similar arrangement. If Robledo gave her a cheque, Fernández would cash it on the 15th too. Robledo again agreed. However, the next day, the 13th, Fernández returned to Robledo's business. She threatened to cash the cheque if Robledo did not move out of the house she was renting. Brandishing the cheque, Fernández warned that Robledo could go to jail.

If Robledo's telling of the events was true, it seems likely that Robledo rejected Fernández's threat, and the two women raced to the bank: Fernández tried to cash the cheque at 9.30 that morning, and, later that day, Robledo deposited enough funds to cover it. Robledo's recounting did not end with the bounced cheque, however. Rather, it ends two days later. On the 15th, a representative for Fernández – described only as a *licenciado* (someone with an undergraduate degree) – approached Robledo with an offer: Fernández would give Robledo an amount equivalent to two months rent if Robledo moved out; otherwise, Fernández would send Robledo to jail. Robledo refused. She then tried several times to send rent payment, but when Fernández refused to receive the funds, Robledo deposited the corresponding amount with Nacional Financiera through her account at Banco de Industria y Comercio. Notably, Fernández's refusal to accept payment was the sort of machination that jurists had anticipated for centuries, from the mediaeval *Siete Partidas* to the 1871 Civil Code (see Chapter 2). Not only did Robledo ask the court to review those accounts, she had two witnesses testify that she had given the cheque to be cashed at a later time. Still, the judge denied Robledo's appeal. There were insufficient funds in her account when she wrote the cheque and when it was cashed. In the end, Robledo paid the 2,500 pesos and was released.[84]

Raquel Robledo's account, if true, is a tale of economic woe and coercion, and a perfect example of why a *librador* might give a *beneficiario* the power of an uncovered cheque despite the risks. Tenants struggled to pay rent, got into trouble when they fell into arrears, and sometimes faced duplicitous machinations by their landlords. If untrue, however, this same story shows the troubles that landlords faced with delinquent tenants. Landlords struggled to collect when tenants could not pay, and they sometimes also had to deal with tenants' creative attempts to evade the obligation. This dynamic could involve costly and extended legal battles. At the end of the day, regardless of the truthfulness of Robledo's story, Fernández had an uncovered cheque in her possession, and it put her in the position to evict or otherwise pressure Robledo. It was a huge amount of power.

Libradores likely knew that giving an uncovered cheque was a risky move. In Raquel Robledo's case, it is possible that she did not consider the consequences when she gave Bertha Fernández the cheque, realising only afterwards what was at stake and rushing to deposit funds. But *libradores* who had had prior arrests for violations of Article 193 of the *Ley General de Títulos y Operaciones de Crédito* (bounced cheques) must have deliberately decided to give the *beneficiario* such power. Alfredo Fisher was one such *librador*. Arrested for writing an uncovered cheque in January 1966, he had a prior arrest for a problem with cheques. Although his file had no further details about what happened in the earlier arrest, it did concern Article 193, suggesting a repeat offender. Fisher was not the only *librador* in the *cheques sin fondos* files with previous legal problems, often of the same sort. Twenty *libradores* from the sample (17.4 per cent) had previously been processed in the Lecumberri prison. Their files included the label '*ingresos anteriores*', but they do not give much information about the prior event. In this subset of 20 files, 45 per cent (9) of the *ingresos anteriores* were for fraud, 10 per cent (2) were for bad cheques, and the rest were processed for other offences.[85] Statistically, *libradores* with prior arrests looked much like first-timers. There was no significant relationship between *libradores* with prior arrests and other variables, including demographic variables such as gender, 'problem' variables (for example, if a *librador* admitted to the crime), and 'justice' variables like the outcome of the case.[86]

At the time of his new arrest in 1966, Fisher was a married, 28-year-old Catholic who had completed the first year of *preparatoria* and lived in the

Santa María la Ribera neighbourhood. He worked in sales and reported an income of 100 pesos per day. Fisher was accused of malfeasance by Constantino Barrios, who worked as a bookie (*corredor*) at Frontón Mexico, a casino as well as the famous arena for the Basque sport *jai alai*. Barrios claimed that Fisher had given him, in December 1962, a cheque for 3,000 pesos drawn on an account at the Banco de Londres México. Barrios was unable to cash the cheque because, he discovered, Fisher did not have an account with the bank. It turned out that Fisher had tried to open an account with Banco de Londres México in December 1962, and he had submitted, as a guarantee, a cheque drawn on the Banco de Oriente. Banco de Londres México denied Fisher's application when it discovered that Fisher had insufficient funds in his Banco de Oriente account to cover the cheque, but it had already given Fisher a chequebook when he submitted his application. He did not return the chequebook when the bank denied his application, which put him in possession of a very tempting tool for committing fraud.

The Fisher case provides one example of how a *librador* could write a cheque on a non-existent account: even though he had a chequebook, he had never had an account with Banco de Londres México. So Fisher used the chequebook to do what he typically did when he lost a bet in the Frontón casino: he gave a cheque as a guarantee while he repaid in instalments. In August 1967, the judge found Fisher guilty of fraud and sentenced him to six months in prison or 800 pesos. Fisher chose to pay.[87] While historians cannot know what was in Fisher's mind, it seems probable, based on his previous arrest, that he knowingly gave Constantino Barrios tremendous power over his life when he handed him the bad cheque. What is more, his application for an account with Banco de Londres México had been denied because he had included a cheque with insufficient funds with his paperwork. Experienced as he was with bad cheques, Fisher must have known the risk he took.

Risk increased with endorsed cheques. A *beneficiario* could sign a cheque over to a third person, thus transferring ownership of the cheque, which introduced another person into the relationship. With that new person came the possibility of new risk: the understanding between the *librador* and the original *beneficiario* could be unknown or unacceptable to the new *beneficiario*. This might have been what happened when José Barnes was arrested in October 1973. At the time of his arrest, the 40-year-old Barnes was working in commerce. He had some secondary schooling, he was married, he lived in the Polanco neighbourhood, and he earned approximately 200 pesos per day. He had a prior arrest, but no further details are given. On 5 September 1971, he had given Rodrigo Pérez, the owner of a travel agency, a cheque for 3,000 pesos for services related to arranging a trip to the USA. Barnes explained that he had given Pérez the cheque as a guarantee of future payment, and that the travel agent knew the account balance was only 215 pesos. However, Pérez endorsed the cheque and gave it to his colleague, Óscar Rivera. When Rivera tried to cash the cheque on 17 September, it was rejected due to insufficient funds. The judge found Barnes guilty and sentenced him to a fine of 400 pesos and one year of prison. Because of his previous arrest, he was not given the option of commutation.[88]

Barnes might have been telling the truth, and Pérez might have promised to hold the cheque as a guarantee of future payment. But Rivera, who presumably had no connection to Barnes, was not bound by Pérez's promise. Endorsement increased the *librador*'s risk of a bad outcome by introducing a third party who had no moral relationship with the *librador*. Unwritten agreements – illegal or not – could be unknown or more easily ignored by strangers. And while negotiability had long been a feature of credit instruments, as shown in previous chapters, the high penalties for uncovered cheques substantively changed the meaning of debt transfer. It was not only a transfer of debt, but a transfer of the power to send someone to jail. Of the files in the sample, 14.8 per cent (17) involved endorsed cheques.[89]

Risk further increased if the cheque amount was unspecified (a blank cheque), as this opened wide the door for fraud. This risk of writing a blank cheque became real for Eloy Donoso in February 1975, when Simón Romero denounced him for writing a cheque for 10,000 pesos without sufficient funds in the account. Donoso was a married, 34-year-old, Catholic cabinetmaker who was originally from Puebla (Xochiapulco) and now lived in the neighbourhood of La Perla, Mexico City. He had originally given the cheque to a man named Enrique Benavides Reyes as part of a sale contract. Enrique Benavides Reyes had then endorsed the cheque to Simón Romero, at which point it bounced when Romero tried to cash it.

Donoso admitted to writing the cheque, but claimed he had given a blank cheque to Enrique Benavides Reyes. In other words, he had signed the cheque to Enrique Benavides Reyes but had not filled out the amount. When Enrique Benavides Reyes transferred the cheque to Simón Romero, Donoso was left financially exposed. Of the files in the sample, only 2 involved blank cheques (1.7 per cent), likely reflecting the enormity of the risk involved. And in this case, it was a particularly perplexing situation. The cheque account in question was shared between Donoso and Rosario Salazar Benavides, his godmother. Was Rosario Salazar Benavides related to Enrique Benavides Reyes? Why had Donoso signed a blank cheque, when it was such a risky move? Possibly, he had a close relationship with Enrique Benavides Reyes, as it is difficult to imagine extending this level of trust beyond one's inner circle. If, indeed, that is what had happened, it was likely an extreme violation of trust for Enrique Benavides Reyes to then endorse the cheque to Simón Romero, especially since it had been left blank.

Regardless, the judge did not consider Donoso's explanation exculpatory. He found Donoso guilty and sentenced him to eight months in prison, which could be commuted to 2,000 pesos, as well as a fine of 30 pesos or three days in jail. The file does not indicate which alternative Donoso chose.[90] What it does indicate is how, with endorsed cheques, the original risks were increased with each degree of separation.

Latent coercion became physical violence only twice in the sample, in each case when *libradores* were forced to write uncovered cheques. It happened to Felipe Rivera in August 1957. He claimed that he had been forced to write three cheques for 3,000 pesos each. A 34-year-old single haberdasher, he had a daily income of approximately 30 pesos. He lived in the Morelos neighbourhood, and he had a primary education. Of the event in question, Felipe Rivera said that he had purchased some merchandise from León Solís in 1955 with the intention of selling it in Tepito, one Mexico City's famous markets. Because of poor sales (*malas ventas*), he fell into arrears repaying Solís. In his statement, Felipe Rivera described how he had asked Solís for more time.

Instead, he recounted, there was a violent encounter. A few days after asking Solís for a reprieve, Felipe was out with his brother, José Rivera. After they had taken a steam bath and had had a drink in the Morelos neighbourhood, they were surrounded by Solís and three companions (two police officers and a lawyer) who forced the brothers into a car. Solís detained Felipe Rivera until his brother returned with a chequebook: '[A]ny chequebook in his possession,' Solís had said (*cualquier chequera que fuera de su propiedad*). Solís then forced Felipe Rivera to write the three cheques, despite José Rivera's warning that the account had been cancelled. And, in fact, the cheques bounced because the account had been cancelled five years earlier. Felipe Rivera was initially released on bail, but he spent two embattled years embroiled in the legal wrangling of the case. Luckily, the brother and another witness corroborated Felipe Rivera's account of the forced detention, and he was eventually found not guilty.[91]

Such violence was unusual in the archive. Writing a bad cheque was typically a white-collar crime. It was a non-violent transgression characterised by bad faith and breach of trust. 'White-collar' generally describes economic crimes, although, as historians Hartmut Berghoff and Uwe Spiekermann emphasise, it is 'a very large subject area' that is 'fraught with definitional fuzziness'.[92] White-collar crime might include stock market manipulation and tax avoidance, cronyism and nepotism, embezzlement and misappropriation, price-fixing and collusion, Ponzi schemes and money-laundering, and so on. Much of the scholarship has focused on malfeasance by firms or corporations or on offences by public officials. The *cheques sin fondos* files, in contrast, show how the creation of white-collar crime impacted ordinary people. In this regard, I am following the work of historian James Taylor, who shows how new legal categories were invented (fraud went from a tort to an offence) to capture the new types of financial misdeeds that accompanied industrialisation in Victorian Britain.[93]

The punishment for uncovered cheques bucked a long-standing historical trend in New Spain and Mexico. Since at least the time of the Bourbons, the movement had been away from detention and other serious penalties for unpaid debts. Then, in the 1930s, financial modernisation engendered a modernisation of violence whereby *beneficiarios* wielded considerable power over *libradores*. The modern criminalisation of uncovered cheques, in the longer historical chronology, looks a bit like debt imprisonment. It was, at the minimum, a major blow to the interests of debtors. A new form of coercion had been introduced into the power struggle between debtors and creditors.

FROM DELINQUENCY TO VULNERABILITY

Transformative moments in the history of capitalism involve changing laws and changing customary practices. Legislators can write new laws, but they cannot easily transform everyday economic habits and long-standing ideas about fairness. Leaders often struggle to establish a new moral economy, as scholars have shown for key moments in the history of private property rights, from the enclosure of the commons in England to the privatisation of community lands under Porfirio Díaz.[94] Such struggles might be extended, incomplete, and violent. Historians have long debated the role of the law as a hegemonic tool of elites, and there exists an extensive historiography about the criminalisation of economic relations. For example, social historians of crime, especially in the British historiography, have shown how the enclosure of the commons and the criminalisation of customary economic relations was part of how the establishment of private property rights facilitated the emergence of capitalism. Debate centres, of course, on what different scholars mean by 'part of': was the law a tool of the emerging capitalist class that dispossessed ordinary people? Or was the law autonomous – or relatively autonomous – vis-à-vis the economy and society?[95]

The answer, in the Mexicanist historiography, is that bankers set the rules to their benefit. The Mexican Revolution and the 1917 Constitution transformed land and labour relations, and the banking laws that passed in the 1920s and 1930s transformed credit relations. Financialisation generated coercion. The potential for exploitation and intimidation between debtors and creditors – which had shaped their relationship for a very long time, as previous chapters have shown – was given new form in the shift to financial capitalism. Indeed, the sort of abuse by creditors that jurists had tried to prevent, from the mediaeval *Siete Partidas* to the nineteenth-century Civil Code, was given a new outlet.

When the new rules for credit in post-revolutionary Mexico began landing delinquent debtors in prison, it signalled the resuscitation of a coercive legal consequence that had been eliminated from legal codes a full century earlier. The coercion of financialisation was not the sort of physical violence that accompanied the enclosures of the commons in seventeenth-century England or land theft under Porfirio Díaz. Yet the difference was only one of degree: the violence of capitalist expansion was re-signified in different times and places as the market economy for land, for labour, and for credit deepened.[96] In the mid twentieth century, the latent violence of coercion left debtors distinctly, and often painfully, vulnerable.

Some of Mexico's leading legal minds in the middle of the century argued that the consequences for writing uncovered cheques were too harsh. José Becerra Bautista, for example, wrote in 1942 on the practice of giving a postdated cheque with insufficient funds. He considered that this scenario did not meet the bar for the 'deceitfulness' (*dolo*) required for fraud because the *beneficiario* had plainly accepted the cheque with a future date. Giving a cheque as a guarantee, Becerra Bautista wrote, might be similarly interpreted. But the latter scenario depended on the circumstances, such as if the *beneficiario* had accepted the cheque as a guarantee only, and whether they had been duly informed of insufficient funds. In Becerra Bautista's analysis, therefore, the law should accept a degree of ambiguity related to intent, which should be determined on a case-by-case basis.[97]

Newspaper coverage of uncovered cheques also presented criticism of the harsh penalties imposed after 1932. This criticism ranged from the superficial to the serious. A gossip columnist in March 1970, for example, between speculation about the actress Natalie Wood and the singer Nadia Milton, indicated that the consequences for uncovered cheques, even for smaller amounts, were overly severe.[98] More serious was *El Nacional*'s report from March 1983 detailing critiques on the state of affairs presented at a legal conference chaired by Attorney General Sergio García Ramírez. The Querétaro lawyers' association described how one-third of judicial processes in the first-instance courts, nationwide, were cases of uncovered cheques.[99] Jurists and lawyers argued that it was time 'to change the actual codes ... and reorient national consciousness'.[100]

The question of appropriate penalty was a topic of so much debate because of the tension that existed between the juridical nature of cheques and the fact that people actually used them in ways that were based on custom. The essential juridical nature of a cheque was that it was an instrument of payment, not a credit instrument. Common practices, especially giving cheques as guarantees, thus violated its intended usage. And according to the 1932 legislation, writing a cheque with insufficient funds was automatically fraudulent, irrespective of circumstances.

Critics of the harsh penalties eventually prevailed. The second paragraph of Article 193 was repealed in 1984.[101] At that point, fraud ceased to be a constitutive feature of writing a bad cheque. It was still possible for *libradores* to be charged with fraud, of course, but only if they acted with criminal intent for illicit gain. The question of fraud now hinged on intent. The new framework did not eliminate ambiguity – the intent of *libradores* and *beneficiarios* was far from clear in the cases above, for example – but it did shift the default penalties.

Unfortunately for the *libradores* in the conflicts studied here, their cases transpired before 1984, when *beneficiarios* still had outsized power over *libradores*. But their cases show how high the stakes were for the repeal of the second paragraph of Article 193. It was, after all, about saving people from jail time and substantial monetary fines. And, in the wake of the repeal, the consensus was that the change was positive. Indeed, in a textbook on the *Ley General de Títulos y Operaciones de Crédito*, legal scholar Carlos Felipe Dávalos Mejía lauds the repeal of 'the disastrous [*nefasto*] second paragraph of Article 193'.[102]

The historical arc of uncovered cheques encapsulated the changing financial and moral economy of the twentieth century. In the early post-revolutionary decades, political leaders had given bankers the power to shape legislation. At that time, financial modernisation was a tool to support consumption, which was so important to the mid-century development model. Politicians gave bankers substantial power in an effort to transform how people used and thought about financial tools and credit instruments. The question of whether legislators succeeded in changing the behaviour of ordinary people remains open. Political leaders did successfully inculcate new ideas about economic justice, however. By the time celebrities such as Silvia Pinal and Roberto Gómez Bolaños enacted the consequences of writing uncovered cheques in the 1970 film *La hermana trinquete* (related at the beginning of this chapter), the new framework of financial culture was mainstream.

In the later twentieth century, however, the economic order was shifting. By the time the second paragraph of Article 193 was repealed in 1984, the Mexican miracle had ended. Many middle-class citizens lived through years of economic instability and crisis. And financial modernisation was no longer just a tool for consumption: finance itself was becoming the goal. Cheques had starred in an early chapter in the history of financialisation, enabling growing numbers of ordinary people to use increasingly immaterial financial products. By the 1980s, these products included credit cards and much more. It was becoming clear that citizens needed protection from the abuses of financial service providers, and political elites took notice and action. Legislators scaled back the penalties for *cheques sin fondos* in an effort to institute better protections for *libradores*. Yet, as Chapter 5 suggests, the repeal was only a superficial win for vulnerable debtors. It belied a fundamental continuity in the power struggle: creditors were still winning the game.

5

Asking for Help

Letters About Fairness and Dispossession, 1990s–2000s

In November 2002, Esther García, a 52-year-old unemployed office worker, wrote to President Vicente Fox. She was asking for help, as she could no longer afford her monthly mortgage payments to Scotiabank.[1] García was one of many citizens who wrote letters about their unpaid debts to President Fox, who held office from 2000 to 2006. Some citizens, like García, posted typed missives. Some sent handwritten letters, and a few wrote emails. Explaining how they got into economic trouble in the first place, these citizens lamented the long-term consequences. They also attributed blame, and they pled for assistance.

By the turn of the twenty-first century, the Mexican government had established new channels for communicating with citizens. Most importantly to individuals like García, it had created a Public Attention Commission in the president's office (Coordinación de Atención Ciudadana de la Presidencia de la República), which received letters directly. President Ernesto Zedillo, who held office from 1994 to 2000, created the commission in 1996. Later, Vicente Fox reorganised and renamed the commission, and in 2003 it became the Citizen Service Federal Network (Red Federal de Servicio a la Ciudadanía).[2] Because most people addressed their letters directly to the president, the documents connected society and state, citizen and president. The Citizen Service Office passed along requests to various government entities and, in theory, monitored the process until the matter was resolved. Citizens could submit complaints, suggestions, opinions, and compliments. The only guidance was that their letters should be 'clearly written, respectful, peaceable [*pacífica*] and as brief as possible'.[3]

The new communication channels belonged to a broader government response to economic crises. Citizens such as García wrote their letters in the aftermath of the first major crisis of neoliberal capitalism. A wave of privatisation in the late 1980s and early 1990s led to a banking crisis in 1994 and 1995, followed by a deep recession. The crisis left many citizens with unpayable debts, and it became an origin story for the instability of the new economic order.

The macroeconomic shocks were the canary in the coalmine for debt trouble in the neoliberal era, but the economic troubles contained in the letters were much bigger than one banking crisis or one development model. The trouble was the changing power balance between debtors and creditors. Starting in the 1970s, citizens had become vulnerable to new types of exploitation as financial instruments multiplied and consumer and banking services became more sophisticated. Indeed, Esther García acquired her home mortgage in the twilight of state-led development, when big government programmes helped some citizens participate in the process of financialisation. That process had begun in the middle of the century with instruments like the cheques studied in Chapter 4. In the 1970s, the government established new credit schemes for home mortgages and consumer credit. At the same time, it worked to protect citizens from exploitation in the increasingly sophisticated financial landscape, including by strengthening consumer rights.

As credit products multiplied in the later 1980s and early 1990s, their growth was spurred in part by the privatised banks. When Esther García wrote to President Fox in 2002, the neoliberal vision of a trim state supporting a robust private sector had taken hold. Her economic troubles thus spanned different development models and cannot be explained by the promise and peril of a single one. Instead, Esther García's story illuminates the contours of economic transformation as financialisation spread and deepened. By the new millennium, the power struggle between debtors and creditors played out between individuals like García and big institutions. And the power differential was stark. García wrote to Fox through the Citizen Service Office, while Scotiabank relied on its well-staffed collections department.

To unpack the power struggle represented in these letters, this chapter first examines the new ways in which citizens became increasingly vulnerable to debt trouble by the turn of the millennium. Then it turns to the narratives that debtors wrote about their troubles, showing how they interpreted the economic order as a wrathful God wreaking havoc in the lives of middle-class people. Financial companies had expanded into more people's lives, and into more areas of life, and citizens experienced the impact of financial booms and busts in new ways. Macroeconomic shocks became emotional sagas as everyday people tried to navigate cycles of financial vulnerability in the face of opaque and impersonal institutions. In the ever-evolving web of debt and credit, the question of economic justice became more pressing than ever.

FROM CITIZENS TO FINANCIAL SERVICE USERS

The process of financialisation, whereby more citizens used a growing number of financial products (like cheques), came into fuller form in the second half of the twentieth century. The available forms of credit had increased, from retail store cards and credit cards to various forms of car loans and home mortgages. Some of these can be traced back to earlier decades, especially store credit – prestige cards from high-end department stores like Palacio de Hierro, for example – which had been available since before the revolution. By the 1940s and 1950s, this sort of credit became available from less rarefied retailers such as Sears and Elektra.[4] Credit cards came to Mexico in the 1960s. The government expanded its credit schemes in the 1970s with mortgage programmes for public employees and consumer credit for citizens who met certain income criteria.[5] Then, after a period of economic austerity in the 1980s, a credit boom took off in the early 1990s, and credit products multiplied. Financialisation, therefore, began as part of state-led development in the 1940s, continued to the 1970s, and accelerated with the neoliberal development model that took hold in the 1980s and 1990s.

As the financial landscape become more sophisticated, with more opportunities for predatory creditors to exploit debtors, political elites took action to protect citizens. In 1976, the government created a consumer rights agency, the Procuraduría Federal del Consumidor (Federal Attorney for the Consumer, or Profeco). Profeco was created by President Luis Echeverría at the end of his six-year term as part of his attempt to reduce the power of the private business sector and foment state-led development. While there are some examples of financial services among Profeco's cases in the 1970s and 1980s, most of its work concerned complaints about upscale housing developers and the prices of basic goods.[6]

Over two decades later, in 1999, President Zedillo created a commission specifically to protect citizens who used financial services (debtors) from the bad behaviour of financial institutions (creditors). This was the Comisión Nacional para la Protección y Defensa de los Usuarios de Servicios Financieros (National Commission for the Protection and Defence of Users of Financial Services, or Condusef).[7] The commission's main objective was ambitious, as described in Article 5: 'to provide equity in the relations between users and financial institutions'.[8] Its activities were also partly educational, such as publicising information about its services, specific financial products, interest rates, and so on.[9] Condusef was an update to the consumer protection of the 1970s, and its mandate reflected the more complex financial services of the 1990s. It did not replace Profeco but rather existed alongside it. Notably, however, Condusef was less powerful.

The difference between Profeco and Condusef illuminates how dynamics of state–society relations changed from 1976 to 1999. Both Echeverría and Zedillo had acted in the context of economic crisis. Echeverría created Profeco as a strategy to mitigate the effects of a crisis in the state-led development model that had been based largely on import substitution and industrialisation policies. Zedillo created Condusef as a strategy to contain the fallout from a crisis in the neoliberal development model of privatisation and trade liberalisation policies. Profeco and Condusef thus represented different ideals of state–society relations. Profeco represented the vision of a welfare state that would take care of citizens through the public programmes of state-led development. Condusef was created according to a neoliberal vision of the private sector advancing the interests of citizens, with a trim public bureaucracy to facilitate the process. Echeverría had created Profeco as a Federal Attorney for the Consumer, and, as such, it had considerable legal power to protect consumers. Condusef, in contrast, was a commission that acted as a mediator without the juridical power to enforce its recommendations. Put simply, Condusef's comparative weakness reveals how the Partido Revolucionario Institucional's (PRI's) commitment to consumer rights had diminished in the intervening decades.

Starting in 1999, citizens could report problems with providers of financial services directly to Condusef within two years of the issue arising. The problems consumers faced could range from irregularities to illegal actions, and the providers could be public entities (like state-run credit programmes) or private enterprises (such as credit card companies). The letters show that people had trouble with car loans and home mortgages, with banks and credit card companies, and with the main credit-rating agency, the Credit Bureau. Because Condusef does not have a public archive, the Citizen Service documents provide an entry into this history.[10] The letters represent the political relationship between society and state, a direct line from a citizen to the president. As such, they are different from the primary sources in previous chapters. The analyses of small claims, precautionary petitions, and uncovered cheques were all based on legal sources such as court cases and arrest records. And the credit reports discussed in Chapter 3 reflect the records of a private financial company. The letters to the president therefore reveal something different about debt trouble: how citizens expected the state to help them.

The letters sampled in this chapter were invariably addressed to the president but then routed to different state agencies, especially Condusef. Citizens had written, sometimes intimately, to President Fox, yet their letters were fed into the government bureaucracy. The Citizen Service archive is housed at the Archivo General de la Nación and the catalogue is digital, well organised, and accurate. My analysis is based on a sample of the letters connected to the economic problems that citizens faced when they could not pay their debts. Researchers can run keyword searches and then photograph the documents. My sample consisted of 10 per cent of the letters with these keywords: Condusef, Credit Bureau, debtor, credit card, guarantee, arrears (*vencida*). The sample also included all the letters with the keywords usury, insolvency, and arrears (*morosidad*), as these keywords returned low numbers. Table 5.1 presents the sample and data universe.

Letters from citizens to the president have been an important source for scholars of post-revolutionary Mexico, especially for the 1920s and 1930s. Historian Christopher Boyer, for example, has used letters from *campesinos* to examine class consciousness and ideas about social justice. And historians such as Adolfo Gilly have explored the paternalistic

TABLE 5.1 *Sample and data universe of citizen letters, 2001–2007*

Year	Cases in sample	Universe	Sample as percentage of data universe
2001	36	333	10.8
2002	9	81	11.1
2003	21	174	12.1
2004	14	86	16.3
2005	18	153	11.8
2006	10	82	12.2
2007	9	81	11.1
Total	117	990	11.8

reputation that President Lázaro Cárdenas cultivated with citizens.[11] This chapter draws on such scholarship about earlier decades and also looks to historian Jennifer Adair's work on 1980s Argentina. Adair analyses the letters that citizens wrote to President Raúl Alfonsín about human rights, democracy, exchange rates, and rising prices to uncover 'a history of diminished hopes and the narrowing of options over the decade'.[12] As most of these scholars point out, historians cannot know if letters to the president were read by anyone, much less by the president.[13] Regardless of the letters' reception, public letter writing was a political act, and both the content and the form give insight into the zeitgeist.

The letters to Fox also help raise historical questions about his presidency: how did state–society relations change under Vicente Fox, whose inauguration in December 2000 unseated the PRI's long rule? Did citizens write these letters with new expectations? It might be that the transition to democracy sparked new hope among citizens that the president could intervene on their behalf. Perhaps this is why the old tradition of writing letters to the president, and especially to Lázaro Cárdenas from 1934 to 1940, was revived, at least for a time. Alternatively, it could be that the intimate pleading never stopped. Perhaps it continued throughout the heyday of the PRI's one-party rule, and historians have simply not yet found those letters in the archives, many of which remain uncatalogued. It is also possible that the personal, intimate nature of these letters could have been a response to Fox's idiosyncratic cowboy persona. No doubt, questions about Fox's presidency will remain open for some time; this chapter is one of the first historical studies of these years. Beyond the rather unique conditions of Fox's presidency, the letters capture a structural change in state–society relations: a shift from group power to individual action.

The best-known history about debtors at the end of the millennium is a collective one. A debtors' social movement, *el Barzón*, emerged in response to the economic crisis in 1994. This de-centralised grassroots movement began when farmers in Colima and Jalisco protested against the restructuring of loan contracts. No longer able to pay their debts as a result, they blocked the roads with their tractors. By 1995, as political scientist Heather Williams shows, it was a social movement with 500,000 members that included small farmers and the urban middle classes.[14]

The word *barzón* refers to a hitch, such as a ring or a belt, that connects a plough to the yoke of oxen, and it comes from an anonymous revolutionary *corrido* or ballad. By adopting the name, the social movement connected the debt protest with Mexico's deep history of revolutionary struggle, linking President Carlos Salinas's neoliberalism with Porfirio Díaz's modernisation. As literary studies scholar Daniel Chávez describes, '[T]he criticism of the Mexican economic structure expressed in the song fits perfectly with *barzonista* claims of illegal property seizures, usury and impossible-to-understand financial statements.'[15] While not as well known as the 1994 Zapatista rebellion in Chiapas, the *barzonista* movement captured the imagination of citizens across Mexico and around the world as a protest against the neoliberal globalisation of the 1990s.[16]

In response to *el Barzón*'s political pressure, the PRI established debtor protection programmes to help people avoid bankruptcy. Overall, the premise of these programmes was twofold. First, to convert the debt from pesos into an *Unidad de Inversión* (indexed account unit) to protect debtors from inflation; and, second, to transfer the debt to a government trust fund with stable interest rates to protect debtors from rate fluctuation.[17] The programmes multiplied, showing both the urgency of the economic crisis and also the impact of *el Barzón*'s political pressure. That said, the social movement refused to endorse the programmes and continued to pressure for better conditions.

Soon, a familiar dynamic between the social movement and the one-party state emerged: *el Barzón* pressed the PRI to address the problems of debtors, and the party responded by creating programmes that aimed to alleviate those problems (and, most likely, to quell some of the discontent). For example, in September 1995, the government established a programme to help debtors with credit card and other consumer debt, as well as with home mortgages. It further shored up support for home mortgages with a complementary programme in May 1996. Shortly thereafter followed programmes for agriculture and for micro, small, and medium businesses in the summer of 1996.[18] The programmes certainly helped some, but, at best, they were considered insufficient.[19] It was lost on no one that programmes to help debtors avoid bankruptcy also protected banks and safeguarded the status quo. Debt forgiveness would have been radical.

El Barzón had been part of a long-standing model of collective action, and its success was largely due to its group power. Indeed, it exemplified the mode of state–society mediation based on group associations (especially unions and corporate groups but also social movements) that neoliberal reforms sought to dismantle or at least decentre. By contrast, the letters to the president reflect individual rather than collective action and, overall, seem to have inspired little change.

In many ways, Esther García's economic life trajectory mirrored the transformations of state–society relations. When she wrote to President Fox in November 2002, she was a single, 52-year-old former public sector office worker. García told Fox that Scotiabank was threatening to foreclose and auction her apartment in the Atizapán de Zaragoza neighbourhood of Mexico City. She had purchased the apartment in 1987, but the macroeconomic crisis of the mid-1990s led to a decline in her income and she fell behind in her payments. García's mortgage had originally been with Multibanco Comermex, a large bank that had been majority-owned by the state until its privatisation. At that point it was integrated into the Inverlat Finance Group, over which Scotiabank later acquired majority control.[20] García had worked as a federal employee for the Instituto Nacional del Consumidor (National Institute for the Consumer, or Inco), which had been created in 1976 alongside Profeco. Profeco protected consumers, and Inco educated them. García had acquired her apartment through the housing credits and mortgage programme for state workers created in 1972, the Fondo de la Vivienda del Instituto de Seguridad y Servicios Sociales de los Trabajadores del Estado (Housing Fund of the Institute for Social Security and Services for State Workers, or Fovissste). Both Inco and Fovissste belonged to the last major government pushes to shore up state-led development in the 1970s before the neoliberal reorientation of Mexico's development model began in 1982.[21]

In short, Esther García had benefited from the sorts of public social programmes that had been the hallmark of state-led development from the revolution until the early 1980s. Considering her home mortgage, she had become a debtor as a worker, by virtue of her employment with Inco. García started working for Inco in 1980, a few years after it opened its doors, and she had been indebted, ultimately, to the state through Multibanco Comermex.

But in November 2002, she could not find dignified work: 'As an older, single woman (52 years old), it has been hard to find work with a dignified salary,' she wrote. 'And I now earn the minimum wage which, as you know, means that I work miracles [*hacer milagros*] to survive, and it is difficult to meet my obligations, and I have been paying what I can.' While historians cannot know why García stopped working at Inco and what other circumstances might explain her trajectory, her letter describes a world in which state-led development, with its promise of employment and housing, was being replaced by a different economic vision. She asked President Fox for help paying her mortgage so that she could live in peace in her old age ('*para poder tener una vejez máz tranquila*'). Her request was routed to Condusef.[22]

The parameters of economic citizenship had changed. Letter writers like García, no doubt, might have belonged to a *Barzón* organisation, or they might even have participated in the protests. But they wrote to the president as private citizens. It was an autonomous action outside the corporatist and formal structures that undergirded much of state–society relations in post-revolutionary Mexico, and which had provided many citizens with an avenue for redress over the years. When García wrote to Fox, the power struggle between debtors and creditors was playing out in a new context: the economic order of neoliberal capitalism. When the letter writers reached out to the president, they did so as individual debtors vulnerable to the predations of powerful institutional creditors.

INSTITUTIONAL BORROWING IN AN ERA OF CRISIS

The stories that citizens recounted in these letters were tales of woe related to being punished for their unpaid debts at a time when the credit economy had spread and deepened into more areas of life. The growing influence of finance coincided with the neoliberal restructuring that, in Mexico, began with trade liberalisation in the 1980s and financial deregulation in the 1990s. Following the privatisation of banks in 1991, citizens from a wider range of socioeconomic backgrounds had access to the growing amounts and types of credit. As the credit economy grew, the power dynamic between debtors and creditors changed.

When more people used financial products, the creditor–debtor relationship became a main locus of profit. This was an important change. The cheques studied in Chapter 4 were financial instruments that supported the growing consumer economy; by the later twentieth century, finance itself had become a goal for politicians and bankers alike. Economist Lena Lavinas describes the new dynamic of capitalist relations: 'a new accumulation regime in which macroeconomics and economic policies are increasingly dominated by the rationale of financial capital … Those directly affected are not only firms, but also ordinary households.'[23] The practical effects, for many such ordinary households, was a rising debt-to-income ratio. Families became indebted as they compensated for declining wages, and financial institutions offered credit products to as many citizens as possible. In broad strokes, in the later twentieth century, as more people used complex financial and credit instruments in more areas of their lives, debt became an increasingly important source of profit in the capitalist economic order.²⁴

By the early twenty-first century, public entitlements began to be channelled through financial institutions. Citizens needed to participate in these institutions to access their rightful benefits. Anti-poverty conditional cash transfers, for example, came to depend on citizens having bank accounts to receive money. In 1997, President Zedillo's administration established the Programa de Educación, Salud y Alimentación (Programme for Education, Health, and Nutrition, or Progresa) to combat increased poverty following the macroeconomic crisis.²⁵ Initially, the government paid benefits in cash at distribution points across the country. In 2003, it began to electronically transfer benefits into savings accounts, and, starting in 2009, it introduced prepaid Visa cards. For many recipients, as economists Serena Masino and Miguel Niño-Zarazúa write, the shift from cash payments to savings accounts was 'the first direct encounter with formal financial services'.²⁶ Many scholars point to the increased savings and reduced transaction costs associated with electronic transfer.²⁷ Although not its intended objective, Progresa increased financial inclusion by getting 'unbanked' people to use financial services because citizens needed bank accounts to access their entitlements.

The emerging economic citizenship described in Chapter 4 – whereby citizens were increasingly participating in financial institutions up to the middle of the twentieth century and beyond – had deepened substantively by the turn of the millennium. When citizens became financial subjects, they often became debtors as well. The spaces for economic life outside the capitalist credit market had contracted, and the power struggle between debtors and creditors shaped more and more of everyday life. Moreover, as the credit economy came to be dominated by private institutions such as banks and credit card companies, a financial logic based on speculation and investment in a global economy penetrated non-financial realms. As part of this shift, the relationship between debtors and creditors became more vulnerable to macroeconomic booms and busts.²⁸

Starting in the 1970s, a series of macroeconomic crises brought instability and uncertainty into the lives of middle-class consumers. The Mexican miracle had ended.²⁹ The mid-century prosperity crested in 1973, after which Mexico became part of a broader international economic downturn. Citizens in Mexico experienced this shift first as consumers. Inflation began to rise erratically and sometimes dramatically starting in 1973; this was a major change from the low and comparably stable inflation rates of earlier decades.³⁰ A fully fledged crisis was averted in 1976 when engineers discovered major oil reserves in the Gulf, but the ensuing oil boom went spectacularly bust in 1981 and 1982. Oil prices collapsed, interest rates rose, and Mexico announced that it could no longer service its national debt.

Inaugurating a global debt crisis, Mexico signed a structural readjustment programme with the International Monetary Fund (IMF), which translated into austerity measures for citizens. Inflation neared 100 per cent in 1982, and the 1980s came to be known as the lost decade. President Miguel de la Madrid was inaugurated in 1982 and responded to the debt crisis with austerity measures, an opening of trade, and privatisation. He led the restructuring of the Mexican economy from a model of state-led capitalism to a more neoliberal one. The fundamental difference in these development models hinged on the proportion of state participation in the economy. In this context, Condusef's comparative weakness vis-à-vis Profeco was part of a reduction in state regulation. Condusef was one of Zedillo's attempts to contain – superficially – the fallout from the ongoing neoliberal reorientation.

Bank privatisation was the financial reform stage of this neoliberal restructuring process, and it sparked a credit boom. Starting in 1989, President Carlos Salinas, who held office from 1988 to 1994, auctioned Mexico's government-owned banks to the highest private bidders. But potential buyers were not inclined to offer high prices. They could easily claim an expropriation risk, a credible claim since the banks had been nationalised in 1982 by José López Portillo in the last months of his presidential term. The government then offered three major incentives to entice buyers, as historian Stephen Haber outlines: the highly concentrated banks would not be broken up, and thus the environment would not be very competitive; the government would allow the Mexican banking sector to continue a dodgy accounting practice for past due loans that allowed bankers to claim the principal as a performing asset; and, finally, the government would essentially guarantee all deposits and all liabilities through a trust fund called the Fondo Bancario de Protección al Ahorro (Fund for the Protection of Bank Savings, or Fobaproa). This fund had access to virtually unlimited resources from the Banco de México.[31] It was a great deal. To be auctioned were oligopolistic banks that were allowed to fiddle the books with the Banco de México poised to absorb all risk.

The sale ignited a credit boom. The privatised banks expanded the credit market and many citizens took out new loans. Haber calculates the 'prodigious' rate of bank credit growth as follows: between 1991 and

1994, real bank lending doubled, and real lending for housing and real estate nearly tripled.[32] As the credit economy precipitously expanded, more people received credit cards, car loans, and home mortgages. These financial products gave people a way to change their lives in small and big ways. Cars and consumer durables, of course, could meaningfully change daily life, but smaller non-essential purchases could also make life easier. Home ownership, in particular, was much more than a financial transaction for most people. A place of one's own could symbolise independence, safety, comfort, family, and the future. Regardless of how people used the credit, the expanded market brought more opportunities to more citizens.

But the boom was short. It went bust in 1994 and 1995 with a banking crisis and recession. Government policy mistakes, banker malfeasance, and capital flight were the main causes behind the dramatic turnaround. The blow-by-blow account of the macro crisis, which came to be called the *tequilazo* (the 'big tequila hit'), is fairly well known.[33] An exchange rate crisis combined with the fragile state of Mexico's banks and changes in global financial conditions. Starting in February 1994, the American Treasury raised interest rates, with gradually increasing hikes scheduled for May, August, and November. Foreign investors became increasingly uneasy throughout the year. They feared that the peso, which was pegged to the American dollar at an adjustable band, was overvalued. Political instability, especially the Zapatista rebellion in Chiapas in January and the assassination of the PRI's presidential candidate at a public rally in March, raised questions about whether Mexico was a stable investment. The result was capital flight driven both by concerns over the situation in Mexico and by the USA's marginally higher interest rates. In response, the government tried to maintain the exchange rate stability by borrowing its way out of the situation, issuing short-term bonds denominated in dollars (*tesobonos*). But to no avail. In mid-December, the government floated the peso, which plummeted. In 1995, Mexico entered a recession.

Global leaders feared that the economic crisis would be contagious – the so-called 'tequila effect' – and might bring down other emerging market economies. In response, the USA and the IMF organised a bailout of 50 billion American dollars. The bailout meant that the government loaned dollars to the banks and that banks transferred their non-performing loans to the government (using the trust fund Fobaproa that had been established for the privatisation process).[34] The transfers included many large insider loans, which banks had issued to their own directors, a practice that Haber describes as 'the looting of the banks by their own directors'.³⁵ Citizens, unsurprisingly, were outraged at the looting and the subsequent bailout of the looters.

In the aftermath of the bust, the credit market tightened. Haber calculates that bank lending to households and business enterprises declined in real terms by 23 per cent from December 1997 to December 2003.³⁶ The decline in available credit applied to consumer credit as well, such as credit cards and store cards. Economists José Luis Negrín and Clara de la Cerda, for example, show that credit-to-consumption rates fell in the years after the crisis. In 1994, consumer credit was 3.6 per cent of the gross domestic product. This fell to 1.7 per cent in 1997; by 2000, it was 1.9 per cent.³⁷ In general, households and private businesses had less access to credit as banks and other lenders were issuing fewer loans.³⁸

This is where many middle-class citizens found themselves at the turn of the millennium. It was a new financial world yet again, and this time there was not only less credit available, it was also more difficult to access. Unsurprisingly, the consequences of falling into arrears also evolved.

INDEBTEDNESS AND DEHUMANISATION

In 1995, a century after R. G. Dun inaugurated modern financial surveillance with credit-reporting in the late 1800s, the Credit Bureau (Buró de Crédito) opened its doors. Offering a private financial service to lending institutions that wanted better information about potential clients, it entered the scene with a new solution to the trust problem that early credit-rating agencies had tried to address with credit reports. How could creditors trust debtors? According to the Credit Bureau, the solution was a credit score. With credit-scoring, creditors had a new tool to monitor and discipline debtors. People who made late payments, who missed payments, or who defaulted on their loans could be blacklisted from the credit economy. Once again, the power dynamic had changed. Debtors now had little control over the enormous and often multinational institutions that held their debts, or over the opaque financial services like the Credit Bureau that shaped so much of their economic lives.

Indebtedness is one of the most relatable economic conditions. People feel the subject of debt personally. Whether the subject is household debt or sovereign debt, or whether the question is about the parameters of fairness and interest rates or about the politics of loan restructuring and bank bailouts, people tend to think about debt in relation to their own finances. With prudence and luck, credit can be productive and liberating, but too much debt can be bad, and if people cross a line, they might never catch up. They might have to make hard choices, or they might go bankrupt. Indebtedness has been a psychosocial economic condition for a very long time.[39] But at the turn of the millennium, when capitalist credit relations expanded into more areas of economic life, macroeconomic booms and busts became, for many middle-class citizens, intimate and emotional sagas. And as the credit economy came to be dominated by financial institutions, people's lives were increasingly connected to macroeconomic conditions.

In 1995, pop icon Gloria Trevi sang about the emotional fallout from the financial collapse. The lyrics of 'Colapso Financiero' connect intimate and macroeconomic instability. The song captures the average citizen's anxieties as they face lost savings and unpayable debts, critiquing the almost invisible financial logic that shapes everyday life with a central question: where is the money? This question forms Trevi's refrain, repeated throughout the song in a high-tempo, almost manic chorus as she sings of financial meltdown:

> Estoy en medio de un
> Colapso financiero
> ¿Dónde, dónde, dónde
> Dónde, dónde
> Está el dinero?
>> Gloria Trevi, 'Colapso Financiero', 1995.
>> Reprinted by permission of Hal Leonard LLC.

> I'm in the middle of a
> financial meltdown
> Where, where, where
> Where, where
> Is the money?

The song depicts financial precarity with high drama and a touch of humour, deftly capturing the fear and uncertainty shaping Mexican economic life in the 1990s. As the song's protagonist faces financial panic, her body deteriorates. The stress makes her ill. She engages in all manner of quotidian subterfuge to avoid her collectors. She hides from her landlord collecting rent. She avoids her local *puesto de abarrotes* (corner kiosk) by donning a hat-and-moustache disguise, but her ruse fails when she is mistaken for someone else who owes even more money. At one point, she considers playing dead.

> Sufro convulsiones
> En mi pobre cuerpo

Y hasta uno que otro
Tic de nervios
Sufro convulsiones
En mi pobre cuerpo
Y hasta uno que otro
Tic de nervios
me encierro en el baño
si viene el casero,
si tira la puerta
fingiré estar muerta
...
Yo le debo tanto al puesto de abarrotes
que ando disfrazada de gorra y bigotes,
pero que me agarran pues me confundieron
con otro que debe mucho más dinero.

I suffer from convulsions
in my poor body
and between them
a nervous tick
I suffer from convulsions
in my poor body
and between them
a nervous tick
I lock myself in the bathroom
if the landlord comes
and opens the door
I'll pretend to be dead
...
I'm so indebted to the corner kiosk
that I go disguised, hat and moustache
but they grabbed me, confused me
With another who owes even more money.

Verse by verse, the lyrics convey the panic of being excluded from the credit market and expose the precarity of middle-class indebtedness. As the protagonist discovers when she seeks a bank loan (which she ultimately plans to repay by getting another loan), 'they only lend to millionaires'.

Y me voy al banco
a pedirles prestado
pero sólo prestan a los millonarios
les doy mi palabra de que
si les pago,

> en cuanto me presten
> en el otro banco
>
> And I'm going to the bank
> to ask for a loan
> but they only lend to millionaires
> I give my word that
> I'll pay
> as soon as they lend me
> in another bank

Pervasive indebtedness generated a personal precarity. Trevi's 'Colapso Financiero' shows how the emotional toll of indebtedness infused popular culture at the turn of the millennium.[40] Indebtedness was emotional and intimate because it concerned the dehumanisation of a person. As Karl Marx wrote in 1844, the credit system was the extreme example of dehumanisation that produced the estrangement of man from his moral and social existence and, indeed, from 'the *inmost depths* of his heart'.[41] The modern credit and banking system, which Marx saw spreading around him, alienated man from himself by transforming him into the guarantee of repayment:

> [T]he life of the poor man and his talents and activity serve the rich man as a *guarantee* of the repayment of the money lent ... all the social virtues of the poor man, the content of his vital activity, his existence itself, represent for the rich man the reimbursement of his capital with the customary interest.[42]

Put simply, a person's labour and character became the collateral that secured a debt.

Marx was writing as credit-rating agencies emerged. Tappan's Mercantile Agency, the precursor to R. G. Dun (see Chapter 3), had been founded just three years earlier in 1841. These kinds of agencies sped up the dehumanisation of capitalism by institutionalising the commodification of a person's morality. Within the credit relationship, wrote Marx:

> [I]t is not the case that money is transcended in man, but that man himself is turned into *money*, or money is *incorporated* in him. *Human individuality*, human *morality* itself, has become both an object of commerce and the material in which money exists. Instead of money, or paper, it is my own personal existence, my flesh and blood, my social virtue and importance, which constitutes the material, corporeal form of the *spirit of money*.[43]

When a person becomes the medium of exchange, the dehumanisation is complete. For sociologist Maurizio Lazzarato, who analyses the relevance of Marx's text in the neoliberal era, this process of commodification and dehumanisation makes debt the archetypical social relation of power and domination.⁴⁴

By the time Trevi belted out the chorus to 'Colapso Financiero' in stadium concerts, middle-class citizens were fused to their debts. Trevi's song reflected the new reality facing would-be borrowers. Not only did banks and other lenders issue fewer loans after the crisis, they also tightened the criteria for assessing the creditworthiness of potential debtors. As Trevi sang, banks would only lend to millionaires. The newly established Credit Bureau provided lenders with new kinds of economic information derived from its new mechanisms of financial surveillance, which had developed considerably since the Dun reports.⁴⁵ As Josh Lauer shows, for example, American credit-rating agencies in the 1960s experimented with statistical scores, which became common in the USA by the late 1970s.⁴⁶ And historian Dan Bouk describes how the economic crises of the 1970s sent a generation of American physicists and mathematicians whose predecessors had worked in universities or government to work in corporate data analysis. This movement inaugurated the age of big data that identified, computed, commoditised, and monetised an individual's statistical data, from FICO (Fair, Isaac and Company) scores in the 1970s to Facebook profiles in the 2000s.⁴⁷ By the new millennium, the dehumanisation that Marx had described was powered by algorithms.

The emotional toll of pervasive indebtedness stemmed from having pledged oneself – one's moral character, one's labour, one's future – with the promise to repay the debt. Unpaid debts have long been associated with personal failure. But when capitalist credit relations expanded into more areas and narrowed the possibilities for a dignified economic life outside the credit economy, the moral framework of indebtedness as a personal failing also took on new dimensions.⁴⁸ Figure 5.1 captures the devastation of being without credit. The advertisement promotes a government credit scheme for small and medium businesses offered through Bancomext (the state-owned Banco National de Comercio Exterior). It was published in the business magazine *El Economista* in December 2001 just as Vicente Fox celebrated his first year in the president's office. With its drawing of the hangman game, Bancomext connected the state of being without credit to death.

When citizens found themselves in the no man's land of the credit economy, they wrote to President Fox. Their letters, analysed together, present a social history of the practical and emotional costs of being cast out from the credit economy. I examined the socioeconomic variables relating to the letter writer and the economic problem they faced,

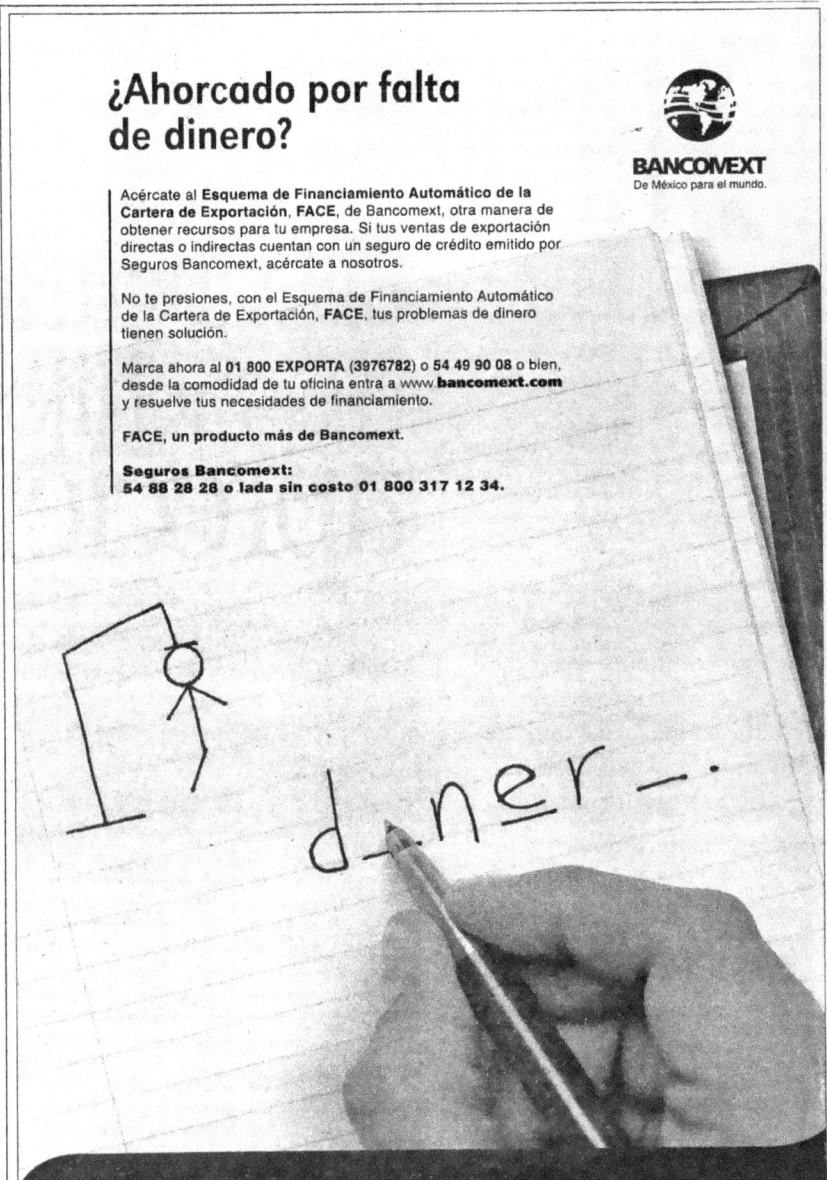

FIGURE 5.1 'Without Credit: To the Hanged Man', advertisement in *El Economista*, December 2001. *Source*: El Economista.

including gender, where the writer was from, the amount they owed, and the type of institution involved (private, public, or other). Unfortunately, in most instances, the files do not include the final resolution. Rather, most of the time the matter is simply referred on to another government agency or entity. Using the available variables, I ran a variety of tests, including chi-squared tests, Fisher's exact tests, and t-tests, to explore the relationships. As in the previous chapters, the quantitative work was exploratory, and I used the results as a starting point for interpretation rather than the basis for conclusive arguments.

The letters were written by a broad spectrum of people, by men and women from across the republic, from the wealthy to the more modest. Of the 117 letters in the sample, women penned 39.3 per cent (46) and men wrote 60.7 per cent (71). Notably, this is a story about Mexico City and about the republic as a whole: 20.5 per cent of writers (24) hailed from the Federal District, 77.8 per cent (91) were from across the republic, and 1.7 per cent (2) were from the USA. Letter writers from the greater Mexico City metropolitan area constituted 34.2 per cent of the sample (40). The financial amounts involved were moderate: 25 per cent of letters were about amounts lower than or equal to 19,270 pesos; 50 per cent were about amounts lower than or equal to 64,000 pesos; and 75 per cent were about amounts lower than or equal to 200,000 pesos. The minimum amount was 200 pesos and the maximum was 13,530,000 pesos, with the mean amount at stake for letter writers being 473,428 pesos.[49] A handy, if crude, strategy for interpreting these amounts lies in the exchange rate between the peso and the American dollar, which was approximately 10:1 between 2000 and 2008. Table 5.2 presents some of the amounts discussed in this chapter in context. Together, the letters represent a diverse array of citizens and their different economic lives.

While both struggled, men and women had problems with different institutions. The authors described the economic problems they faced with government agencies (33.3 per cent, or 39 writers) and with banks (41 per cent, or 48 writers); the rest of the letters concerned other sorts of institutions.[50] There was a significant relationship between the gender of the letter writer and the type of institution involved. Men had problems with government agencies: an examination of the conditional percentages shows that a higher proportion of men wrote about government agencies than did women letter writers.[51] And tests found that women had more problems with banks.[52] This disparity might indicate that women had a better relationship with the state, as they were less likely to experience or complain about their interactions with government agencies.

TABLE 5.2 *Value of amounts in citizen letters, 2001–2007*

Year	Amounts discussed in citizen letters in nominal pesos (minimum amount)	Amounts discussed in citizen letters in nominal pesos (maximum amount)	Amounts discussed in citizen letters in nominal pesos (mean)	Value in historical American dollars (mean)[a]
2001 (n=18)	655	13,530,000	981,722	105,143
2002 (n=5)	4,138	240,000	111,428	11,531
2003 (n=9)	32,629	3,003,622	434,157	40,226
2004 (n=4)	1,890	230,000	75,472	6,685
2005 (n=7)	25,000	280,000	77,303	7,096
2006 (n=2)	19,270	150,000	84,635	7,760
2007 (n=4)	200	30,000	12,538	1,147

[a] The amount discussed in each letter was converted to American dollars and then averaged for the year. Conversion calculated using Lawrence H. Officer, 'Exchange Rates Between the United States Dollar and Forty-one Currencies', MeasuringWorth, 2024.

When Ernestina Romero wrote to President Fox in December 2000, it was no surprise that she was writing about her bank. A senior citizen without a pension, she told Fox that she and her husband had bought their home in Querétaro (in the Las Plazas neighbourhood) in March 1993, during the boom years. When the boom went bust in 1994, she could no longer afford her monthly mortgage payments. The mortgage was held by Bancomer, and the bank was threatening foreclosure. Hers was a modest home, part of social housing, although she does not mention the specific programme ('*el contrato que adquirimos fue por una casa de interés social pequeña*'). For their down payment, Romero and her husband had used their life savings and also borrowed money from family. The mortgage was 118,400 pesos, and it was secured by the house itself. Romero wrote that she had made mortgage payments to the tune of 59,243 pesos in the year or so after signing the contract. But, she explained, she could no longer afford monthly payments because of the devaluation and interest rate increase. When she tried to clear the debt later, Bancomer told her she owed 420,459 pesos, an amount that she described as 'too high, impossible to liquidate, completely unreal [*completamente fuera de la realidad*]'. The precise chronology is unclear, but it seems likely that Romero stopped making payments around 1995 and then wanted to clear her debt sometime around 1999 or 2000, whereupon Bancomer informed her of the new amount.

Citizens' letters like Romero's are about blame and accountability. In her letter to President Fox, Romero complained that it was impossible to fight a bank. She therefore pleaded with Fox to intervene to help her save her home. It was their only asset, she explained, and neither she nor her husband had a pension. Her request was routed to Condusef.[53]

Notably, the connection between gender and institution was the only example where gender showed a significant relationship to other variables. Gender was not significantly associated with the debt amount, for example. Tests did not find a significant difference in the mean amount owed in letters written by women and the mean amount owed in letters written by men.[54] Neither were women associated with specific explanations for their problems: tests did not find a statistically significant relationship between the gender of the author and how they explained their quandary.[55] Nor were women writers associated with any specific geographical origin: there is no statistically significant relationship between gender and geographical unit.[56] And, finally, there is no statistically significant relationship between the gender of the author and the involvement of a legal proceeding, indicating that women writers were not associated with more litigiousness.[57] The significant relationship between women and banks thus stands out.

Similarly, the amounts owed were not significantly connected to other variables. For example, the different institutions (government, bank, or other) were not significantly related to debt amounts. Tests did not find a significant difference in the mean amount owed in cases involving a government agency and the mean amount owed in cases involving a different institution.[58] The different explanations letter writers offered for their debt problems were not significantly related to the amounts involved either. For example, the mean amount owed in cases involving a 'macro event' explanation is not significantly different from the mean amount owed in cases involving a different kind of explanation.[59] Neither were the amounts owed significantly related to litigiousness: tests did not find a significant difference in the mean amount owed when the letter writer was involved in a legal proceeding and the mean amount owed when letter writers were not involved in such proceedings.[60] And finally, the different geographic units were not related to the amounts involved.

Asking for Help 189

The mean amount owed in cases from the Federal District, for example, was not significantly different from the mean amount owed in cases from beyond the city limits.[61]

The experiences of people like Ernestina Romero belonged to the era of neoliberal capitalism, but they were also part of a much deeper history. For a very long time, people around the world have lived through cycles of economic boom and bust. And scholars have chronicled their experiences, such as historian Barbara Weinstein's study of a rubber boom in the Brazilian Amazon and anthropologist James Ferguson's examination of a mining bust in the Zambian Copperbelt, among many examples.[62] The economics of boom and bust for those sorts of commodities are comprehensible to most people, who understand the risks associated: depending on someone else's willingness to pay the same or higher prices, assuming transportation costs remain stable or decrease, hoping that another region does not begin to offer higher quality at lower price, and so on. And citizens make political decisions based on their understanding of the world systems in which rubber and copper circulate.

The booms and busts of high financial capitalism, in contrast, are less readily understandable. In the words of Ernestina Romero, the new economic reality felt 'completely unreal'. From the perspective of everyday men and women caught in the churn of macroeconomic crisis and change, it was much easier to hold the individual credit institution responsible for the seemingly insurmountable debt so many citizens found themselves facing.

ECONOMIC STORYTELLING AND THE POWER OF
THE PRESIDENT

When letter writers explained how they got into trouble, they wrote economic stories. Their narratives countered the official story, which was written in financial statements for their home mortgages, credit cards, and loan agreements. While the official story was full of bureaucratic legalise and algorithmic credit scores – fine print that was incomprehensible to many citizens – the letter writers crafted dramas. They had villains and victims, suspense, moral codes, and ideological arguments; these were riches to rags narratives, whereby citizens found themselves unable to meet their obligations and were shut out of the credit economy.

The letters show how debtors tried to take control of their own narratives in vulnerable times. In their letters, citizens reframed ideas about blame and fairness by anchoring their unpaid debts in stories about the economy and explaining how they found themselves in trouble. Their narratives revealed alternative moral economies to the credit score produced by the Credit Bureau's algorithms, and they described how the parameters of fairness and proper behaviour had been breached.

What kind of a story was Ernestina Romero's? It depends on whose contract and property rights are valued. Romero blamed her difficulties on both the macroeconomic crisis and Bancomer, even describing one of their representatives as 'despotic and overbearing'.[63] Hers is a riches to rags story – a narrative featuring a fall from prosperity and a decline in happiness – which is one of the fundamental plot shapes identified by structuralist literary scholars.[64] In this reading, Romero is a victim, her decline driven by events beyond her control. Alternatively, her story can be read along Kurt Vonnegut's axis of great fortune–ill fortune. Ernestina Romero's narrative takes the form of a 'sudden drop in fortune' in Vonnegut's formulation, placing her story alongside the likes of Adam and Eve's ejection from the Garden of Eden and the plight of the protagonist in Franz Kafka's *The Metamorphosis*.[65] Or perhaps Romero was the villain, albeit a tragic one. After all, she could not fulfil her obligations, and surely a bank, and society at large, needs to depend on people paying their debts. Both interpretations are plausible, and emphasising or embracing one analytical frame – victim or villain – is an ideological decision.

Studying these letters, my method is inspired by cultural history analysis of narratives. The citizens' letters can be analysed for their storytelling skills, what historian Natalie Zemon Davis calls 'the crafting of a narrative'.[66] Davis's close readings of pardon tales from sixteenth-century France show how murderers fashioned their experiences into a narrative form designed to persuade the king that they were worthy of a pardon.[67] In this case, the letter writers pleaded with President Fox for help, and they provided what they thought made a good story when they accounted for their plights.[68] In the pages to come, I also draw on quantitative literary analysis and the Russian formalist concept of fundamental plots, examining the letters as a data universe with abstract relationships between variables, to explore underlying themes within the stories.[69] The abstract statistical analysis shows how citizens made sense of the world around them, and how they connected economic, political, and personal realms. The letter writers believed they had little control over macroeconomic phenomena, but they lived its effects. When I coded the explanations that people gave for their economic troubles (who or what they blamed), I drew on the work of business strategy scholars studying mental maps.⁷⁰ Classifying the explanations was both a formulaic and a subjective process, and I discuss some of the coding decisions below.

The stories in these letters work as counternarratives to the economic information in financial statements and official paperwork, whether that information be a credit score or a foreclosure notification. The analysis in this section, then, is more meta-analytical than in the previous chapters. These letters are about 'what happened' when people did not pay their debts, and they are about the experiences of ordinary citizens. In endeavouring to bring their stories to light, I have continued the method of previous chapters by presenting a quantitative social history of the sample and offering close readings of individual examples. But the following pages focus more on the narratives that people constructed about their experiences. Social science traditions of studying popular recounting offer models for analysing how people talk about the economy: from anthropological and sociological studies of how people interpret macroeconomic phenomena to economic analyses of how narratives shape those macro phenomena.⁷¹ Some scholars might argue that all the sources in this book are stories, and they would not be wrong. Such an analysis, perhaps inspired by literary theorist Hayden White, might emphasise the overlap between history and fiction to suggest that legal records are stories presented by litigants or notaries and that the credit reports are stories written by Dun agents.⁷² This alternative postmodernist analysis notwithstanding, however, I distinguish between 'what happened' and stories about what happened. Put simply, I read the letters to understand how people explained their situations, and I then classified these into five categories.

Some writers described how their financial troubles were caused by macroeconomic events such as the *tequilazo*. Marco Antonio Ramos, for example, was a 62-year-old retired doctor from Mexico City (Tlalpan) who blamed the 1994 crisis for the crushing burden of his monthly mortgage payments to Banamex. He framed his letter as an almost academic overview of the crisis, and even sent a 'graphic presentation' of the bank's misbehaviour (sadly, the appendix is not included in the file). When he described his situation, he put himself into a broader universe of families who had the misfortune of holding a home mortgage when the crisis began, and who had similarly suffered from both the lack of credit and the legalisation of 'anatocism' (here, he was using the classical term for compound interest). The debt adjustment programmes, Ramos argued, had benefited only the wealthy. 'The majority, who lack financial means,' he wrote, 'were subjected to restructurings that did not take into account, as in my case, that I was retired; there was no consideration of my economic capacity; I was forced, under threat of losing everything, to sign a contract with monthly payments equal to 70 per cent of my income and these increase every month with market variations.' Now, he was in danger of losing his home.

Ramos wrote to President Fox in July 2001, seven months after Fox took office and ended the PRI's seventy-one-year rule. He contrasted Fox's 'humanist' policies with the 'voracious policies of previous administrations that did not care about the common good'. He appealed to Fox to intervene, to help him and other pensioners by establishing better mortgage conditions; this would be a 'worthwhile' (*valiosa*) action that would help pensioners reach the levels of security and well-being that Fox had promised during his presidential campaign. In this way, Ramos cast Fox in the role of saviour, valiantly saving pensioners from the wrongdoings of previous administrations. His request was routed to Condusef.[73]

The second phenomenon that writers blamed their problems on was the bad actions of private companies. Nicolás García, a 45-year-old employee from Mexico State (Juchitepec), wrote to President Fox in June 2001 to complain about the bad actions (or in this case, inaction) of a private financing company. Nearly two years after making his final payment, he was still waiting for proof that he had cleared his debt. He had originally received credit from a financial factoring company called Cominsa Factoraje S.A. de C.V., although he gave no information about this original agreement. He fell into arrears because of the devaluation of the peso and rising interest rates, and his debt was transferred (*canalizado*) to another financing company, Auritec S.A. de C.V. Following a judicial agreement, García was directed to repay his debt through regular deposits into a Bancomer account.

Whereas Ramos had described his situation as part of the broader problems facing pensioners with home mortgages, García emphasised his individual trajectory and suffering. García described his humble origins as someone with little education or training (*sin preparación*) from the countryside. With the grace of God and through 'superhuman force' (*esfuerzo sobre humano*), as well as by selling some assets, he had cleared the debt in May 1999. Yet he was still waiting for Auritec to give him the loan discharge documents, which he urgently needed for other matters. He had requested the documents many times and from all three institutions, only to be met with 'evasion, apology and, on some occasions, refusal to look'. He wrote to President Fox about the anguish (*angustia*) caused by the missing paperwork. He begged Fox to help get the documents and resolve the 'anomalies' in these financial institutions. García thus cast Fox as the fixer of damage caused by the arbitrary administrative disfunctions of the private sector wreaking havoc in the lives of humble and hardworking citizens like himself. His request was routed to Condusef.[74]

Third, writers attributed their problems to the bad actions of public agencies or institutions, as did Pedro Gómez in November 2000. Despite the fact that Gómez's trouble began with a private company, he blamed government agencies for not resolving the situation. The trouble started in January 2000, when Gómez purchased a Chevy cargo van that had been modified to be used as a *pesero*, a microbus common in Mexican cities and towns for public transportation. The 52-year-old Gómez worked with his son as a driver in Tultitlán, Mexico State. Unfortunately, the tyres on his new van blew after less than six weeks. The dispute concerned the maximum load: the van could support 1,600 kilograms, but the tyres that the dealership had sold with the van could support only 790 kilograms. Gómez filed a claim with the insurance company Seguros Aba, but the company denied the claim. In fact, Seguros Aba blamed Gómez for overloading the van, which, the company claimed, had a maximum capacity of 937 kilograms. Gómez disputed the decision, showing the bill of sale indicating the 1,600 kilogram capacity.

Eventually, Gómez sought help from the government. He wrote to Profeco (the office of the Federal Attorney for the Consumer) and Atención Ciudadana (the precursor to the Citizen Service) in August 2000, but to no avail. Then, in September 2000, he wrote a letter to President Zedillo, with a copy to President-elect Fox, asking for help with the insurance company. Trying to capture his readers' attention, he invoked the Ford–Firestone scandal, which led to hundreds of fatalities and injuries in the late 1990s: 'Mr President, must we wait for accidents like those that happened with FORD/FIRESTONE in the USA before resolving the matter?'

Indeed, Gómez attributed his economic problems to inadequate government action as well as to the perfidy of private corporations. He was not making headway, however. So, a few weeks after his first letters, he changed tactics: his subsequent letters focused on the inaction of various government agencies, barely mentioning the insurance company at all. In a letter to President-elect Fox written in November 2000, Gómez decried several public agencies. 'These offices are useless [*no sirven para nada*],' he asserted, 'and they only cost us a lot of money.' At this point,

Gómez was referring specifically to Profeco and to Atención Ciudadana. He asked Fox to intervene to help save him, his livelihood, and his patrimony. As the operator of a small transportation business, Gómez appealed to Fox's 'entrepreneurial vision', and he also emphasised the bigger economic consequences of an unproductive bureaucracy. Addressing Fox, he wrote, '[Y]ou know that one should not lose time going in circles and circles, that the country should have PRODUCTIVITY and EFFECTIVITY.' He explained that he had voted for Fox because he wanted 'CHANGE'. Gómez wrote that Mexico's future depended on everyone 'WORKING VERY HARD', and concluded that he wanted to advance his family and contribute 'my little grain of sand' to Fox's national goals.

Gómez sent a nearly identical letter in February 2001, and then another a few weeks later in March 2001. In the third instalment, he added that he had also sought recourse with Condusef, but that the agency had 'so far done nothing'. At this point, the Atención Ciudadana office replied, referring Gómez to Condusef for help with the insurance company. While the file contains no further communication on the matter, it seems unlikely that Gómez would have been satisfied with this suggestion considering that he was already disappointed with Condusef's response.

Gómez's file is unusual because it contains multiple correspondence, as well as a printed summary of a separate request that Gómez submitted to Atención Ciudadana when he wrote to request help finding work in 1996.[75] Gómez's letters thus offer a unique insight into the relationship between citizens and the state. He was a very active citizen who exercised his rights in seeking assistance from various government institutions. But he was frustrated by what he perceived as dysfunctional bureaucracy. The failure of government institutions to protect him ended up overshadowing the bad actions of the private insurance company that had, in his telling, wrongfully denied his claim. Throughout his correspondence, Gómez cast Fox as an entrepreneur who had the ability to bring productivity into the public sector so that the government could do its job to protect hard-working small businesspeople like himself from deceitful private financial institutions.

The fourth phenomenon on which writers blamed their troubles was the fraudulent or illegal actions of others. Here, I return to the story of Efrén Romano, who I first mentioned in the Introduction to this book. Romano wrote to President Fox in February 2004, requesting that he be released from his role as guarantor (*fiador*) for an instalment plan contract with the electronics retailer Elektra. In his letter, he described how his daughter, Irma Romano, had tricked him two years earlier into becoming a *fiador* for two mobile telephones that she had purchased on instalment from the company. Although it is unclear how the deception happened, his daughter connived with her husband, Jorge González, to establish Efrén Romano as guarantor. Since then, Efrén Romano had been in economic trouble. His daughter and son-in-law had not paid the instalments, and Elektra's corporate collections department was demanding payment from him. Efrén Romano, who lived in the Coyoacán borough of Mexico City, described himself as a senior citizen with very low income. He explained that he was barely able to cover his most basic necessities. His daughter and son-in-law also lived in the capital, in the El Centro neighbourhood.

Efrén Romano asked President Fox for help, appealing to his powerful position. 'I know that you have all the means necessary to help me,' he pleaded. Specifically, he wanted the president to either oblige his daughter and son-in-law to pay the debt or face jail time. Either scenario, he believed, would liberate him from his role as *fiador*. He added, at the end of his short letter, that Jorge González was a lowlife (*mal viviente*) who 'drank wine, smoked marijuana, etc., and beat his wife and children'. Notably, Efrén Romano neither critiqued the economic order (he expressed no concern with Elektra's contract) nor deployed the discourse of democratic hope (he made no reference to Fox's historic election). Rather, his letter cast Fox as a protector with the power to save the vulnerable from the wicked. The request was routed to the city government's legal services.[76]

The fifth and final phenomenon that writers blamed their difficult economic situations on was their personal circumstances. They blamed themselves and asked for help. These requests tended to reference trouble paying for health or education expenses. Javier Lozano, for example, was a 55-year-old from the Ricardo Flores Magón neighbourhood in Tijuana who could not afford a hernia operation. He sent a handwritten letter to President Fox in April 2004 appealing to Fox as a fellow patient, as the president had had a hernia the previous year. 'As you know,' the letter reads, 'it is very painful.' Lozano explained that he worked as a construction worker (*abañil*) to support his family, but that now the hernia was preventing him from working. He could not afford the associated costs for the operation at the public hospital, although he does not specify what those costs might be. In his letter, he asked if there were a programme that could help cover the costs, or if the president could help find a clinic that would operate without charge, perhaps even where Fox himself had been treated. Lozano asked for help so that he could support his family. 'Mr President,' he begged, 'please help me to get well and keep working, for my family and to meet my obligations to pay the water and electricity.' He did not blame anyone else. There were no deceitful institutions or macroeconomic conditions that bore responsibility for his circumstances. Casting Fox as a healer, he simply emphasised his bond with the president due to their shared physical condition, and then asked for help. His request was routed to the Ministry of Health.[77]

No matter who they blamed for their troubles, letter writers cast President Fox as the hero of their stories: he was a saviour, fixer, entrepreneur, protector, healer. Writers supplicated and attempted to persuade. Some invoked the collective good and others emphasised their individual connection with the president. Before the letters were sent into the machinery of government bureaucracy, routed to the appropriate ministry or agency, they were a direct line from citizens to the president, even though it is unlikely that the president read them. The letters created a dialogue rife with political messages, and reading them as stories shows how writers adopted a humble literary posture to appeal to the president's mercy and benevolence.

Yet even as citizens wrote to the president as if he were a powerful hero who could save them from their woes, the embedded themes underpinning their stories paint a slightly different picture: a president who did not have enough political power to challenge the almost superhuman power of economic forces. Quantitative analysis uncovers how some of these themes shaped the letter writers' narratives. Examining relationships between variables, especially the different explanations that people gave for their economic troubles, uncovers underlying interpretations about fairness and power. Of the five different explanations I coded in the letters, blaming one's personal circumstances was the most common, at 41.3 per cent. Blaming fraud was the second most common theme (24.5 per cent), followed by macroeconomic events in 12.5 per cent of the letters. Writers blamed bad private and bad public action at 10.9 per cent each.[78] Table 5.3 presents the frequency of these explanations. Because writers blamed multiple situations or entities, these percentages are calculated on the base of the total 184 explanations that appear in the 117 letters.

When they deployed multiple explanations for their financial woes, letter writers connected economic, political, and personal realms. Writers who put forward only one explanation for their troubles had something

TABLE 5.3 *Explanation frequency in citizen letters, 2001–2007*

Explanation	Frequency	Percentage
Personal economy	76	41.3
Fraud/illegal action	45	24.5
Macroeconomics	23	12.5
Bad government action	20	10.9
Bad private action	20	10.9
Total	184	100.0

clear that they wanted to communicate to the authorities; they often advanced more solid explanations about what had happened to them than writers who combined two or more explanations. But analysis of intersecting explanations uncovers moral codes and ideological arguments embedded in these economic stories. Put simply, the intersecting explanations people offered for their financial problems show how they understood the economy and their economic lives. Table 5.4 presents these intersecting explanations in the format of an UpSet plot that visualises the relationships between sets and the frequency of relationships.[79] Of the 117 letters, 52.1 per cent (61 letters) include only one explanation for the financial trouble; 39.3 per cent (46) include two explanations; 7.7 per cent (9) include three; and 1 letter (0.9 per cent) manages to incorporate four explanations. Table 5.4 also shows which explanations letter writers used in combination, as well as the frequency of the different combinations. For letters with two explanations, for example, the most frequent combination was to blame both macro conditions and personal circumstances for the trouble at hand; the combination appears in 16 of the letters. The second most frequent combination was when letter writers blamed both personal circumstances and fraud, which occurred in 12 of the letters. Table 5.4 thus presents a descriptive snapshot of how and how often writers used multiple explanations to explain their financial problems to President Fox.

The underlying themes of the letters and the relationships between different variables not only expose the economic stories the writers embedded in their letters; they also indicate how writers may have conceptualised the economic order. The letter writers seem to have seen macroeconomic phenomena as unconnected to politics but deeply connected to their personal circumstances. Three groups of findings, together, conjure up the figure of a wrathful God at work. It is the first set of findings that suggest letter writers did not conceptualise macroeconomics

TABLE 5.4 *Multiple explanation combinations in citizen letters (with intersection size), 2001–2007*

Number of explanations and types of combination

Number of explanations	Macro-economic conditions	Bad actions (public)	Bad actions (private)	Personal circumstances	Fraud or illegal actions	Frequency	Intersection size
1 explanation	X					2	2
		X				8	8
			X			2	2
				X		33	33
					X	16	16
2 explanations	X	X				1	1
	X		X			0	0
	X			X		16	16
	X				X	0	0
		X	X			1	1
		X		X		2	2
		X			X	3	3
			X	X		4	4
			X		X	7	7
				X	X	12	12
3 explanations	X	X	X			0	0
	X	X		X		1	1
	X		X	X		2	2
		X	X	X		1	1
		X	X		X	1	1
		X		X	X	2	2
			X	X	X	2	2
4 explanations	X	X	X	X		1	1

as inherently political. Writers who explained their problems as related to macroeconomics tended to have issues connected to banks. Tests found that a higher proportion of writers used a 'macro event' explanation when the problem was about a bank rather than a different type of institution.[80] This was the case, for example, with Ernestina Romero's letter.[81] Writers who offered macroeconomic explanations also tended to have problems that were not connected to government agencies. Tests found that a lower proportion of letter writers used a 'macro event' explanation when the problem was about a government agency rather than a different type of institution.[82] These results suggest that people might have considered macroeconomics as being more connected to the private business world than to the government. By extension, this might suggest that macroeconomics were seen as separate from the political sphere and thus beyond the influence of ordinary people, at least in theory. As citizens, letter writers could vote and ostensibly impact politics. They had no such direct influence over the banks.

The second finding suggests that letter writers viewed macroeconomics as beyond human influence altogether. Writers who blamed macroeconomic phenomena were less inclined to also blame fraudulent or illegal action for their woes. Tests found that a lower proportion of letters with a 'fraud/illegal' explanation also presented a 'macroeconomics' explanation in comparison with letters that did not deploy a 'fraud/illegal' explanation.[83] In other words, people who blamed macroeconomics for their troubles did not tend to also blame other people. This suggests that letter writers may have perceived macroeconomics as separate from fraudulent human action, as though the macroeconomy were a cloud floating above the hustle and bustle of their lives, unmediated by deliberate human action.

The third group of findings suggests that letter writers connected the macroeconomic with the intimate. When letter writers described the macroeconomic issues affecting them, they also tended to blame their personal circumstances for their economic troubles. Tests found that a higher proportion of letter writers whose explanation included 'personal circumstances' also presented a 'macroeconomic' explanation for their troubles, in comparison with letters that did not deploy a 'personal circumstances' explanation.[84] These writers described divorces, illnesses, and deaths alongside the macroeconomic phenomena they associated with their problems. For example, Raúl Barros, a 65-year-old from Mexico State (Amecameca de Juárez), was a retiree with a social security pension (from the Instituto Mexicano de Seguro Social) who also owned a small electronics materials shop. He wrote to President Fox in December 2000 because his loan payments to Banca Serfin had ballooned due to the macroeconomic crisis. In 1993, his monthly payments were less than 2,000 pesos; in 1994, they were less than 3,000 pesos; in 1995, they were over 4,000 pesos; and since 1996, they were over 5,500 pesos. In his letter, Barros described how his wife had fallen ill and his 17-year-old son had left school to work.[85] In contrast, writers who blamed others for their problems (using explanations such as bad government action, bad private action, and fraudulent or illegal action) tended not to offer any personal circumstances as an explanation.[86] When they blamed macroeconomic phenomena for their troubles, letter writers also had a tendency to blame their personal circumstances, but, perhaps unsurprisingly, those who blamed others were uninclined to blame themselves.

The relationship between economic life and macroeconomics was almost one of divine punishment, whereby people suffered the consequences of unpredictable, unstable, and unforgiving forces. The consequence, often, was excommunication from the credit economy. Letter writers conceptualised macroeconomics as a separate realm, beyond the influence of human action, and they blamed themselves for the blowback. Despite their direct appeals to President Fox, it is certainly possible that they did not believe that he (or any other politician or the state apparatus) could do much to help them. Of course, the spectre of a wrathful God is speculative interpretation, but the method behind it is an approach to understanding how people articulated and advanced notions of fairness. Analysing the themes of their stories shows how citizens understood wealth and economic justice at the turn of the millennium.

USURY AND THE NEW PURGATORY

When they described unfair practices, writers articulated their personal view of property rights and property crimes. What actually happened when people did not pay their debts? And was this different from the rules on the books, from what should have happened? Whose property rights were protected and whose were not? Writers answered these questions in different ways.

Some accused the villains in their stories of usury. One of the oldest transgressions in history, it is an offence that sits at the intersection of religion and the economy. Usury prohibitions sent rapacious creditors charging interest above an established rate straight to purgatory, a cosmological detention for minor crimes invented by mediaeval Catholicism.

When claiming that they were the victims of unreasonably high interest rates, the letter writers might have hoped that their creditors would be found guilty of usury, or they might have been trying to infuse their pleas with gravitas, or both. Whatever their strategy, when writers invoked usury, they captured the contradiction between law and reality: usury was prohibited, which in theory constituted meaningful protection for debtors, but the prohibition was generally ignored, giving creditors the advantage. Unenforced prohibitions of this sort show the tension between ideas about fairness in contracts and whose rights were, in fact, protected.

Usury was prohibited in Mexico, as it had been in New Spain. However, the criteria and definition of the term varied. For much of the colonial period and the nineteenth century, interest above 5 or 6 per cent was considered usurious, except under the economic liberalism of the late nineteenth century.[87] After the revolution, as historian Nicole Mottier has shown, leading intellectuals and political officials in the 1920s and 1930s decried usury, but they rarely quantified what constituted a usurious rate. Instead, as Mottier writes, they left the numeric rate 'to their reader's imagination'.[88]

Indeed, usury was defined differently in the different legal codes that emerged in the two centuries examined in this book. Federal Civil, Penal, and Commercial Codes, as well as various State and Federal District Codes, all had different rules that changed over time. Furthermore, each code had different rules for related situations: some, for example, allowed creditors to charge a higher 'penalty' interest if a debtor fell into arrears. Some legislation specified an actual interest rate; some used other criteria.[89] The 1928 Federal Civil Code distinguished, in Article 2395, between a legal annual rate of 9 per cent (*interés legal*) and a conventional rate, which was simply what parties agreed. The conventional rate (*interés convencional*) could be higher or lower than the 9 per cent legal annual rate. Article 2395 elaborated on how the different rates might be used. 'If the interest rate is so disproportionally high that it is clear that [the creditor] has abused of the pecuniary hardship, the inexperience, or the ignorance of the debtor,' the text intoned, 'the judge, following the debtor's petition, and considering the special circumstances of the case, can lower the interest rate, equitably, to the legal interest.'[90] Usury, defined in this way, was both objective and subjective. In contrast, the 1931 Federal Penal Code prohibited usury in Article 386, number 8, as a fraudulent act, defining it as 'one who using the ignorance, or the economic bad standing of a person, benefits from the said person by means of contracts or agreements that stipulate revenues or gains higher than those usual in the market'.[91] Usury was thus defined as above-market interest rates. In yet another example – perhaps the broadest definition of usury in the post-revolutionary decades – Article 21, number 3, of the American Convention on Human Rights (which Mexico ratified in 1981) declared: 'Usury and any other form of exploitation of man by man shall be prohibited by law.'[92]

Whatever the definition, usury prohibitions were a regular feature of Mexican legal codes. The law, however, was often not enforced. Scholars have documented how both creditors and debtors avoided usury prohibitions throughout history using strategies as wide-ranging as keeping two sets of books or by hiding the real interest rate in the cost of transactions.[93] Those who wrote to President Fox might have wished for more, but the government focused on protecting consumer interests through information campaigns rather than taking legal steps against creditors who violated the law. Condusef warned citizens about usury through announcements in its publications, on its website, and through newspaper coverage. In 2005, for example, newspapers covered Condusef's warning that pawnshops were charging upwards of 110 per cent interest.[94]

The most detailed denunciation of usury in my sample came from Evaristo Bolaños, a 66-year-old from Irapuato, Guanajuato, who wrote to President Fox in February 2005.[95] He and his wife, Guadalupe García, had five adult children. They lived in the Primero de Mayo Infonavit neighbourhood with two of their daughters, both of whom had been abandoned by their husbands, and their grandchildren: 4-year-old Cristián and 3-year-old Toñito. Bolaños did not have a pension, and the household depended on support from the five children. According to his letter, his trouble had begun over a decade earlier with the onset of kidney problems. In September 1993, he found himself in 'urgent need' of a private loan, so he borrowed 25,000 pesos from Francisco Corona. For collateral, Bolaños and his wife put up the only property they owned: their home, which they had purchased in 1986 through the government's mortgage programme, the Instituto del Fondo Nacional de la Vivienda para los Trabajadores (Institute of the National Fund for Workers' Housing, or Infonavit).[96] They signed a loan agreement (*contrato de mutuo*) with a monthly interest rate of 3 per cent on the outstanding capital and an 8 per cent penalty for late payment (*interes moratorio*).

The crux of Bolaños's usury denunciation centres on the penalty interest. Bolaños argued that the loan agreement had an 11 per cent monthly interest rate. For Bolaños, the 3 per cent interest and 8 per cent penalty interest came together. According to his letter, they 'transformed into a penalty interest of 11% ELEVEN PER CENT MONTHLY, a percentage that far exceeds the legal monthly interest rate'. However, penalty interest was often allowed, and the precise amount varied in different legal codes. Thus, Bolaños may have been wrong, depending on which law he had in mind. For example, according to the Federal Civil Code discussed above, the 11 per cent would have been usurious; according to the Federal Penal Code, it would depend on market variation. And according to the State of Guanajuato Penal Code, the 11 per cent would not be considered usurious at all.[97] While the legal basis for his denunciation was uncertain, Bolaños was most likely writing in more general terms.

Bolaños's denunciation, however, went beyond the 11 per cent interest rate. It also includes a description of Corona's machinations in the servicing of the loan. According to Bolaños, Corona (a retired army major) had a long history of usurious moneylending to modest homeowners in Irapuato. Bolaños wrote that his neighbours had had similar experiences borrowing money from him. In Bolaños's case, he claimed that he had made several payments to Corona in the first year, totalling 10,000 pesos. Corona had applied these payments to the interest rather than the capital. Corona then filed a civil suit against Bolaños in December 1994 for the full 25,000 pesos. The letter does not indicate what prompted the suit, but it was decided against Bolaños and a lien was placed on his home in January 1995. When Bolaños appealed, the conflict continued for several years. The heart of the matter, according to Bolaños, was that Corona had used manipulative mathematics. Bolaños claimed that he continued to make payments on the principal, and that, by February 2005, he had paid 20,000 pesos. Corona, meanwhile, had continued to calculate a penalty interest on the original loan amount of 25,000 pesos.

The calculation, Bolaños claimed, was fantastical. The interest owed calculations had been submitted to the court by Corona's daughter, Irma Corona, whom he described as persuasive with the authorities ('*tiene mucha labia*') but arrogant and rude to the debtors. In 1996, she submitted interest adjustment paperwork calculating the debt owed at 91,241 pesos; in 1999, she submitted further adjustment paperwork that claimed the debt owed was 144,408 pesos; finally, in 2005, she claimed that Bolaños owed 280,000 pesos. If Bolaños's chronicle of events is accurate, the father and daughter likely manoeuvred the peso devaluation to their advantage.

Incredibly, however, this part of the saga was still not the core rationale for Bolaños taking the time to document his economic troubles in a letter to President Fox. Writing in February 2005, more than a decade after the trouble with the loan began, Bolaños pleaded, '[W]e don't want a handout, we want JUSTICE, we want to pay our creditor a fair amount.' Bolaños was desperate, unsure if even the president himself could help. 'I don't know if it's in your power to help with these sorts of economic problems,' he wrote, then asked if Fox could intervene in the judicial process or help him renegotiate his Infonavit mortgage. Perhaps the president could give him a direct loan? Finally, he asked if there was some sort of relief programme that might help. He described how his family lived in a constant state of tension. He and his wife were worn out; they had fallen ill. They feared losing their home.

If Bolaños's story were true, the Corona family had adopted a classic strategy of the 'haves' against the 'have nots': dispossession by paperwork. Bolaños's narrative belongs to a long tradition of world historical narratives about dispossession – most notably land theft – from the enclosures of eighteenth-century England to the land taken from the peasants of Anenecuilco in the years before the revolution.[98] The financial statements and manipulative mathematics rendered Bolaños's debt unjustly unpayable. It was the same dispossession by paperwork that rendered '*fuera de la realidad*' the amount that Ernestina Romero owed to Bancomer. And it was the same sort of inflated instalment payments that the peasants owed the landowner in the traditional revolutionary *corrido* 'El Barzón' from which the *barzonista* social movement took its name:

> Cuando llegué a mi casita,
> me decía mi prenda amada:
> ¿on'ta el maíz que te tocó?
> Le respondí yo muy triste:
> – El patron se lo llevó
> por lo que debía en la hacienda
> pero me dijo el patrón
> que contara con la tienda.
> Ora voy a trabajar
> para seguirle abonando,
> veinte pesos, diez centavos
> son los que salgo restando,
> me decía mi prenda amada
> – ¡Ya no trabajes con ese hombre
> nomás nos está robando!
>
> When I got home
> my beloved said:
> where's your share of corn?

> Sadly I answered:
> – The master took it
> for what I owed the *hacienda*
> but the master said
> I should count on his store.
> Now I'll work
> to keep paying installments,
> twenty pesos, ten cents
> is what I owe,
> my beloved said:
> – Work no more for that man,
> he is just robbing us!⁹⁹

Indeed, Bolaños's villains could be characters in a *corrido*. The dispossession by paperwork strategy would certainly be as familiar to Vicente Fox – and to any bureaucrat who might have read Bolaños's letter – as folk singer Amparo Ochoa's rendition of the *corrido*. The financial statements submitted by Corona's daughter purporting to document the amount Bolaños owed were the land surveys and company store chits of the new millennium. And by invoking usury, Bolaños advanced a notion of economic justice infused with religious moralism, whether out of genuine belief, political strategy, or both. He did not stint with his words. Bolaños wrote that President Fox was on the side of the most vulnerable citizens and that Fox fought against the corruption of those who did not fear God. Bolaños repeatedly described Corona and his daughter as usurers, juxtaposing their corruption with the innocence of his grandchildren, Cristián and Toñito, who might lose their home. He concluded, '[I]t's an injustice what they're doing to us, this house is all that we have.' His request was routed to the Guanajuato State Government.

Bolaños's invocation of usury was incongruous with the values of the neoliberal order. Long-standing ideas about guilt in economic justice had been turned on their head by the twenty-first century. The roles of sinner and sinned against had reversed. Previously, Roman Catholic doctrine dating back to the thirteenth century had held that the souls of usurers were sent to purgatory where they would be cleansed of their sin before going to heaven. As historian Jacques Le Goff shows, the invention of purgatory was an adaption to changing financial practices. Usury had long been forbidden, but merchants had found ways to circumvent the prohibition. As trade grew in the midst of a commercial revolution underway in the thirteenth century, usury became increasingly commonplace. The church created a way station after death to ease the pressure. Usurers could purify themselves in purgatory and still enter heaven, which meant that usurers could continue the practice without the fear of going to hell.[100]

But by the time Bolaños wrote to President Fox in the twenty-first century, it was debtors – not creditors – who had to expiate their sins. Now it was debtors who found themselves in purgatory. And they did their penance in the purgatory of the new millennium: the Credit Bureau's feared Black List. In their letters to the president about the Credit Bureau, citizens enacted a sort of religious supplication. They confessed their sin (an unpaid debt); they described their fall from grace (their economic trouble); and they sought absolution (to be removed from the Black List).

THE CREDIT BUREAU AND THE BLACK LIST

The Buró de Crédito opened in 1995. A private company, it was regulated by the Comisión Nacional Bancaria, the Secretaría de Hacienda, and the Banco de México. Its *raison d'être* was clear. The credit boom and bust of the early 1990s created both opportunity and need. There was a new and lucrative business opportunity in providing an ostensibly necessary financial service that the government was disposed to facilitate based on the perception that 'better' credit information might help Mexico avoid another crisis. As José Negrín shows, several companies entered the market, but it was the Credit Bureau that succeeded. The Credit Bureau displaced a public registry of credit information called Servicio Nacional de Información de Crédito Bancario (National Service of Bank Credit Information, or Senicreb) that had been established in 1964 and whose institutional roots could be traced back to 1934.[101] Senicreb had functioned on a limited basis from the 1960s to the credit boom of the early 1990s, when the business opportunity for private credit-rating services became apparent.[102] Following the *tequilazo*, potential profitability increased, as did the potential political support for such private initiatives.

The Credit Bureau belongs to the history of modern economic honour that began when Banamex subscribed to R. G. Dun's credit-rating service a century earlier. Initially, the Credit Bureau focused on generating credit reports about individuals and was an arm of the American credit bureau Trans Union. Then, in 1997, when it partnered with Dun & Bradstreet (the successor to the R. G. Dun credit-rating agency analysed in Chapter 3), it began reporting on companies, too.[103] It thus connected that longer history of credit-reporting with a new technology: the computerised financial surveillance system. Josh Lauer traces the emergence of this system in his history of American credit-rating. In the 1970s, when the automated calculation of a person's credit (a numerical score) replaced textual appraisals such as the Dun reports, it created, in Lauer's words, 'a powerful system of surveillance' that evaluated the economic value of individual citizens.[104] Business leaders celebrated the computerised credit-reporting and credit-scoring system. 'For hundreds of years, the lending of money has been an art form in the sense that judgments have had to be based on the intuitive consideration of qualitative information,' wrote a representative from FICO in 1972. 'Only in the last two decades have innovations in technology changed the money lending activity from an art form to a scientific process, which enables people to reach decisions based on quantitative data.'[105] Leaders in the industry anticipated business expansion. In an algorithmic future, one expert foresaw, credit scores would determine much of a person's economic life: 'We will see point tables to make decisions such as: lease/don't lease, promote/don't promote, insure/don't insure, hire/don't hire, open/ don't open a checking account, and so forth.'[106] Lauer sums up the changes in credit-reporting in the 1970s as follows: 'Big Brother had not arrived in the guise of Orwellian technocrats, but rather as a business system for controlling consumers.'[107]

When the Credit Bureau opened in Mexico, it raised the question of how to protect citizens if the Credit Bureau itself abused its power. After all, unlike the public credit registry it displaced, it was an opaque private institution with considerable power. Debtors deemed unworthy by the Credit Bureau could, in broad strokes, be shut out of the formal credit economy. Indeed, the potential negative consequences of the Credit Bureau provide one example of why the government created Condusef in 1999. The government wanted to balance supporting the Credit Bureau's role in creating useful economic information with protecting citizens from being unjustly excluded from financial institutions.

Citizens wrote letters to the president asking him to protect their rights. In part, they were worried because the Credit Bureau was rumoured to have a Black List. Condusef tried to assure citizens that the Credit Bureau did not, in fact, maintain a Black List. But to no avail. Indeed, the myth was so pervasive that Condusef warned citizens of fraudulent services that promised to erase their names from the list.[108] Instead of a Black List, what the Credit Bureau actually had was something resembling more of a red zone reflecting when a consumer's credit score fell into a range that essentially blocked their access to credit. Yet the notion of a Black List felt very real to the debtors who found themselves deemed unworthy of credit. After all, an actual Black List need not exist for people to be

FIGURE 5.2 'Pursued by Past Debts', announcement in *La Jornada*, October 2007. Source: *La Jornada*.

blacklisted. Figure 5.2 captures the threat of blacklisting, and shows how government messaging sought to balance assistance and penalty. The announcement for a federal government programme to write off a substantial portion of tax debts appeared in various newspapers in October 2007.[109] It asks readers if they are 'pursued by their past' unpaid tax bills.

Asking for Help

The picture communicates sympathy for a person burdened by the weight of an unpaid debt (the man does indeed look hounded by his history). The announcement combines a meaningful offer of help sorting out tax debts with an exhortation to 'maintain a clear credit history', and then warns that indebted taxpayers will be reported to the Credit Bureau.

A bad record with the Credit Bureau could limit the opportunities for households to prosper and for businesses to survive. Those deemed unworthy might turn to creditors who advertised, in the back pages of newspapers, that they did not consult the Credit Bureau ('*no importa Buró de Crédito*').[110]

Ten of the letters in the sample are about the Credit Bureau and its Black List. In them, writers articulated ideas about justice and honour, and they described the intimate consequences of being excluded from the credit economy. These letters, in fact, advance some of the most trenchant critiques of corruption and unfairness in the sample as a whole. Roberto Monsalve, for example, denounced the Credit Bureau in a letter he wrote in April 2007.[111] As he put it, 'the Credit Bureau is the guillotine of Mexicans'. Monsalve did not describe any specific problem that he was facing. Instead, he penned a blanket condemnation of a corrupt institution that he felt was anathema to Mexicans. Monsalve claimed that millions of Mexicans were on the Black List because of the *tequilazo*, and he described how these people had been 'marked with a stigma'. The letter was routed to Condusef, and the agency notified Monsalve that he could submit a specific complaint. Otherwise, the agency stated, the matter was closed.[112]

Monsalve's letter stands out: he denounced the Credit Bureau in broad strokes and asked for justice for all Mexicans. Most citizens who wrote about the Black List, in contrast, pleaded with President Fox to help with their specific problem. Bertha Rivas wrote to Fox in April 2003. She was a 37-year-old single mother of two girls, aged 2 and 9 years, from Nuevo León (the Cadereyta Jiménez neighbourhood). She worked as a federal employee in a Pemex refinery. Rivas dreamed of owning her own home, and she had been about to realise this dream through Pemex's mortgage programme when she discovered she had been placed on the Credit Bureau's Black List. 'They list me as having a bad credit history,' Rivas explained.

Rivas had previously been a client of Banco Unión, where she claimed she had been cheated by the banker Carlos Cabal Peniche. In fact, Cabal Peniche was no average banker. He had bought Banco Unión in the 1991 privatisation, then famously went on the run after being accused of massive bank fraud in 1994. He was apprehended in Australia in 1998 and extradited to Mexico in 2001, where many of the charges were subsequently dropped. At the time Rivas wrote her letter (2003), Cabal Peniche was about to launch a banana and pineapple export business. He had started out as a fruit magnate, a 'banana baron', before banking, and his investor group had purchased both Del Monte Fresh Produce and Del Monte Foods Co. in the 1990s.[113]

During the course of the Banco Unión scandal, Rivas explained, she had been reported for a bad transaction. The transaction was, essentially, the original sin that landed her on the Black List, but her letter was vague on the matter. She did not include details about what Banco Unión claimed had happened, and she did not even assert her innocence or guilt. Whatever the case was, she had sought recourse from the Comisión Nacional Bancaria and the Credit Bureau, among others. She had received no help. 'How,' she asked, 'could the ghost of this bank affect me so?' 'I am desperate,' she pleaded. Her request was routed to Condusef.[114]

While Rivas had obfuscated on the exact nature of her bad transaction, other writers were more direct in describing the transaction that landed them in trouble with the so-called Black List. Some proclaimed their innocence and others confessed, but they generally described the transaction in question. Florentino Fernández was one who proclaimed his innocence. Fernández was a 27-year-old employee from Guanajuato. When he wrote to President Fox in March 2005, he had recently applied for a bank loan and was surprised to learn that he was on the Credit Bureau's Black List. He had no debt and had never had a credit card or retail card. The request was routed to Condusef.[115] Raúl Robledo, by contrast, performed a sort of confession and sought absolution. Robledo was a 32-year-old from Tabasco who worked in the oil industry. When he wrote to President Fox to ask for help in May 2003, he admitted to having misused a credit card, which had landed him on the Black List. He explained that he had cleared his debt, and so wanted Fox's help to clear his credit history so that he could get a bank loan. The request was routed to Condusef. When Robledo wrote again in April 2007, he confessed that he had once again fallen into arrears with his credit card, and he again explained that he had cleared the debt. Like the previous time, he asked for help clearing his credit history, and his request was routed to Condusef.[116]

Seven years was one of the Credit Bureau's signature timelines. After seven years of good behaviour, a person's uncreditworthy behaviour would be purged from the record. But seven years was a long time to be excluded from the world of credit, and Robledo was not alone in wanting out of the Credit Bureau's seven-year purgatory. César Marín, for example, had fallen into arrears on his mortgage payments, had lost his house, and was blacklisted by the Credit Bureau. A retired senior citizen from Sinaloa, Marín wrote to President Fox to protest against the seven-year period. He was sick and needed to apply for another loan; he could not wait.[117] Likewise, María de los Ángeles Ríos, a 41-year-old federal employee from Mexico City (Iztapalapa, El Rosario), wrote to President Fox in July 2004 asking for help because she was on the 'famous Black List' after falling into arrears with a loan from Banamex. She explained that she had cleared that debt the previous year, but complained that she would now be blacklisted for another six years. She wanted to apply for a new line of credit with Bancomer, and this loan would be repaid directly via salary deduction. But the loan would not be approved until she was off the Black List. 'It is unjust,' she declared.[118] Both Marín and Ríos had cleared their debts – expiated their sins – and they wanted out of purgatory. Both cases were routed to Condusef.

VILLAINS AND VICTIMS

A good story has a conflict, with a villain and a victim. In these economic stories, the villains were bankers such as Carlos Cabal Peniche, moneylenders like Francisco Corona, or faceless institutions like the Credit Bureau. The victims were Mexican citizens who had been excluded from the credit economy and who were in danger of losing their homes. Good and bad faith existed on both sides. Rich and powerful creditors made mistakes and also cheated and stole. So did ordinary debtors. At the turn of the millennium, however, it was more common to discipline debtors than to police creditors.

When citizens wrote to the president with their problems, their concerns reflected a new iteration of an age-old question: what was considered fair within the inherently asymmetrical relationship between debtors and creditors? This same question, which has guided the research running through each chapter of this book, was no less pressing for Mexican citizens experiencing macroeconomic vulnerability in the increasingly depersonalised market economy of the twenty-first century. The debtor–creditor relationship had changed in three important ways over the course of two centuries. First, capitalist credit relations had reached into many areas of life, and there was less space outside them.

Second, with few exceptions, the creditors in this chapter tended to be impersonal institutions that operated on finance logics to increase profits. Both these first two changes could be good for both debtors and creditors: the former had access to loans and the latter could earn profit. However, creditors and debtors alike had become more vulnerable to macroeconomic shocks. Whereas Mexico's massive macroeconomic crises in the nineteenth century had not manifested in the everyday lending and borrowing of ordinary and middling people, citizens lived the shock of the 1990s as an intimate and emotional saga. The third change to the debtor–creditor relationship was also felt on a very personal level by everyday borrowers. By the turn of the millennium, creditors had more power to punish debtors who did not meet their obligations.

For many citizens in the early twenty-first century, the parameters of fairness were strained in new ways. Letters by citizens show exactly how they thought the game was rigged. How could they prevail against the ghost of Cabal Peniche's Banco Unión or against an amorphous entity like Elektra? They faced the prospect of losing their homes or languishing in the Credit Bureau's purgatory through a slow and systematic dispossession by paperwork. Their letters illuminate a tense moral economy whereby the line between exploitation and opportunity had become unstable in novel ways. Importantly, many of the people who wrote to Fox wanted to continue participating in the capitalist credit economy, such as those who wanted to be taken off the Credit Bureau's Black List so they might qualify for new loans in the hopes of improving their lot in life. The credit economy had spread deep into their lives, and they wanted new loans. They also wanted guardrails to protect them from exploitation. The government had put creative measures in place, like Condusef, to give citizens a sense of recourse and, thus, balance out their vulnerability. And in this context, letter writers offered the role of hero to President Fox, asking him to help and to rectify their circumstances. But he did not accept the mantle. Instead, the letters were sent to Condusef.

Conclusion

Debts Unpaid examines one problem over a long chronological horizon: what happened when people did not pay their debts? This question puts the small-scale troubles of ordinary people at the centre of economic transformation. Each chapter has presented a deep sounding of conflicts between debtors and creditors in Mexico City across different historical epochs. Drawing on evidence from discrete archival collections, each chapter has offered a specific lens through which to explore the debtor–creditor relationship. Together, they show that the power struggle between debtors and creditors was a stress test for the stability of the economic order, and that debt trouble was a driving force in the history of accumulation and justice in the modern world.

The power struggle between debtors and creditors in Mexico City was a core arena of contestation over capitalist expansion. Studying malfunction – examining what happened when contracts broke or strained – exposes this power struggle. However small the value of the loan might have been, debtors and creditors were backed by a legal framework, they deployed the best economic information available, and they relied on long-standing notions about fairness as they navigated changing circumstances.

From mediaeval Iberia to nineteenth-century Mexico, jurists worked to establish fair and functional laws concerning unpaid debts to strengthen the economic power of the territory. In the eighteenth and nineteenth centuries, as New Spain became Mexico, new legal institutions shaped by liberalism began serving the needs of debtors and creditors now freed from older constraints. Two of the most important changes were that debtors no longer faced the possibility of debt prison, and creditors no longer faced usury prohibitions. Yet debt litigation rose in the nineteenth century, with greater numbers of creditors and debtors appearing before magistrates and judges. As Chapter 1 shows, the number of small claims conflicts soared; Chapter 2 suggests that this pattern held true for property sequestration and a range of other conflicts. Notably, increased debt litigation indicates that economic justice was working and that people had enough faith in the system to try their luck, but it also suggests that debtors and creditors were having more problems with each other. Something was not working when they entered into agreements. As increasingly impersonal economic relations expanded into the world of ordinary people with their small and medium enterprises, the older frameworks they had long relied on – frameworks based on trust and personal relationships – started to strain.

Debt litigation suggested that creditors were not getting good enough information to make smart decisions about who to trust. A growing disjuncture between the expanding economy and traditional trust mechanisms left creditors worried. Luckily for them, economic justice generally worked in their favour. Magistrates and judges acted on creditors' worries, and creditors usually prevailed in their legal petitions. But, as Chapters 1 and 2 show, magistrates and judges also worked to protect debtors throughout the nineteenth century, delivering economic justice for ordinary people. Although it favoured creditors, the law did not oppress debtors. And, overall, this balance was good for debtors because they wanted creditors to lend to them. In short, the prospects of ordinary debtors and creditors rose during much of the nineteenth century. Navigating debt conflicts with the aid of local magistrates and judges enabled the wheels of trade and commerce to function more or less smoothly for small and middling enterprise even as macroeconomic change began to transform Mexico's economy.

At the turn of the twentieth century, however, the power dynamic tipped dramatically in favour of creditors. As Chapter 3 shows, when credit-rating agencies produced a new type of economic information – the credit report – they facilitated the growth of impersonal lending by financial institutions. By modernising the trust mechanism, credit-rating agencies set the conditions for lenders such as banks to reach into the economic lives of ordinary people. The early credit reports transformed the power struggle between debtors and creditors by providing a new tool to allay creditors' anxieties. They gave creditors, especially institutional creditors, a leg up that fundamentally changed the power balance in everyday lending. This was good and bad for debtors. By helping creditors trust them, credit reports could unlock credit for ordinary people and possibly lead to new opportunity and greater prosperity. However, those who were deemed unworthy by credit-reporting were excluded from the growing credit economy.

Conclusion

From that point on, the debtor–creditor relationship became a frontier of capitalist expansion as market relations spread into the world of small-scale loans. There was a lot at stake for middling people and their enterprises: the credit reports set the parameters for inclusion in and exclusion from modern financial institutions. The power of creditors only grew as the credit market expanded through increasingly impersonal institutions, and the intersection of modern banking and traditional ideas about trust and fair dealing created serious tension. After the Mexican Revolution, more and more citizens opened bank accounts and used financial instruments like cheques. As Chapter 4 shows, this early financialisation gave creditors enormous power over debtors, especially those who used cheques as a stand-in for more traditional modes of exchange such as guarantees and IOUs. Legislators, keen to encourage financial modernisation to further their development goals, established serious consequences for misusing cheques at the very same time as growing numbers of middle-class citizens were starting to use these modern financial products.

The growing pains of financialisation were painful indeed: debtors who wrote uncovered cheques became vulnerable to coercion by creditors who could threaten them with high fines and jail time. The potential for exploitation and intimidation between debtors and creditors, which had shaped their relationship for a very long time, was given new form. For the first time in a century, a form of debt imprisonment was back on the docket. Indeed, the very sort of abuse by creditors that jurists had been trying to prevent in both mediaeval and liberal legal codes was given a new outlet that left many debtors more vulnerable than ever. By the middle of the twentieth century, the power balance had decidedly shifted to favour creditors, and debtors were increasingly found guilty of fraud. Financialisation, it seemed, depended on the coercion of ordinary and middle-class debtors.

At the turn of the millennium, the power differentials were stark. Debtors had lost much of their power, while the debtor–creditor relationship became one of the main areas of profit in the new economic order. The early financialisation of bank accounts and chequebooks deepened in the later twentieth century, as Chapter 5 shows. There was less space for economic life outside the credit economy. Capitalist credit relations, especially between individual debtors and institutional lenders, had spread into homes through mortgages, into transportation through car loans, and into monthly consumption through credit cards. Financial institutions also came between state and society, as citizens increasingly accessed their entitlement payments – some of their most tangible rights – through bank accounts. More people were being included in financial institutions, for good or ill, than ever before. And as citizens became economic citizens, they often became debtors who were vulnerable to losing their patrimony.

The historical arc of the power struggle between debtors and creditors was one of freedom and constraint: during the long nineteenth century, both did well. In the long twentieth century, the power balance shifted to favour creditors. Over two centuries, their power struggle was one of the fundamental struggles of capitalist expansion. The centre of this changing economic order was the firmament of ordinary people. The smooth functioning of their conflicts was key to the economic power of the territory, a dynamic understood by monarchs and elected leaders alike. The world of wealthy merchants and macro phenomena such as international trade and public revenues was, of course, important to the broader economy. But without the centre, without the world of modest people with their contracts and enterprises, there was no whole.

Ordinary people were neither wealthy nor poor; they were simply middling or middle-class citizens. Their world began to change when credit-rating agencies began helping institutional lenders trust people of modest means in the later nineteenth century. Thereafter, capitalist financial institutions sought to lend to a wider array of citizens. It was a story that unfolded over the span of two hundred years, but was supercharged with the technological changes of the twentieth century. Increasingly, citizens accessed credit as individuals, consumers, workers, bank account holders, and financial service users. And these citizens played two key roles in the history of economic transformation: their lives were a space for capitalist credit relations to deepen and spread, and the smooth resolution of their conflicts buttressed the hegemony of expanding capitalism.

The debt troubles faced by ordinary people tested the legitimacy of the economic order. Studying different types of troubles over the *longue durée* shows that no matter how much might change in different historical eras – and the chapters in this book show that much did, indeed, change – the core function of debt trouble in history remained the same. Debt trouble was about the legitimation of the broader economic system, regardless of whether the mode of accumulation was mercantilist or capitalist. As described in the Introduction, the concept of hegemony is often used to study the establishment of legitimate political authority through a combination of consent (usually from below, from the ruled) and coercion (usually from above, from the rulers). Legitimacy of the economic order was just as important, if not more so. Legitimacy (and the stability it supported) was about striking a balance between opportunity and exploitation: opportunities for debtors to borrow so they might advance their plans, and opportunities for creditors to lend and make a profit. People wanted to participate in the credit economy, and political leaders, for their part, encouraged more and more people into it.

The main historical questions that shaped economic relations over time were how much exploitation and coercion was acceptable to debtors and creditors, and how much would be allowed by the political authority. Neither leaders nor ordinary people envisioned or expected equality between debtors and creditors. Given the power differential – creditors were, after all, the owners of the money or asset being loaned – equality was not an important consideration. The moral economy of the debtor–creditor relationship centred on the proper functioning of both parties within a contract bound by an acceptable amount of exploitation. The boundaries of exploitation were political and ideological, and they changed over time. As Chapter 2 shows, shifting boundaries of exploitation occurred alongside changing rules for contracts. Chapter 4 demonstrates this dynamic in relation to changing penalties for misusing financial instruments. For ordinary debtors and creditors, fairness was about how much one party could or could not benefit at the expense of the other.

Economic justice is the drudgery that serves a lofty purpose. The key is defining fair terms for contracts and delivering fair resolutions when disputes arise. For the economic order to be stable and thrive, most people need to feel that they have some recourse if their agreements sour. The contract is one of the basic economic relationships in human history: it is a mutually binding agreement or promise that might or might not have been written down. As Chapter 2 shows, contract law facilitated exchange and legitimised the authority of the monarchy and, later, the republic. The rules for contract terms and the resolutions of contract disputes had to be fair enough for people to borrow and lend. Fairness, in this economic register, was shorthand for consistency and legibility. Much depended on the smooth resolution of the almost relentless problems of ordinary and middle-class people. Economic justice sustained the economic order and (by extension) political authority. As this book has argued, disputes over small sums constituted a relentless test for the broader economic order as massive transformations altered the dominant mode of accumulation, from commercial to industrial to financial capitalism. Even the veneer of fairness could help underpin the economic order. As Chapter 5 shows, the government established avenues such as Condusef and the Citizen Service Office for people to denounce unfair terms. Although the outcomes of the complaints are not always clear, the possibility of recourse offered by such venues helped establish a sense of governmental concern for vulnerable debtors when the power of creditors felt unfair.

A large part of economic justice happened in the legal sphere. Jurists articulated the parameters of exploitation in legal codes, and the rules had to work when creditors and debtors faced each other in the courtroom.

In terms of legal conflicts, creditors usually prevailed. But within that context, economic justice worked fairly in two important ways: men and women could expect similar outcomes; and it appears that magistrates and judges did not act differently when the matter concerned smaller or larger sums. Chapter 1 shows such fairness in small claims conflicts, Chapter 2 shows it for asset seizure petitions, and Chapter 4 shows it for the legal sagas of people arrested for writing uncovered cheques. Considering adjudication, economic justice seems to have been fair, and consistently so in different conflicts and historical moments. Outside the legal sphere, ideas about economic justice and fairness were theological, ideological, and cultural. As Chapters 2 and 5 show, concerns about unjust gain in lending at interest persisted and recurred from mediaeval Iberia to the new millennium.

Economic justice changed over time, but on a long chronological horizon. It provided a bedrock for transformation. It was humdrum and prosaic: vulgar, to borrow Plato's word. And that was its power. Economic justice provided a consistency and a persistence that underpinned massive historical change, from mercantilism and feudalism to capitalism, and through different modes of capitalist accumulation. Looking at different debt troubles over the *longue durée* thus reveals the interplay between continuity and change in a cosmopolitan city at a dynamic nexus in the global economy.

The relationship between debtors and creditors is one of the most basic in economic life. It has been re-signified over the past two hundred years: shaped by both freedom and constraint, created by both personal and impersonal connections, and constituting both a minor and a major part of the economic order. Yet some of its primary characteristics are remarkably durable. It is, and has always been, a power struggle between two parties with opposing interests, with a constant tension between trust and distrust, the moral and the material. It is a relationship that can be exploitative and liberating, but, most fundamentally, it is dyadic: debtors and creditors exist only in relation to one another. The struggle between them has been a driving force in historical transformations from the colonial twilight to the recent past.

Debt trouble, as a category of analysis, illuminates the temporalities of accumulation and justice in modern history. Looking forward, the power struggle between debtors and creditors will no doubt remain a core relationship in human history. *Debts Unpaid*, for the most part, has studied the problem of what happened when people did not pay their debts in Mexico City in the capitalist era, but this same power struggle has been fundamental to all manner of economic orders around the world and throughout history. It will remain at the heart of whatever comes next.

Notes

Introduction

1 ERM to Fox, dated 11 February 2004 in Archivo General de la Nación (AGN), Presidentes, V. Fox, Red Federal de Servicio a la Ciudadanía (RFSC), *caja* (c.) 394, *expediente* (exp.) 1175549.
2 Archivo Histórico de la Ciudad de México 'Carlos de Sigüenza y Góngora' (AHCDMX), Ayuntamiento-Justicia (AJ), vol. 2763, exp. 1, folio (f.) 45v, 16 August 1813.
3 I define capitalism as an embedded economic system of capital accumulation that is based on a set of social property relations which force people into a dependence on market exchange (through different forms of violence, alienation, and enticement) and that is characterised by an almost continuous movement into new areas for material reproduction. These new areas range widely (from territorial geography to intimate spaces to the digital realm) and include, importantly for this book, the credit economy. Within this economic system, profit maximisation is often pursued through market competition and/or state control, technological innovation and/or monopoly, and de jure and/or de facto political power. The emergence of capitalism as a dominant mode of accumulation took different forms in different places; in the Iberian world it was a long and often fitful process of coexisting and superseding mercantilism and feudalism. I have drawn on scholars of political economy, especially Brenner, 'Agrarian Class Structure'; Cardoso and Faletto, *Dependency and Development*; Harvey, *New Imperialism*; Polanyi, *Great Transformation*; Schwartz, *Slaves, Peasants, and Rebels*; Semo, *History of Capitalism in Mexico*; Thompson, *Whigs and Hunters*; Wood, *Origin of Capitalism*. My approach in this book emphasises capitalism as an historical process; future scholars might develop the topic of unpaid small debts by engaging more thoroughly with philosophical theorisations of economic science.
4 Matthew O'Hara describes how, in the early modern world, the intellectual framework shifted from an earlier view of money as something static and unchanging to a new understanding of it as unstable and fertile. O'Hara, *History of the Future*, chapter 4.

5 On ecclesiastic credit in the eighteenth century, see von Wobeser, *Crédito eclesiástico*. On increased circulation of credit instruments in the later eighteenth century, see Pérez Herrero, *Plata y libranzas*.
6 Von Wobeser, 'Mecanismos crediticios'; see also Martínez López-Cano, *Crédito a largo plazo*; O'Hara, *History of the Future*, chapter 4.
7 The shift from the *censo* to the *depósito irregular* is evident in loans issued by ecclesiastical institutions. O'Hara, *History of the Future*, chapter 4; Von Wobeser, *Crédito eclesiástico*, chapter 3; see also Martínez López-Cano, 'Usuras'.
8 Guerra, *Modernidad e independencias*, 13.
9 Much of the scholarship about the economic dimension of liberalism has focused on free trade and on the dismantling of corporate-owned property. Economic liberalism also transformed credit and debt relations for ordinary people: in contracts, by eliminating debt imprisonment and usury protections, and, more indirectly, by facilitating the growth of non-ecclesiastic lenders. The scholarship on liberalism is considered in Chapter 1; the changing rules for contracts are examined in Chapter 2; and non-ecclesiastic lenders are examined in Chapter 3. For an overview, see Adelman, 'Liberalism and Constitutionalism'; see also Lurtz, *From the Grounds Up*, on everyday economic liberalism.
10 On the nationalisation of church wealth, see Bazant, *Alienation of Church Wealth*.
11 As part of a broader effort to understand the Porfiriato, the revolution, and the state consolidation of the 1920s, scholarship on late nineteenth- and early twentieth-century Mexico has offered some of the best studies of changing property rights and the growing credit economy in Latin American history, such as Noel Maurer's work on banking. In Chapter 3, I follow one thread of that scholarship to explore how honour, risk, and information technologies changed the dynamics between debtors and creditors during these decades. See Haber et al., *Politics of Property Rights*; Maurer, *Power and the Money*. More generally, the breakup of communal property and the causes of the Mexican Revolution are among the most studied topics in modern Latin American history. For recent overviews, see Garciadiego, 'Revolución mexicana'; Joseph and Buchenau, *Mexico's Once and Future Revolution*.
12 The historiography on the 1920s and 1930s is substantial, and much of the scholarship addresses the political consolidation of the ruling elite and the negotiation of hegemony with peasant, worker, and popular sectors. On the former, see, for example, Joseph and Nugent, eds, *Everyday Forms of State Formation*. On land redistribution, see, among others, Fallaw, *Cárdenas Compromised*. Historical scholarship on the mid-century decades has grown in recent years, especially for the 1940s to the 1970s. See, for example, Gillingham and Smith, eds, *Dictablanda*; Pensado and Ochoa, eds, *México Beyond 1968*.
13 Historians of New Spain and nineteenth-century Mexico have examined kinship credit networks among wealthy merchants and families, formal lending by ecclesiastic institutions and banks, and questions of sovereign debt. The scholarship is extensive, but the following studies are particularly helpful:

Baskes, *Staying Afloat*; Chowning, *Wealth and Power*; Galindo Rodríguez, *Ethnic Entrepreneurs*; Marichal, *Bankruptcy of Empire*; Maurer, *Power and the Money*; Salvucci, *Politics, Markets*; von Wobeser, *Crédito eclesiástico*; Walker, *Kinship, Business, and Politics*.

14 Francois's study on pawnshops and precarious middle-income household finances in Mexico City, as well as Levy's analysis of non-bank credit and notaries as trust brokers in Mérida, bring debt and credit into a social history tradition that reconstructs the urban world of late New Spain and nineteenth-century Mexico. Francois, *Culture of Everyday Credit*; Levy, *Making of the Market*. The social history scholarship is extensive; seminal texts include Arrom, *Women of Mexico City*; Pérez Toledo, *Hijos del trabajo*.

15 The first line of enquiry guides the institutional model of economic history, much of which was inspired by North's *Institutions, Institutional Change, and Economic Performance*. Emblematic of the second is Linebaugh, *London Hanged*. The distinction here is overly schematic; it is examined in greater detail throughout the chapters, especially in Chapter 4.

16 Danzig, '"True Justice" in the "Republic"'; Schiller, 'Just Men and Just Acts'; see also Arnold, 'Vulgar and Elegant'.

17 I am drawing on E. P. Thompson's definition of moral economy as 'the proper economic functions of several parties within the community'. Thompson, 'Moral Economy of the English Crowd', 79.

18 On the economic anthropology of debt and credit, I am drawing on the review essay Peebles, 'Anthropology of Credit'.

19 Historians of the national era have shown how gendered notions of honour were at the core of political legitimacy, state-building projects, and modern social hierarchies. In their introduction to an influential volume, Caulfield et al. describe how notions of masculine and feminine honour were central to the shift from corporate society to liberal individualism in the nineteenth century: 'honor played a crucial new role after independence, mediating liberalism's competing commitments to individual equality and social order' (2). In his study of the Mexican public sphere, Piccato shows how masculine honour was 'the keystone in the building of a modern public sphere in Mexico' (4). This book contributes an analysis of economic and financial honour to the scholarship that is inspired by Piccato's study of national economic honour and his examination of the public reaction to the renegotiation of Mexico's British debt in 1884. Caulfield et al., *Honor, Status, and Law*; Piccato, *Tyranny of Opinion*.

20 Taylor, *Fugitive Freedom*, x.

21 Trivellato's examination of merchant letters across the Mediterranean and Bishara's analysis of *khiyār* sales in the Indian Ocean world, as well as debates over public and private institutions in the Champagne fairs, represent some of the wide-ranging studies about trust mechanisms. See Bishara, *Sea of Debt*; Edwards and Ogilvie, 'What Lessons'; Greif, 'Institutions and Impersonal Exchange'; Trivellato, *Familiarity of Strangers*.

22 My framework also draws on other disciplines where pressing present-day questions have been addressed, including the economics of rumours, the sociology of reputation and trust, and the study of information and big data.

See, especially, Banerjee, 'Economics of Rumours'; Diekmann and Przepiorka, 'Trust and Reputation in Markets'; Bouk, 'History and Political Economy of Personal Data'.
23 Scott, *Seeing Like a State*.
24 For example, see parallels between the small claims examined in Chapter 1 and the analysis by Sen et al. of debt litigation in colonial Virginia, 'When Good Little Debts Went Bad'.
25 Within the *Annales* school, there are different approaches to a long duration. It could include chronologies that go beyond the scale of human memory. Most often, the *longue durée* approach encompasses several centuries, such as Le Roy Ladurie's study of agrarian cycles in southern France. There is also the *très longue durée* of almost geological time, applied most famously in Braudel's analysis of millennia in *Mediterranean*. As Dale Tomich writes, the *longue durée* 'forms the stabilizing ground against which cyclical variations of other temporal structures are established'. In this book, the broader cyclical change in the debtor–creditor relationship is highlighted by putting the conflicts studied, which took place between 1808 and 2008, into the context of longer political and legal histories. Braudel, *Mediterranean*; Le Roy Ladurie, *Peasants of Languedoc*; Tomich, 'Order of Historical Time', 10.
26 These terms reflect different historical moments and connect with distinct historiographies. In broad strokes, these people did not constitute the largest segment of the economy when considering population and wealth. For example, considering inequality as measured by deciles of wealth distribution, most would be in between a tiny group of rich people and a very large number of poor people. And their transactions probably did not represent the lion's share of wealth traded. Nevertheless, the volume and velocity of their transactions across all sectors transformed their world into the core of the local economy.
27 Bleynat, *Venders' Capitalism*, 2. Historians of early modern England write about independent trading households and middling sorts. Barry and Brooks, *Middling Sort of People*.
28 Le Roy Ladurie, 'Motionless History'; see also McCants, 'Editor's Introduction'.
29 I have drawn on the scholarship on liberalism and conservativism in the late eighteenth and nineteenth centuries – and in particular the emphasis on popular politics and political culture – to think about popular economic hegemony. See, for example, Echeverri, *Indian and Slave Royalists*; Guardino, *Time of Liberty*; Mallon, *Peasant and Nation*.
30 This is the analytical benefit of studying a problem across a long national period. Most historical scholarship on modern Mexico, including my first book, focuses on more discrete time periods, such as a long nineteenth century from the Bourbon reforms to the outbreak of the revolution, the struggle for independence, the postcolonial wars, the dictatorship of Porfirio Díaz, the revolution and its immediate aftermath, the consolidation and heyday of one-party rule, and so on. In this regard, scholarship on the colonial era offers more models for studying a problem over an extensive chronology.
31 The *juicios verbales* (small claims) are from the 'Justicia' collection at the AHCDMX. The *providencias precautorias* (precautionary asset sequestration

petitions) are part of the *Tribunal Superior de Justicia del Distrito Federal* collection at the AGN. The credit reports are from the R. G. Dun books at the Archivo Histórico del Banco Nacional de México. The arrest records are from the 'Lecumberri' collection at the AHCDMX. And the letters to Fox are part of the 'Presidentes' collection at the AGN.

32 Exploring unpaid debts is only part of the potential use of these sources. Some of these collections hold countless more conflicts (economic and otherwise) awaiting future researchers.

33 I finished this book in 2023, when artificial intelligence (AI) tools had become available to the public. These raise questions about authorship and integrity for the scholarly research community, but best practice guidelines had not yet been established. In the interests of transparency, I include this note: I did not use any artificial intelligence programs or tools in any capacity.

34 These tests were suitable for my small sample sizes. Elsewhere, I have examined the small claims dataset using regression analysis, with substantively similar results and interpretations. I decided against including regressions in this book to maintain consistency across the chapters: because the small claims dataset is the largest, more regressions were possible; for the other datasets, fewer were possible. See Walker, 'Everyday Economic Justice'.

35 See Alan Knight's discussion of the problematics of testing hypotheses as a methodology for historians of Mexico. Knight, 'Subalterns, Signifiers, and Statistics', 153–156.

36 While the 'significant' results in this study meet the conventional threshold, some models with significant results have low numbers of observations. Throughout the book, I present both the percentages and the numbers to show the low numbers and to emphasise that the quantitative analysis is suggestive (percentages may not sum to 100 due to rounding). Similarly, the 'not significant' results do not give direct evidence that there was no relationship between variables (such as between the gender of defendant and the outcome of a legal conflict), only that the test did not find a relationship. There are different reasons to be circumspect about basing too much historical interpretation on the inferential statistics. In addition to concerns about simple dichotomies, statisticians in health sciences and other disciplines have described the challenges of reproducibility and the effects of edge cases. See Spiegelhalter, *Art of Statistics* for a recent example. On 'dichotomania' and 'harm', see Amrhein et al., 'Scientists Rise Up Against Statistical Significance', 306–307.

37 For example, Solow, 'Economic History and Economics'.

38 See, for example, Guillory, 'Sokal Affair'.

39 Throughout the chapters, I describe methodological limitations. I detail the sampling strategies. I explain coding decisions and consider how other scholars might have classified cases differently. I include the numbers of observations when reporting the statistical results to underscore the limitations of the quantitative analysis. I also advance alternative readings of case studies to highlight the limitations of impressionistic interpretation. The datasets are public and are housed at Northeastern University Library's Digital Repository Service.

Chapter 1

1 An abridged version of this chapter was published as Walker, 'Everyday Economic Justice'. I am grateful to *The American Historical Review* and Oxford University Press for permission to use.
2 Archivo Histórico de la Ciudad de México 'Carlos de Sigüenza y Góngora' (AHCDMX) Ayuntamiento Justicia (AJ), vol. 2887, expediente (exp.) 1, folio (f.) 11v, 31 July 1832. The archive was renamed in 2016; it was previously the Archivo Histórico del Distrito Federal (AHDF).
3 These hearings represented, in terms of legal system hierarchy, a lower level than the first-instance cases that were heard by legally trained judges. *Juicios verbales* were also called *juicios ordinaries* and *juicios sumarios*. On the earlier history of *juicios verbales*, see Borah, *Justice by Insurance*, 13–15.
4 Arnold, 'Introduction: Juzgados Constitucionales', 9–10; Arnold, 'Juicios verbales y conciliatorios', 911.
5 The Constitution of Cádiz, Article 312. I am using the translation in Mirow, *Florida's First Constitution*.
6 On the transformations and continuities of Cádiz liberalism, see Breña, ed., *Cádiz a debate*. On Cádiz and judicial organisation, see López González, *Organización para la administración*, 42–43, 100–110.
7 Escanilla Huerta, 'They Will Live', 201, 213.
8 See, for example, Richard Warren's analysis of popular participation in Mexico City. Warren *Vagrants and Citizens*.
9 There was a brief period from 6 July 1848 to 19 May 1849 when magistrates were appointed rather than elected. More generally, Mexico City's judicial structure changed considerably from 1813 to 1863. Legislators created new jurisdictions and eliminated, renamed, or changed the mandate of others. These were not clean breaks, and other scholars have analysed the changes. I refer to all the different kinds of magistrates who heard *juicios verbales* in this archive as, simply, magistrates. The possible impact of legislative and jurisdictional changes is considered below. On the legislative changes, see Arnold, 'Juicios verbales y conciliatorios'; Flores Flores, *Justicia criminal ordinaria*; James, 'Lay Magistrates'; Pulido Esteva, 'Después del alcalde de barrio'.
10 Articles 249 and 250 of the Constitution of Cádiz carved out exceptions for the church and the military; the *juicios verbales* were subsequently extended to ecclesiastics and soldiers in 1821. See Arnold, 'Juicios verbales y conciliatorios', 911; Arnold, 'Dos demandantes, un demandado'.
11 The *alcaldes constitucionales* also heard the *juicios conciliatorios* (cases with amounts over 100 pesos). After 1812, the *juicios conciliatorios* became a mandatory first step for civil litigation: in order to appear before a first-instance judge, plaintiffs needed to present a certificate of conciliation. See Arnold, 'Juicios verbales y conciliatorios', 911.
12 Guerra, *Modernidad e independencias*, 13.
13 Guerra, *Modernidad e independencias*, 85, 89.
14 Guerra, *Modernidad e independencias*, chapter 3.
15 O'Hara, *History of the Future*, chapter 5.
16 On the revisionist historiography, see Eastman, 'Introduction', 7–10.

Notes to pages 22–25   225

17 Lira González, *Comunidades indígenas*.
18 The archive collection ends in 1863, but the *juicios verbales* continued (as did the *juicios conciliatorios*). On the procedural and administrative changes from 1812 to the 1880s, see Arnold, 'Juicios verbales y conciliatorios'.
19 The plaintiff's gender is unknown in 11 cases; the defendant's gender is unknown in 7 cases.
20 There were no guidelines for location: for example, Luis de Ezeta's 1845 manual simply instructs magistrates to name the time and place. In her introduction to the archive collection, Linda Arnold describes residents going to magistrates' homes, which was common in the cases in my sample; Flores Flores describes the same for the cases she studies. Ezeta, *Manual de alcaldes y jueces de paz*, 61; Arnold, 'Introduction: Juzgados Constitucionales', 10; see also Flores Flores, *Ciudad judicial*, 49.
21 From 1848 to 1863, the *juicios verbales* summaries were lodged in books with various other cases. Ezeta, *Manual de alcaldes y jueces de paz*, 60–64. Relevant excerpts of Ezeta's guidelines are reproduced in Arnold, *Catálogo*, 13–27.
22 Because the volume increased dramatically over time, the sample includes all records from the 1810s; 10 per cent of the cases in all the books for the 1820s; and 5 per cent of the cases in selected books for the following decades, with at least two books for each year (one short and one long, to include both popular magistrates and those who were not very busy). After the sample was analysed against the larger data universe, additional cases were transcribed for the decades from the 1830s to the 1860s to ensure that the sample reached close to 1 per cent of the total cases for each year (again alternating between short and long books). The data universe is based on a conservative estimate of 1 case per page.
23 Unless otherwise noted, the results given are for all years. Analysis of the magistrates is based on a selection: the eleven magistrates with more than twenty cases. See the Introduction for additional information about the methods used.
24 Here, I am following a social history tradition, and I acknowledge two main weaknesses: the concept of 'ordinary people' has a vagueness that is methodologically imperfect, and there is an implicit condescension in the reification of such broad categories. See Samuel, 'What Is Social History?', 34–38.
25 On artisans and urban economies, see Pérez Toledo, *Hijos del trabajo*. On factories, wage labour, and gender in Puebla and Durango during these years and Mexico City in the later nineteenth century, see Ramos Escandón, *Industrialización, género*. On middle-class household economies, see Francois, *Culture of Everyday Credit*. On tributary Indians, see Granados, 'Cosmopolitan Indians'.
26 See Vinson, *Before Mestizaje*.
27 Granados, 'Cosmopolitan Indians', 275.
28 My demographic description is deliberately vague because there is not a complete time series. Instead, there are snapshots of the city's demographic distributions from different sources before and during the years studied here. My overview is based on Pérez Toledo and Klein, *Población y estructura*, 79, 97, 165–168, 180, 189; Sánchez Santiró, 'Población', table on p. 39.

29 Arrom, *Containing the Poor*, 8–9.
30 Challú and Gómez-Galvarriato, 'Mexico's Real Wages', 97.
31 John Tutino has shown a similar dynamic for the Bajío, where national economic collapse encased in political conflict allowed regular groups to claim gains, on the ground if not ideologically or legislatively. See, for example, Tutino, 'Revolution in Mexican Independence'; see also, for the regions around Mexico City, Tutino, *Mexican Heartland*, especially chapters 7 and 8.
32 Where possible, examples are given in five-year increments with two examples for each year. When the sample does not include two cases with an item whose full monetary value is clear for a given year, examples from the nearest year are used.
33 I am following Juliette Levy's use of an estate inventory from nineteenth-century Yucatán to explain the value of a peso. Levy, *Making of the Market*, 130–133.
34 The average rent data, developed by Andrés Calderón Fernández, is for rooms in the Vizcaínas building. The three rooms that he describes have been restored to their original dimensions: room 7 is 69.03 square metres; room 30 is 68.82 square metres; and room 60 is 65.30 square metres. I am grateful to Amílcar Challú for suggesting monthly rent as a gauge of value. Calderón Fernández, 'Mirando a Nueva España', 184, table 4.2.
35 The daily wage was close to 4 reales for the 1810s, but it stabilised at around 3.25 reales for most of the years under study here. Challú and Gómez-Galvarriato, 'Mexico's Real Wages', 97. For the historical exchange rate, see Instituto Nacional de Estadística, Geografía e Informática, *Estadísticas históricas de México*, 884, table 20.6.
36 Szmrecsanyi and Topik, 'Business History', 179. See also Gibson, ed., *Black Legend*; Kagan, *Spain in America*.
37 Coatsworth, 'Obstacles to Economic Growth', 94, 100. See also Coatsworth, 'Inequality, Institutions', 557–559.
38 Dye, 'Institutional Framework'.
39 Until this institutional revolution, Coatsworth writes, late colonial and early republican elites 'had no choice but to accept a legal system that failed to define property rights clearly or to provide an efficient court system to enforce them'. Coatsworth, 'Inequality, Institutions', 557.
40 The scholarship on New Institutional Economics and the institutional model of economic history is extensive; for an overview, see Dye, 'Institutional Framework'.
41 Scholars of other regions have challenged similar 'significant misconceptions' about economic and legal institutions. Despite it being 'generally assumed that property rights in China were ill defined and not enforced by the state', for example, scholars of late imperial China have shown that property rights did exist in town and country and that they are recorded in vast quantities of contracts lodged in archives. Zelin et al., 'Introduction', 2. See also Austin, 'African Economic Development'. On the persistence of the institutional deficiency narrative, see, for example, Ho, 'Endogenous Theory'.
42 The collection has probably not attracted much attention because the books are catalogued only by magistrate and year, with no information about cases.

Notes to pages 29–33

The exception is some of the books from the 1850s, for which the catalogue provides short summaries of individual cases. The most helpful analyses of this archive are Linda Arnold's essays, cited above in note 4.

43 Castillo Hernández, 'Ley y el honor'; Teitelbaum, 'Sectores populares'.
44 Flores Flores, *Ciudad judicial*, 21–75. In another publication, Flores Flores includes *juicios verbales* and *concilitorios* in her study of judicial institutions and administrative structures. Flores Flores, *Justicia criminal ordinaria*.
45 My approach is closest to Laura Shelton's brief analysis of *juicios verbales* to underscore the importance of petty credit for workers, farmers, and artisans in early republican Sonora. Shelton, *For Tranquillity and Order*, 104–105.
46 My arguments about the historiographical assumptions about deficient legal institutions are indebted to conversations with Christopher Albi, Silvia Arrom, and Timothy James at the Conference on Latin American History panel 'Legal History, Capitalism, and Economic Life: New Research from Mexico', Chicago, January 2019.
47 Flores Flores, *Ciudad judicial*, 43.
48 Flores Flores, *Ciudad judicial*, 13, 14.
49 Scardaville, 'Crime and the Urban Poor'; Scardaville, '(Hapsburg) Law and (Bourbon) Order'.
50 The nineteenth-century legal historiography is extensive. On criminal cases (*justicia ordinaria criminal*), see Piccato, *City of Suspects*; Speckman Guerra, *Crimen y castigo*. On legislation and administrative structures, see Flores Flores, *Justicia criminal ordinaria*; López González, *Organización para la administración*. There is less scholarship on civil conflicts (*justicia ordinaria civil*), although this is changing among historians of the early nineteenth century. For example, Schaefer examines civil and criminal litigation to analyse popular legal culture and how ordinary people used the language of equality, rights, and freedoms in their commonplace conflicts. Schaefer, *Liberalism as Utopia*. The scholarship that uses the Mexico City *juicios verbales* is discussed in the text with citation provided. See, in addition, Mijangos y González's historiography essay *El nuevo pasado jurídico mexicano*.
51 Table 1.4 should be considered a general sketch, as population estimates by leading demographic historians vary considerably. See Ariel Rodríguez Kuri's discussion of the difficulty with population estimates in *Experiencia olvidada*, 82–91. While the details vary depending on the population estimate, the general picture is one of growing numbers of *juicios verbales*. The spikes and dips are discussed in the final section of this chapter.
52 Flores Flores, *Ciudad judicial*, 54–75.
53 On the notary public, see Burns, *Into the Archive*; Levy, *Making of the Market*. On the scholarship using bankruptcy court records and wealthy litigants, see, for example, Adelman *Republic of Capital*; Baskes, *Staying Afloat*; Chowning, *Wealth and Power*.
54 Of the 293 cases involving disputed cases (and for which there is also information on resolutions), 160 (54.6 per cent) resulted in repayment plans. Of the 621 undisputed cases (and for which there is also information on resolutions), 516 (83.1 per cent) resulted in repayment plans. A chi-squared test (x^2test)

found the observed difference in proportions (54.6 versus 83.1) to be statistically significant. See the Introduction for more on the method used. Hereafter, x^2test results (and Fisher's exact test results) will be abbreviated to telegraph essential information; subsequent notes will give a shortform version of the fuller format provided here, similar to shortform archival references.
55 A t-test found a significant means difference. There is no mention of interest on the debt; amortisation here means the period of time to full repayment.
56 Of 293 total disputed cases that also give information on postponement, 59 were postponed (20.1 per cent); of 621 total undisputed cases, 21 were postponed (3.4 per cent). A x^2test found a significant proportion difference.
57 See Covarrubias, *Moneda de cobre*; Romano, *Moneda, seudomonedas y circulación monetaria*. One study on the late colony has challenged the traditional view of low currency supply, showing instead active monetary circulation in Mexico City with a high volume of small currency used daily; see Quiroz, 'Moneda menuda en la circulación monetaria'.
58 These studies often emerge through a focus on the pivotal role played by notaries. See Hoffman, Postel-Vinay, and Rosenthal, for example, on notaries as credit brokers in eighteenth- and nineteenth-century Paris, and Levy on notaries in later nineteenth-century Yucatán. Hoffman et al., 'Information and Economic History'; Hoffman et al., 'Private Credit Markets'; Levy, *Making of the Market*.
59 Escriche, *Diccionario razonado*, sv. '*obligación de dar*'; Rael Academia Española (RAE), *Diccionario de la lengua española*, sv. '*obligación*'. To maintain the specificity of each instrument, and because not all have direct translations, I use the Spanish terms throughout, with a gloss at first mention.
60 AHCDMX AJ, vol. 4476, exp. 1, ff. 66r–66v, 9 December 1842.
61 The minimum number of days to full repayment of instalments is 7.5 days; the maximum is 1,980 days; and the average number is 249.2 days. In terms of frequency distribution, 25 per cent of cases required 87.5 days or fewer; 75 per cent of cases required 330.6 days or fewer.
62 It is possible that the instrument here was a *carta de crédito* (instruments that were payable to the bearer). I think it is more likely to be a *carta* because these documents appear throughout the sample and there is no mention of a *carta de crédito*. Escriche, *Diccionario razonado*, svv. '*carta*': '*carta de crédito*', '*instrumento público*'.
63 AHCDMX AJ, vol. 2868, exp. 1, ff. 92v–92r, 10 August 1831.
64 AHCDMX AJ, vol. 4499, exp. 1, ff. 22v–22r, 11 April 1844.
65 AHCDMX AJ, vol. 2857, exp. 1, ff. 63v–64v, 22 October 1830.
66 There is a weak, positive, statistically significant correlation between a credit instrument being involved and a case being postponed.
67 The mean amount owed in cases involving a credit instrument is 45.2 pesos (98 cases). The mean amount owed in cases not involving a credit instrument is 34.1 pesos (701 cases). A t-test found that observed differences in means are not statistically significant. Hereafter, results from t-tests will be abbreviated.
68 A *pagaré a la orden* was issued 'to order'. Escriche, *Diccionario razonado*, svv. '*pagaré*', '*pagaré a la orden*'.
69 AHCDMX AJ, vol. 2948, exp. 1, f. 186v, 2 May 1856.

Notes to pages 37–40   229

70 The reason is given in 837 cases of the 934 cases, with 97 missing values.
71 Of 220 total rent cases that also give information on contestation, 36 were disputed (16.4 per cent); of 614 total non-rent cases, 245 were disputed (39.9 per cent). A x^2test found a significant proportion difference.
72 Calderón Fernández, 'Serie de precios', 33–40; Scardaville, 'Crime and the Urban Poor', 60, 156; von Wobeser, *Crédito eclesiástico*, 79–81.
73 Of 217 total rent cases that also give information on outcome, 183 resulted in repayment plans (84.3 per cent); of 610 total non-rent cases, 415 resulted in repayment plans (68 per cent). A x^2test found a significant proportion difference.
74 Rent cases have a mean amortisation period of 339.2 days (82 cases); non-rent cases have mean amortisation period of 187.9 days (143 cases). A t-test found a significant means difference.
75 AHCDMX AJ, vol. 2765, exp. 1, ff. 18r–19r, 6 November 1820.
76 AHCDMX AJ, vol. 2765 bis., exp. 2, ff. 90v–91v, 3 October 1814.
77 Of 119 total cases with female defendants that also give information on reason, 51 stem from rent reasons (42.9 per cent); of 670 total cases with male defendants, 135 stem from rent reasons (20.1 per cent). A x^2test found a significant proportion difference.
78 AHCDMX AJ, vol. 4484, exp. 1, ff. 11r–12v, 18 October 1843.
79 The gendered dynamics visible within the *juicios verbales* fit with the findings of other scholars who have analysed gender and the city's economy. Marie Francois has analysed the women who depended on pawning to run economically vulnerable middle-class households. Carmen Ramos Escandón describes how the transformation of textiles with the introduction of industrialised spinning and later weaving displaced poor women workers and artisans. Francois, *Culture of Everyday Credit*; Ramos Escandón, *Industrialización, género*.
80 Of 142 total cases with female plaintiffs that also give information on defendant gender, 37 have a female defendant (26.1 per cent); of 738 total cases with a male plaintiff, 92 have a female defendant (12.5 per cent). A x^2test found a significant proportion difference.
81 See, for example, for Latin America, Herzog, *Administración como un fenómeno*; Owensby, *Empire of Law*; Premo, *Enlightenment on Trial*.
82 These models are based on the full sample (n=998). Of 177 total cases with female plaintiffs that also give information on outcome, 33 have an outcome of 'no or light penalty' (18.6 per cent); of 753 total cases with a male plaintiffs, 41 have an outcome of 'no or light penalty' (5.4 per cent). A x^2test found a significant proportion difference. Of 150 total cases with female defendants that also give information on outcome, 22 have an outcome of 'no or light penalty' (14.7 per cent); of 780 total cases with male defendants, 52 have an outcome of 'no or light penalty' (6.7 per cent). A x^2test found a significant proportion difference.
83 These models are based on the subset of the sample (n=934). Of 140 total cases with female plaintiffs that also give information on outcome, 95 have an outcome of a repayment plan (67.9 per cent); of 728 total cases with male plaintiffs, 547 have an outcome of a repayment plan (75.1 per cent). A x^2test did not find a significant proportion difference. Of 140 total cases with female

plaintiffs that also give information on outcome, 6 have an outcome of 'no or light penalty' (4.3 per cent); of 728 total cases with male plaintiffs, 20 have an outcome of 'no or light penalty' (2.7 per cent). A Fisher's exact test (FET) did not find a significant proportion difference. Of 140 total cases with female plaintiffs that also give information on outcome, 11 had the outcome postponed (7.9 per cent); of 728 total cases with male plaintiffs, 63 had the outcome postponed (8.7 per cent). A x^2 test did not find a significant proportion difference. There was one exception when looking at the relationships in the decade clusters. From 1833 to 1842, magistrates were uninclined to reward women plaintiffs with repayment plans: of 20 total cases with female plaintiffs, 11 have the outcome of a repayment plan (55 per cent); of 146 total cases with male plaintiffs, 121 have the outcome of a repayment plan (82.9 per cent). An FET found a significant proportion difference. Whether something might have been different during these years remains an open question; I do not have enough observations to further investigate.

84 These models are based on the subset of the sample (n=934). Of 128 total cases with female defendants that also give information on outcome, 95 have the outcome of a repayment plan (74.2 per cent); of 740 total cases with male defendants, 547 have the outcome of a repayment plan (73.9 per cent). A x^2 test did not find a significant proportion difference. Of 128 total cases with female defendants that also give information on outcome, 3 have an outcome of 'no or light penalty' (2.3 per cent); of 740 total cases with male defendants, 23 have an outcome of 'no or light penalty' (3.1 per cent). An FET did not find a significant proportion difference. Of 128 total cases with female defendants that also give information on outcome, 7 had the outcome postponed (5.5 per cent); of 740 total cases with male defendants, 67 had the outcome postponed (9.1 per cent). A x^2 test did not find a significant proportion difference.

85 I discuss the decision in more detail and present some examples from the omitted cases, in Walker, 'Everyday Economic Justice'.

86 Male plaintiffs have a mean amount owed of 35.6 pesos (641 cases); female plaintiffs have a mean amount owed of 33.1 pesos (118 cases). A t-test did not find a significant means difference. Male defendants have a mean amount owed of 36.1 pesos (681 cases); female defendants have a mean amount owed of 32 pesos (115 cases). A t-test did not find a significant means difference. This is true for the entire sample and for the year and decade clusters (when there were enough observations to run models), with the following exception: in the 1850s, female defendants are generally associated with lower amounts than their male counterparts. Because the collection ends in 1863, it is unknown if this is the beginning of a new trend whereby women defendants are involved in disputes over lower amounts.

87 Of 37 total cases with entity plaintiffs that also give information about reasons, 30 stem from rent reasons (81.1 per cent); of 793 total cases with person plaintiffs, 187 stem from rent reasons (23.6 per cent). A x^2 test found a significant proportion difference.

88 The process of confiscating property began in the colonial twilight but was fitful until the major liberal reforms in 1856. Bazant, *Alienation of Church Wealth*.

89 There were no significant relationships found between entity plaintiffs (compared with men and women plaintiffs together) and the other variables. Tests run included: FETs and x^2 tests for entity plaintiffs and outcomes; t-tests for entity plaintiffs and amounts; and FETs and x^2 tests for entity plaintiffs and the other reasons. No statistical significance was found.
90 Of 37 total cases with entity plaintiffs that also give information about contestation, 6 are disputed (16.2 per cent); of 880 total cases with person plaintiffs, 290 are disputed (33 per cent). A x^2 test found a significant proportion difference.
91 AHCDMX AJ, vol. 2769, exp. 1, f. 49r, 12 June 1823.
92 AHCDMX AJ, vol. 4729, exp. 1, ff. 80f–81f (magistrate unnamed), 10 June 1844.
93 Buchenau, *Tools of Progress*; Galindo Rodriguéz, *Ethnic Entrepreneurs*; Vinson, *Before Mestizaje*.
94 Burns, *Into the Archive*, 2.
95 Scardaville, 'Justice by Paperwork'.
96 Flores Flores, *Ciudad judicial*, 55.
97 The analysis of magistrates is based on a subset of the eleven magistrates with twenty or more cases (from the 934 subset).
98 The mean amounts owed in cases before the eleven magistrates range from 25.6 pesos to 45.2 pesos. An analysis of variance shows that the differences between means are not statistically significant.
99 There are no significant differences found in the proportion of male and female plaintiffs who appeared before the magistrates (each of the eleven magistrates compared with all the other magistrates). This result is for the subset (n=934). In the full sample (n=998), magistrate Jacinto Flores stood out from the others: he saw a significantly higher proportion of female plaintiffs; he heard a significantly higher proportion of cases of personal and marital conflict; and he issued a significantly higher proportion of light or no penalties. With regards to variables that were not obviously related to marital or personal conflicts, such as whether a *juicio verbal* involved a credit instrument or a conflict over rent, Flores was not significantly different from the other magistrates. Flores ran a marriage court. Many of Flores's records were part of the 64 *injurias leves* conflicts omitted from the subset (n=934). His cases are in AHCDMX AJ, vol. 2767 VI.
100 Mean amortisation is not significantly different between the eleven magistrates (each magistrate compared with all the others subsumed into one group).
101 Teitelbaum, 'Sectores populares', 1248–1250.
102 Payno, *Fistol del diablo*, vol. 1 (the episode is in chapter 11 and the quote on p. 166).
103 Payno, *Fistol del diablo*, quote on p. 159.
104 Payno, *Fistol del diablo*, quote on p. 172.
105 Palti, 'Narrar lo inenarrable', 11–13, quote on p. 12. On Payno, see also Rosa, 'Finance and Literature'. On the *Fistol del Diablo*, see also Sandoval, 'Figura del diablo'.
106 James, 'Lay Magistrates', 5.

107 Flores Flores, *Ciudad Judicial*, 48–49.
108 *Fiadores* were required in 9.3 per cent of cases (87); garnishment of wages was ordered in 3.6 per cent (34).
109 Cases were repeat *juicios verbales* in 10.5 per cent of 932 cases, with two missing values.
110 O'Hara, *History of the Future*, 4.
111 Adelman, ed., *Colonial Legacies*, quotes on pp. ix, 1.
112 For early New Spain, Borah's *Justice by Insurance* looks at summary justice for indigenous claimants. Most of the colonial legal historiography focuses on first-instance disputes, which are the topic of Chapter 2. See Yannakakis, *Since Time Immemorial*; Premo and Yannakakis, 'Court of Sticks and Branches'.
113 Scardaville, 'Crime and the Urban Poor'. For a judicial history on some of these *libros de reos* focusing on alcohol crimes, sex crimes, robbery, and homicide, see also Sánchez-Arcilla Bernal, *Jueces, criminalidad*.
114 Scardaville describes how the 1798 breakdown is representative: '[T]he overall distribution of arrests remained relatively similar.' His debt data is therefore assumed to be about 155 debt cases for 1798 and about 255 debt cases for all years. Scardaville, 'Crime and the Urban Poor', data from tables 6, 7, 8 on pp. 38–40, quote on p. 13.
115 Scardaville, 'Crime and the Urban Poor', 130–138, tables 39, 41, 49, 51, 40, 44. Scardaville analyses the demographic details of property crimes in chapter 3.
116 Scardaville, 'Crime and the Urban Poor', especially chapter 6, quote on p. 309, on speed 312–313, on less severe sentences 276.
117 Scardaville, '(Hapsburg) Law and (Bourbon) Order'.
118 Scardaville, 'Crime and the Urban Poor', 274. Bourbon reformers were especially concerned with drunkenness, thus the preponderance of related crimes in the books (231).
119 Scardaville, '(Hapsburg) Law and (Bourbon) Order', 513–515.
120 Scardaville, '(Hapsburg) Law and (Bourbon) Order', 514.
121 Scardaville, '(Hapsburg) Law and (Bourbon) Order', 513
122 Scardaville draws on Colin MacLachlan's philosophical matrix in *Spain's Empire*.
123 For review of the extensive scholarship, see Yannakakis, 'Indigenous People and Legal Culture'.
124 William Taylor describes how some people preferred the Inquisition to crown courts for this reason. Taylor, *Fugitive Freedom*, 18–19. Sylvia Sellers-García describes a 'policing wave' in late colonial Guatemala City. Sellers-García, 'Walking While Indian'.
125 A larger sample might confirm some of my findings and revise others. This is the first attempt to analyse Mexico City's small claims collection for all years. Future researchers would do a great service by collecting more data for a more robust sample. A larger sample would allow for more analysis in the five-year and decade clusters. This work would be ideally undertaken by a team of researchers: because the city archive does not permit photographs, the records must be transcribed in situ, which puts stress on the budgets of most historians.

Notes to pages 49–56   233

126 On the shift from elected to appointed magistrates, see Arnold, 'Juicios verbales y conciliatorios', 914–916; James, 'Lay Magistrates', 3–4.
127 Adelman, 'Liberalism and Constitutionalism', 511–512.
128 In addition to Guerra's study of New Spain, discussed above, see scholarship on individualism by historians of the USA. Scholars have studied manifestations of individualism from the daguerreotype to the census. See, especially, Bouk, 'History and Political Economy'; also Hodes, 'Fractions and Fictions'; Masur, 'Age of the First Person Singular'.
129 Hilda Sábato describes how earlier generations of scholars 'minimized' the relevance of elections and how these decades had previously been characterised as a period of turbulent and corrupt *caudillo* rule. See Sábato, *Republics of the New World*, 51.
130 See, for example, Guardino, *Time of Liberty*; Mallon, *Peasant and Nation*.
131 See, for example, Premo, *Enlightenment on Trial*; Schaefer, *Liberalism as Utopia*.
132 The *juicios verbales* connect to a legal historiography that approaches law and legal categories 'in action' (in addition to 'on the books') in the colonial and national eras: for example, Yannakakis's examination of Native custom in New Spain forged through social practice from below; Herzog's analysis of citizenship forged through the claims of merchants in colonial Quito; and Fallaw and Nugent's contrasting of formal and lived citizenship in Mexico and Peru after 1850. Yannakakis, *Since Time Immemorial*; Herzog, *Defining Nations*; Fallaw and Nugent, eds, *State Formation in the Liberal Era*.
133 Herzog uncovers the parameters of citizenship in her study of how merchants claimed *vecindad* and *naturaleza* in colonial Quito. Herzog, *Defining Nations*; Herzog, 'Merchants and Citizens'.

Chapter 2

1 'Juan Cortázar contra Hilario Jiménez Providencia Precautoria', 21 January 1865, Archivo General de la Nación (AGN), Tribunal Superior de Justicia del Distrito Federal (TSJDF), *caja* (c.) 399. If the mules were worth less than 100 pesos, the matter might have found its way to a *juicio verbal*. Otherwise, given the 250 peso debt, it would likely have become a *juicio conciliatorio*. These proceedings are the subject of Chapter 1.
2 *Siete Partidas*, Partida 5, 'Introduction', 1007. I am using Burns's edition, which uses Scott's translation; the code is discussed in detail in the final section.
3 Aristotle, *Rhetoric* (trans. Roberts, ed. Barnes), 2192.
4 Some of the people and businesses examined below, no doubt, were poorer or wealthier than others and could be described with different analytical terms. I am not positing a clear sociological boundary, but rather advancing a capacious category of small and medium enterprise.
5 *Novísima Recopilación*, Book 11, Title 31, Law 19, p. 295. This is discussed in detail in the final section.

6   *Providencias precautorias* were different from *embargos*, which a plaintiff could request once they had initiated civil litigation. A plaintiff could request a *providencia precautoria* at the same time that they initiated civil litigation. My description of the *providencias precautorias* is based on *Código de Procedimientos Civiles para el Distrito Federal y Territorio de la Baja California*, Chapter V, Articles 479–515 (hereafter *Código Procedimientos Civiles DF y BC*). The Civil Procedure Code was companion to the 1870 Civil Code that is analysed in the final section of the chapter. See also Rodríguez de San Miguel and Galván Rivera, *Curia Filípica Mexicana*, 182–187.
7   *Código procedimientos civiles DF y BC* [1872], Articles 479, 483.
8   Overview based on *Código procedimientos civiles DF y BC* [1872], Chapter V, Articles 479–515.
9   Other scholars have examined the city's changing judicial structure: legislators created new *juzgados*, suppressed or renamed others, and revised the responsibilities of different jurisdictions (for example, some *juzgados* assumed policing duties), and so on. For detailed analysis of these changes, see Flores Flores, *Justicia criminal ordinaria*.
10 The reality was not quite so neat, as there was occasional overlap in jurisdiction between the *Tribunal Superior* and the *Suprema Corte*. See Mijangos y González, *Historia mínima*, especially chapter 1.
11 I did my research in 2013 and 2014. At that time, researchers could request documents by year and were given the corresponding boxes of documents.
12 I worked with Lance Ingwersen. I was researching cases about unpaid debts, and he was researching cases related to theatres. My cases included *providencias precautorias*, *embargos*, and *tercerías*. Because there were far fewer theatre cases, we chose six years with the most promising leads for theatres. Dividing the boxes, we photographed the related files. The catalogue, while generally accurate, was incomplete (for all years, we found many of the theatre files listed in the catalogue, but we also found additional theatre files that were not listed or where the listing was inaccurate or incomplete in the catalogue). Because of the overwhelming number of conflicts over unpaid debts, we stopped going through the boxes for any given year once we had found the theatre cases that we were seeking. My sample, therefore, was determined by the theatre research. This method was the most efficient strategy to get a potentially random sample: there is no reason to believe that any connection exists between theatres (in comparison to other businesses) and unpaid debts. The TSJDF collection has tremendous offerings, especially for teams of researchers; with time and funds, more robust samples could be examined. Among the possibilities, the collection has many '*sobre pesos*' conflicts that promise another entry point into economic life and conflict. On this archive, see also Santiago Aparicio and García González, 'Guerra de guerrillas', especially 185–187.
13 In addition, litigiousness could be appraised across the late colonial and early national divide to gauge trends. Future research could also use debt litigation to approximate the size of the credit market, which is not the topic of this book. Craig Muldrew has shown, for early modern England, a dynamic whereby expanding credit markets led to rising debt litigation.

My provisional findings suggest that a similar dynamic existed in Mexico. Muldrew, *Economy of Obligation*.
14 See note 12.
15 See Antonio García Cubas's estimates in Instituto Nacional de Estadística, Geografía e Informática, *Estadísticas históricas de México*, 1990, vol. 1, p. 24.
16 I counted approximately 100 *providencias precautorias* from 1850 to 1859; around 550 in the 1860s; around 380 in the 1870s; and around 360 in the 1880s.
17 I counted approximately 100 *concursos* from 1850 to 1859; around 220 in the 1860s; around 300 in the 1870s; and around 400 in the 1880s.
18 I counted approximately 40 *cesiones* from 1850 to 1859; around 100 in the 1860s; around 135 in the 1870s; and around 130 in the 1880s.
19 I counted approximately 65 *tercerías* from 1850 to 1859; around 350 in the 1860s; around 600 in the 1870s; and around 1,900 in the 1880s.
20 I estimated the size of the collection by counting the number of pages in the catalogue and estimating 40 cases per page. I counted approximately 9,400 cases from 1850 to 1859; around 33,400 in the 1860s; around 51,800 in the 1870s; and around 129,000 in the 1880s. Another type of economic litigation gives further context, the '*sobre pesos*' and '*pesos*' cases. The TSJDF boxes hold vast numbers of these, and they also increase dramatically. There were approximately 2,500 from 1850–1859; around 14,000 in the 1860s; around 27,000 in the 1870s; and around 50,000 in the 1880s. These cases include many instances of unpaid debts among all sorts of other economic troubles awaiting future researchers.
21 I relied entirely on the TSJDF catalogue, which is incomplete and not always accurate, and I simply counted the number of cases listed by decade. Given the numbers of *providencias precautorias* suggested in the catalogue, reviewing each file would be feasible for a team of researchers.
22 Kuntz Ficker, 'Introducción', 21; Kuntz Ficker, 'De las reformas liberales a la gran depression', 16–17, quote on p. 17.
23 The Porfiriato is one of the most studied periods in Mexican economic history. See Kuntz Ficker's analysis in 'De las reformas liberales a la gran depression'.
24 Beatty, *Technology*, 3–8, quote on p. 3. Beatty writes that the technologies 'were intimately linked to the broader needs, ambitions, dreams and frustrations of Mexicans across the social spectrum' (7).
25 Sánchez Santiró, 'Población de la Ciudad de México', 277–278, quote on p. 297.
26 Bleynat, *Vendors' Capitalism*, 13–14.
27 Kuntz Ficker, 'De las reformas liberales a la gran depresión', 316.
28 Kuntz Flicker emphasises that this institutional change created the legal conditions for modern economic activity, even if the legal framework did not materialise until the Restored Republic. Kuntz Ficker, 'De las reformas liberales a la gran depresión', 311–312, quote on p. 311.
29 For an overview of the many elements of this transformation, see Kuntz Ficker, 'De las reformas liberales a la gran depresión', especially 317–334.
30 Harris, 'Glossary', xli.
31 Harris, 'Glossary', xli.

32 Tönnies, *Community and Civil Society*, 52.
33 These sociological constructions suggest ways to interpret conflicts examined in this chapter, but with important methodological limitations: there is always the danger of reducing historical phenomena to abstract categories. These concepts are helpful tools alongside others, such as Vickers' analytical categories described below in note 54.
34 Tönnies, *Community and Civil Society*, 19; Harris, 'General Introduction', xi.
35 The *providencias precautorias* capture the liminality better than the *juicios verbales*, in part as the result of different primary sources. As part of first-instance litigation, the *providencias precautorias* are longer documents with much more detail offering more insight into how people trusted each other.
36 Banerjee et al. define a gossip as a person who is a 'good diffuser[s] of information'. They distinguish between gossip and rumour: 'We use the term "gossip" to refer to the spreading of information about particular people. Our diffusion process is focused on basic information that is not subject to the biases or manipulations that might accompany some "rumors".' Banerjee et al., 'Using Gossips to Spread Information', 3, fn5.
37 Banerjee, 'Economics of Rumours', 309. Economists examine the function of gossip using methods from game theory to field experiments, with the goal of understanding decision-making, optimising behaviour, market volatility, and reputation management.
38 See, for example, White, 'Telling More'.
39 On the Latin Americanist historiography, see, most recently, the contributions to Foss et al., eds, 'Interpretative Challenges'. Elsewhere, I have examined the economic and political function of rumours in the 1970s. Walker, *Waking from the Dream*, especially 51–54.
40 Piccato, *Tyranny of Opinion*, 163–172. Piccato also describes an in-between period, from the late colonial and early national romantic ideas about individual self-esteem.
41 In their literature review, Francesca Giardini and Rafael Wittek describe strategic behaviour as one of six characteristics of gossip and reputation: 'both are relational and triadic, morally laden, multifunctional, and context-dependent social phenomena that have an evolutionary base and are subject to strategic behaviour'. Giardini and Wittek, 'Introduction: Gossip and Reputation', 1. For their discussion of reputation mechanisms, see p. 11.
42 'Navarro Ángel Apoderado de Miguel P. Gallardo contra Antonio Picazo. Providencia Precautoria', 9 November 1878, AGN, TSJDF, c. 642.
43 Of the 40 cases that involve witnesses, 80 per cent (32) involve only witnesses for the plaintiffs, 15 per cent (6) involve only witnesses for the defendants, and in 5 per cent (2) witnesses appeared for both the plaintiffs and the defendants.
44 Of the 85 cases involving male plaintiffs and for which there is also information on witnesses, 34 of the cases (40 per cent) involve a witness. Of the 9 cases involving female plaintiffs and for which there is also information on witnesses, 6 of the cases (66.7 per cent) involve a witness. A Fisher's exact test (FET) found that the observed difference in proportions (40 versus 66.7) is not statistically significant. See the Introduction for more on the method used. Hereafter, FET results (and chi-squared tests) will be abbreviated to telegraph

essential information; subsequent notes will give a shortform version of the fuller format provided here, similar to shortform archival references. Of the 88 total cases with a male defendant, 35 have witnesses (39.8 per cent); of the 5 total cases with a female defendant, 3 have witnesses (60 per cent). An FET did not find a significant proportion difference. Further, an FET did not find a significant proportion difference between litigant gender and cases with witnesses for the plaintiff. Likewise, an FET did not find a significant proportion difference found between litigant gender and cases with witnesses for the defendant.

45 The mean amount owed in cases involving a witness is 459.7 pesos (33 cases); the mean amount owed in cases not involving a witness is 289.2 pesos (43 cases). This observed difference in means is not statistically significant (t-test). However, when using the non-parametric Mann-Whitney U test (MW-U test), which replaces values by ranks, a significant difference emerges: cases with witnesses were associated with higher amounts than cases not involving witnesses. This difference is statistically significant. If the distributions of amounts owed between cases with and without witnesses are identical, it could be expected that the mean ranks would be similar. The relatively big difference in ranks suggests that the two distributions are different and that the observed higher amounts among cases with witnesses are not due to random variation. Hereafter, results from t-tests and MW-U tests will be abbreviated.

46 Cases with witnesses for the plaintiff have a mean amount owed of 497.8 pesos (28 cases); cases without witnesses for the plaintiff have a mean amount owed of 284.7 (48 cases). A t-test did not find a significant means difference, but an MW-U test found that cases with witnesses for the plaintiff are significantly associated with higher amounts. Cases with witnesses for the defendant have a mean amount owed of 221 pesos (7 cases); cases without witnesses for the defendant have a mean amount owed of 377.6 pesos (69 cases). A t-test did not find significant means difference; likewise, an MW-U test did not find significant difference in mean ranks.

47 Of 34 total cases with witnesses present that also give information on outcome, 31 were approved (91.2 per cent); of 53 total cases with witnesses not present, 50 were approved (94.3 per cent). An FET did not find a significant proportion difference. Of 29 total cases with witnesses for the plaintiff present, 27 were approved (93.1 per cent); of 58 total cases with no witnesses for the plaintiff, 54 were approved (93.1 per cent). An FET did not find a significant proportion difference. Of 6 total cases with witnesses for the defendant present, 5 were approved (83.3 per cent); of 81 total cases with no witnesses for the defendant, 76 were approved (93.8 per cent). An FET did not find a significant proportion difference.

48 Muldrew, *Economy of Obligation*.

49 'Providencia Precautoria Solicitada por Mónica Sánchez contra Juan Castro', 30 October 1865, AGN, TSJDF, c. 399.

50 'Ángel González contra Florencio Hernández. Providencia Precautoria', 28 January 1878, AGN, TSJDF, c. 652.

51 Vickers, 'Errors Expected', 1055.

52 'Adam Francisco Pidiendo Providencia Precautoria contra Doña Soledad Montes', 18 November 1878, AGN, TSJDF, c. 645.

53 Beatty, *Technology*, 23.
54 In his history of economic relationships in early New Hampshire, Daniel Vickers describes how people operated in two modes: what he called monetary and non-monetary exchange. He also describes these as formal and informal economies, as individualist and communal dimensions, as political economy and moral economy, and as inside and outside the market. Vickers, 'Errors Expected', especially 1035, 1038, 1055.
55 From considering uncertainty to gauging risk, other scholars have shown a slow shift in economic relations from the conquest to independence. On changing ideas about risk and risk management in the colonial twilight, see Mathew O'Hara's study of usury and Jeremy Baskes's analysis of maritime insurance. Baskes, *Staying Afloat*; O'Hara, *History of the Future*. The distinction between risk and uncertainty is part of the history of insurance. Dan Bouk, for example, describes the early life insurance industry in the USA as having 'the sorts of certainty that could be grasped' in tension with 'the hopelessness of forecasting' in relation to an individual life and sudden, unexpected death. Bouk, *How Our Days Became Numbered*, 16–17. For a helpful discussion of risk and uncertainty, see Hansson, 'Risk', 1–5. For a literary approach, see the analysis of suspense and risk in eighteenth- and nineteenth-century American literature in Burnham, *Transoceanic America*.
56 The judges are not considered in the statistical analysis. The nature of both the archive and the sampling strategy does not allow for many tests (compared, for example, with the tests run for the *juicios verbales* chapter). In the 97 cases, there are 47 judges, only 3 of whom heard more than 5 cases.
57 Because of low numbers of observations, very few logistic and linear regressions were possible, and I decided not to include those results in the chapter. See the Introduction for more on method.
58 There are six unknown or missing values for plaintiff gender.
59 There are eight unknown or missing values for defendant gender.
60 The reason is given in all of the 97 cases. The other reasons are scattershot, such as two disputes over embargos and one agricultural conflict.
61 Amount owed is known in 76 of the 97 cases, with 21 missing values.
62 I limited the examples to assets valued over 100 pesos to complement the information in Table 1.3 in Chapter 1, which overviews values under 100 pesos between 1813 and 1861.
63 'Juan Dupeux Pidiendo una Providencia Provisional y Precautoria contra D. Romero Acho', 1 November 1861, AGN, TSJDF, c. 350.
64 Notably, the litigants did not fight over that amount; rather, the buyer of the *zapatería* worried about the transfer of the property and requested that equipment and furniture be sequestered. The file does not include a description of which items would be sequestered. The value of the *zapatería*, therefore, helps explain the value of a peso but does not constitute an observation for the 'amounts disputed' variable. (In the dataset, I coded the amount disputed as 'not available' for this case.)
65 Arrom, *Containing the Poor*, 269.
66 Arrom, *Containing the Poor*, 268.

67 The peso:dollar exchange rate ranged from 0.93:1.00 in 1860 to 1.10:1.00 in 1880. See Instituto Nacional de Estadística, Geografía e Informática, *Estadísticas históricas de México*, 884, table 20.6.
68 Cass Sunstein, among others, traces the origins of the precautionary principle to the concept of *vorsorgeprinzip* in 1970s German environmental policy. Sunstein, *Laws of Fear*, 16. See also Morris, ed., *Rethinking Risk*; Randall, *Risk and Precaution*.
69 While, to my knowledge, other historians have not used these petitions as a principal archival source, the *providencias precautorias* are not unusual or little known. See, for example, Aguilar Aguilar, 'Régimen legislativo y de propiedad'; Hernández Elizondo, 'Propietarios, especuladores y renta'.
70 Of 76 total cases with male plaintiffs that also give information on outcome, 70 were approved (92.1 per cent); of 8 total cases with female plaintiffs, 8 were approved (100 per cent). An FET did not find a significant proportion difference. Of 79 total cases with male defendants that also give information on outcome, 73 were approved (92.4 per cent); of 4 total cases with female defendants, 4 were approved (100 per cent). An FET did not find significant proportion difference.
71 Approved cases (63 cases) have a mean amount owed of 348.3 pesos; cases not approved (5 cases) have a mean amount owed of 378.7 pesos. A t-test did not find a significant means difference; likewise, an MW-U test did not find a significant difference in mean ranks.
72 Because of the number of different reasons, each reason was tested separately. For example, of 9 cases where rent was the reason that also give information about outcome, 8 were approved (88.9 per cent); of 78 total non-rent cases, 73 were approved (93.6 per cent). An FET did not find a significant proportion difference. FETs were performed for each reason and did not find significant relationships between any reasons and outcomes.
73 There might still be a pattern, of course, but either the tests did not pick up on it or I did not have the variables that would explain it. See the Introduction on the limitations of interpreting the results when tests did not find statistical significance.
74 'Providencia Precautoria Pedida por D. José Rufino, contra Las Sras. Peraire y Ca.', 7 January 1878, AGN, TSJDF, c. 646.
75 Diekmann and Przepiorka describe how the trust problem can be addressed by contract law, but 'taking legal action involves costs and uncertainties, so that problems arising between trading partners who are repeatedly engaged in business transactions are usually settled outside the courts'. Diekmann and Przepiorka, 'Trust and Reputation in Markets', 386–387.
76 'Providencia Precautoria. Luna Carlota contra Francisco Trejo', 27 May 1878, AGN, TSJDF, c. 639. A *libranza* could be a simple, non-transferable promise of payment. However, if it was between merchants, a transferable *libranza* could also function as a commercial bill similar to a *letra de cambio* (a uniform bill of exchange). The archival record for Luna v Trejo does not give further details about the *libranza*. See Escriche, *Diccionario razonado*, sv. '*libranza*'.

77 Of 85 total cases with male plaintiffs that also give information about outcome, 13 were withdrawn (15.3 per cent); of 9 total cases with female plaintiffs, 1 was withdrawn (11.1 per cent). An FET did not find a significant proportion difference. Of 88 total cases with male defendants that also give information about outcome, 88 were withdrawn (100 per cent); of 5 total cases with female defendants, 0 were withdrawn (0 per cent). An FET did not find a significant proportion difference. Withdrawn cases (12 cases) have a mean amount owed of 731.8 pesos; cases not withdrawn (64 cases) have a mean amount owed of 294.1 pesos. A t-test did not find a significant means difference; likewise, an MW-U test did not find a significant difference in mean ranks.
78 'Editorial: Providencias precautorias', *El Siglo Diez y Nueve*, 5 December 1869, 1.
79 'Editorial: Administración de justicia en el ramo civil', *El Monitor Constitucional*, 22 May 1877, 1.
80 Haber et al., *Politics of Property Rights*, definition on pp. 21–23. In this definition, which comes from the New Institutional Economics model of economic history, property rights are considered a bundle of rights. As Jonathan Ocko writes in his overview of different approaches to property rights, another scholarly tradition emphasises property rights as the exclusive dominion over a thing; this tradition might be traced to William Blackstone's 'sole and despotic dominion' (see also Rose on Blackstone, 'Cannons of Property Talk', quote on p. 1). The theoretical difference between these approaches, as Ocko writes, concerns the sacrality of property and the strength of private property. Ocko, 'Missing Metaphor', especially 184–190.
81 I am borrowing the term 'interface' from American legal scholarship about the relationship between property and contract rights. As Merges writes on anonymity and intimacy: '[O]nce parties cross the bridge between the anonymity of property and the intimacy of contract, property continues as an important presence in the relationship. Property ownership gives a contracting party many small additional options that become collectively valuable if the contract goes bad – if enforcement becomes necessary. And so the power of the state-backed property right continues to exert influence even after the legal actors are no longer strangers.' Merges, 'Transactional View of Property Rights', 1519–1520. See also Merrill and Smith, 'Property/Contract Interface'.
82 For an overview of this extensive historiography, see Adelman, 'Liberalism and Constitutionalism'; Sábato, *Republics of the New World*.
83 For a historiographical review, see Palacios, 'Introducción'.
84 Much of the scholarship addresses questions about the causes of the Mexican Revolution. For an overview, see Escobar Ohmstede and Butler, 'Introduction: Transitions and Closures'.
85 Aurora Gómez Galvarriato has shown how scholarly assumptions about vulnerable debtors can lead to misunderstandings about exploitation and resistance. Her research on company stores overturned a long-standing historiographical interpretation that company stores exploited workers through debt peonage; in contrast, she suggests that the stores offered credit on comparatively favourable terms. Gómez Galvarriato, 'Myth and Reality'.

86 I examine scholarly interpretations of institutional deficiency in Chapter 1; that argumentation is further extended in Walker, 'Everyday Economic Justice'. For an overview of the institutional scholarship, see Dye, 'Institutional Framework', especially 172–175.
87 Deliberate deception was, in part, a successful lie. I am following Arnold Isenberg's definition of lying: 'A lie is a statement made by one who does not believe it with the intention that someone else shall be led to believe it.' Isenberg, 'Deontology and the Ethics of Lying', quote on p. 248. My definition, however, does not require an actual lie (a literal falsehood); deliberate deception could be misleading. On this, I am following Stuart P. Green's framework: 'Fraud and the other misleading offenses do not require a literal falsehood.' Green, 'Lying, Misleading, and Falsely Denying', especially 182–201, quote on p. 186. See also Perez Zagorin's distinction between dissimulation and simulation and William Taylor's discussion of the importance of the latter in early modern Spain and New Spain. Zagorin, *Ways of Lying*, 3; Taylor, *Fugitive Freedom*, 13–15.
88 Zamora-Pierce, *Fraude*, 11 (the Penal Code's Fifth Chapter, concerning fraud, is reproduced on pp. 11–14).
89 Of 85 total cases with male plaintiffs that also give information about deception, 21 involve deception (24.7 per cent); of 9 total cases with female plaintiffs, 2 involve deception (22.2 per cent). An FET did not find a significant proportion difference. Of 88 total cases with male defendants that also give information about deception, 22 involve deception (25 per cent); of 5 total cases with female plaintiffs, 2 involve deception (40 per cent). An FET did not find a significant proportion difference.
90 Cases with deliberate deception have a mean amount owed of 391.9 pesos (18 cases); cases with no deliberate deception have a mean amount owed of 354.3 pesos (58 cases). A t-test did not find a significant means difference; likewise, an MW-U test did not find a significant difference in mean ranks.
91 Regarding reasons and deliberate deception, each reason was tested separately. For example, of the 11 cases with rent reasons that also give information about deception, 2 involve deception (18.2 per cent); of the 86 cases with no rent reason, 22 involve deception (25.6 per cent). An FET did not find a significant proportion difference. FETs were performed for each reason and did not find significant relationships between the reasons and deliberate deception. Of 23 total cases with deliberate deception, 22 were approved (95.7 per cent); of 64 total cases with no deliberate deception, 59 were approved (92.2 per cent). An FET did not find a significant proportion difference.
92 'Vicente Arnaiz Solicitando una Providencia Precautoria contra Manuel Carrera', 26 October 1861, AGN, TSJDF, c. 348.
93 Groebner, *Who are You?*
94 Groebner emphasises connections between the early modern period and the present, such as between identity fraud by early modern imposters and identity theft by twenty-first-century hackers. In contrast, when looking only at the relationship between debtors and creditors, I see a substantive change in the late nineteenth century with new technologies to surveil debtors (the topic of Chapter 3). Groebner, *Who are You?*, 241.

95 Escriche's definition is as follows: 'the opposition made by a third party, that is presented in a lawsuit filed by two or more litigants, either contributing to the right of one of them, or deducting their own with the exclusion of others.' Escriche, *Diccionario razonado*, sv. *'Tercería'*. Most civil and commercial codes until the nineteenth century address *tercerías* with overall continuity. See *Novísima Recopilación*, Book 11, Title 28, Laws 16 and 17; Romero Gil, *Código de procedimientos*, Articles 646–652; *Código de Comercio de México*, Articles 1002–1010; *Código Procedimientos Civiles DF y BC*, Articles 1420–1451.

96 'Las Señoritas Carmen y Francisca Vicente Interponiendo Tercera a Los Muebles Embargados Al C. Manuel de Vicente', 8 January 1878, AGN, TSJDF, c. 632.

97 'El C. Sánchez y Sánchez por La de Luz Gayosso a Las Intenciones Tiene a Su Objeto Embargado al C. Gayosso por El de Gutiérrez', 25 November 1878, AGN, TSJDF, c. 648.

98 As described above, the *tercerías* are not included in the subset for statistical analysis, which uses only the 97 *providencias precautorias*. Of the 137 cases that I collected while researching in the TSJDF archive, 7 are *tercerías*.

99 *Novísima Recopilación*, Book 11, Title 28, Laws 16 and 17 (quote from Law 17).

100 'Emilio Duviard Pide una Providencia Precautoria contra Ferrary', 14 June 1861, AGN, TSJDF, c. 349.

101 'Don Maximino Río de La Loza contra Florencia Delmotte Sobre Que por Providencia Precautoria Se Asegure la Fábrica de Ácidos Situada en la Casa Llamada Guerrero, en el Paseo de La Viga', 23 October 1865, AGN, TSJDF, c. 402.

102 Of 85 total cases with male plaintiffs that also give information about defendants moving, 17 have defendants moving (20 per cent); of 9 total cases with female plaintiffs, 1 has a defendant moving (11.1 per cent). An FET did not find a significant proportion difference. Likewise, an FET was performed for defendant gender and did not find a significant relationship between defendant gender and defendants moving. Cases with defendants moving have a mean amount owed of 342.3 pesos (16 cases); cases with no defendant moving have a mean amount owed of 368.8 (60 cases). A t-test did not find a significant means difference; likewise, an MW-U test did not find a significant difference in mean ranks. Regarding reasons and defendant moving, each reason was tested separately. For example, of 11 total cases with a rent reason, 1 defendant was moving (9.1 per cent); of 86 total cases with no rent reason, 17 defendants were moving (19.8 per cent). An FET did not find a significant proportion difference. FETs were performed for each reason, and tests did not find significant relationships between reasons and defendants moving. Of 14 total cases with a defendant moving, 13 were approved (92.9 per cent); of 73 total cases with a defendant not moving, 68 were approved (93.2 per cent). An FET did not find a significant proportion difference.

103 'Precautoria Promovida por D. Francisco Reyna', 7 December 1861, AGN, TSJDF, c. 350.

104 These form the topic of Chapter 3. On the modern state-formation project of rendering citizens legible, see Scott's foundational analysis and, for example, Bouk's history of statistics in the USA. In Mexico, similar projects began in earnest after the revolution; see the volume edited by Joseph and Nugent. Credit-rating is examined in Chapter 3; see Lauer for more on financial surveillance. Bouk, *How Our Days Became Numbered*; Joseph and Nugent, eds, *Everyday Forms of State Formation*; Lauer, *Creditworthy*; Scott, *Seeing Like a State*.
105 Recent social science research on reputation is inspired by the internet economy and systems of online reviews. As Diekmann and Przepiorka write: 'Reputation is always based on perception and perception can be deceptive. This is true for gossip and title-tattle and equally so for online reputation indices. In particular, a good reputation can also be faked to a certain extent. This used to be called swindling but is nowadays termed reputation management.' Diekmann and Przepiorka, 'Trust and Reputation in Markets', 395.
106 Taylor, *Fugitive Freedom*, xi. See also, for example, Eliav-Feldon and Herzig, eds, *Dissimulation and Deceit*.
107 Taylor, *Fugitive Freedom*, 142.
108 *Siete Partidas*; *Novísima Recopilación*; *Código Civil del Distrito Federal y Territorio de la Baja-California* (*Código Civil 1870*).
109 Burns, 'Introduction to the Fifth *Partida*', xxxiii. Most of the relevant rules are in the fifth *Partida*, entitled 'Which Treats of Loans, Sales, Purchases, and Exchanges, and All Other Contracts and Agreements Which Men Have With One Another of Every Description Whatsoever'. Some are also from the fourth *Partida*, which describes the marriage contract and contains some relevant rules about property. A final set of rules from the seventh *Partida* outlines a range of crimes including fraud. Burns describes the seventh *Partida* as the beginning of a separation between criminal and civil law (and many of the topics in the seventh Partida have their corresponding sections in the 1871 Penal Code). Burns, 'Introduction to the Seventh *Partida*', ix.
110 Most of the relevant rules are in the Third Book, 'De los contratos'. This analysis focuses on the first five titles, which present the general rules for contracts, loans, mortgages, and other obligations; the remaining titles of the Third Book deal with specific types of contracts. On civil codification from independence to the early post-revolution, see González, 'Notas para el estudio'.
111 On codification, see Cruz Barney, *Historia del derecho*, 702–734. The Commercial Code (1883), like earlier merchant law, is omitted from this analysis because my focus is on ordinary people. Merchant law has been the subject of extensive scholarship. See, for example, Baskes, *Staying Afloat*. More broadly, see Sicking and Wijffels, eds, *Conflict Management*. The commission explained its motives in the *Exposición* (exposition): *Exposición de los cuatro libros del Código Civil del Distrito Federal y Territorio de la Baja California que hizo la comisión al presenter el proyecto al supremo gobierno* (*Exposición del Código Civil* [1870]).
112 Cruz Barney, *Historia del derecho*, 118–124. Many of the relevant rules in the *Novísima Recompilación* echo or directly reference the *Siete Partidas*, and in these pages I focus on the material that does not overlap.

113 Most of the relevant rules are in Book Ten about contracts ('De los contratos y obligaciones; testamentos y herencias'), in Book Eleven about procedures when problems arise ('De los juicios civiles, ordinarios y executivos'), and Book Twelve, which has some rules concerning economic crimes ('De los delitos, y sus penas: y de los juicios criminals').

114 For an overview of rules for these procedures in the early nineteenth century, see, for example, *Novísima Recopilación*, Book 11, Titles 32–34, pp. 295–302. For a description of these procedures, see Pugliese, 'Prisión por deudas'. Bankruptcy litigation provides abundant material for historians, and other scholars have studied conflicts, especially vis-à-vis wealthier merchants. See, for example, Adelman, *Republic of Capital*; Chowning, *Wealth and Power*.

115 *Siete Partidas*, Partida 5, Title 15, Law 4, pp. 1170–1171.

116 On the jurisprudence of *privación de libertad* vis-à-vis unpaid debts in mediaeval and early modern Spain and its territories, see Ramos Vázquez, 'Detenciones cautelares', especially 714–732. On prisons in Mexico City at the turn of the nineteenth century, see Sánchez Michel, *Usos y funcionamiento de la cárcel*.

117 *Novísima Recopilación*, Book 11, Title 32, Law 7, p. 297.

118 For more on debt prisons, especially the rules and procedures, with case examples from late colonial Río de la Plata, see Pugliese, 'Prisión por deudas'. See also Tomás y Valiente, 'Prisión por deudas' on Castilian and Aragonese jurisprudence from the Visigoth Code to the nineteenth century; Ramos Vázquez, 'Detenciones cautelares'.

119 *Novísima Recopilación*, Book 11, Title 31, Law 19, p. 295.

120 For example, a *real orden* from June 1790 protected customs employees from civil debt imprisonment; see *Recopilación de leyes, decretos, reglamentos, circulares y providencias de los Supremos Poderes y otras autoridades de la República Mexicana formada de orden del Supremo Gobierno*, 470–471.

121 The 1786 law referenced a 1683 law that had protected silk manufacturers from having their tools seized because of civil debts. The 1683 law aimed to promote production: 'being so important the recovery of commerce, and that the silk factories do not fade away, rather that they do increase'. *Novísima Recopilación*, Book 11, Title 31, Law 18, p. 295. Carlos III's decree began by lauding the achievements of the 1683 law: '[E]xperience has shown the benefit and the common good,' it read. In the interests of 'promoting everything that leads to the well-being of the State', the king extended the protection from tool seizure to all labourers and artisans. The king then radically expanded the rights to include protection from debt imprisonment. *Novísima Recopilación*, Book 11, Title 31, Law 19, p. 295.

122 Romero Gil, *Código de procedimientos civiles y criminales de México*, Title 13, Section 6, Article 591. Romero Gil described his text as a 'resumén de las leyes vigentes' (p. 6).

123 *Siete Partidas*, Partida 3, Title 9, 'Introduction', p. 620.

124 *Siete Partidas*, Partida 3, Title 9, Law 1, p. 620.

125 *Siete Partidas*, Partida 5, Title 15, Introduction', p. 1169.

126 *Siete Partidas*, Partida 5, Title 15, Law 7, Laws 11 and 12, pp. 1172–1174.

127 Many of these rules came from late mediaeval and early modern legislation and are compiled in *Novísima Recopilación*, Book 11, Title 31, pp. 289–294.
128 *Siete Partidas*, Partida 5, Title 11, Law 13, p. 1098.
129 *Siete Partidas*, Partida 5, Title 15, Law 10, p. 1173.
130 *Exposición Código Civil* [1870], 60.
131 *Código Civil 1870*, Book 3, Title 4, Chapter 1, Article 1637, p. 272.
132 *Siete Partidas*, Partida 5, Title 14, Law 8, p. 1150.
133 *Exposición Código Civil* [1870], 62.
134 *Exposición Código Civil* [1870], 55.
135 *Código Civil 1870*, Book 3, Title 1, Chapter 4, Article 1430, p. 243.
136 *Exposición Código Civil* [1870], 55.
137 *Exposición Código Civil* [1870], 55.
138 *Código Civil 1870*, Book 3, Title 1, Chapter 4, Article 1432, p. 243.
139 The first category, outlined in Title 7, included a notary falsifying records and anyone who counterfeits money; these were 'closely connected with treason' and the punishments were correspondingly severe. These are described in *Siete Partidas*, Partida 7, Title 7, pp. 1337–1341, quote from the introduction on p. 1337.
140 *Siete Partidas*, Partida 7, Title 16, Law 1, p. 1406.
141 *Siete Partidas*, Partida 7, Title 16, Law 3, pp. 1406–1407.
142 *Siete Partidas*, Partida 7, Title 16, Law 3, pp. 1406–1407; also *Siete Partidas*, Partida 5, Title 5, Law 57, pp. 1049–1050.
143 First quote from *Siete Partidas*, Partida 7, Title 16, Law 3, pp. 1406–1407; second quote from *Siete Partidas*, Partida 7, Title 16, Law 7, p. 1408; punishment in *Siete Partidas*, Partida 7, Title 16, Law 12, p. 1410.
144 Zamora-Pierce, *Fraude*, 3–9. Also in 1871, the German Penal Code included a general conceptualisation of fraud. The Spanish Penal Code developed one in 1983.
145 *Código Penal* [1871], Book 3, Title 1, Chapter 5, Article 413, p. 190. See also Zamora-Pierce, *Fraude*, 11–14.
146 *Código Penal* [1871], Book 3, Title 1, Chapter 5, Article 414, pp. 190–191. On *falsedad*, see the Exposition in the *Código Penal*, pp. 60–61.
147 When the defrauded value was under 5 pesos, punishment was a fine of three times that value or corresponding prison time. Between 5 and 50 pesos, the punishment was minor jail time (*arresto menor*). Between 50 and 100 pesos, the perpetrator received major jail time (*arresto mayor*). Between 100 and 500 pesos, the perpetrator received one year of jail time, with two years for values from 500 to 1,000 pesos. For frauds and robberies over 1,000 pesos, additional jail time was calculated by adding one month per 100 pesos up to a maximum of four years. *Código Penal* [1871], Book 3, Title 1, Chapter 2, Article 376, p. 180; *Código Penal* [1871], Book 3, Title 1, Chapter 5, Article 415, p. 191.
148 *Código Penal* [1871], Book 3, Title 1, Chapter 5, Articles 416–433, pp. 191–195. The *Código Penal* dedicated the next chapter to frauds associated with unpaid debts: fraudulent bankruptcy (*quiebra fraudulenta*). These rules pertained specifically to merchants (*comerciantes*) who hid assets or otherwise deceived creditors in the bankruptcy proceedings. Such fraud was

punished by jail time corresponding to the amount involved. *Código Penal* [1871], Book 3, Title 1, Chapter 6, Articles 434–441, pp. 196–197.
149 *Siete Partidas*, Partida 5, Title 5, Law 9, pp. 1029–1030.
150 *Siete Partidas*, Partida 5, Title 5, Law 56, pp. 1049–1050.
151 *Exposición Código Civil* [1870], 64.
152 *Código Civil 1870*, Book 3, Title 5, Chapter 1, Articles 1771–1772, p. 290; *Código Civil 1870*, Book 3, Title 18, Chapter 6, Article 3023, p. 466. The carveout for just prices continued in the 1884 update to the Civil Code; see *Código Civil* (1884), Book 3, Title 5, Chapter 1, Article 1658.
153 Burns, 'Introduction to the Fifth *Partida*', xi.
154 *Siete Partidas*, Partida 5, Title 11, Laws 31 (and editor's note), p. 1105; *Novísima Recompilación*, Book 10, Title 1, Laws 20 and 22, p. 7; *Novísima Recompilación*, Book 12, Title 22, pp. 399–401.
155 *Novísima Recompilación*, Book 12, Title 22, Law 4, p. 401.
156 On 15 March 1861, Benito Juárez abrogated the usury prohibition and decreed that '*en consecuencia, la tasa o interés queda a voluntad de las partes*'. *Leyes de Reforma*, p. 775. See also Levy, *Making of the Market*, 34.
157 Before Juárez, various liberal regimes had lifted the ban only to see it reinstated by conservatives during the nineteenth century civil wars. See Levy, 'Cuestión de intereses'; Francois, *Culture of Everyday Credit*.
158 Levy, *Making of the Market*, 38. Levy shows how the repeal led to major changes in the Yucatecan credit market: debtors and creditors adapted quickly to the new rules, and contracts had explicit interest rates well above the previous usury maximum (38–53). See also Levy, 'Cuestión de intereses'.
159 Levy, *Making of the Market*, 37–38.

Chapter 3

1 United States Department of State, *Credit Systems of the Several Countries*, 413. I am grateful to Graciela Márquez Colín for sharing this report.
2 United States Department of State, *Credit Systems of the Several Countries*, 423, 431.
3 Of course, when Banamex arrived on the scene, it was hardly the first financial lending institution to extend credit in local urban economies. Banamex was formed by merging two existing banks, Banco Mercantil and Banco Nacional; see Maurer, *Power and the Money*, especially chapter 1.
4 Bazant, *Alienation of Church Wealth*. See also Chapter 1.
5 For a map of the historiography, see Tenorio-Trillo and Gómez Galvarriato, *El Porfiriato*.
6 Maurer, *Power and the Money*, 6.
7 Gustavo del Ángel and Carlos Marichal synthesised the scholarship in their 2003 historiography essay 'Poder y crisis', especially 679–692. Recent scholarship includes Wasserman's examination of capital and credit flows through case studies of foreign investors in *Pesos and Politics*.
8 Wyatt-Brown, 'God and Dun & Bradstreet', 437.
9 The early years of the Mercantile Agency and R. G. Dun & Company are well known. See Madison, 'Evolution of Commercial Credit Reporting'; Wyatt-Brown, 'God and Dun & Bradstreet'.

10 Flandreau and Geisler Mesevage, 'Untold History of Transparency'.
11 I refer to the company by its second nomenclature, which corresponds to the years under study.
12 Lauer, 'From Rumor to Written Record'; Olegario, *Engine of Enterprise*; Olegario, *Culture of Credit*.
13 Tom Baker and Jonathan Simon use the term 'embracing risk' to combine the concepts of risk spreading and risk taking. Baker and Simon, 'Embracing Risk', 1–2.
14 Lauer, *Creditworthy*, 17.
15 Lauer, *Creditworthy*, 17.
16 Lauer, 'From Rumor to Written Record', 301–304.
17 Wyatt-Brown, 'God and Dun & Bradstreet', 432–434.
18 Bouk, 'History and Political Economy of Personal Data', 86.
19 Credit reports such as those produced by Dun stand out in Bouk's chronology of personal data in American history. Other forms of personal information were commoditised later, once 'data doubles' had been aggregated (most notably by actuarial statisticians). Until then, the economic utility of other kinds of data doubles was limited. Bouk, 'History and Political Economy of Personal Data', 94.
20 Lauer, 'From Rumor to Written Record', 301.
21 The question about who created the six Banamex books is further complicated because they are marked as 'property of R. G. Dun'. This suggests a second interpretation: that these are indeed official legers that Dun either loaned to Banamex or created upon special request from the bank. But that would not have been typical of Dun's services. And the handwritten index at the beginning of each Banamex book is almost certainly the work of a Banamex employee. A third possibility is that these scrapbooks were assembled some time after the 1920s (the final reports in the books are from 1923) when they entered the bank's archive. I am grateful to Tim Mahoney, archivist of the Dun collection at the Baker Library, for help puzzling out possible explanations.
22 For example, scholars of American history have used the Baker collection to study patterns of African American entrepreneurship in the 1800s. See Kenzer, 'Black Businessman in the Postwar South'. See also Murphy, 'Business Ladies'; Spellman, 'Trust Brokers'; Tulchinsky, 'Said to Be a Very Honest Jew'; Walker, 'Racism, Slavery, and Free Enterprise'; Wheaton, 'Trade in This Place'.
23 During my research in 2013 and 2014, the Archivo Histórico del Banco Nacional de México (AHBNM) did not have a formal enumeration system for the six Dun books. I created my own system, with the books in chronological order. The five books are cited as follows, with the dates given corresponding to the first and last report in each book: AHBNM, *Fondo Libros Contables, Serie R. G. Dun y Cia* (Dun) Book 1, August 1899–January 1904; Dun Book 2, Zamora book (omitted from analysis); Dun Book 3, June 1920 (the first and last reports are from the same month); Dun Book 4, November 1918–April 1922; Dun Book 5, October 1920–October 1922; Dun Book 6, June 1922–March 1923.

24 Lizama Silva, 'Capitales zamoranos'.
25 I am grateful to Robert Kenzer for his advice on methodology and interpretation. Many of the variables in my database are inspired by his work on black entrepreneurs in the American South. Kenzer, 'Black Businessman in the Postwar South'.
26 See the Introduction for more on method.
27 The economics scholarship is extensive. For recent scholarship on Mexico, see Cruz-García et al., 'Financial Inclusion and Exclusion'.
28 Gender is known for 120 of the 123 reports, with three missing values. Of the 120 reports, only 1 is about a woman (99.2 per cent are about men). A second woman appears in the sample, but that report was part of the group of reports omitted because they contained no information: these are short notes about people who had died, moved, or could not be located.
29 AHBNM, Dun Book 1, 14 September 1903, p. 282; AHBNM, Dun Book 1, 18 October 1904, p. 313.
30 Information about net wealth is given for 102 of the 123 reports, with 21 missing values. Analysing Pérez's wealth in another way, 6.9 per cent of the sample have a net wealth less than or equal to 3,000 pesos.
31 Length of time is known for 118 of the 119 reports about men. The minimum length of time in these 118 reports is zero years and the maximum is 57 years. An observation of 'zero' indicates that the report gives a snapshot of the present with no substantive information about the person's past.
32 Age of person is known for 93 of the 123 reports. The minimum age in these 93 reports is 21 years and the maximum is 72 years.
33 The reports covered many sectors: the most common was commerce, with 40.7 per cent (48) of the reports focused on people engaged in this activity. Sector is known for 118 of the 123 reports. The second most common was commissions, at 14.4 per cent (17); the third was tied between manufacturing and mining at 11 per cent (13) each. Other sectors were scattershot, ranging from agriculture to finance, and none reached 10 per cent of the sample.
34 Information on business ability is given in 102 of the 123 reports, with 21 missing values. Of those 102 people, 79.4 per cent (81) were described as having positive business ability, 11.8 per cent (12) were described as having negative business ability, and 8.8 per cent (9) were described as having neutral business ability.
35 Marital status is known for 88 of the 123 reports, with 35 missing values; of these, 73.9 per cent (65) were married, 23.9 per cent (21) were single, and 2.3 per cent (2) were widowed. Information about where a person originally hailed from is given in 89 of the 123 reports, with 34 missing values: 30.3 (27) per cent of the people were from Mexico and 69.7 per cent (62) were from outside Mexico.
36 See note 35 on married people in the sample.
37 Future researchers could design a different study of the books to explore the question.
38 My wealth size categories are based on those developed by Lizama Silva. She created two alternative schemata, and her second was more basic: under 50,000 pesos; from 50,000 to 80,000 pesos; and more than 100,000 pesos.

I prefer her four-tier schema, because it offers a sharper separation of both the wealthy and the modest. I did, however, run all the tests for both schemata and found minimal substantive differences in the results.

39 Of the 17 reports that involve a net wealth in Group A (and for which there is also information on evaluations), 3 of the reports (17.6 per cent) have the 'desirable' evaluation. Of the 73 reports that involve a net wealth in Groups B, C, and D (and for which there is also information on evaluations), 1 report (1.4 per cent) has the 'desirable' evaluation. A Fisher's exact test (FET) found the observed difference in proportions (17.6 versus 1.4) to be statistically significant. Hereafter, FET results and chi-squared tests (x^2 tests) will be abbreviated to telegraph essential information; subsequent notes will give a shortform version of the fuller format provided here, similar to shortform archival references.

40 Of the 27 reports that involve a net wealth in Group D (and which also give information on evaluations), 7 have 'not creditworthy' evaluations (25.9 per cent); for Groups A, B, and C, of 63 reports, 4 have 'not creditworthy' evaluations (6.3 per cent). An FET found a significant proportion difference.

41 The mean net wealth for 'desirable' evaluations is 2,458,157.5 pesos (4 reports). The mean net wealth for 'fair' evaluations is 238,089.4 pesos (53 reports). The mean net wealth for 'not creditworthy' evaluations is 27,136.4 pesos (11 reports). The mean net wealth in evaluations that mention a guarantee is 27,930 pesos (10 reports). T-tests found statistically significant observed differences between the net wealth of the 'desirable' evaluation and each of the three other evaluations. A t-test did not find a significant observed difference between the mean net wealth for a 'desirable' evaluation and the mean net wealth of a 'good' evaluation (which is 984,629.1 pesos). Looking at mean net wealth of the other evaluations (e.g. good v. fair), tests did not find any statistically significant observed differences. Hereafter, t-tests results will be abbreviated. There might still be a pattern, but the tests did not pick up on it. See the Introduction on the challenges of interpreting the results when tests did not find statistical significance.

42 Tests did not find significant difference between the mean net wealth of single and married people (t-test) and did not find significant proportion differences of single and married people in any of the wealth size categories (x^2 tests and FETs). Several tests were run regarding business reach. For example, t-tests did not find significant differences in the mean net wealth of businesses with an international reach and the mean net wealth of businesses with a reach within Mexico. Regarding age, the results are mixed. Older people are associated with higher net wealth: there is a positive, moderate, statistically significant correlation between age and net wealth. But t-tests did not find significant differences in the mean ages of individuals in different wealth categories. Further, t-tests did not find a significant difference between the mean age of individuals in reports that have missing values for net wealth and the mean age of individuals in reports that have information on net wealth.

43 Reports on the finance sector have a mean net wealth of 2,826,090 pesos (7 reports); reports on the commerce sector have a mean amount owed of 82,680.8 pesos (43 reports). A t-test found a significant means difference.

Similarly, t-tests found significant means differences between finance and each of the other sectors, with finance being higher.
44 Dun had moved towards a ratings system in the USA by the 1860s, with companies listed in a reference book. The numbers of businesses and individuals in the reference books increased massively, from around 20,000 in the 1870s to 800,000 in the 1880s. Madison, 'Evolution of Commercial Credit Reporting', 172–173. For example, the 1918 manual discussed in this chapter includes instructions on how to categorise people and businesses: there was an alphabetical system for capital ratings, with AA the best and M the worst; and there was a numerical system for credit ratings that ranged from 1 (the top score) to 4. The manual noted that 'the credit rating is always based upon outside information and should reflect nothing more than the opinions obtained'; it was based on reports such as those in the Banamex archive. None of the reports in the Banamex archive, however, use the system. Mercantile Agency, *Mercantile Agency Reporters' Manual* (1918), 32, 91.
45 United States Department of State, *Credit Systems of the Several Countries*, 427; 'naturally lazy' is on p. 426.
46 Mercantile Agency, *Mercantile Agency Reporters' Manual* (1918), 25, italics in original. See note 78 for another example of italics.
47 There were too many agents to test for each one. Of the 28 distinct agents in the sample, I tested the six agents with 9 or more reports. These were Agents 6, 11, 42, 52, 81, and 82. Each of these agents was compared with all other agents together.
48 Each agent was tested against all others (subsumed into a group) vis-à-vis the different evaluations. With the exception of Agents 11 and 82, described below, FETs and x^2 tests did not find any significant proportion differences.
49 Looking only at the subset of reports written by the six agents in the quantitative analysis: of the 67 reports written by agents with more than 9 reports, 28.4 per cent (19) were written by Agents 11 and 82.
50 For Agent 11, of the 8 reports that also give information on evaluations, 4 have 'good' evaluations (50 per cent); for the other agents, of the 81 total reports, 9 are 'good' (11.1 per cent). An FET found a significant proportion difference.
51 For Agent 82, of the 9 reports that also give information on evaluations, 4 have 'guarantee' evaluations (44.4 per cent); for the other agents, of the 80 total reports, 7 have 'guarantee' evaluations (8.8 per cent). An FET found a significant proportion difference.
52 T-tests of mean net wealth for each individual agent (compared with all other agents) were conducted for Agents 6, 11, 42, 52, 81, and 82. T-tests found no significant means differences.
53 Mercantile Agency, *Mercantile Agency Reporters' Manual* (1918), 24.
54 Mercantile Agency, *Mercantile Agency Reporters' Manual* (1918), 34.
55 Mercantile Agency, *Mercantile Agency Reporters' Manual* (1918), 39.
56 Mercantile Agency, *Mercantile Agency Reporters' Manual* (1918), 35.
57 AHBNM, Dun Book 5, 4 August 1921.
58 The high proportion of foreigners is not surprising, given the well-established history of foreigners doing business in Mexico. Among others, see Buchenau,

Tools of Progress; Galindo Rodríguez, *Ethnic Entrepreneurs*; Wasserman, *Pesos and Politics*. Information about a person's origins was given in 89 of the reports: of these, 30.3 per cent were from Mexico (27 individuals) and 69.7 per cent were from abroad (62 individuals). Of 27 total reports on people of Mexican origin that also give information about evaluations, 15 have 'fair' evaluations (55.6 per cent); of 59 total reports on people from abroad, 35 have 'fair' evaluations (59.3 per cent). A x^2 test did not find a significant proportion difference. Regarding the other evaluations, FETs were performed for Mexican origin (v from abroad) and each evaluation; the tests did not find significant proportion differences.

59 The evaluation is given in 109 of the 123 reports, with 14 missing values. Lizama Silva, in contrast, developed a three-tier classification of the evaluations in the Zamora book: good, acceptable with a guarantee, and bad. My five-tier evaluations, I think, better capture the range of evaluations in the Mexico City books. I did, however, run all the tests for both the five-tier and three-tier schemata and found minimal substantive differences. (I created a three-tier schema by merging 'desirable' and 'good' and by merging 'fair' and 'guarantee'.)

60 FETs were conducted for each category of evaluation (desirable, good, fair, guarantee required, not creditworthy) with each wealth size category (Groups A, B, C, and D).

61 AHBNM, Dun Book 1, 25 January 1903, p. 108; related reports in the same book are on pp. 38–40 and 79.

62 AHBNM, Dun Book 1, 26 August 1902, p. 337, agent number unknown.

63 AHBNM, Dun Book 3, 4 February 1920, p. 110.

64 AHBNM, Dun Book 6, 12 February 1923, p. 69; 19 January 1922, p. 69.

65 Mercantile Agency, *Mercantile Agency Reporters' Manual* (1918), 47.

66 AHBNM, Dun Book 3, June 1920, p. 1, agent number unknown.

67 The mean known history of 'fair' evaluations is 10.2 years (60 reports); the mean length of time for reports in all other categories (combined into one) is 6.7 years (49 reports). A t-test found a significant means difference.

68 The mean known history of 'guarantee' evaluations is 3.6 years (14 reports); the mean length of time for reports in all other categories (combined into one) is 9.4 years (95 reports). A t-test found a significant means difference. Otherwise, no significant association was found between the length of a person's known history and the other evaluations. T-tests were performed for the other evaluations and did not find significant differences between the mean known histories.

69 Mercantile Agency, *Mercantile Agency Reporters' Manual* (1902), 7; Mercantile Agency, *Mercantile Agency Reporters' Manual* (1918), 18. In her study of how banks in England and Wales assessed the reputation, virtue, and character of their potential borrowing customers between 1870 and 1920, Lucy Newton finds that length of time was very important. Although Newton's focus is different – she examines the length of established relationships between banks and their customers – the importance of known history in both contexts suggests directions for future research. Newton, 'Trust and Virtue', especially 184–185.

70 There are 43 reports that explicitly reference fire insurance. Of the 123 reports, 9.8 per cent (12) involve businesses with fire insurance, 25.2 per cent (31) mention that the business does not have fire insurance, and 65 per cent (80) have no mention of insurance. For coding, I assumed that if it was not mentioned, there was no insurance. (I also ran models with only the 43 reports with explicit mention of insurance and the tests did not find significant relationships.) I tested each evaluation separately. Where insurance is mentioned, of the 12 total reports that also give information about evaluations, 9 have 'fair' evaluations (75 per cent); for businesses with no insurance, of 97 total reports, 51 have 'fair' evaluations (52.6 per cent). A x^2 test of association found no statistically significant difference in observed proportions. FETs were also performed for insurance (v no insurance) and each evaluation; these tests did not find significant proportion differences.

71 Alexander, *City on Fire*, 113. The effect of having fire insurance, especially for the later decades, remains an open question that could be examined by future researchers with a bigger sample.

72 In order, AHBNM, Dun Book 3, 24 December 1920, p. 100; AHBNM, Dun Book 4, 28 February 1919, p. 72; AHBNM, Dun Book 3, 23 October 1919, p. 11; AHBNM, Dun Book 5, 19 November 1920, p. 189; AHBNM, Dun Book 1, 9 April 1904, p. 249.

73 The mean age of those with insurance is 40.2 years (11 reports); the mean age without insurance is 42.6 years (82 reports). A t-test did not find a significant difference. The mean net wealth with insurance is 126,905.4 pesos (12 reports); the mean net wealth without insurance is 568,403.3 pesos (90 reports). A t-test did not find a significant difference. For those with insurance, of the 12 total reports that also give information about wealth size categories, 4 are in Group C (33.3 per cent); for those with no insurance, of the 90 total reports, 21 are in Group C (23.3 per cent). An FET did not find a significant proportion difference. For the other wealth categories, FETs were performed for insurance (v no insurance) and each group; the tests did not find significant proportion differences. In the commerce sector, of the 48 total reports that also give information about insurance, 9 have insurance (18.8 per cent); in other sectors, of 70 total reports, 3 have insurance (4.3 per cent). A x^2 test found a significant proportion difference.

74 Where there is no wealth information, of 19 total reports that also give information about evaluations, 7 have 'fair' evaluations (36.8 per cent); with known wealth, of 90 total reports, 53 have 'fair' evaluations (58.9 per cent). A x^2 test found a significant proportion difference. FETs were also performed for known (v unknown) net wealth and each evaluation; the tests did not find significant proportion differences.

75 AHBNM, Dun Book 1, 9 September 1904, p. 309, agent number unknown.

76 AHBNM, Dun Book 1, 25 June 1904, p. 235.

77 AHBNM, Dun Book 1, 3 March 1904, p. 288.

78 The mean age in reports with unknown wealth is 43.1 years (15 reports); the mean age with known wealth is 42.2 years (78 reports). A t-test did not find a significant proportion difference. Of 21 total reports where wealth is unknown

and that also give information about sector, 5 are in the commerce sector (23.8 per cent); of 97 total reports with known wealth, 43 are in commerce (44.3 per cent). A x^2test did not find a significant proportion difference. FETs were also performed for known (v unknown) net wealth and each sector; the tests did not find significant proportion differences. Of 9 total reports where wealth is unknown, 2 have national reach (22.2 per cent); of 56 total reports with known wealth, 14 have national reach (25.0 per cent). An FET did not find a significant proportion difference. FETs were performed for known (v unknown) net wealth and national and international reach; the tests did not find significant proportion differences.

79 Mercantile Agency, *Mercantile Agency Reporters' Manual* (1918), 90, italics in original. This is one of only two times that italics are used for emphasis. See also note 45.
80 The historiography is vast. For a recent synthetic account, see Joseph and Buchenau, *Mexico's Once and Future Revolution*. For recent scholarship, see Ristow, *Revolution Unfinished*. There are also many historiographical overviews. See Garciadiego, 'Revolución mexicana'.
81 Crain, 'War Exclusion Clauses'.
82 McCaa estimates a total human loss of 2.1 million, which also includes lost births (about one-quarter) and emigration (less than one-tenth). McCaa, 'Missing Millions', 394–397. 'Excess deaths' is defined as the difference between the number of dead in a crisis (such as a civil war or pandemic) and what would have been expected under normal conditions. See Msemburi et al., 'WHO Estimates of Excess Mortality', 130.
83 Maurer, *Power and the Money*, 134.
84 Maurer, *Power and the Money*, 158.
85 Maurer, *Power and the Money*, 159.
86 AHBNM, Dun Book 5, 22 March 1916, p. 367. The company had been formed in 1904 to develop rail and irrigation in the Yaqui River Valley as well as agricultural and real estate development. It would later be expropriated by the post-revolutionary government. For more on the company, see Cerutti and Gustavo Lorenzana Durán, 'Irrigación, expansión de la frontera agrícola'; Dwyer, *Agrarian Dispute*, chapter 1.
87 The 1916 report was excluded from all models that examined relationships between variables before and after the revolution.
88 Before 1910, of the 38 total reports that also give information about evaluations, 4 have the 'desirable' evaluation (10.5 per cent); after 1917, of the 71 total reports, 1 has a 'desirable' evaluation (1.4 per cent). An FET found a significant proportion difference. Before 1910, of the 38 total reports, 10 have a 'good' evaluation (26.3 per cent); after 1917, of the 71 total reports, 6 have a 'good' evaluation (8.5 per cent). A x^2test found a significant proportion difference.
89 Before 1910, of the 38 total reports that also give information about evaluations, 15 have a 'fair' evaluation (39.5 per cent); after 1917, of the 71 total reports, 45 have a 'fair' evaluation (63.4 per cent). A x^2test found a significant proportion difference.

90 Before 1910, of the 38 total reports that also give information about evaluations, 5 have a 'guarantee' evaluation (13.2 per cent); after 1917, of the 71 total reports, 9 have a 'guarantee' evaluation (12.7 per cent). An FET did not find a significant proportion difference. Before 1910, of the 38 total reports, 4 have a 'not creditworthy' evaluation (10.5 per cent); after 1917, of the 71 total reports, 10 have a 'not creditworthy' evaluation (14.1 per cent). An FET did not find a significant proportion difference.

91 Before 1910, of the 43 total reports that also give information about sector, 5 are in agriculture (11.6 per cent); after 1917, of the 74 total reports, 1 is in agriculture (1.4 per cent). An FET found a significant proportion difference. FETs and x^2 tests were performed for other sectors before 1910 and after 1917; the tests did not find significant proportion differences.

92 Before 1910, the mean net wealth is 756,323.4 pesos (34 reports); after the revolution it is 401,704 pesos (67 reports). A t-test did not find a significant means difference. Before 1910, for the 34 reports that give information about net wealth, the minimum net wealth is 0 pesos; the second lowest is 2,000 pesos; and the maximum is 10,000,000 pesos. After 1917, for the 67 reports, the minimum net wealth is 0 pesos; the second lowest is 1,000 pesos; and the maximum is 10,000,000 pesos.

93 Before 1910, 25 per cent of reports involve a net wealth of 14,000 pesos or less; 50 per cent are 41,250 pesos or less; and 75 per cent are 500,000 pesos or less. After 1917, 25 per cent of reports involve a net wealth of 23,750 pesos or less; 50 per cent are 51,000 pesos or less; and 75 per cent are 144,327.4 pesos or less. The distributions of the two subsets are not significantly different from each other (Kolmogorov-Smirnov test). Likewise, the medians of the two subsets are not statistically significantly different from each other (Mann-Whitney U test).

94 Before 1910, of the 34 total reports, 6 relate to Group C (17.6 per cent); after 1917, of the 67 total reports, 18 relate to Group C (26.9 per cent). A x^2 test did not find a significant proportion difference. X^2 tests were performed for other wealth categories before 1910 and after 1917; the tests did not find significant proportion differences.

95 AHBNM, Dun Book 3, 28 September 1920, p. 164.

96 Dividing the sample into subsets for before and after the revolution, I ran a series of x^2 tests and FETs analysing relationships between the evaluations and the net wealth and wealth size categories. Richer people were over-represented in the better evaluation categories both before and after the revolution.

97 Despite Strother's implication, the function of honour in financial transactions was not unique to the Hispanic world; for example, Matthew Barrett has shown how financial honour functioned in British and Canadian culture during the First World War. Barrett, 'Worthless Cheques and Financial Honour'; United States Department of State, *Credit Systems of the Several Countries*, 411

98 For modern Mexico, Piccato's study of masculine honour and political legitimacy is an influential and representative study. Piccato, *Tyranny of Opinion*. The historiography of honour is considered in greater detail in the Introduction.

99 Mercantile Agency, *Mercantile Agency Reporters' Manual* (1918), 19–20.
100 Mercantile Agency, *Mercantile Agency Reporters' Manual* (1918), 23.
101 For example, historians of banking in Britain have shown how 'respectability' or 'reputation' had more to do with financial probity than moral or social virtue. See Newton, 'Trust and Virtue', especially 187–192.
102 There is a moderate, positive, statistically significant correlation between positive character and positive capacity. There is a weak, positive, statistically significant correlation between negative character and negative capacity.
103 Of the 90 total reports with positive character comments that also give information about evaluations, 8 have a 'not creditworthy' evaluation (8.9 per cent); of the 19 total reports with other character comments, 6 have a 'not creditworthy' evaluation (31.6 per cent). An FET found a significant proportion difference. Of 77 total reports with positive comments on capacity, 3 have a 'not creditworthy' evaluation (3.9 per cent); of 32 total reports with other capacity comments, 11 have a 'not creditworthy' evaluation (34.4 per cent). An FET found a significant proportion difference.
104 AHBNM, Dun Book 5, 28 July 1921, p. 127.
105 AHBNM, Dun Book 1, 19 February 1902, p. 27.
106 AHBNM, Dun Book 5, 28 January 1921, p. 117.
107 AHBNM, Dun Book 1, 28 April 1903, p. 211, agent number unknown.
108 AHBNM, Dun Book 1, 2 May 1903, p. 113.
109 AHBNM, Dun Book 1, 7 August 1901, p. 146; 18 April 1902, p. 146; 7 May 1903, p. 146.
110 AHBNM, Dun Book 5, 24 November 1921, p. 209.
111 There is information on the net wealth in 11 of the 14 reports with 'not creditworthy' evaluations. The minimum net wealth in the 11 reports is 0 pesos, the maximum is 100,000 pesos, and the average net wealth is 27,136.4 pesos. In terms of distribution, 25 per cent of reports involve people or businesses with a net wealth of 4,750 pesos or less; 50 per cent are 10,000 pesos or less; and 75 per cent are 46,250 pesos or less.
112 AHBNM, Dun Book 3, April 1921, p. 153, agent number unknown.
113 AHBNM, Dun Book 1, 26 August 1903, p. 137.
114 AHBNM, Dun Book 1, 21 July 1903, p. 120.
115 AHBNM, Dun Book 4, 10 September 1918, p. 11.
116 AHBNM, Dun Book 5, 16 August 1921, p. 1; 14 October 1920, p. 1.
117 On the strategic value of lies, manipulation, and selective disclosure, see Giardini and Wittek, 'Introduction: Gossip and Reputation', 2.
118 Mercantile Agency, *Mercantile Agency Manual* (1897), 18.
119 Mercantile Agency, *Mercantile Agency Manual* (1897), 18.
120 Flandreau and Geisler Mesevage, 'Untold History of Transparency'.
121 Mercantile Agency, *Mercantile Agency Manual* (1897), 18–19. The approach to gossip was strikingly different from instructions about self-reported information (the financial statements that people gave agents): 'Care should be taken not to rate on statements only. It is absurd to believe everything that people say about themselves.' Gossip among one's business associates (or rivals) was acceptable, but self-presentation was scrutinised. Mercantile Agency, *Mercantile Agency Manual* (1897), 53.

122 This in-between state was also, of course, evident in the American reports. Lauer describes how early credit rating traded in 'quasi-empirical facts'. Lauer, 'From Rumor to Written Record', 305.
123 Mercantile Agency, *Mercantile Agency Reporters' Manual* (1918), 38.
124 Mercantile Agency, *Mercantile Agency Manual* (1897), 62.
125 Mercantile Agency, *Mercantile Agency Reporters' Manual* (1918), 9.
126 Mercantile Agency, *Mercantile Agency Reporters' Manual* (1918), 9.
127 Sociologists have studied the downsides to the 'scientific' approach to information, and much of the scholarship is connected to the role of reviews and ratings in the internet economy. See, for example, Diekmann and Przepiorka, 'Trust and Reputation in Markets'. See also Lauer's discussion of black box algorithms, *Creditworthy*, 15–16.

Chapter 4

1 *La hermana trinquete*, directed by René Cardona (1970), quote at 00:10:20. The film is so representative of the era that it is quoted in Alfonso Cuarón's film *Roma*, when Adela and Ramón watch *La hermana trinquete* in Mexico City's famous Metropolitan theatre. See also Perez Reyna, 'Auteurs on Netflix', 47.
2 'Reforma al Art. 193 de la Ley General de Títulos y Operaciones de Crédito. Iniciativa para que la expedición de un cheque sin fondos no se considere como fraude sino como un delito especial', 9 November 1972, Legislature XLVIII (1970–1973). Text of the proposed reform is published online by the Fundación Miguel Estrata Iturbide.
3 Cheques were widely used in the Muslim world by the tenth century and began to appear in Europe around 1400. Negotiability (transfer by endorsement) was introduced in Amsterdam in the late sixteenth and early seventeenth centuries; usage spread and increased thereafter. Quinn and Roberds, 'Evolution of the Check', 2–7. Troubles associated with endorsed cheques are considered later in the chapter.
4 Dávalos Mejía, *Títulos y operaciones de crédito*, 272–273.
5 See Noel Maurer on the establishment of the central bank, Banco de México, in 1925: Maurer, *Power and the Money*, especially 173–181. See also Gustavo del Ángel on the new relationship between business groups and banks: del Ángel, 'Nexus Between Business Groups'.
6 Maurer, *Power and the Money*, 174.
7 Maurer, *Power and the Money*, 174–175. As Maurer sums up, the history of banking and finance under Porfirio Díaz and in the post-revolutionary period was 'fundamentally political' (p. 2).
8 Dávalos Mejía, *Títulos y operaciones de crédito*, 272–273.
9 For overviews of the scholarship, see Hansen, 'From Finance Capitalism to Financialization'; Lai, 'Financialization of Everyday Life'; Martin, *Financialization of Daily Life*.
10 '[D]uring the postwar period there was a certain idea of the nation as a community even if only an imagined community. What kept the nation together was the narrative of the social state, a narrative that gradually lost

its coherence from around 1980 when neo-liberalism, financialization, individualism and the competition state began to take over.' Hansen, 'From Finance Capitalism to Financialization', 618.
11 Gómez Gordoa, *Títulos de Crédito*, 201.
12 Thompson articulated the moral economy of the poor. I use the concept to examine the views of middle-class account holders regarding the social norms and obligations of economic behaviour. Thompson, 'Moral Economy of the English Crowd', 79.
13 See Acemoglu and Robinson, 'De Facto Political Power'; Acemoglu, Johnson, and Robinson, 'Rise of Europe'.
14 On tensions between the political and economic elites, see Anaya Merchant, *Colapso y reform*, especially chapter 5. For relevant analysis of a slightly later period, see also Knight, 'Cardenismo: Juggernaut or Jalopy?'; Romero Sotelo, 'Los secretarios de Hacienda a debate'.
15 The *Ley General de Títulos y Operaciones de Crédito* was published in the *Diario Oficial* on 27 August 1932. It is still in force today. The original law, as well as the current legislation and the various modifications since 1932, are available on the Mexican congress's website.
16 *Diario Oficial*, 27 August 1932, 15.
17 *Diario Oficial*, 9 March 1946, 3. Further revisions included using multiples of the minimum wage in lieu of nominal pesos.
18 For example, McAndrews and Roberds, 'General Equilibrium Analysis of Check Float'. Mediaeval jurists also focused on the 'use' of property in a debt relationship, and many of the rules about unpaid debts examined in Chapter 2 concerned if and how an asset was used while a creditor awaited repayment or the return of a good.
19 As economists Quinn and Roberds write, 'anyone who has written a check the day before payday knows that a check can also function as an instrument of credit. Such credit is generally quite short term, however.' Quinn and Roberds, 'Evolution of the Check', 4, fn8.
20 Research done in 2013, 2014, and 2019.
21 See the Introduction for more on methodology.
22 Because some of the *libradores* and *beneficiarios* might be alive, I have changed the names of all litigants and others, such as their family and friends, who played a role in the events.
23 The analysis of consumption often uses the term consumer citizens, and the central conceptual text for Mexico and Latin America is García Canclini, *Consumidores y ciudadanos*. See also the influential analysis of the topic in American history in Cohen, *Consumer's Republic*. I used the term to examine consumer rights in 1970s Mexico in chapter 4 of my first book, *Waking from the Dream*. On mass consumption in mid-century Mexico, see Bayardo Rodríguez, *Entre el lujo, el deseo y la necesidad*; on the welfare state, see Sanders, *Gender and Welfare*; on consumerism, see essays in Aguilar and García Canclini, *Cultura y Comunicación*. On mid-century Argentina, see Elena, *Dignifying Argentina*.
24 On financial inclusion in Mexico, see, for example, Cruz-García et al., 'Financial Inclusion and Exclusion'.

25 Zamora-Pierce, *Fraude*, 366.
26 The historical scholarship on small and medium enterprises in Mexico is mostly concentrated on the nineteenth century. Ingrid Bleynat's study of public market vendors in Mexico City from 1867 to 1966 connects the nineteenth-century historiography with a new approach to post-revolutionary political economy. There is more scholarship on consumption, such as Enrique Ochoa's study of the politics of food and nutrition and Lilia Bayardo Rodríguez's examination of consumer values, as well as analyses of larger retailers such as Julio Moreno's work on Sears. These studies offer models for studying other entrepreneurial sectors in post-revolutionary Mexico. Sabine Effosse provides another example, focusing on consumption and credit in postwar France. Bayardo Rodríguez, *Entre el lujo, el deseo y la necesidad*; Bleynat, *Vendors' Capitalism*; Effosse, *Crédit à la consommation*; Moreno, *Yankee, Don't Go Home!*; Ochoa, *Feeding Mexico*.
27 I have written elsewhere about the mid-century economic boom and one-party rule. The description in the next four paragraphs is drawn from *Waking from the Dream*, 1–12.
28 While the evolution involved more than mere nomenclature, I am following a scholarly tradition that takes 1929 as the beginning of one-party rule, emphasising the longevity and institutional flexibility of the PRI's system.
29 On electoral contests at the national level, see Loaeza, *Partido Acción Nacional*; Servín, *Ruptura y oposición*. For Morelos, see Padilla, *Rural Resistance*. For Guerrero and Veracruz, see Gillingham, *Unrevolutionary Mexico*.
30 The scholarship on mid-century Mexico is growing. See, for example, Cedillo and Calderón, eds, *Challenging Authoritarianism*; del Castillo Troncoso, ed., *Reflexión y crítica*; Gillingham and Smith, eds, *Dictablanda*; Gillingham et al., eds, *Journalism, Satire, and Censorship*; Padilla and Walker, eds, 'Spy Reports'; Pensado and Ochoa, eds, *México Beyond 1968*.
31 In the post-revolutionary scholarship, analysis of state-sponsored repression and resistance is a particularly rich line of enquiry. See, for example, a growing number of studies on education, students, and teachers: Allier, *68*; Aviña, *Specters of Revolution*; Dillingham, *Oaxaca Resurgent*; Padilla, *Unintended Lessons*; Pensado, *Rebel Mexico*.
32 Population statistics from Wilkie and Wilkins, 'Quantifying the Class Structure', 585; see also Walker, *Waking from the Dream*, 213, table A.1.
33 The middle classes are the topic of my book *Waking from the Dream*.
34 Paz, 'Other Mexico', 260, 271.
35 *El Siglo de Torreón*, 3 August 1942, 3.
36 'Individuo elegante probablemente cajero, afuera de una oficina de cobro', ca. 1935–1940. I am grateful to the Fototeca Nacional, Instituto Nacional de Antropología e Historia, Secretaría de Cultura, México, for authorisation to reproduce.
37 'Empleado atendiendo clientes tras una ventanilla en un camión de prestamos del Banco del Pequeño Comercio', 5 April 1962. I am grateful to the Fototeca Nacional, Instituto Nacional de Antropología e Historia, Secretaría de Cultura, México, for authorisation to reproduce.

38 On the mid-century finance industry, see del Ángel, 'Paradoja del desarrollo financiero'. On the growth in Mexico more generally, see Cárdenas, 'Economía mexicana'; Márquez, 'Evolución y estructura del PIB'; Moreno-Brid and Ros, *Development and Growth*.
39 Spallanzani, 'Note on Florentine Banking', 156–157, 64.
40 Drawing on Spallanzani and other scholars, Quinn and Roberds describe how, in early modern Europe, cheques and bills of exchange had complementary roles. Quinn and Roberds, 'Evolution of the Check', 5.
41 'Violación a la Ley General de Títulos y Operaciones de Crédito', 29 January 1955, Archivo Histórico de la Ciudad de México 'Carlos de Sigüenza y Góngora' (AHCDMX), Cárceles, *caja* (c.) 1627, *partida* (ptda.) 961.
42 The outcome is given in 104 of the 115 files, with 11 missing values; percentages are based on 104 files. Of those 104 files, other outcomes happened in 10.6 per cent of files (11).
43 Gender is known for all *libradores*. For *beneficiarios*, gender is known in 93 files with 22 missing values; analyses of *beneficiario* gender are based on 86 reports, omitting the unknowns and the entities.
44 These scholars give incomes in monthly pesos, and I calculated the daily pesos assuming 20 working days. Cline estimated 300–9,999 monthly pesos: Cline, *Mexico*, 116. González Cosío put it at 2,693 monthly pesos: González Cosío, 'Clases y estratos sociales', 62–64. For more on the limitations of the income estimates, see my examination of these and other estimates in Walker, *Waking from the Dream*, appendix.
45 The peso value of the cheque is known in 88 of the 115 files, with 27 missing values; percentages are based on 88 files. If a conflict involves multiple bad cheques, the amount given is the total amount.
46 'Le dieron cheque sin fondos a Tito Bauche', *Avance*, 4 January 1975, 8. Coverage also included local political and economic elites caught up in cases with uncovered cheques: for example, municipal politicians in Coahuila and bank leaders in Tabasco. 'Humberto Murciaga, Principal Responable de la Privación Ilegal de Priístas en Monclova; Se exigirá un Informe Financiero', *El Nacional*, 5 January 1985, 2; 'Consignado un funcionario de Banamex', *El Nacional*, 5 May 1984, 5.
47 'Ecos de la voz popular', *Jueves de Excelsior*, 17 June 1948, 3.
48 'Daniel L. Benson fue aprehendido', *El Universal*, 16 April 1952, 1.
49 There is information on what went wrong in 94 of the 115 files, with 21 missing values.
50 'Violación a la Ley General de Títulos y Operaciones de Crédito', 29 September 1962, AHCDMX, Cárceles, c. 2232, ptda. 6906.
51 In terms of percentiles, 25 per cent of the *libradores* are 31 years old or younger; 50 per cent are 39 or younger; and 75 per cent are 45 or younger. The files have no information about *beneficiario* age.
52 The mean age of *libradores* with the problem of insufficient funds is 40.8 years (52 files). The mean age of *libradores* with the other problems (subsumed into one) is 35.1 years (17 files). A t-test found the observed difference in means to be statistically significant. See the Introduction for more on method. Hereafter, t-test results will be abbreviated.

53 Of the *libradores* from Mexico, 45.9 per cent (34) are from the Distrito Federal and 54.1 per cent (40) are from across the republic.
54 'Violación a la Ley General de Títulos y Operaciones de Crédito', AHCDMX, Cárceles, c. 2207, ptda 3826.
55 Based on a review of coverage of '*cheques sin fondos*' in the Hemeroteca National digital catalogue.
56 'Capturado el que defraudaba a los carniceros', *Avance*, 10 February 1976, 10.
57 Cases with a 'not guilty' outcome have a mean daily *librador* income of 69.3 pesos (8 files); other outcomes have a mean daily *librador* income of 118.1 pesos (19 files). A t-test found a significant means difference. T-tests were performed for mean income and each outcome (compared with all other outcomes grouped together), and these did not find significant relationships.
58 'Violación a la Ley General de Títulos y Operaciones de Crédito', 31 October 1975, AHCDMX, Cárceles, c. 3588, ptda. 9263.
59 Bátiz-Lazo, *Cash and Dash*, 228.
60 'Control de Cheques', undated, in Banco de México Archivo Histórico, Fondo Rodrigo Gómez, c. 18, exp. 1. The document is undated but corresponds to the 1950s or 1960s: it was produced during Rodrigo Gómez Gómez's tenure as director of the Banco de México (1952–1970).
61 The gender of the individual involved is given in 120 of the 123 Dun credit reports, with 3 missing values. Of the 120 reports, only 1 is about a woman (99.2 per cent are about men). A second woman appears in the sample but that report was part of the group of reports omitted because they contain no information: these are short notes about people who have died or moved or could not be located.
62 There is information on gender for all *libradores*. For *beneficiarios*, gender is known in 93 files, with 22 missing values; analyses of *beneficiario* gender are based on 86 reports, omitting the unknowns and the entities. Among *beneficiarios*, 7.5 per cent (7) are entities.
63 The plaintiff's gender is unknown in 11 *juicios verbales* records; the defendant's gender is unknown in 7 cases. Of the plaintiffs, 15.6 per cent are women (144), 80.4 per cent are men (742), and 4.0 per cent are entities (37) such as religious institutions. Of the defendants, 14.6 per cent are women (145), 85.3 per cent are men (791), and there is 1 (0.1 per cent) entity. See Chapter 1.
64 The plaintiff's gender is unknown in 6 *providencias precautorias* files; the defendant's gender is unknown in 8 files. Of the plaintiffs, 87.6 per cent (85 cases) are men and 9.3 per cent (9) are women. Of the defendants, 90.7 (88) per cent are men and 5.2 per cent (5) are women. See Chapter 2.
65 The exceptions were unsurprising, such as female *libradoras* being significantly associated with the profession of homemaker.
66 For example, tests did not find significant association between male *beneficiarios* and younger *libradores*: the mean age of *libradores* is not significantly different for files with a male *beneficiario* and files with a female *beneficiaria*. Files with female *beneficiarias* have a mean *librador* age of 42.6 years (7 cases); those with male *beneficiarios* have a mean *librador* age of 38.9 years (56 cases). A t-test did not find a significant means difference. Likewise, tests

did not find significant relationships between *beneficiario* gender and the other demographic variables. The following tests were run: Fisher's exact test (FET) for *beneficiario* gender and *librador* prior arrests; t-test for *beneficiario* gender and *librador* mean daily income; and FET for *beneficiario* gender and where the *librador* was from.

67 For female *libradoras*, of the 9 total files that also give information about outcome, 3 of these have a 'not guilty' outcome (33.3 per cent). For male *libradores*, of the 95 total files that also give information about outcome, 33 have a 'not guilty' outcome (34.7 per cent). An FET did not find a significant proportion difference. FETs were performed for *librador* gender and other outcomes; these did not find significant relationships. For female *beneficiarias*, out of 8 total files, 1 has a 'not guilty' outcome (12.5 per cent). For male *beneficiarios*, out of 70 total files, 21 have a 'not guilty' outcome (30 per cent). An FET did not find a significant proportion difference. Hereafter, FET results and chi-squared tests (x^2 tests) will be abbreviated to telegraph essential information. FETs were performed for *beneficiario* gender and other outcomes; these did not find significant relationships.

68 The duration is known for 114 of the 115 files, with 1 missing value; percentages are based on 114 files. In terms of frequency distribution, 25 per cent of files have a duration of 92 days or less; 50 per cent are 372.5 days or less; and 75 per cent are 843 days or less.

69 This was true when analysing the gender of *libradores* and *beneficiarios*. The mean duration for female *libradoras* is 641.9 days (10 files); for male *libradores* it is 663 days (104 files). A t-test did not find a significant means difference. The mean duration for female *beneficiarias* is 805.8 days (8 files); for male *beneficiarios* it is 701.5 days (78 files). A t-test did not find a significant means difference.

70 As with much of the statistical work in this book, the examination of the *cheques sin fondos* files is the first attempt, to my knowledge, to create a dataset for statistical analysis. Some of the quantitative research questions could be explored by future researchers; larger samples and different tests could add nuance or revise the picture.

71 Tests did not find significant relationships between amounts and the demographic variables. The following tests were run: t-test for *beneficiario* gender and amount; t-test for *librador* gender and amount; t-test for where the *librador* came from and amount; correlation for mean *librador* income and amount; and t-test for *librador* prior arrests and amount.

72 Files with a 'not guilty' outcome have a mean total amount 4,852.8 pesos (23 files); files with other outcomes have a mean total amount of 7,214.5 pesos (58 files). A t-test did not find a significant means difference. T-tests were performed for mean amounts and other outcomes and did not find significant relationships.

73 There are 88 cases for which both variables were observed.

74 For example, see Goux, 'Cash, Check, or Charge?'

75 Economists examine friction in terms of the transaction costs of different transfer mechanisms, especially in the present or very recent past, with

'frictionless' considered an ideal that is 'riskless, costless, and instantaneous'. Berger et al., 'Framework for Analyzing Efficiency', 701. See also Brynjolfsson and Smith, 'Frictionless Commerce?' My discussion of friction is drawn from anthropologist Bill Maurer's analysis, which incorporates cultural and emotional dimensions over a longer chronological arc; see especially Maurer, 'Foreword: Friction and Fantasies'.

76 Maurer, 'Foreword: Friction and Fantasies', vi.
77 Berger et al., 'Framework for Analyzing Efficiency', 701; see also Brynjolfsson and Smith, 'Frictionless Commerce?'
78 Bátiz-Lazo, *Cash and Dash*, 29.
79 Bátiz-Lazo et al., 'Origins of the Modern Concept of a Cashless Society', 99–101.
80 The economics scholarship on cheques in the USA, such as the work of Roberds, focuses on the technological and regulatory changes that reduced costs. McAndrews and Roberds, 'General Equilibrium Analysis of Check Float'; Quinn and Roberds, 'Evolution of the Check'.
81 A 1960 example by journalist Frank Gibney captures the sentiment at mid-century: 'Check kiting is a different and more complex process than forging ... Few up-and-coming businessmen can claim to have resisted the temptation to write a pressing check just a day or two before some money is due, in the prayerful expectation that their deposit will get into the bank's ledgers before the check they have cashed comes home to roost'. Gibney, *The Operators*, 158; also quoted in the *Oxford English Dictionary*, which traces the first usage of 'check kiting' to 1872.
82 Husz, 'Comment les salariés suédois', especially 114–117; see also Husz, 'Bank Identity', 398–401. Husz is the main historian, to my knowledge, who has examined cheques in the post-World War II period. There exists tremendous potential for future enquiry, both local and comparative. Other scholars offer glimpses of that potential. Historian Sabine Effosse, for example, has shown a slightly different timeline for cheques in France, where usage was initially slower but lasted longer than in other European countries, with broad use beginning in the late 1960s and lasting into the twenty-first century. She attributes the difference to the particularities in French banking law and the fact that marketing campaigns targeted women consumers. In addition, economists Matthew Jaremski and Gabriel Mathy examine the history of cheques in the USA, where the mode of payment enjoyed heavy and long usage until the late 1990s. They focus on clearing houses to help explain their usage. Effosse, 'Cheque en Francia'; Jaremski and Mathy, 'Mirada retrospectiva'.
83 Information about reasons is given in 64 cases, with 51 missing values.
84 'Violación a la Ley General de Títulos y Operaciones de Crédito', 7 September 1963, AHCDMX, Cárceles, c. 2290, ptda. 5875.
85 Information about *librador* prior arrests is given in all of the 115 files. Information about the prior charge is given in all of the 20 files with prior arrests.

Notes to pages 160–164   263

86 For female *beneficiarias*, of the 8 total files that also give information about *librador* prior arrests, 1 of these has a *librador* with a prior arrest (12.5 per cent); for male *beneficiarios*, of the 78 total files, 14 have a *librador* with a prior arrest (17.9 per cent). An FET did not find a significant proportion difference. For *libradores* with prior arrests, out of 20 total files, in 18 the *librador* admitted the offence (90 per cent); for *libradores* with no prior arrests, out of 95 total files, in 70 the *librador* admitted the offence (73.7 per cent). An FET did not find a significant proportion difference. For *libradores* with prior arrests, out of 17 total files, 7 have an outcome 'guilty and fined' (41.2 per cent); for *libradores* with no prior arrests, out of 87 total files, 31 have an outcome 'guilty and fined' (35.6 per cent). A x^2 test did not find a significant proportion difference. FETs and x^2 tests were performed for prior arrests and other outcomes, and did not find significant proportion differences.
87 'Violación a la Ley General de Títulos y Operaciones de Crédito', 15 January 1966, AHCDMX, Cárceles, c. 2447, ptda. 250.
88 'Violación a la Ley General de Títulos y Operaciones de Crédito', 5 October 1973, AHCDMX, Cárceles, c. 3327, ptda. 9964.
89 Information about endorsement is known for all of the 115 cases; there are no missing values.
90 'Violación a la Ley General de Títulos y Operaciones de Crédito', 23 July 1975, AHCDMX Cárceles, c. 3571, ptda. 7512.
91 'Violación a la Ley General de Títulos y Operaciones de Crédito', 15 October 1957, AHCDMX, Cárceles, c. 1885, ptda. 9456. The only other prison file that referenced physical violence gives less detail about the events. María del Refugio Espinosa del Prado, a 33-year-old housewife, was arrested in September 1966. José Curiel Pavía claimed that Espinosa had given him a cheque for 8,203.50 pesos, drawn on Banco Comercial Mexicano, and that the cheque bounced because Espinosa's account had been cancelled. Espinosa admitted that she wrote the cheque, but said she had done so 'under threat of injury'. She was found guilty and paid a fine of 1,000 pesos. 'Violación a la Ley General de Títulos y Operaciones de Crédito', 10 September 1966, AHCDMX, Cárceles, c. 2502, ptda. 6940; quote from document dated 26 February 1968.
92 Berghoff and Spiekermann propose six characteristics of white-collar crime, many of which could describe the *cheques sin fondos* examined here: delinquents were from middle- or upper-class backgrounds; they were motivated by financial gain; the crime was non-violent; it involved a breach of trust or an abuse of good faith; and it was systemic in nature, such as part of the culture at a firm; finally, the crime appeared victimless because the cost or harm was spread out over many people. Berghoff and Spiekermann, 'Shady Business', 290–291, quote on p. 299.
93 Taylor, 'White-Collar Crime'.
94 On the former, see, for example, Linebaugh, *London Hanged*; Thompson, *Whigs and Hunters*. On the latter, see, for example, Joseph, *Revolution from Without*; Womack, *Zapata*.

95 While much of the debate concerned eighteenth-century English history, the sources and methods of social history of crime inspired historians around the world. One entry into these questions is to study the tension between the content and the conclusion of E. P. Thompson's *Whigs and Hunters* and the resulting reviews and debates. Thompson had showed how the law was used by the oligarchic Hanoverian Whigs to steal resources from common forest dwellers, and his famous conclusion – that the rule of law was an 'unqualified human good' – seemed, to many scholars, to contradict his findings. Another entry into these debates is the exchange between John Langbein and Peter Linebaugh over the influential edited volume *Albion's Fatal Tree*, and in particularly Douglas Hay's introductory essay. Hay, 'Property, Authority'; Langbein, 'Albion's Fatal Flaws'; Linebaugh, '(Marxist) Social History'.

96 While there exists an extensive scholarship on land and labour rights, historians have given less attention to the everyday struggles that accompanied the deepening of financial capitalism; much of the historical scholarship for Mexico and beyond has been focused on macroeconomic questions. Exceptions include Sharon Murphy's analysis of life insurance in early nineteenth-century American history; Murphy, *Investing in Life*. Among the more influential macro analyses, see Ferguson, *Ascent of Money*. For a unique combination of micro and macro financial history, see Costeloe, *Bubbles and Bonanzas*.

97 Becerra Bautista, 'Expedición de cheques', especially 271–272, 288–289.

98 'F de L [Federico de León]', *Avance*, 2 March 1970, 5.

99 'De los procesos judiciales en el país, 33% es por Extender Cheques sin Fondos', *El Nacional*, 16 March 1983, 3. I have not been able to confirm the proportion of *cheques sin fondos* cases in first-instance proceedings for these decades. I also have not found information about the number of bounced cheques as a proportion of all cheque transactions for these decades. Instead, I have found glimpses from newspaper reporting. Banks in Acapulco reported, for example, that the percentage of bounced cheques was 1.73 per cent in November–December 1984 and 1.65 per cent in January–February 1985. 'Evitan en Acapulco el mal uso de chequeras otorgadas por la Banca', *El Nacional*, 29 April 1985, 5.

100 'De los procesos judiciales en el país, 33% es por Extender Cheques sin Fondos', *El Nacional*, 16 March 1983, 3.

101 A first attempt to eliminate fraud as a defining feature of uncovered cheques failed in 1972. The PAN (Partido Acción Nacional) deputy and legal scholar Francisco Peniche Bolio introduced a reform proposal to the Cámara de Diputados, to no avail. See 'Reforma al Art. 193 de la Ley General de Títulos y Operaciones de Crédito. Iniciativa para que la expedición de un cheque sin fondos no se considere como fraude sino como un delito especial', 9 November 1972, Legislature XLVIII (1970–1973). Text of the proposed reform is published online by the Fundación Miguel Estrata Iturbide.

102 Dávalos Mejía, *Títulos y operaciones de crédito*, 320.

Chapter 5

1. EGG to Fox, dated 6 November 2002, in Archivo General de la Nación (AGN), Presidentes, V. Fox, Red Federal de Servicio a la Ciudadanía (RFSC), *caja* (c.) 33, *expediente* (exp.) 9702 (note that the file name and date sometimes differ from the letter, and I include both; file name and date: EGG, Condusef, 23 January 2003). As in Chapter 4, I have changed the names of all the letter writers and others, such as their family and friends, who played a role in the events, and I have abbreviated to initials in the citations.
2. *Diario Oficial*, 13 August 2003.
3. Presidencia de la República, 'Mecanismos de participación ciudadana de la Red Federal de Servicio a la Ciudadanía', information flyer, n.d.
4. On department store credit in Porfirian Mexico, see Bunker, *Creating Mexican Consumer Culture*, especially chapter 4. On Sears store credit, see Moreno, *Yankee, Don't Go Home!*, especially chapter 6. On Elektra, see Ruiz, 'From Pawn Shops to Banks'.
5. Elsewhere, I have written about credit cards and government credit schemes; see Walker, *Waking from the Dream*, chapter 4.
6. Elsewhere I have written about Profeco; see Walker, *Waking from the Dream*, 122–125.
7. Full text published in *Diario Oficial*, 18 January 1999. The commission was created by the *Ley de Protección y Defensa al Usuario de Servicios Financieros* (Law for the Protection and Defence of the Users of Financial Services).
8. *Diario Oficial*, 18 January 1999.
9. The educational charge is outlined in Article 52.
10. Condusef did not, at the time of research (2014–2015), have an historical archive open to the public.
11. Among several publications, see, recently, Boyer, 'Ecology of Class', especially 47–49; Gilly, *El cardenismo*; see also Becker, *Setting the Virgin on Fire*; Knight, 'Cardenismo'.
12. Adair, *In Search of the Lost Decade*, 106. See also the letters to Cuauhtémoc Cárdenas collected by Adolfo Gilly and Rhina Roux in *Cartas a Cuauhtémoc Cárdenas*.
13. Becker, in contrast, argues the Lázaro Cárdenas read and learned from the letters. Becker, *Setting the Virgin on Fire*.
14. de Grammont, *Barzón: clase media, ciudadanía y democracia*; Williams, *Social Movements and Economic Transition*.
15. Chávez, 'El Barzón', see 97–101 for Chávez's analysis of the *barzonista* use of the *corrido* and the history of the song; quote on p. 98.
16. Rodríguez Gómez, 'Making a Globalized Nation'. There were several books published about *el Barzón* that combine popular history, journalism, *testimonio*, and collective history, many of which reproduce important historical primary sources. See, for example, Gómez Caballero, *Barzonistas*; Samperio, *Se nos reventó el Barzón*.
17. Haber, 'Mexico's Experiments', 2341.
18. On these plans, see Ibarra, 'México: Plan y coyuntura', especially 122–124.

19 Huerta González, *Debate del Fobaproa*, 39–50. See also Solís Rosales, ed., *Del Fobaproa al IPAB*. For an analysis of the *barzonista* struggles against Fobaproa, see also de Grammont, *Barzón: clase media, ciudadanía y democracia*, especially chapters 5–8.
20 On the history of Multibanco Comermex, see Álvarez, 'Venturing Abroad'.
21 I have written about Inco in *Waking from the Dream*, 125–128. On Fovissste, see Patiño, 'Fondo de Vivienda', 279–317. For comparative analysis of housing policy in the 1970s and 2000s, see Heeg et al., 'Financialization of Housing'.
22 EGG to Fox, dated 6 November 2002, in AGN, Presidentes, V. Fox, RFSC, c. 33, exp. 9702 (file name and date: EGG, Condusef, 23 January 2003).
23 Lavinas, *Takeover of Social Policy*, 7.
24 Scholars who have theorised this stage of capitalism and have studied its real-world effects use different terms to describe the economic order: financialisation, financialised capitalism, neoliberalism, the debt economy, credit-led accumulation, debtfarism, rentier capitalism, finance-dominated capitalism, and more. While these terms represent important distinctions, the broad picture is a shift in profit-making from trade and commodity production to finance. The pace and degree of the shift, of course, was different in different places (and is ongoing). I am using the term neoliberal capitalism because it connects the history of the early twenty-first century with the economic and political liberalism of the late eighteenth and early nineteenth centuries with which this book opened: putting the struggles between debtors and creditors into a longer chronology exposes both change and continuity. But many of these other terms could also describe the history examined in this chapter. For an overview of the scholarship, see Lavinas, *Takeover of Social Policy*, 7–8.
25 Progresa was renamed 'Opportunidades' in 2001 and 'Prospera' in 2010. See Masino and Niño-Zarazúa, 'Improving Financial Inclusion'; Parker and Todd, 'Conditional Cash Transfers'.
26 Masino and Niño-Zarazúa, 'Improving Financial Inclusion', 153.
27 See review in Masino and Niño-Zarazúa, 'Improving Financial Inclusion', 153–155.
28 On the financial logic conquering non-financial realms, see Pellandini-Simányi et al., 'Financialization of Everyday Life'.
29 I have written about the economic crises of the 1970s and 1980s in *Waking from the Dream*. The description in this paragraph and the next one draws on chapter 2 for the 1970s crisis, on chapter 4 for consumer protection, and on chapter 5 for the 1980s crisis.
30 From 1950 to 1972, the annual inflation rate was almost always under 5 per cent; in 1973 it shot up to 12 per cent; and for the next nine years it oscillated erratically between about 15 and 30 per cent. Messmacher and Werner, 'Inflación en México', 54, table 3. Cited in Walker, *Waking from the Dream*, 107.
31 Haber, 'Mexico's Experiments', 2325–2353. These and other incentives are described on pp. 2327–2333. Of course, the relationship between Fobaproa and the Banco de México was more complex than my quick summary, and readers should consult Haber for his description of the fine points.

He concludes: 'In short, the Banco de México explicitly stated that it was not only guaranteeing all deposits (*including inter-bank deposits*), it was also guaranteeing virtually all bank liabilities (deposits, loans, and credits) with the exception of subordinated debt.' Haber, 'Mexico's Experiments', 2333.

32 Haber estimates, however, that the actual rate of growth for housing loans might have been twice that, given the accounting practices. Haber, 'Mexico's Experiments', 2336–2338, especially table 3.

33 My bare-bones summary is based on Lustig, 'Mexican Peso Crisis' and Musacchio 'Mexico's Financial Crisis'.

34 As Haber writes, bank loan portfolios grew as a percentage of Fobaproa bonds from 9 per cent in 1995 to 20 per cent in 1996 to 29 per cent in 1997 and 1998; they peaked at 35 per cent in 1999. Haber, 'Mexico's Experiments', 2342.

35 Haber, 'Mexico's Experiments', 2340–2343, quote on p. 2342.

36 Haber cautions that this is a conservative calculation: 'Inasmuch as many types of loans, particularly those for housing, automobiles, and other consumer durables, have multi-year terms, the stock of loans is serially correlated. The implication is that the flow of new loans for private purposes has declined more dramatically than the data we present here.' Haber, 'Mexico's Experiments', 2345–2346, quote on p. 2346, fn18.

37 Negrín and de la Cerda, 'Evolución de la calidad', 3–7. While scholars do not yet have a time series that brings together information about the many different types of consumer credit before and after 1994, focused studies like Negrín and de la Cerda's show that specific kinds of consumer credit declined after the crisis. Most studies begin in 1994 because the available data changed after the crisis. Changes to Mexico's household income survey meant they gave more granulated information about household debt after the crisis. New surveys about consumption and finance also began after the *tequilazo*. Meanwhile, economists with access to Credit Bureau and other data unavailable to historians tend to focus on financial inclusion in recent years.

38 Haber, 'Mexico's Experiments', 2345–2346.

39 Anthropologists have studied the debtor–creditor relationship in archaic societies. The classic modern text is Maus's 1925 essay on reciprocity, *The Gift*. More recently, Graeber examines debt and the origins of social inequality over a long chronology in *Debt: 5,000 Years*. Philosophers have also studied the primordial function of debt vis-à-vis faith, guilt, and trust in moral systems; for example, Nietzsche's classic *Genealogy of Morality* and more recently Goodchild's *Credit and Faith*. I am drawing on sociologist Maurizio Lazzarato, who historicises the more theoretical scholarship and argues that indebtedness is the human condition of neoliberal capitalism. See Lazzarato, *Making of the Indebted Man*.

40 On Trevi as a protagonist of Mexican urban popular culture in the early 1990s, see Monsiváis, *Los rituals del caos*, 166–177.

41 Marx, 'Comments on James Mill' [1844], in *Marx and Engels: Collected Works*, translated by Richard Dixon, vol. 3, 211–228, quote on p. 214, italics in original.

42 Marx, 'Comments on James Mill', 215, italics in original.

43 Marx, 'Comments on James Mill', 215, italics in original.
44 Lazzarato, *Making of the Indebted Man*, 33–34.
45 Negrín, 'Mecanismos para compartir información crediticia'.
46 Lauer, *Creditworthy*, 200–211.
47 Bouk, 'History and Political Economy of Personal Data', 101–106. See also Poon, 'Scorecards as Devices for Consumer Credit'; Zuboff, 'Big Other'.
48 On the emotional toll generated when capitalist credit relationships dominate new areas of economic life, see Clara Han's study of healthcare debt in Chile in the early 2000s. Han, *Life in Debt*.
49 There is information about the amount in 49 of the 117 letters, with 68 missing values.
50 There is information about the institution in 108 of the 117 letters, with 9 missing values. Some writers reference more than one institution. Of the 117 letters, 87 per cent (94) are about 1 type of institution, 12 per cent (13) are about 2 types of institution, and 1 letter (0.9 per cent) is about more than 2 types of institution. Looking at 13 letters that reference 2 types of institution, 6 of these are about a government agency/institution and a bank; 6 are about a bank and another kind of institution; and 1 is about a government institution and another kind of institution.
51 Of the 39 letters with female authors and for which there is also information on institutions, 9 (23.1 per cent) are about government institutions. Of the 69 letters with male authors and for which there is also information on institutions, 30 (43.5 per cent) are about government institutions. A chi-squared test (x^2test) found that the observed difference in proportions (23.1 versus 43.5) is statistically significant. Hereafter, x^2tests and Fisher's exact tests (FETs) are abbreviated to telegraph essential information, and subsequent notes give a shortform version of the fuller format provided here.
52 Of the 39 letters with female authors that also give information on institutions, 23 concern a bank (59 per cent). Of the 69 letters with male authors, 25 are about a bank (36.2 per cent). A x^2test found a significant proportion difference.
53 ERV to Fox, dated 11 December 2000, in AGN, Presidentes, V. Fox, RFSC, c. 7, exp. 1802 (file name and date: ERV, Condusef, 31 January 2001).
54 The mean debt amount in letters with female authors is 185,785.1 pesos (22 letters). The mean amount in letters with male authors is 707,804 pesos (27 letters). A t-test did not find a statistical significance in the observed differences in means. Hereafter, results from t-tests are abbreviated. As in previous chapters, the 'not significant' results show only that the test did not uncover a significant connection. There may well exist a statistically significant relationship between the variables, but the tests are not finding one for myriad reasons. See the Introduction for more on method.
55 For explanation and writer gender, I tested each explanation separately. For example, of the 46 letters with female authors that also give information about explanation, 10 have a macro explanation (21.7 per cent); of the 71 with male authors, 13 have a macro explanation (18.3 per cent). A x^2test did not find a significant proportion difference. X^2tests were performed for writer gender and each explanation; they did not find significant proportion differences.

56 For geography and writer gender, I tested each geographical unit separately. For example, of the 46 letters with female authors that also give information about geography, 10 of the writers are from the Federal District (21.7 per cent); of the 71 letters with male authors, 14 writers are from the Federal District (19.7 per cent). A x^2 test did not find a significant proportion difference. FETs and x^2 tests were performed for writer gender and each geographical unit; they did not find significant proportion differences.

57 Of the 46 letters with female authors that give information about legal proceedings, 27 reference legal proceeding (58.7 per cent). Of the 71 letters with male authors, 38 reference legal proceeding (53.5 per cent). A x^2 test did not find a significant proportion difference.

58 Letters involving a government institution have a mean amount of 1,317,514.4 pesos (11 letters); letters with a different type of institution have a mean amount of 237,370.1 pesos (36 letters). A t-test did not find a significant means difference. T-tests were performed for amount and each institution type; they did not find significant means differences.

59 Letters involving macro explanations have a mean amount of 314,507.2 pesos (14 letters); letters with a different type of explanation have a mean amount of 536,996.6 pesos (35 letters). A t-test did not find a significant means difference. T-tests were performed for amount and each explanation; they did not find significant means differences.

60 Letters involving legal proceedings have a mean amount of 646,403.4 pesos (34 letters); letters not involving legal proceedings have a mean amount of 81,351.1 pesos (15 letters). A t-test did not find a significant means difference.

61 Letters with writers from the Federal District have a mean amount of 331,591.1 pesos (10 letters); letters with writers not from the Federal District have a mean amount of 509,796.7 (39 letters). A t-test did not find a significant means difference. T-tests were performed for amount and each geographic unit; they did not find significant means differences.

62 Ferguson, *Expectations of Modernity*; Weinstein, *Amazon Rubber Boom*.

63 ERV to Fox, dated 11 December 2000, in AGN, Presidentes, V. Fox, RFSC, c. 7, exp. 1802 (file name and date: ERV, Condusef, 31 January 2001).

64 See, most recently, Reagan et al., 'Emotional Arcs of Stories'.

65 Vonnegut, *Palm Sunday*, 311–316, especially 314.

66 Davis, *Fiction in the Archives*, 3.

67 Davis frames the French pardon letters as a mixed genre and shows how they were an aspect of state-building. She describes the letters as serving three interrelated needs: they were 'a judicial supplication to persuade the king and courts, a historical account of one's past actions, and a story. In all three there was a role for crafting and shaping.' Davis, *Fiction in the Archives*, 4.

68 I am echoing some of the research questions that Davis raises about her pardon tales. While her study focuses on how people explained their murderous rage, her questions can also be asked regarding how ordinary people crafted stories about commonplace problems. Davis, *Fiction in the Archives*, 4.

69 Vladimir Propp's classification of the thirty-one functions of Russian folktales inspired a wave of structuralist analysis. See Propp, *Morphology of the Folktale*.

70 For a methodological model, see Barr et al., 'Cognitive Change'. Relatedly, psychologists Peter Lunt and Sonia Livingstone show how ordinary people in Britain around 1990 attributed indebtedness to both personal causes and societal ones. Their network analysis of two psychological experiments shows how people attributed indebtedness to both personal responsibility and control and commercial and institutional forces. Lunt and Livingstone, 'Everyday Explanations for Personal Debt'.

71 On the former, see, for example, James Ferguson's ethnography of modernity and abjection among Zambian copper miners from boom to bust, and Viviana Zelizer's analysis of the sacred, social, and moral meanings of money, from life insurance to household economics. Ferguson, *Expectations of Modernity*; Zelizer, *Social Meaning of Money*. Regarding the latter, see, for example, Shiller's argument that stories matter because, whether true or not, narratives have an impact on macroeconomic fluctuations when they spread or 'go viral'. Shiller, 'Narrative Economics'. See also my own examination of the economic function of rumour, discussed in Chapter 2.

72 White, *Content of the Form*.

73 MARM to Fox, dated 10 July 2001, AGN, Presidentes, V. Fox, RFSC, c. 214, exp. 63236 (file name and date: MARM, Condusef, 6 August 2001).

74 NSGM to Fox, dated 1 July 2001, in AGN, Presidentes, V. Fox, RFSC, c. 169, exp. 49786 (file name and date: NSGM, Condusef, 10 July 2001).

75 PGM to Fox and Zedillo, dated 4 September 2000; PGM to Fox, dated 23 November 2000; PGM to Fox, dated 13 February 2001; PGM to Fox, dated 21 March 2001; Atención Ciudadana to PGM, dated 26 March 2001; all letters in AGN Presidentes, V. Fox, RFSC, c. 42, exp. 12165 (file name and date: PGM, Condusef, 5 April 2001); emphasis in original. On active citizenship, I am drawing on Fallaw and Nugent, eds, *State Formation in the Liberal Era*; see also Chapter 1.

76 ERM to Fox, dated 11 February 2004, in AGN, Presidentes, V. Fox, RFSC, c. 394, exp. 117549 (file name and date: ERM, GDF, 20 February 2004).

77 JFLA to Fox, dated 20 April 2004, in AGN, Presidentes, V. Fox, RFSC, c. 477, exp. 13348 (file name and date: JFLA, SS, 6 May 2004).

78 Because writers often used multiple explanations, these percentages are calculated on the base of the total 184 explanations that appear in the sample as opposed to the 117 letters. Throughout this section I report the numbers in the notes because the numbers are counterintuitive given the sample size of 117 letters.

79 The format is based on the work of biologists and visual data analysts. See Conway et al., 'UpSetR'; Lex et al., 'UpSet'.

80 Of the 48 letters about banks that also give information about explanations, 16 have a macro explanation (33.3 per cent); of the 60 letters about other institutions, 7 have a macro explanation (11.7 per cent). A x^2 test found a significant proportion difference.

81 ERV to Fox, dated 11 December 2000, in AGN, Presidentes, V. Fox, RFSC, c. 7, exp. 1802 (file name and date: ERV, Condusef, 31 January 2001).

82 Of the 39 letters about government institutions that also give information about explanations, 4 have a macro explanation (10.3 per cent); of the

69 letters about other institutions, 19 have a macro explanation (27.5 per cent). A x^2 test found a significant proportion difference.
83 Of the 45 letters that use the fraud explanation and also give other explanations, 2 also use a macro explanation (4.4 per cent); of the 72 letters without a fraud explanation, 21 use a macro explanation (29.2 per cent). A x^2 test found a significant proportion difference.
84 Of the 76 letters with a personal circumstances explanation that also give other explanations, 20 also give a macro explanation (26.3 per cent); of the 41 letters without a personal circumstances explanation, 3 also use a macro explanation (7.3 per cent). A x^2 test found a significant proportion difference.
85 RBM to Fox, dated 2 December 2000, in AGN, Presidentes, V. Fox, RFSC, c. 1, exp. 112 (file name and date: RBM, Condusef, 23 January 2001).
86 Of the 76 letters with a personal circumstances explanation that also give other explanations, 6 also give a bad government action explanation (7.9 per cent); of the 41 letters without a personal circumstances explanation, 14 give a bad government action explanation (34.1 per cent). A x^2 test found a significant proportion difference. Of the 76 letters with a personal circumstances explanation, 9 also give a bad private action explanation (11.8 per cent); of the 41 letters without a personal circumstances explanation, 11 also give a bad private action explanation (26.8 per cent). A x^2 test found a significant proportion difference. Of the 45 letters with a fraud explanation, 18 also give a personal circumstances explanation (40 per cent); of the 72 letters without a fraud explanation, 58 also give a personal circumstances explanation (80.6 per cent). A x^2 test found a significant proportion difference.
87 Juárez lifted the usury ban in 1861 as part of his liberal reforms, and the prohibition was reinstated after the revolution. See Levy, 'Cuestión de intereses'. The nineteenth-century usury legislation is examined in Chapter 2.
88 Mottier, 'Moneylending', 152.
89 For an overview, see Licona Vite, *Usura*, 392–564. See also Borja Martínez, 'Régimen jurídico'; Heredia Vázquez, *Usura*.
90 *Diario Oficial*, 26 May 1928, 487–488; see also Licona Vite, *Usura*, 427–431, especially 427.
91 *Diario Oficial*, 14 August 1931, 81–82; see also Karon, 'Law and Popular Credit'; Licona Vite, *Usura*, 523–526.
92 *Diario Oficial*, 7 May 1981, 6.
93 The scholarship on usury is vast. For a cultural history approach, see Le Goff, *Your Money or Your Life*. For intellectual history, see Kerridge, *Usury, Interest, and the Reformation*. For economic history, see Koyama, 'Evading the "Taint of Usury"'. For Mexico, see Levy, 'Cuestión de Intereses'; Levy, *Making of the Market*, especially chapter 3; Martínez López-Cano, 'Usuras'; Mottier, 'Moneylending'; O'Hara, *History of the Future*, especially chapter 4.
94 Verónica Reynold Reyes, 'Alertan sobre usura en casas de empeño', *El Economista*, 15 August 2005, 1.
95 EBA to Fox, 4 February 2005, in AGN, Presidentes, V. Fox, c. 710, exp. 210992 (file name and date: EBA, Gobierno del Estado de Guanajuato, n.d.); emphasis in original.

96 The Infonavit programme was passed in 1972 to provide home mortgages to low-income workers. It was complementary to the Fovissste programme that provided mortgages to state employees, also passed in 1972, through which Esther García, with whom I opened this chapter, had received her mortgage. On the early years of Infonavit, see Buchanan, 'Working for the Workers?' See also Schteingart and Graizbord, eds, *Vivienda y vida urbana*. On Fovissste, see note 21.

97 The State Code defined usury as greater than four times the *Costo Porcentual Promedio*, as fixed by the Banco de México; defined in this way, in September 1993 an 11 per cent interest rate would not have been usurious. *Código Penal para el Estado de Guanajuato*, 14 May 1978, Article 205.

98 On enclosures, see Thompson, *Whigs and Hunters*. On Anenecuilco, see Sotelo Inclán, *Raíz y razón*; Womack, *Zapata*.

99 Translation from Chávez, 'El Barzón', 98–99; original from Kuri-Aldana and Mendoza Martínez, *Cancionero popular mexicano*, 420.

100 Le Goff, *Your Money or Your Life*.

101 Negrín, 'Mecanismos para compartir información crediticia', 437–439.

102 Negrín, 'Mecanismos para compartir información crediticia', 439–444.

103 Negrín, 'Mecanismos para compartir información crediticia', 449–450. Note that the Buró was initially called the Buró Nacional de Crédito but changed its name so that it would not be mistaken for a government institution.

104 Lauer, *Creditworthy*, 200–217. On surveillance systems in late twentieth-century USA, see also Bouk, 'History and Political Economy of Personal Data'.

105 Quoted in Lauer, *Creditworthy*, 213; original Roy, 'Why Credit Scoring', 27.

106 Quoted in Lauer, *Creditworthy*, 211; original Nelson, 'Credit Scoring', 36.

107 Lauer, *Creditworthy*, 212. Indeed, some scholars describe the mode of accumulation at the turn of the millennium as one of 'surveillance capitalism'. I prefer the term 'neoliberal capitalism' because the *longue durée* history of power struggles between debtors and creditors suggests that surveillance was a fundamental but not a uniquely defining aspect of capitalism at the turn of the millennium. The Credit Bureau in the 2000s had an equivalent in the close observation and collection of economic information in a butcher's shop in the 1870s (examined in Chapter 2). The economic information of the late twentieth and early twenty-first centuries belongs to a long history of projects to inscribe and discipline ordinary people in the structures of modern states and capitalist relations. On the political economy of the digital era, see especially Zuboff, 'Big Other'. On the growing interest among historians of the USA in the concept of surveillance capitalism, see, for example, Lauer and Lipartito, eds, *Surveillance Capitalism in America*.

108 Credit history 'cleaning services' appeared in newspaper back pages, such as this text, which was followed by a mobile phone number: '¿!PROBLEMAS EN BURO?! ¡¡NADIE TE DA CREDITO?! NOSOTROS SOMOS TU SOLUCIÓN!!! LIMPIAMOS SU HISTORIAL CREDITICIO!!', *El Informador*, 6 October 2006, 7-D (punctuation and spelling errors in original).

109 *La Jornada*, 29 October 2007, 21.

110 These were a regular feature in the back pages. For example, *El Informador*, 27 November 2007, 6-D.
111 Monsalve's letter is one of 9 in the sample addressed to President Calderón.
112 RAMC to Calderón, dated 7 April 2007, in AGN, Presidentes, F. Calderón, RFSC, c. 1359, exp. 02-1S.3-97346 (file name and date: RAMC, Condusef, 4 December 2007).
113 'Cabal Buys Rest of Del Monte', *The Independent* (London), 28 June 1994. See also 'Esta es la historia de Carlos Cabal Peniche, uno de los principales banqueros en el rescate del Fobaproa y exinversionista de Interjet', *Business Insider Mexico*, 24 November 2020; 'Extraditado banquero Cabal Peniche regresa a los negocios', *La Nación* (San José), 24 January 2004; Armando Guzmán, 'Retorno de Cabal Peniche', *Proceso*, 26 December 2014; Rosen, '$55 Billion Bank-Bailout Scandal'.
114 BARE to Fox, dated 4 April 2003, in AGN, Presidentes, V. Fox, RFSC, c. 126, exp. 37331 (file name and date: BARE, Condusef, 16 May 2003).
115 FFG to Fox, dated 4 March 2005 in AGN, Presidentes, V. Fox, RFSC, c. 689, exp. 204636 (file name and date: FFG, Condusef, 8 April 2005).
116 RRC to Fox, dated 9 May 2003, in AGN, Presidentes, V. Fox, RFSC, c. 276, exp. 82419 (file name and date: RRC, Condusef, 31 October 2003). RRC to Calderón, dated 26 April 2007, in AGN, Presidentes, F. Calderón, RFSC, c. 636, exp. 02-1S.3-47105 (file name and date: RRC, Condusef, 1 June 2007). Robledo's second letter was addressed to Calderón.
117 CGMC to Fox, dated 10 November 2004, in AGN, Presidentes, V. Fox, RFSC, c. 630, exp. 187354 (file name and date: CGMC, Condusef, 14 January 2005).
118 MARV to Fox, dated 14 July 2004, in AGN, Presidentes, V. Fox, RFSC, c. 524, exp. 156155 (file name and date: MARV, Condusef, 24 November 2004).

References

ARCHIVES CITED

Archivo General de la Nación (AGN)
    Collection Presidenciales
    Collection Tribunal Superior de Justicia del Distrito Federal (TSJDF)
Archivo Histórico de la Ciudad de México 'Carlos de Sigüenza y Góngora' (AHCDMX)
    Collection Ayuntamiento Justicia
    Collection Cárceles
Archivo Histórico del Banco de México
    Collection Fondo Rodrigo Gómez
Archivo Histórico del Banco Nacional de México (AHBNM)
    Collection Libros Contables, Serie R. G. Dun y Cia
Baker Library, Harvard Business School
Fototeca Nacional, Instituto de Antropología e Historia
    Collection Archivo Casasola
Hemeroteca Nacional de México

PERIODICALS

Avance
Business Insider México
Diario Oficial
El Economista
La Iberia
The Independent (London)
El Informador
La Jornada
Jueves de Excelsior
El Monitor Constitucional

La Nación (San José)
El Nacional
Proceso
El Siglo de Torréon
El Siglo Diez y Nueve
El Universal

PRIMARY SOURCES

Alfonso, X. *Las Siete Partidas*, edited by Robert I. Burns, translated by S. P. Scott. Philadelphia: University of Pennsylvania Press, 2001 [1256–1265].

Cardona René, Jr., dir. *La hermana trinquete*. Mexico City: Churubusco-Azteca, 1970.

Código Civil del Distrito Federal y Territorio de la Baja-California. Mexico City: Imprenta Dirigida por Jose Batiza, 1870.

Código de Comercio de México. Mexico City: Imprenta de José Mariano Lara, 1854.

Código de Procedimientos Civiles para el Distrito Federal y el Territorio de la Baja California. Mexico: Imprenta del Gobierno en Palacio, 1872.

Código Penal para el Distrito Federal y Territorio De La Baja-California sobre delitos del Fuero Común y para toda La República Mexicana sobre delitos contra La Federación. Veracruz: Librerías 'La Ilustración', 1891 [1871].

Constitución de Cádiz. Translated by M. C. Mirow. In *Florida's First Constitution: The Constitution of Cádiz, Introduction, Translation, and Text*, introduction, translation, and text by M. C. Mirow. Durham, NC: Carolina Academic Press, 2012 [1812].

Cuarón, Alfonso, dir. *Roma*. Mexico and USA: Espectáculos Fílmicos, El Coyúl, and Netflix, 2018.

Escriche, Joaquín and Juan Rodríguez de San Miguel. *Diccionario razonado de legislación civil, penal, comercial y forense*. Mexico City: UNAM, Instituto de Investigaciones Jurídicas, 1998 [1837].

Exposicion de los cuatro libros del Codigo Civil del Distrito Federal y Territorio de la Baja California que hizo la comisión al presenter el proyecto al supremo gobierno. Mexico City: Aguilar e hijos, 1882 [1870].

Ezeta, Luis G. de. *Manual de alcaldes y jueces de paz*. Mexico City: Impreso por Leandro J. Valdes, 1845.

INEGI. *Estadísticas Históricas de México*, 4th edition. Aguascalientes: Instituto Nacional de Estadística, Geografía e Informática (INEGI), 1999.

Leyes de Reforma: Colección de las disposiciones que se conocen con este nombre, publicadas desde el año de 1855 al de 1868. Tomo 2. Parte 2. Nacionalización de bienes eclesiásticos. Constitución. Compiled and annotated by Licenciado Blas José Gutiérrez Flores Alatorre. Mexico City: Impresor Miguel Zornoza, 1870.

Mercantile Agency. *The Mercantile Agency Manual: A Compilation of Rules and Regulations for the General Conduct of the Business*, 3rd edition. New York: R. G. Dun & Co., 1897.

The Mercantile Agency Reporters' Manual, 2nd edition. New York: R. G. Dun & Co., 1902.
The Mercantile Agency Reporters' Manual, 4th edition. New York: R. G. Dun & Co., 1918.
Novísima Recopilación de las Leyes de España. Madrid: no publisher, 1805–1807.
Payno, Manuel. *El fistol del diablo: novela de costumbres mexicanas*, 2nd edition. Mexico City: Imprenta de F. Díaz de León y Santiago White, 1871.
Recopilación de leyes, decretos, reglamentos, circulares y providencias de los Supremos Poderes y otras autoridades de la República Mexicana formada de orden del Supremo Gobierno: Año de 1831. Mexico City: Imprenta de J. M. Fernandez de Lara, 1835.
Rodríguez de San Miguel, Juan and Mariano Galván Rivera. *Curia Filípica Mexicana*. Mexico: Universidad Nacional Autónoma de México, 1978 [1850].
Romero Gil, Hilarión José. *Código de procedimientos civiles y criminales de México*. Mexico City: Imprenta de Tomás S. Guardiola, 1854.
Trevi, Gloria. 'Colapso Financiero.' On *Si me llevas contigo*. Sony International, 1995.
United States Department of State. 'Credit Systems of the Several Countries: Reports from the Consuls of the United States on the Credit and Trade Systems of Their Several Districts, in Answer to a Circular from the Department of State.' Consular Report 43. Washington, DC: Government Printing Office, 1884.

SECONDARY SOURCES

Acemoglu, Daron and James A Robinson. 'De Facto Political Power and Institutional Persistence.' *American Economic Review* 96, no. 2 (2006): 325–330.
Acemoglu, Daron, Simon Johnson, and James A Robinson. 'The Rise of Europe: Atlantic Trade, Institutional Change, and Economic Growth.' *American Economic Review* 95, no. 3 (2005): 546–579.
Adair, Jennifer. *In Search of the Lost Decade: Everyday Rights in Post-Dictatorship Argentina*. Oakland: University of California Press, 2020.
 ed. *Colonial Legacies: The Problem of Persistence in Latin American History*. New York: Routledge, 1999.
 'Liberalism and Constitutionalism in Latin America in the 19th Century.' *History Compass* 12, no. 6 (2014): 508–516.
 Republic of Capital: Buenos Aires and the Legal Transformation of the Atlantic World. Stanford, CA: Stanford University Press, 1999.
Aguilar, Miguel Ángel and Néstor García Canclini, eds. *Cultura y comunicación en la Ciudad de México*. Mexico City and Iztapalapa: Universidad Autónoma Metropolitana and Editorial Grijalbo, 1998.
Aguilar Aguilar, Cándido Eugenio. 'Régimen legislativo y de propiedad durante la Revolución Mexicana: Los casos de las haciendas petroleras de Chapopote y

El Álamo, en el norte veracruzano (1925–1937).' *Revista de El Colegio de San Luis* 8, no. 15 (2018): 13–45.

Alexander, Anna Rose. *City on Fire: Technology, Social Change, and the Hazards of Progress in Mexico City, 1860–1910*. Pittsburgh: University of Pittsburgh Press, 2016.

Allier, Eugenia. *68 el movimiento que triunfo en el futuro: historias, memorias y presente*. Mexico City: Universidad Nacional Autónoma de México, 2021.

Álvarez, Sebastián. 'Venturing Abroad: The Internationalisation of Mexican Banks Prior to the 1982 Crisis.' *Journal of Latin American Studies* 49, no. 3 (2017): 517–548.

Amrhein, Valentin, Sander Greenland, and Blake McShane. 'Scientists Rise Up Against Statistical Significance.' *Nature* 567, no. 7748 (2019): 305–307.

Anaya Merchant, Luis. *Colapso y reforma: la Integración del sistema bancario en el México Revolucionario, 1913–1932*. Zacatecas: Universidad Autónoma de Zacatecas, 2002.

Aristotle. *Rhetoric*. In *The Complete Works of Aristotle. Volume 2: The Revised Oxford Translation*, edited by Johnathan Barnes, translated by W. Rhys Roberts, 2152–2269. Princeton, NJ: Princeton University Press, 1984.

Arnold, Linda. *Catálogo de los libros de juicios verbales y conciliatorios del ayuntamiento de la Ciudad de México*. Mexico City: Ilustre y Nacional Colegio de Abogados de México, AC, Ayuntamiento de la Ciudad de México, and Archivo Histórico del Distrito Federal, 2001.

'Dos demandantes, un demandado: El juicio verbal en el fuero militar o ¿Qué pasó con mi caballo?' In *Construcción de la Legitimidad Política en México*, edited by Brian Conaughton, Carlos Illades, and Sonia Pérez Toledo, 195–205. Mexico City: UAM-Iztapalapa, UNAM, and Colegio de México, 2009.

'Introduction: Juzgados Constitucionales (1813–1848).' In *Catálogo de los libros de juicios verbales y conciliatorios del ayuntamiento de la Ciudad de México*, 9–12. Mexico City: Ilustre y Nacional Colegio de Abogados de México, AC, Ayuntamiento de la Ciudad de México, and Archivo Histórico del Distrito Federal, 2001.

'Juicios verbales y conciliatorios.' In *Diccionario histórico judicial de México: Ideas e instituciones II*, 910–919. Mexico City: Suprema Corte de Justicia de la Nación, 2010.

'Vulgar and Elegant: Politics and Procedure in Early National Mexico.' *The Americas* 50, no. 4 (1994): 481–500.

Arrom, Silvia Marina. *Containing the Poor: The Mexico City Poor House, 1774–1871*. Durham, NC: Duke University Press, 2000.

The Women of Mexico City, 1790–1857. Stanford, CA: Stanford University Press, 1985.

Austin, Gareth. 'African Economic Development and Colonial Legacies.' *Revue Internationale de Politique de Développement* 1, no. 1 (2010): 11–32.

Aviña, Alexander. *Specters of Revolution: Peasant Guerrillas in the Cold War Mexican Countryside*. Oxford: Oxford University Press, 2014.

Baker, Tom and Jonathan Simon. 'Embracing Risk.' In *Embracing Risk: The Changing Culture of Insurance and Responsibility*, edited by Tom Baker and Jonathan Simon, 1–26. Chicago: University of Chicago Press, 2002.

Banerjee, Abhijit V. 'The Economics of Rumours.' *Review of Economic Studies* 60, no. 2 (1993): 309–327.
Banerjee, Abhijit, Arun G. Chandrasekhar, Esther Duflo, and Matthew O. Jackson. 'Using Gossips to Spread Information: Theory and Evidence from Two Randomized Controlled Trials.' *Review of Economic Studies* 86, no. 6 (2019): 2453–2490.
Barr, Pamela S., J. L. Stimpert, and Anne S. Huff. 'Cognitive Change, Strategic Action, and Organizational Renewal.' *Strategic Management Journal* 13, no. S1 (1992): 15–36.
Barrett, Matthew. 'Worthless Cheques and Financial Honour: Cheque Fraud and Canadian Gentlemen Officers During the First World War.' *Histoire Sociale* 51, no. 104 (2018): 301–328.
Barry, Jonathan and Christopher Brooks. *The Middling Sort of People: Culture, Society and Politics in England, 1550–1800*. New York: St Martin's Press, 1994.
Baskes, Jeremy. *Staying Afloat: Risk and Uncertainty in Spanish Atlantic World Trade, 1760–1820*. Stanford, CA: Stanford University Press, 2013.
Bátiz-Lazo, Bernardo. *Cash and Dash: How ATMs and Computers Changed Banking*. Oxford: Oxford University Press, 2018.
Bátiz-Lazo, Bernardo, Thomas Haigh, and David L. Stearns. 'Origins of the Modern Concept of a Cashless Society, 1950s–1970s.' In *The Book of Payments: Historical and Contemporary Views on the Cashless Society*, edited by Bernardo Bátiz-Lazo and Leonidas Efthymiou, 95–106. London: Palgrave Macmillan, 2016.
Bayardo Rodríguez, Lilia Esthela. *Entre el lujo, el deseo y la necesidad: Historia del gasto familiar y del consumo moderno en la Ciudad de México, 1909–1970*. Zapopan, Jalisco: El Colegio de Jalisco, 2018.
Bazant, Jan. *Alienation of Church Wealth in Mexico: Social and Economic Aspects of the Liberal Revolution, 1856–1875*. Cambridge: Cambridge University Press, 2008.
Beatty, Edward. *Technology and the Search for Progress in Modern Mexico*. Oakland: University of California Press, 2015.
Becerra Bautista, José. 'Expedición de cheques sin fondos.' *Revista de la Escuela Nacional de Jurisprudencia* IV, no. 15 (1942): 267–292.
Becker, Marjorie. *Setting the Virgin on Fire: Lázaro Cárdenas, Michoacán Peasants, and the Redemption of the Mexican Revolution*. Berkeley: University of California Press, 2006.
Berger, Allen N., Diana Hancock, and Jeffrey C. Marquardt. 'A Framework for Analyzing Efficiency, Risks, Costs, and Innovations in the Payments System.' *Journal of Money, Credit and Banking* 28, no. 4 (1996): 696–732.
Berghoff, Hartmut and Uwe Spiekermann. 'Shady Business: On the History of White-Collar Crime.' *Business History* 60, no. 3 (2018): 289–304.
Bishara, Fahad Ahmad. *A Sea of Debt: Law and Economic Life in the Western Indian Ocean, 1780–1950*. Cambridge: Cambridge University Press, 2017.
Bleynat, Ingrid. *Vendors' Capitalism: A Political Economy of Public Markets in Mexico City*. Stanford, CA: Stanford University Press, 2021.

Borah, Woodrow. *Justice by Insurance the General Indian Court of Colonial Mexico and the Legal Aides of the Half-Real*. Berkeley: University of California Press, 1983.

Borja Martínez, Francisco. 'Régimen jurídico aplicable en materia de tasas de interés.' *Jurídica* 13 (1981): 305–314.

Bouk, Dan. 'The History and Political Economy of Personal Data over the Last Two Centuries in Three Acts.' *Osiris* 32, no. 1 (2017): 85–106.

How Our Days Became Numbered: Risk and the Rise of the Statistical Individual. Chicago: University of Chicago Press, 2015.

Boyer, Christopher R. 'The Ecology of Class: Revolution, Weaponized Nature, and the Making of 'Campesino' Consciousness.' *Historical Reflections* 41, no. 1 (2015): 40–53.

Braudel, Fernand. *The Mediterranean and the Mediterranean World in the Age of Philip II*. New York: Harper & Row, 1972.

Breña, Roberto, ed. *Cádiz a debate: Actualidad, context y legado*. Mexico City: Colegio de México, 2014.

Brenner, Robert. 'Agrarian Class Structure and Economic Development in Pre-Industrial Europe.' *Past & Present* 70, no. 1 (1976): 30–75.

Brynjolfsson, Erik and Michael D. Smith. 'Frictionless Commerce? A Comparison of Internet and Conventional Retailers.' *Management Science* 46, no. 4 (2000): 563–585.

Buchanan, Jordan. 'Working for the Workers? Infonavit's Creation and Its Foundational Motivations, 1972–1976.' *Journal of Urban History* (Prepublished 23 October 2024) https://doi.org/10.1177/00961442241288520.

Buchenau, Jürgen. *Tools of Progress: A German Merchant Family in Mexico City, 1865–Present*. Albuquerque: University of New Mexico Press, 2004.

Bunker, Steven B. *Creating Mexican Consumer Culture in the Age of Porfirio Díaz*. Albuquerque: University of New Mexico Press, 2012.

Burnham, Michelle. *Transoceanic America: Risk, Writing, and Revolution in the Global Pacific*. Oxford: Oxford University Press, 2019.

Burns, Kathryn. *Into the Archive: Writing and Power in Colonial Peru*. Durham, NC: Duke University Press, 2010.

Calderón Fernández, Andrés. 'Mirando a Nueva España en otros espejos: Cuatros ensayos sobre demografía y niveles de vida, siglos XVI–XIX.' PhD thesis, Universidad Compultense de Madrid, 2016.

Caldéron Fernández, Andrés. 'Una serie de precios de vivienda: las Accesorias del Real Colegio de San Ignacio de Loyola de los Señores Vizcaínos, 1771–1821.' *Gaceta Vizcaínas* 4, no. x (2009): 1–53.

Cárdenas, Enrique. 'La economía mexicana en el dilatado siglo XX, 1929–2009.' In *Historia económica general de México: de la colonia a nuestros días*, edited by Sandra Kuntz Ficker, 503–548. Mexico City: El Colegio de Mexico, 2010.

Cardoso, Fernando Henrique and Enzo Faletto. *Dependency and Development in Latin America*. Berkeley and Los Angeles: University of California Press, 1979.

Castillo Hernández, Diego. 'La ley y el honor: Jueces menores en la ciudad de México, 1846–1850.' *Signos históricos* 13, no. 26 (2011): 78–109.

Caulfield, Sueann, Sarah C. Chambers, and Lara Putnam. *Honor, Status, and Law in Modern Latin America*. Durham, NC: Duke University Press, 2005.

Cedillo, Adela and Fernando Calderón. *Challenging Authoritarianism in Mexico: Revolutionary Struggles and the Dirty War, 1964–1982*. New York: Routledge, 2012.

Cerutti Pignat, Mario Italo, and Gustavo Lorenzana Durán. 'Irrigación, expansión de la frontera agrícola y empresariado en el Yaqui (1925–1965).' *America Latina en la Historia Económica* 16, no. 1 (2009): 5–36.

Challú Amílcar E. and Aurora Gómez-Galvarriato. 'Mexico's Real Wages in the Age of the Great Divergence, 1730–1930.' *Revista de Historia Economical Journal of Iberian and Latin American Economic History* 33, no. 1 (2015): 83–122.

Chávez, Daniel. 'El Barzón: Performing Resistance in Contemporary Mexico.' *Arizona Journal of Hispanic Cultural Studies* 2, no. 1 (1998): 87–112.

Chowning, Margaret. *Wealth and Power in Provincial Mexico: Michoacán from the Late Colony to the Revolution*. Stanford, CA: Stanford University Press, 1999.

Cline, Howard Francis. *Mexico: Revolution to Evolution, 1940–1960*. London: Oxford University Press, 1962.

Coatsworth, John H. 'Inequality, Institutions and Economic Growth in Latin America.' *Journal of Latin American Studies* 40, no. 3 (2008): 545–569.

'Obstacles to Economic Growth in Nineteenth-Century Mexico.' *The American Historical Review* 83, no. 1 (1978): 80–100.

Cohen, Lizabeth. *A Consumer's Republic: The Politics of Mass Consumption in Postwar America*. New York: Vintage Books, 2004.

Conway, Jake R, Alexander Lex, and Nils Gehlenborg. 'UpSetR: An R Package for the Visualization of Intersecting Sets and Their Properties.' *Bioinformatics* 33, no. 18 (2017): 2938–2940.

Costeloe, Michael P. *Bubbles and Bonanzas: British Investors and Investments in Mexico, 1821–1860*. Lanham, MD: Lexington Books, 2011.

Covarrubias, José Enrique. *La moneda de cobre en México, 1760–1842: Un problema administrativo*. Mexico City: Universidad Nacional Autónoma de México and Instituto de Investigaciones Dr José María Luis Mora, 2000.

Crain, James M. 'War Exclusion Clauses and Undeclared Wars.' *Tennessee Law Review* 39, no. 2 (1972): 328–340.

Cruz Barney, Oscar. *Historia del Derecho en Mexico*. Mexico City: Oxford University Press, 2004.

Cruz-García, Paula, María del Carmen Dircio Palacios Macedo, and Emili Tortosa-Ausina. 'Financial Inclusion and Exclusion Across Mexican Municipalities.' *Regional Science Policy & Practice* 13, no. 5 (2021): 1496–1526.

Danzig, Gabriel. '"True Justice" in the "Republic".' *Illinois Classical Studies* 23 (1998): 85–99.

Dávalos Mejía, Luis Carlos Felipe. *Títulos y operaciones de crédito: análisis teórico práctico de la ley general de títulos y operaciones de crédito y temas afines*. Mexico City: Oxford University Press, 2012.

Davies, Keith A. 'Tendencias demográficas urbanas durante el siglo XIX en México.' *Historia mexicana* 21, no. 3 (1972): 481–524.
Davis, Natalie Zemon. *Fiction in the Archives: Pardon Tales and Their Tellers in Sixteenth-Century France*. Stanford, CA: Stanford University Press, 1987.
de Grammont, Hubert C. *El barzón: clase media, ciudadanía y democracia*. Mexico City: UNAM, 2001.
del Ángel, Gustavo A. 'The Nexus Between Business Groups and Banks: Mexico, 1932–1982.' *Business History* 58, no. 1 (2016): 111–128.
  'La paradoja del desarrollo financiero.' In *Historia económica general de México: de la colonia a nuestros días*, edited by Sandra Kuntz Ficker, 635–666. Mexico City: El Colegio de Mexico, 2010.
del Ángel, Gustavo A. and Carlos Marichal. 'Poder y crisis: historiografía reciente del crédito y la banca en México, siglos XIX y XX.' *Historia mexicana* 52, no. 3 (2003): 677–724.
del Castillo Troncoso, Alberto, ed. *Reflexión y crítica en torno al movimiento estudiantil de 1968: nuevos enfoques y líneas de investigación*. Mexico City: Instituto Mora, 2012.
Diekmann, Andreas and Wojtek Przepiorka. 'Trust and Reputation in Markets.' In *The Oxford Handbook of Gossip and Reputation*, edited by Francesca Giardini and Rafael Wittek, 382–400. Oxford: Oxford University Press, 2019.
Dillingham, Alan Shane. *Oaxaca Resurgent: Indigeneity, Development, and Inequality in Twentieth-Century Mexico*. Stanford, CA: Stanford University Press, 2021.
Dwyer, John Joseph. *The Agrarian Dispute: The Expropriation of American-Owned Rural Land in Postrevolutionary Mexico*. Durham, NC: Duke University Press, 2008.
Dye, Alan. 'The Institutional Framework.' In *The Cambridge Economic History of Latin America*, edited by Victor Bulmer-Thomas, John H. Coatsworth, and Roberto Cortés Conde, vol. 2, 167–208. Cambridge: Cambridge University Press, 2006.
Eastman, Scott. 'Introduction: The Sacred Mantle of the Constitution of 1812.' In *The Rise of Constitutional Government in the Iberian Atlantic World*, edited by Scott Eastman and Natalia Sobrevilla Perea, 1–18. Tuscaloosa: University of Alabama Press, 2015.
Echeverri, Marcela. *Indian and Slave Royalists in the Age of Revolution: Reform, Revolution, and Royalism in the Northern Andes, 1780–1825*. New York: Cambridge University Press, 2017.
Edwards, Jeremy and Sheilagh Ogilvie. 'What Lessons for Economic Development Can We Draw from the Champagne Fairs?' *Explorations in Economic History* 49, no. 2 (2012): 131–148.
Effosse, Sabine. 'El cheque en Francia: El lento ascenso de un medio de pago de masas (1918–1975).' *Revista de la Historia de la Economica y de la Empresa* 11 (2017): 77–94.
  Le crédit à la consommation en France, 1947–1965: De la stigmatisation à la réglementation. Paris: Comité pour l'histoire économique et financière de la France, 2014.

Elena, Eduardo. *Dignifying Argentina : Peronism, Citizenship, and Mass Consumption*. Pittsburgh: University of Pittsburgh Press, 2011.

Eliav-Feldon, Miriam and Tamar Herzig, eds. *Dissimulation and Deceit in Early Modern Europe*. Houndmills: Palgrave Macmillan, 2015.

Escanilla Huerta, Silvia. '"They Will Live Without Law or Religion": Cádiz, Indigenous People, and Political Change in the Viceroyalty of Peru, 1812–1820.' *The Hispanic American Historical Review* 101, no. 2 (2021): 199–230.

Escobar Ohmstede, Antonio and Matthew Butler. 'Introduction: Transitions and Closures in Nineteenth- and Twentieth-Century Mexican Agrarian History.' In *Mexico in Transition: New Perspectives on Mexican Agrarian History, Nineteenth and Twentieth Centuries*, edited by Antonio Escobar Ohmstede and Matthew Butler, 33–76. Mexico City: CIESAS, 2013.

Fallaw, Ben. *Cárdenas Compromised: The Failure of Reform in Postrevolutionary Yucatán*. Durham, NC: Duke University Press, 2001.

Fallaw, Ben and David Nugent, eds. *State Formation in the Liberal Era: Capitalisms and Claims of Citizenship in Mexico and Peru*. Tucson: University of Arizona Press, 2020.

Ferguson, James. *Expectations of Modernity: Myths and Meanings of Urban Life on the Zambian Copperbelt*. Berkeley: University of California Press, 1999.

Ferguson, Niall. *The Ascent of Money: A Financial History of the World*. New York: Penguin, 2008.

Flandreau, Marc and Gabriel Geisler Mesevage. 'The Untold History of Transparency: Mercantile Agencies, the Law, and the Lawyers (1851–1916).' *Enterprise & Society* 15, no. 2 (2014): 213–251.

Flores Flores, Graciela. *La ciudad judicial: una aproximación a los lugares de y para la justicia criminal en la ciudad de México (1824–1846)*. Mexico City: Tirant lo Blanch, 2020.

La justicia criminal ordinaria en tiempos de transición: la construcción de un nuevo orden judicial (Ciudad de México, 1824–1871). Mexico City: Universidad Nacional Autónoma de México, 2019.

Foss, Sarah, Vanessa Freije, and Rachel Nolan, eds. 'Interpretative Challenges in the Archive: Rumor, Forgery, and Denunciation in Latin America and the Caribbean.' *Journal of Social History* 55, no. 1 (2021) [special section].

Francois, Marie Eileen. *A Culture of Everyday Credit: Housekeeping, Pawnbroking, and Governance in Mexico City, 1750–1920*. Lincoln: University of Nebraska Press, 2007.

Galindo Rodríguez, José. *Ethnic Entrepreneurs, Crony Capitalism, and the Making of the Franco-Mexican Elite*. Tuscaloosa: University of Alabama Press, 2021.

García Canclini, Néstor. *Consumidores y ciudadanos: Conflictos multiculturales de la globalización*. Mexico City: Grijalbo, 1995.

Garciadiego, Javier. 'La revolución mexicana: el reto de la historia reciente.' *Historia Mexicana*, 71, no. 1 (2021): 249–269.

Giardini, Francesca and Rafael Wittek. 'Introduction: Gossip and Reputation, A Multidisciplinary Research Program.' In *The Oxford Handbook of Gossip and Reputation*, edited by Francesca Giardini and Rafael Wittek, 1–20. Oxford: Oxford University Press, 2019.

Gibney, Frank. *The Operators*. Westport, CT: Greenwood Press, 1960.
Gibson, Charles, ed. *The Black Legend: Anti-Spanish Attitudes in the Old World and the New*. New York: Alfred A. Knopf, 1971.
Gillingham, Paul. *Unrevolutionary Mexico: The Birth of a Strange Dictatorship*. New Haven, CT: Yale University Press, 2021.
Gillingham, Paul and Benjamin T. Smith, eds. *Dictablanda Politics, Work, and Culture in Mexico, 1938–1968*. Durham, NC: Duke University Press, 2014.
Gillingham, Paul, Michael Lettieri, and Benjamin T. Smith, eds. *Journalism, Satire, and Censorship in Mexico*. Albuquerque: University of New Mexico Press, 2018.
Gilly, Adolfo. *El cardenismo: una utopía mexicana*. Mexico City: Cal y Arena, 1994.
Gilly, Adolfo and Rhina Roux, eds. *Cartas a Cuauhtémoc Cárdenas*. Mexico City: Ediciones Era, 1989.
Gómez Caballero, Alma. *Barzonistas: el palpitar de un corazón colectivo, el barzón Chihuahua*. Mexico City: Consejo Nacional para la Cultura y las Artes, 2002.
Gómez Galvarriato, Aurora. *Industry and Revolution: Social and Economic Change in the Orizaba Valley, Mexico*. Cambridge, MA: Harvard University Press, 2013.
 'Myth and Reality of Company Stores during the Porfiriato: The *tiendas de raya* of Orizaba's Textile Mills.' Working Paper 317. Mexico City: Centro de Investigación y Docencia Económicas, 2005.
Gómez Gordoa, José. *Títulos de Crédito*. Mexico City: Porrúa, 2013 [1988].
González Cosío, Arturo. 'Clases y estratos sociales.' In *Mexico: cincuenta años de revolución. II: La vida social*, edited by Julio Duran Ochoa et al., 31–77. Mexico City: Fondo de Cultura Economica, 1961.
Goodchild, Philip. *Credit and Faith*. London: Rowman & Littlefield, 2020.
Goux, Jean-Joseph. 'Cash, Check, or Charge?' In *New Economic Criticism: Studies at the Intersection of Literature and Economics*, edited by Martha Woodmansee and Mark Osteen, 114–127. New York: Routledge, 1999.
Graeber, David. *Debt: The First 5,000 Years*. Brooklyn: Melville House, 2011.
Granados, Luis Fernando. 'Cosmopolitan Indians and Mesoamerican Barrios in Bourbon Mexico City: Tribute, Community, Family and Work in 1800.' PhD thesis, Georgetown University, 2008.
Green, Stuart P. 'Lying, Misleading, and Falsely Denying: How Moral Concepts Inform the Law of Perjury, Fraud, and False Statements.' *The Hastings Law Journal* 53, no. 1 (2001): 157–212.
Greif, Avner. 'Institutions and Impersonal Exchange: From Communal to Individual Responsibility.' *Journal of Institutional and Theoretical Economics* 158, no. 1 (2002): 168–204.
Groebner, Valentin. *Who Are You?: Identification, Deception, and Surveillance in Early Modern Europe*. Brooklyn: Zone Books, 2007.
Guardino, Peter. *The Time of Liberty: Popular Political Culture in Oaxaca, 1750–1850*. Durham, NC: Duke University Press, 2005.
Guerra, François-Xavier. *Modernidad e independencias: Ensayos sobre las revoluciones hispánicas*. Mexico City: Fondo de Cultura Económica, 1993.

Guillory, John. 'The Sokal Affair and the History of Criticism.' *Critical Inquiry* 28, no. 2 (2002): 470–508.
Haber, Stephen. 'Mexico's Experiments with Bank Privatization and Liberalization, 1991–2003.' *Journal of Banking & Finance* 29, nos. 8–9 (2005): 2325–2353.
Haber, Stephen H., Noel Maurer, and Armando Razo. *The Politics of Property Rights: Political Instability, Credible Commitments, and Economic Growth in Mexico, 1876–1929.* Cambridge: Cambridge University Press, 2003.
Han, Clara. *Life in Debt: Times of Care and Violence in Neoliberal Chile.* Berkeley: University of California Press, 2012.
Hansen, Per H. 'From Finance Capitalism to Financialization: A Cultural and Narrative Perspective on 150 Years of Financial History.' *Enterprise & Society* 15, no. 4 (2014): 605–642.
Hansson, Sven Ove. 'Risk.' In *The Stanford Encyclopedia of Philosophy*, edited by Edward N. Zalta and Uri Nodelman (Fall 2018 Edition) [online].
Harris, Jose. 'General Introduction.' In *Tönnies: Community and Civil Society*, edited by Jose Harris, ix–xxx. Cambridge: Cambridge University Press, 2001.
  'Glossary.' In *Tönnies: Community and Civil Society*, edited by Jose Harris, xli–xliv. Cambridge: Cambridge University Press, 2001.
Harvey, David. *The New Imperialism.* Oxford: Oxford University Press, 2005.
Hay, Douglas. 'Property, Authority and the Criminal Law.' In *Albion's Fatal Tree: Crime and Society in Eighteenth-Century England*, edited by Douglas Hay et al., 17–63. Harmondsworth: Penguin Books.
Heeg, Susanne, Maria Verónica Ibarra García, and Luis Alberto Salinas Arreortua. 'Financialization of Housing in Mexico: The Case of Cuautitlan Izcalli and Huehuetoca in the Metropolitan Region of Mexico City.' *Housing Policy Debate* 30, no. 4 (2020): 512–532.
Heredia Vázquez, Horacio. *Usura: serie decisiones relevantes de la Suprema Corte de Justicia de la Nación.* Mexico City: Suprema Corte de Justicia de la Nación and Instituto de Investigaciones Jurídicas, 2018.
Hernández Elizondo, César. 'Propietarios, especuladores y renta petrolera en las regiones del Golfo de México (1900–1926).' *Sotavento* 5 (1998–1999): 33–66.
Herzog, Tamar. *La administración como un fenómeno social: la justicia penal de la Ciudad de Quito, 1650–1750.* Madrid: Centro de Estudios Constitucionales, 1995.
  Defining Nations: Immigrants and Citizens in Early Modern Spain and Spanish America. New Haven, CT: Yale University Press, 2003.
  'Merchants and Citizens: On the Making and Un-Making of Merchants in Early Modern Spain and Spanish America.' *Journal of European Economic History* 42, no. 1 (2013): 137–163.
Ho, Peter. 'An Endogenous Theory of Property Rights: Opening the Black Box of Institutions.' *Journal of Peasant Studies* 43, no. 6 (2016): 1121–1144.
Hodes, Martha. 'Fractions and Fictions in the United States Census of 1890.' In *Haunted by Empire: Geographies of Intimacy in North American History*, edited by Ann Stoler, 240–270. Durham, NC: Duke University Press, 2006.
Hoffman, Philip T., Gilles Postel-Vinay, and Jean-Laurent Rosenthal. 'Information and Economic History: How the Credit Market in Old

Regime Paris Forces Us to Rethink the Transition to Capitalism.' *The American Historical Review* 104, no. 1 (1999): 69–94.

'Private Credit Markets in Paris, 1690–1840.' *Journal of Economic History* 52, no. 2 (1992): 293–306.

Huerta González, Arturo. *El debate del Fobaproa: orígenes y consecuencias del 'rescate bancario'*. Mexico City: Editorial Diana, 1999.

Husz, Orsi. 'Bank Identity: Banks, ID Cards, and the Emergence of a Financial Identification Society in Sweden.' *Enterprise & Society* 19, no. 2 (2018): 391–429.

'Comment les salariés suédois sont devenus des consommateurs de produits financiers: l'expérience des "comptes chèques salariaux" dans les années 1950 et 1960.' *Critique internationale* 69, no. 4 (2015): 99–118.

Ibarra, David. 'México: Plan y coyuntura.' *Revista de la CEPAL* 58 (1996): 115–127.

Isenberg, Arnold. 'Deontology and the Ethics of Lying.' In *Aesthetics and Theory of Criticism: Selected Essays of Arnold Isenberg*, edited by Isenberg William Callaghan, 245–264. Chicago: University of Chicago Press, 1973.

James, Timothy. 'Lay Magistrates and the Administration of Justice in Mexico City, 1840s–50s.' Paper presented at the Annual Meeting of the Conference on Latin American History at the American Historical Association, Chicago, January 2019.

Jaremski, Mathew and Gabriel Mathy. 'Una mirada retrospectiva la era del cheque personal en América, 1800–1960.' *Revista de la Historia de la Economica y de la Empresa* 11 (2017): 41–74.

Joseph, Gilbert M. *Revolution from Without: Yucatán, Mexico, and the United States, 1880–1924*. Cambridge: Cambridge University Press, 1982.

Joseph, Gilbert M. and Daniel Nugent, eds. *Everyday Forms of State Formation: Revolution and the Negotiation of Rule in Modern Mexico*. Durham, NC: Duke University Press, 1994.

Joseph, Gilbert M. and Jürgen Buchenau. *Mexico's Once and Future Revolution: Social Upheaval and the Challenge of Rule since the Late Nineteenth Century*. Durham, NC: Duke University Press, 2013.

Kagan, Richard L. *Spain in America: The Origins of Hispanism in the United States*. Urbana: University of Illinois Press, 2002.

Karon, Paul. 'Law and Popular Credit in Mexico.' *Arizona Journal of International and Comparative Law* 1, no. 1 (1982): 88–121.

Kenzer, Robert C. 'The Black Businessman in the Postwar South: North Carolina, 1865–1880.' *Business History Review* 63, no. 1 (1989): 61–87.

Kerridge, Eric. *Usury, Interest and the Reformation*. Aldershot: Ashgate, 2002.

Klein, Herbert S. 'The Demographic Structure of Mexico City in 1811.' *Journal of Urban History* 23, no. 1 (1996): 66–93.

Knight, Alan. 'Cardenismo: Juggernaut or Jalopy?' *Journal of Latin American Studies* 26, no. 1 (1994): 73–107.

'Subalterns, Signifiers, and Statistics: Perspectives on Mexican Historiography.' *Latin American Research Review* 37, no. 2 (2002): 136–158.

Koyama, Mark. 'Evading the "Taint of Usury": The Usury Prohibition as a Barrier to Entry.' *Explorations in Economic History* 47, no. 4 (2010): 420–442.

Kuntz Ficker, Sandra. 'De las reformas liberales a la gran depression, 1856–1929.' In *Historia económica general de México: de la colonia a nuestros días*, edited by Sandra Kuntz Ficker, 305–352. Mexico City: El Colegio de Mexico, 2010.

— 'Introducción.' In *Historia económica general de México: de la colonia a nuestros días*, edited by Sandra Kuntz Ficker, 13–38. Mexico City: Colegio de Mexico, 2010.

Kuri-Aldana, Mario and Mendoza Martínez Vicente. *Cancionero popular mexicano*. Mexico City: Consejo Nacional para la Cultura y las Artes, 1996.

Lai, Karen. 'Financialization of Everyday Life.' In *The New Oxford Handbook of Economic Geography*, edited by Gordon L. Clark, Maryann Feldman, Meric S. Gertler, and Dariusz Wójcik, 611–627. Oxford: Oxford University Press, 2018.

Langbein, John. 'Albion's Fatal Flaws.' *Past & Present* 98 (1983): 96–120.

Lauer, Josh. *Creditworthy: A History of Consumer Surveillance and Financial Identity in America*. New York: Columbia University Press, 2017.

— 'From Rumor to Written Record: Credit Reporting and the Invention of Financial Identity in Nineteenth-Century America.' *Technology and Culture* 49, no. 2 (2008): 301–324.

Lauer, Josh and Kenneth Lipartito, eds. *Surveillance Capitalism in America*. Philadelphia: University of Pennsylvania Press, 2021.

Lavinas, Lena. *The Takeover of Social Policy by Financialization: The Brazilian Paradox*. New York: Palgrave Macmillan, 2017.

Lazzarato, Maurizio. *The Making of the Indebted Man: An Essay on the Neoliberal Condition*, translated by Joshua David Jordan. South Pasadena: Semiotext(e), 2012.

Lear, John. 'Mexico City: Space and Class in the Porfirian Capital, 1884–1910.' *Journal of Urban History* 22, no. 4 (1996): 454–492.

Le Goff, Jacques. *Your Money or Your Life: Economy and Religion in the Middle Ages*. New York: Zone Books, 2004.

Le Roy Ladurie, Emmanuel. 'Motionless History.' *Social Science History* 1, no. 2 (1977): 115–136.

— *The Peasants of Languedoc*. Urbana: University of Illinois Press, 1974.

Levy, Juliette. 'Una cuestión de intereses: Entre Benito, Maximiliano y Porfirio. Una reforma liberal y la liberación de tasas de interés en Yucatán, 1850–1900.' *America Latina en la Historia Económica* 19, no. 1 (2012): 157–177.

— *The Making of the Market: Credit, Henequen and Notaries in Yucatán 1850–1900*. University Park: Pennsylvania State University Press, 2012.

Lex, Alexander, Nils Gehlenborg, Hendrik Strobelt, Romain Vuillemot, and Hanspeter Pfister. 'UpSet: Visualization of Intersecting Sets.' *IEEE Transactions on Visualization and Computer Graphics* 20, no. 12 (2014): 1983–1992.

Licona Vite, Cecilia. *Usura: la lesión en los contratos*. Mexico City: Porrúa, 2008.

Linebaugh, Peter. *The London Hanged: Crime and Civil Society in the Eighteenth Century*. Cambridge: Cambridge University Press, 1992.

'(Marxist) Social History and (Conservative) Legal History: A Reply to Professor Langbein.' *New York University Law Review* 60, no. 2 (1985): 212–243.

Lira González, Andrés. *Comunidades indígenas frente a la ciudad de México: Tenochtitlan y Tlatelolco, sus Pueblos y Barrios, 1812–1919*. Zamora: Colegio de México, 1983.

Lizama Silva, Gladys. 'Los capitales zamoranos a principios del siglo XX.' *Historia mexicana* 39, no. 4 (1990): 1029–1061.

Loaeza, Soledad. *El Partido Acción Nacional, la larga marcha, 1939–1994: oposición leal y partido de protesta*. Mexico City: Fondo de Cultura Económica, 1999.

López González, Georgina. *La organización para la administración de la justicia ordinaria en el segundo imperio: modernidad institucional y continuidad jurídica en México*. Mexico City: Colegio de México, 2014.

Lunt, Peter K. and Sonia M. Livingstone. 'Everyday Explanations for Personal Debt: A Network Approach.' *British Journal of Social Psychology* 30, no. 4 (1991): 309–323.

Lurtz, Casey. *From the Grounds Up: Building an Export Economy in Southern Mexico*. Stanford, CA: Stanford University Press, 2019.

Lustig, Nora. 'The Mexican Peso Crisis: The Foreseeable and the Surprise.' Brookings Discussion Papers in International Economics 114. Washington, DC: Bookings Institution, 1995.

MacLachlan, Colin M. *Spain's Empire in the New World: The Role of Ideas in Institutional and Social Change*. Berkeley: University of California Press, 1988.

Madison, James H. 'The Evolution of Commercial Credit Reporting Agencies in Nineteenth-Century America.' *Business History Review* 48, no. 2 (1974): 164–186.

Mallon, Florencia E. *Peasant and Nation: The Making of Postcolonial Mexico and Peru*. Berkeley: University of California Press, 1995.

Marichal, Carlos. *Bankruptcy of Empire: Mexican Silver and the Wars between Spain, Britain, and France, 1760–1810*. Cambridge: Cambridge University Press, 2010.

Márquez, Graciela. 'Evolución y estructura del PIB, 1921–2010.' In *Historia económica general de México: de la colonia a nuestros días*, edited by Sandra Kuntz Ficker, 549–572. Mexico City: Colegio de Mexico, 2010.

Martin, Randy. *Financialization of Daily Life*. Philadelphia: Temple University Press, 2002.

Martínez López-Cano, María del Pilar. *El crédito a largo plazo en el siglo XVI: Ciudad de México, 1550–1620*. Mexico City: Universidad Nacional Autónoma de México, 1995.

'Usuras.' Research Paper Series 2020-01. Frankfurt: Max Planck Institute for European Legal History, 2019.

Marx, Karl. 'Comments on James Mill' [1844]. In *Marx and Engels: Collected Works by Karl Marx and Frederick Engels*, translated by Richard Dixon, vol. 3, 211–228. New York: International Publishers, 1975.

Masino, Serena and Miguel Niño-Zarazúa. 'Improving Financial Inclusion through the Delivery of Cash Transfer Programmes: The Case of Mexico's Progresa-Oportunidades-Prospera Programme.' *Journal of Development Studies* 56, no. 1 (2020): 151–168.
Masur, Louis P. '"Age of the First Person Singular": The Vocabulary of the Self in New England, 1780–1850.' *Journal of American Studies* 25, no. 2 (1991): 189–211.
Maurer, Bill. 'Foreword: Friction and Fantasies of the Cashless Future.' In *The Book of Payments: Historical and Contemporary Views on the Cashless Society*, edited by Bernardo Bátiz-Lazo and Leonidas Efthymiou, v–vii. London: Palgrave Macmillan.
Maurer, Noel. *The Power and the Money: The Mexican Financial System, 1876–1932*. Stanford, CA: Stanford University Press, 2002.
Mauss, Marcel. *The Gift: Forms and Functions of Exchange in Archaic Societies*, translated by Ian Cunnison. Glencoe: Free Press, 1954.
McAndrews, James and William Roberds. 'A General Equilibrium Analysis of Check Float.' *Journal of Financial Intermediation* 8, no. 4 (1999): 353–377.
McCaa, Robert. 'Missing Millions: The Demographic Costs of the Mexican Revolution.' *Mexican Studies* 19, no. 2 (2003): 367–400.
  'Peopling of 19th Century Mexico: Critical Scrutiny of a Censured Century.' In *Statistical Abstract of Latin America*, edited by James Wilkie et al., 603–633. Los Angeles: University of California Press, 1993.
McCants, Anne. 'Editor's Introduction to 40th Anniversary Issue: History and the Social Sciences: Past Imperfect; Future Promising.' *Social Science History* 40, no. 4 (2016): 525–534.
Merrill, Thomas W. and Henry E. Smith. 'The Property/Contract Interface.' *Columbia Law Review* 101, no. 4 (2001): 773–852.
Merges, Robert P. 'A Transactional View of Property Rights.' *Berkeley Technology Law Journal* 20, no. 4 (2005): 1477–1520.
Messmacher, Miguel and Alejandro Werner. 'Inflación en México: 1950–2000.' *Gaceta de Economía* (2002): 19–60 [special issue].
Mijangos y González, Pablo. *Historia mínima de la suprema corte de justicia de México*. Mexico City: El Colegio de México, 2019.
  El nuevo pasado jurídico mexicano: una revisión de la historiografía jurídica mexicana durante los últimos 20 años. Madrid: Universidad Carlos III de Madrid, 2011.
Monsiváis, Carlos. *Los rituales del caos*. Mexico City: Ediciones Era, 1995.
Moreno, Julio. *Yankee, Don't Go Home!: Mexican Nationalism, American Business Culture, and the Shaping of Modern Mexico, 1920–1950*. Chapel Hill: University of North Carolina Press, 2003.
Moreno-Brid, Juan Carlos and Jaime Ros. *Development and Growth in the Mexican Economy: A Historical Perspective*. Oxford: Oxford University Press, 2009.
Morris, Julian, ed. *Rethinking Risk and the Precautionary Principle*. Oxford: Butterworth-Heinemann, 2000.
Mottier, Nicole. 'Moneylending in Myth and Practice in Twentieth-Century Mexico.' *Mexican Studies* 34, no. 2 (2018): 143–164.

Msemburi, William, Ariel Karlinsky, Victoria Knutson, Serge Aleshin-Guendel, Somnath Chatterji, and Jon Wakefield. 'The WHO Estimates of Excess Mortality Associated with the COVID-19 Pandemic.' *Nature* 613, no. 7942 (2023): 130–137.

Muldrew, Craig. *The Economy of Obligation: The Culture of Credit and Social Relations in Early Modern England*. New York: St Martin's Press, 1998.

Murphy, Lucy Eldersveld. 'Business Ladies: Midwestern Women and Enterprise, 1850–1880.' *Journal of Women's History* 3, no. 1 (1991): 65–89.

Murphy, Sharon Ann. *Investing in Life: Insurance in Antebellum America*. Baltimore: Johns Hopkins University Press, 2010.

Musacchio, Aldo. 'Mexico's Financial Crisis of 1994–1995.' Harvard Business School Working Paper 12-101. Cambridge, MA: Harvard University, 2011.

Negrín, José Luis. 'Mecanismos para compartir información crediticia: evidencia internacional y la experiencia mexicana.' *Trimestre económico* 68, no. 271 (2001): 405–466.

Negrín, José Luis and Clara de la Cerda. 'Evolución de la calidad de los usuarios de tarjetas de crédito en México: un enfoque microeconómico.' Serie Documentos de Investigación. Mexico City: Banco de México, Dirección General de Investigación Económica, 2002.

Nelson, O. D. 'Credit Scoring: Outlook for the 80s.' *The Credit World* 67, no. 5 (1979): 34–37.

Newton, Lucy. 'Trust and Virtue in English Banking: The Assessment of Borrowers by Bank Managements at the Turn of the Nineteenth Century.' *Financial History Review* 7, no. 2 (2000): 177–199.

Nietzsche, Friedrich Wilhelm. *On the Genealogy of Morals: A Polemic: By Way of Clarification and Supplement to My Last Book, Beyond Good and Evil*, translated by Douglas Smith. Oxford: Oxford University Press, 1996.

North, Douglass C. *Institutions, Institutional Change, and Economic Performance*. Cambridge: Cambridge University Press, 1990.

Ochoa, Enrique. *Feeding Mexico: The Political Uses of Food Since 1910*. Wilmington, DE: Scholarly Resources, 2002.

Ocko, Jonathan K. 'The Missing Metaphor: Applying Western Legal Scholarship to the Study of Contract and Property in Early Modern China.' In *Contract and Property in Early Modern China*, edited by Madeleine Zelin, Jonathan K. Ocko, and Robert Gardella, 178–205. Stanford, CA: Stanford University Press, 2004.

O'Hara, Matthew D. *The History of the Future in Colonial Mexico*. New Haven, CT: Yale University Press, 2018.

Olegario, Rowena. *A Culture of Credit: Embedding Trust and Transparency in American Business*. Cambridge, MA: Harvard University Press, 2006.

  The Engine of Enterprise: Credit in America. Cambridge, MA: Harvard University Press, 2016.

Owensby, Brian P. *Empire of Law and Indian Justice in Colonial Mexico*. Stanford, CA: Stanford University Press, 2008.

Padilla, Tanalís. *Rural Resistance in the Land of Zapata: The Jaramillista Movement and the Myth of the Pax-Priísta 1940–1962*. Durham, NC: Duke University Press, 2009.

Unintended Lessons of Revolution: Student Teachers and Political Radicalism in Twentieth-Century Mexico. Durham, NC: Duke University Press, 2021.
Padilla, Tanalís and Louise E. Walker, eds. 'Spy Reports: Content, Methodology and Historiography in Mexico's Secret Police Archive.' *Journal of Iberian and Latin American Research* 19, no. 1 (2013): 1–102.
Palacios, Guillermo. 'Introducción: entre una "nueva historia" y una "nueva historiografía" para la historia política de América Latina en el siglo XIX.' In *Ensayos sobre la nueva historia política de América Latina, siglo XIX*, edited by Guillermo Palacios, 9–18. Mexico City: Colegio de México, 2007.
Palti, Elias. 'Narrar lo inenarrable: literatura, nación y muerte en "El fistol del diablo" de Manuel Payno.' *Iberoamericana* 5, no. 19 (2005): 7–26.
Parker, Susan and Petra Todd. 'Conditional Cash Transfers: The Case of Progresa/Oportunidades.' *Journal of Economic Literature* 55, no. 3 (2017): 866–915.
Patiño, Luis. 'El Fondo de Vivienda del Instituto de Seguridad y Servicios Sociales de los Trabajadores del Estado (Fovissste).' In *Entre el estdo y el mercado: La vivienda en el México de hoy*, edited by René Coulomb and Martha Schteingart, 279–317. Mexico City: Universidad Autonoma Metropolitana, 2006.
Paz, Octavio. 'The Other Mexico.' In *The Labyrinth of Solitude and Other Writings*, 213–325. New York: Grove Press, 1985 [1970].
Peebles, Gustav. 'The Anthropology of Credit and Debt.' *Annual Review of Anthropology* 39, no. 1 (2010): 225–240.
Pellandini-Simányi, Léna. 'The Financialization of Everyday Life.' In *The Routledge Handbook of Critical Finance Studies*, edited by Christian Borch and Robert Wosnitzer, 278–299. London: Routledge, 2020.
Pellandini-Simányi, Léna, Ferenc Hammer, and Zsuzsanna Vargha. 'The Financialization of Everyday Life or the Domestication of Finance? How Mortgages Engage with Borrowers' Temporal Horizons, Relationships and Rationality in Hungary.' *Cultural Studies* 29, nos. 5–6 (2015): 733–759.
Pensado, Jaime M. *Rebel Mexico: Student Unrest and Authoritarian Political Culture During the Long Sixties*. Stanford, CA: Stanford University Press, 2013.
Pensado, Jaime and Erique Ochoa, eds. *México Beyond 1968: Revolutionaries, Radicals, and Repression During the Global Sixties and Subversive Seventies*. Tucson: University of Arizona Press, 2018.
Pérez Herrero, Pedro. *Plata y libranzas: La articulación comercial del México borbónico*. Mexico City: El Colegio de México, 1988.
Perez Reyna, Paulina. 'Auteurs on Netflix: A Reception Study of Roma (Alfonso Cuarón, 2018).' Masters' thesis, Department of Media and Communication, University of Oslo, 2019.
Pérez Toledo, Sonia. *Los hijos del trabajo: los artesanos de aa Ciudad de México, 1780–1853*. Mexico City: El Colegio de México, 1996.
Pérez Toledo, Sonia and Herbert S. Klein. 'Estructura social de la ciudad de México en 1842.' In *Población y estructura urbana en México, siglos XVIII y XIX*, edited by Carmen Blázquez Dominguez, Carlos Contreras Cruz, and Sonia Pérez Toledo, 251–275. Xalapa: Universidad Veracruzana, 1996.

Población y estructura social de la Ciudad de México, 1790–1842. Mexico City: Universidad Autónoma Metropolitana Iztapalapa, 2004.

Piccato, Pablo. *City of Suspects: Crime in Mexico City, 1900–1931.* Durham, NC: Duke University Press, 2001.

The Tyranny of Opinion: Honor in the Construction of the Mexican Public Sphere. Durham, NC: Duke University Press, 2010.

Polanyi, Karl. *The Great Transformation: The Political and Economic Origins of Our Time.* Boston, MA: Beacon Press, 2001 [1944].

Poon, Martha. 'Scorecards as Devices for Consumer Credit: The Case of Fair, Isaac & Company Incorporated.' *The Sociological Review* 55, no. S2 (2007): 284–306.

Premo, Bianca. *The Enlightenment on Trial: Ordinary Litigants and Colonialism in the Spanish Empire.* New York: Oxford University Press, 2017.

Premo, Bianca and Yanna Yannakakis. 'A Court of Sticks and Branches: Indian Jurisdiction in Colonial Mexico and Beyond.' *The American Historical Review* 124, no. 1 (2019): 28–55.

Propp, V. Y. *Morphology of the Folktale.* 2nd edition, revised and edited with a preface by Louis A. Wagner and a new introduction by Alan Dundes. Austin: University of Texas Press, 1968 [1928].

Pugliese, María Rosa. 'La prisión por deudas en el Río de La Plata a finales del período hispánico.' *Anales de la Universidad de Chile* 20 (1989): 425–472.

Pulido Esteva, Diego. 'Después del alcalde de barrio: experiencias policiales en la Ciudad de México (1824–1861).' *Nuevo mundo, mundos nuevos* (2017): 1–18.

Quinn, Stephen and William Roberds. 'The Evolution of the Check as a Means of Payment: A Historical Survey.' *Economic Review* 93, no. 4 (2008): 1–28.

Quiroz, Enriqueta. 'La moneda menuda en la circulación monetaria de la ciudad de México, siglo XVIII.' *Mexican Studies/Estudios Mexicanos* 22, no. 2 (2006): 219–249.

Ramos Escandón, Carmen. *Industrialización, género y trabajo femenino en el sector textil mexicano: El obraje, la fábrica y La Compañía Industrial.* Mexico City: Centro de Investigaciones y Estudios Superiores en Antropología Social, 2005.

Ramos Vázquez, Isabel. 'Detenciones cautelares, coactivas o punitivas: la privación de libertad en el derecho castellano como instrumento jurídico.' *Anuario de Historia del Derecho Español* 77 (2007): 707–770.

Randall, Alan. *Risk and Precaution.* Cambridge: Cambridge University Press, 2011.

Reagan, Andrew J., Lewis Mitchell, Dilan Kiley, Christopher M Danforth, and Peter Sheridan Dodds. 'The Emotional Arcs of Stories Are Dominated by Six Basic Shapes.' *EPJ Data Science* 5, no. 1 (2016): 1–12.

Ristow, Colby. *A Revolution Unfinished: The Chegomista Rebellion and the Limits of Revolutionary Democracy in Juchitán, Oaxaca.* Lincoln: University of Nebraska Press, 2018.

Ródriguez Gómez, M. Guadalupe. 'Making a Globalized Nation in the Countryside: El Barzón, a Popular Movement in Contemporary Mexico.' *Urban Anthropology and Studies of Cultural Systems and World Economic Development* 27, no. 2 (1998): 197–232.

Rodríguez Kuri, Ariel. *La experiencia olvidada: el ayuntamiento de México: política y gobierno, 1876–1912*. Mexico City: El Colegio de México, 1996.
Romano, Ruggiero. *Moneda, seudomonedas y circulación monetaria en las economías de México*. Mexico City: El Colegio de Mexico, 1998.
Romero Sotelo, María Eugenia. 'Los secretarios de Hacienda a debate: Alberto J. Pani contra Luis Montes de Oca, Eduardo Suárez y Ramón Beteta.' *Economía UNAM* 16, no. 48 (2019): 66–97.
Rosa, Richard. 'Finance and Literature in Nineteenth-Century Spanish America.' *PMLA* 127, no. 1 (2012): 137–144.
Rose, Carol M. 'Canons of Property Talk, or, Blackstone's Anxiety.' *The Yale Law Journal* 108, no. 3 (1998): 601–632.
Rosen, Fred. 'The $55 Billion Bank-Bailout Scandal.' *NACLA Report on the Americas* 32, no. 3 (1998): 11–14.
Roy, H. J. H. 'Why Credit Scoring.' *Burroughs Clearing House* 56, no. 7 (1972): 27, 55–60.
Ruiz, Claudia. 'From Pawn Shops to Banks: The Impact of Formal Credit on Informal Households.' Policy Research Working Paper 6634. Washington, DC: Development Research Group, World Bank, 2013.
Sábato, Hilda. *Republics of the New World: The Revolutionary Political Experiment in Nineteenth-Century Latin America*. Princeton, NJ: Princeton University Press, 2018.
Salvucci, Richard J. *Politics, Markets, and Mexico's 'London Debt', 1823–1887*. New York: Cambridge University Press, 2009.
Samperio, Ana Cristina. *Se nos reventó el barzón: radiografía del movimiento barzonista*. Mexico City: Edivisión, 1996.
Samuel, Raphael, 'What Is Social History?' *History Today* 35, no. 3 (1985): 34–38.
Sánchez-Arcilla Bernal, José. *Jueces, criminalidad y control social en la Ciudad de México a finales del siglo XVIII*. Madrid: Dykinson, 2016.
Sánchez Michel, Valeria. *Usos y funcionamiento de la cárcel novohispana: El caso de la Real Cárcel de Corte a finales del siglo XVIII*. Mexico City: El Colegio de México, 2008.
Sánchez Santiró, Ernest. 'La población de la Ciudad de México en 1777.' *Secuencia: Revista de historia y ciencias sociales* 60 (2004): 31–56.
Sanders, Nichole. *Gender and Welfare in Mexico: The Consolidation of a Postrevolutionary State*. University Park: Pennsylvania State University Press, 2011.
Sandoval, Adriana. 'La figura del diablo en algunos textos y en El fistol del diablo.' *Literatura mexicana* 22 no. 1 (2011): 119–142.
Santiago Aparicio, Eliud and David García González. 'La guerra de guerrillas: un arma de dos filos en la Guerra de 1847. Documentos del Tribunal Superior de Justicia, Distrito Federal.' *Signos Históricos* 16, no. 32 (2014): 184–195.
Scardaville, Michael Charles. 'Crime and the Urban Poor: Mexico City in the Late Colonial Period.' PhD thesis, University of Florida, 1977.
Scardaville, Michael C. '(Hapsburg) Law and (Bourbon) Order: State Authority, Popular Unrest, and the Criminal Justice System in Bourbon Mexico City.' *The Americas* 50, no. 4 (1994): 501–525.

'Justice by Paperwork: A Day in the Life of a Court Scribe in Bourbon Mexico City.' *Journal of Social History* 36, no. 4 (2003): 979–1007.
Schaefer, Timo H. *Liberalism as Utopia: The Rise and Fall of Legal Rule in Post-Colonial Mexico, 1820–1900.* Cambridge: Cambridge University Press, 2017.
Schiller, Jerome P. 'Just Men and Just Acts in Plato's Republic.' *Journal of the History of Philosophy* 6, no. 1 (1968): 1–14.
Schteingart, Martha and Boris Graizbord. *Vivienda y vida urbana en la Ciudad de México: La acción del Infonavit.* Mexico City: El Colegio de México, 1998.
Schwartz, Stuart B. *Slaves, Peasants, and Rebels: Reconsidering Brazilian Slavery.* Urbana: University of Illinois Press, 1992.
Scott, James C. *Seeing Like a State: How Certain Schemes to Improve the Human Condition Have Failed.* New Haven, CT: Yale University Press, 1998.
Sellers-García, Sylvia. 'Walking While Indian, Walking While Black: Policing in a Colonial City.' *The American Historical Review* 126, no. 2 (2020): 455–480.
Semo, Enrique. *The History of Capitalism in Mexico: Its Origins, 1521–1763.* Austin: University of Texas Press, 1993.
Sen, Tinni, Turk McCleskey, and Atin Basuchoudhary. 'When Good Little Debts Went Bad: Civil Litigation on the Virginia Frontier, 1745–1755.' *Journal of Interdisciplinary History* 46, no. 1 (2015): 60–89.
Servín, Elisa. *Ruptura y oposición: el movimiento henriquista, 1945–1954.* Mexico City: Cal y Arena, 2001.
Shaw, Frederick John. 'Poverty and Politics in Mexico City, 1824–1854.' PhD thesis, University of Florida, 1975.
Shelton, Laura. *For Tranquility and Order: Family and Community on Mexico's Northern Frontier, 1800–1850.* Tucson: University of Arizona Press, 2010.
Shiller, Robert J. 'Narrative Economics.' *The American Economic Review* 107, no. 4 (2017): 967–1004.
Sicking, Louis and Alain A. Wijffels, eds. *Conflict Management in the Mediterranean and the Atlantic, 1000–1800: Actors, Institutions and Strategies of Dispute Settlement.* Leiden: Brill and Nijhoff, 2020.
Solís Rosales, Ricardo, ed. *Del Fobaproa al IPAB: testimonios, análisis y propuestas.* Mexico City: Plaza y Valdés Editores, 2000.
Solow, Robert M. 'Economic History and Economics.' *The American Economic Review* 75, no. 2 (1985): 328–331.
Sotelo Inclán, Jesús. *Raíz y razón de Zapata, Anenecuilco.* Mexico City: Editorial Etnos, 1943.
Spallanzani, M. 'A Note on Florentine Banking in the Renaissance: Orders of Payment and Cheques.' *Journal of European Economic History* 7, no. 1 (1978): 145–168.
Speckman Guerra, Elisa. *Crimen y castigo: legislación penal, interpretaciones de la criminalidad y administración de justicia, Ciudad de México, 1872–1910.* Mexico City: El Colegio de México, 2002.
Spellman, Susan V. 'Trust Brokers: Traveling Grocery Salesmen and Confidence in Nineteenth-Century Trade.' *Enterprise & Society* 13, no. 2 (2012): 276–312.
Spiegelhalter, David. *The Art of Statistics: How to Learn from Data.* New York: Basic Books, 2019.

Sunstein, Cass R. *Laws of Fear: Beyond the Precautionary Principle.* Cambridge: Cambridge University Press, 2005.
Szmrecsanyi, Tamás and Steven Topik. 'Business History in Latin America.' *Enterprise & Society* 5, no. 2 (2004): 179–186.
Taylor, James. 'White-Collar Crime and the Law in Nineteenth-Century Britain.' *Business History*, 60, no. 3 (2018): 343–360.
Taylor, William B. *Fugitive Freedom: The Improbable Lives of Two Impostors in Late Colonial Mexico.* Oakland: University of California Press, 2021.
Teitelbaum, Vanesa. 'Sectores populares y "delitos leves" en la ciudad de México a mediados del siglo XIX.' *Historia Mexicana* 55, no. 4 (2006): 1221–1287.
Tenorio-Trillo, Mauricio and Aurora Gomez Galvarriato. *El Porfiriato.* Mexico City: Centro de Investigación y Docencia Económica, 2006.
Thompson, E. P. 'The Moral Economy of the English Crowd in the Eighteenth Century.' *Past & Present* 50 (1971): 76–136.
 Whigs and Hunters: The Origin of the Black Act. New York: Pantheon Books, 1976.
Tomás y Valiente, Francisco. 'La prisión por deudas en los derechos castellano y aragonés.' *Anuario de Historia del Derecho Español* 30 (1960): 248–489.
Tomich, Dale. 'The Order of Historical Time: The *Longue Durée* and Micro-History.' In *The Longue Durée and World-Systems Analysis,* edited by Richard E. Lee, 9–34. Albany: State University of New York Press, 2012.
Tönnies, Ferdinand. *Tönnies: Community and Civil Society,* translated by Margaret Hollis and edited by Jose Harris. Cambridge: Cambridge University Press, 2001.
Trivellato, Francesca. *The Familiarity of Strangers: The Sephardic Diaspora, Livorno, and Cross-Cultural Trade in the Early Modern Period.* New Haven, CT: Yale University Press, 2009.
Tulchinsky, Gerald. '"Said to Be a Very Honest Jew": The R. G. Dun Credit Reports and Jewish Business Activity in Mid-19th Century Montreal.' *Urban History Review* 18, no. 3 (1990): 200–209.
Tutino, John. *The Mexican Heartland: How Communities Shaped Capitalism, a Nation, and World History, 1500–2000.* Princeton, NJ: Princeton University Press, 2017.
 'The Revolution in Mexican Independence: Insurgency and the Renegotiation of Property, Production, and Patriarchy in the Bajío, 1800–1855.' *The Hispanic American Historical Review* 78, no. 3 (1998): 367–418.
Vickers, Daniel. 'Errors Expected: The Culture of Credit in Rural New England, 1750–1800.' *Economic History Review* 63, no. 4 (2010): 1032–1057.
Vinson III, Ben. *Before Mestizaje: The Frontiers of Race and Caste in Colonial Mexico.* New York: Cambridge University Press, 2018.
Vonnegut, Kurt. *Palm Sunday: An Autobiographical Collage.* New York: Dell, 1984.
von Wobeser, Gisela. *El crédito eclesiástico en la nueva españa, siglo XVIII.* Mexico City: Universidad Nacional Autónoma de México, 1994.
 'Mecanismos crediticios en la Nueva Espana: el uso del censo consignativo.' *Mexican Studies* 5, no. 1 (1989): 1–23.

Walker, David W. *Kinship, Business, and Politics: The Martínez del Río Family in Mexico, 1824–1867*. Austin: University of Texas Press, 1986.

Walker, Juliet E. K. 'Racism, Slavery, and Free Enterprise: Black Entrepreneurship in the United States before the Civil War.' *Business History Review* 60, no. 3 (1986): 343–382.

Walker, Louise E. 'Everyday Economic Justice: Mediating Small Claims in Mexico City, 1813–1863.' *The American Historical Review* 128, no. 1 (2023): 120–143.

Waking from the Dream: Mexico's Middle Classes after 1968. Stanford, CA: Stanford University Press, 2013.

Warren, Richard A. *Vagrants and Citizens: Politics and the Masses in Mexico City from Colony to Republic*. Lanham: Rowman & Littlefield, 2007.

Wasserman, Mark. *Pesos and Politics: Business, Elites, Foreigners, and Government in Mexico, 1854–1940*. Stanford, CA: Stanford University Press, 2015.

Weinstein, Barbara. *The Amazon Rubber Boom, 1850–1920*. Stanford, CA: Stanford University Press, 1983.

Wheaton, Carla. '"The Trade in This Place Is in a Very Critical State": R. G. Dun & Company and the St. John's Business Community, 1855–1874.' *Acadiensis* 29, no. 2 (2000): 120–137.

White, Hayden V. *The Content of the Form: Narrative Discourse and Historical Representation*. Baltimore: Johns Hopkins University Press, 1987.

White, Luise. 'Telling More: Lies, Secrets, and History.' *History and Theory* 39, no. 4 (2000): 11–22.

Wilkie, James W. and Paul D. Wilkins. 'Quantifying the Class Structure of Mexico, 1895–1970.' In *Statistical Abstract of Latin America* 21, 578–590. Los Angeles: UCLA Latin American Institute, 1981.

Williams, Heather L. *Social Movements and Economic Transition: Markets and Distributive Conflict in Mexico*. Cambridge: Cambridge University Press, 2001.

Womack, John. *Zapata and the Mexican Revolution*. New York: Vintage House, 1970.

Wood, Ellen Meiksins. *The Origin of Capitalism: A Longer View*. London: Verso, 2002.

Wyatt-Brown, Bertram. 'God and Dun & Bradstreet: 1841–1851.' *Business History Review* XL, no. 4 (1966): 432–450.

Yannakakis, Yanna. 'Indigenous People and Legal Culture in Spanish America.' *History Compass* 11, no. 11 (2013): 931–947.

Since Time Immemorial: Native Custom and Law in Colonial Mexico. Durham, NC: Duke University Press, 2023.

Zagorin, Perez. *Ways of Lying: Dissimulation, Persecution, and Conformity in Early Modern Europe*. Cambridge, MA: Harvard University Press, 1990.

Zamora-Pierce, Jesús. *El Fraude*. Mexico City: Porrúa, 2008 [1992].

Zelin, Madeline, Jonathan Ocko, and Robert Gardella. 'Introduction.' In *Contract and Property in Early Modern China*, edited by Madeline Zelin, Jonathan Ocko, and Robert Gardella, 1–13. CA: Stanford University Press, 2004.

Zelizer, Viviana A. *The Social Meaning of Money*. New York: Basic Books, 1994.

Zuboff, Shoshana. 'Big Other: Surveillance Capitalism and the Prospects of an Information Civilization.' *Journal of Information Technology* 30, no. 1 (2015): 75–89.

Index

Abecilla, Francisco, 39
Adair, Jemmifer, 173
Adam, Francisco, 69–70, 89, 97
Adelman, Jeremy, 47, 50
Aguilar, Luisa, 20, 27, 32–33, 47, 52
Aguirre y Salazar, Ángel, 119
alcaldes, 21
   constitucionales, 20, 30, 51
   del barrio, 30
Alexander, Anna, 118
Alfonsín, Raúl, 173
Alfonso X, 54, 89, 97
algorithms, 8, 184, 190
Amado, Luciano, 35
Amigos de País, 22
amortisation period, 33–34, 38, 41, 45
anatocism, 191
ancien régime, 22, 50, 53, 60, 89
Andino, Leopoldo, 113, 117–118
annual salaries, 75
archival collections, 4, 9, 13–14, 213
Aristotle, 54
Arnaiz, Vicente, 83
arrest records, 4, 11, 14, 18, 172
Arrom, Silvia, 25, 75
artisans, 24–25, 48, 55, 76, 111
   imprisonment of, 13, 56, 91
assets
   concealing, 9, 14, 18, 104
   houses as, 188
   seizure of, 218
   valuation of, 72
Atención Ciudadanía, 193–194

Auritec, 192
austerity measures, 178
Ayala, Félix, 64
Ayme, Louis H., 99
Azipreste, Francisco, 38
Azuceno, José Rufino, 77

bad cheques
   analysis of, 172
   and financial honour, 137
   as fraud, 94, 138, 157
   as guarantees, 18
   as property crime, 138
   as risk, 134
   as symbols of prosperity, 146
   bank efforts to reduce, 153
   cancelled account, 137–138, 141, 149–150, 163
   cheque amounts, 155
   coercion to write, 163, 215
   consequences of writing, 135
   criminalisation of, 5, 18, 135–141, 157, 164
   deliberate use of, 134, 151
   endorsed, 161, 163
   false signatures, 153
   frequency of, 149
   gender differences, 154–155
   history of, 166
   insufficient funds, 13, 135, 137–138, 140–141, 145–147, 149–151, 154, 157–158, 165–166
   newspaper coverage of, 166

bad cheques (cont.)
    on non-existent accounts, 161
    penalties for, 4, 11, 14, 135–136, 138–140, 155, 157–158, 162, 164–167, 215, 218
    reasons for writing, 135, 138, 140, 149
    repeat offenders, 160
    rubber cheques, 151
Banamex, 17, 99–100, 120, 136, 154, 191
    credit reports used by, 107
    evaluating creditworthiness, 111
    and financial exclusion, 107–111
    official status of, 101
    post-revolution changes, 122
    use of credit reports by, 101, 104
Banca Serfin, 200
Banco de Industria y Comercio, 159
Banco de Londres México, 161
Banco de México, 153, 178, 206
Banco de Oriente, 161
Banco de Pequeño Comercio, 143
Banco Industrial y Agrícola, 143
Banco Nacional de México, *See* Banamex
Bancomer, 187, 190, 192, 204, 211
Bancomext, 184
Banerjee, Abhijit, 62
bank accounts, 18, 147, 151, 153, 161, 215
    cancelled, 137, 150
    entitlement payments through, 177, 215
    financialisation of, 215
bankers
    automation and, 156
    bad cheques and, 137, 157–158
    and the debtor/creditor relationship, 18, 133
    finance as goal of, 176
    fraudulent, 179, 209, 211
    looting of banks by, 179
    power of, 136–137, 157, 166
    property rights for, 122, 138
    protection of, 18, 136, 138
    rules benefitting, 165
    Swedish, 157
banking industry
    automation of, 156
    banking laws, 136–137, 157, 165
    citizens' participation in, 141, 143, 147
    citizens' problems with, 186, 199
    and the credit economy, 177, 179, 184
    credit reports used by, 100–102, 107
    crisis (1994 and 1995), 169, 179

    economic citizenship and, 13
    financial capitalism and, 136
    government bailouts, 179–180
    misbehaviour of, 191
    modern system, 124, 136
    modernisation of, 33, 98, 214
    nationalisation of, 178
    privatisation of, 169, 176, 178
    protection for, 174
    redesign of banks, 143
    revolution's effect on, 120
    in Sweden, 157
    uncovered cheques and, 137, 149, 153, 157
    women's dealings with, 186, 188
bankruptcy, 32, 56, 84, 90, 174, 181
Barajas Reyes, Enrique, 162
Barnes, José, 161–162
Barrete, Agustín, 78
Barrios, Constantino, 161
Barros, Raúl, 199
Barzón, el 173–174
barzonista movement, 174
Bátiz-Lazo, Bernardo, 153, 156
Bauche, Tito, 148
Beatty, Edward, 60, 70
Becerra Bautista, José, 165
Benavides Reyes, Enrique, 162
Benítez, Manuel, 65
Berghoff, Hartmut, 164
Berti, Francisco, 78
big data, 184
bills of exchange, 139, 144
Biron, Enrique, 77
Black Legend, 27, 29
Black List, 2, 18, 206–212
blacklisting, 180
Bleynat, Ingrid, 11, 60
Bouk, Dan, 104, 184
Bourbons, 30, 48, 51, 91, 164
Boyer, Christopher, 172
Brazilian Amazon, 189
Breeskin, Elias, 149
bribes, 45, 79
Brito, José, 42
Builla, Francisco, 35
Burns, Kathryn, 43
Burns, Richard, 95
Burns, Robert, 89
Buró de Crédito, 180
Buseta, María Francisca, 2, 4–5, 10, 12, 17

Cádiz Constitution, 17, 20, 30
capital
    expansion of, 165
    financial, 176
    institutionalisation of, 98
    nationalisation of, 100
capital flight, 179
capitalism
    commercial, 10, 97, 217
    and the credit market, 2, 8, 13, 216
    dehumanisation of, 183
    economic relations and, 10
    expansion of, 12, 216
    financial, 10, 102, 135–136, 138, 143, 148, 151, 157, 165, 217
    high financial, 189
    history of, 155, 164, 218
    industrial, 10, 70, 97, 217
    material culture of, 155
    neoliberal, 169, 176, 189
    property rights and, 165
    shift to, 3
    state-led, 178
    support for, 12
car loans, 179, 215
Cárdenas, Lázaro, 173
Carlos III, 13, 56, 91, 97
Carlos IV, 89
Carrera, Manuel, 83
carta, 35
Castaño, Dolores, 146
caste systems, 29
Castro, Juan, 66–67
Catholic Church, 27, 29, 41
censo, 3
Centeno, Benito, 67
Cerda, Clara de la, 180
Cervantes, Guadalupe, 39
Cervantes, Rafael, 35
cesiones, 59
Céspedes, Adela, 145
Chávez, Daniel, 174
Chávez, Nabor, 70
Cheban brothers, 117
cheques, *See also* bad cheques
    as credit instruments, 135, 137, 139, 143
    as financial instrument, 137, 151
    as guarantees, 139, 150, 156–157, 161–162, 165–166, 215
    as instrument of financial capitalism, 136
    as payment tool, 135
    as symbol of financial modernisation, 136
    blank, 162
    and the consumer economy, 142
    decline of, 156
    endorsed, 161, 163
    and the financialisation process, 137, 169–170, 176, 215
    friction and costs of, 156
    increased use of, 142, 144, 147, 153, 156
    misuse of, 137
    postdated, 5, 139, 165
    reasons for writing, 135
    regulation of, 136, 138
    in Renaissance Florence, 144
    in Sweden, 157
citizen letters, 14, 172, 176
    analysis of, 172, 184, 190–191
    blaming macroeconomics, 199
    blaming personal circumstances, 199
    explanation frequency, 196
    gender variables, 188
    multiple explanation combinations in, 197
    value of amounts in, 186
    writers of, 186
Citizen Service Office, 168–169, 217
citizenship, 50–51
    economic, 4, 13, 18, 55, 95, 135, 141–149, 176–177, 215
    political, 141
City Bank of New York, 136
Civil Code, 29, 81, 159, 165
civil justice, 22, 47
civil litigation, 57, 90–91, 98
civil rights, 51–52
Cline, Howard, 147
Coatsworth, John, 28–30
Código Civil, 89, 92
Código de la Reforma, 81, 96
Código Penal, 93–94, 138
'Colapso Financiero', 181–184
collateral, 46, 71, 90, 157
    character as, 183
    flexible, 4
    home as, 202
colonial rule, 29
Cominsa Factoraje, 192
Comisión Nacional para la Protección y Defensa de los Usuarios de Servicios Financieros, 171
Commercial Code, 29, 56, 81

commercial revolution, 56, 89
communal property, 29
community lands, 22, 164
compound interest, 191
concurso de acreedores, 90
concursos, 59
Condusef, 171–172, 178, 194, 202, 207, 217
    letters routed to, 176, 188, 192–193, 209–212
confirmation bias, 16
constitutionalism, 20, 30, 50
consumer credit, 169–170, 180
consumer economy, 142, 176
consumer rights, 169–171
contract fraud, 93
contract law, 9, 56, 80, 89, 97, 217
    agreements regarding, 81
    changes in, 81
    property rights and, 80
contract rights, 2, 56, 190
contracts
    broken, 54, 71–72
    fairness in, 201, 217
    legal backing of, 56
    sale, 94
    between strangers, 55
    terms for voiding, 8
    voiding, 95
contractual society, 4, 21–24
convent of San Lorenzo, 38
Cornejo, Bernardo, 119
corporate collections departments, 4
corporate privileges, 21–22, 29
corporate property, 5
corporate rights, 21–22
Corte, María Gertrudes, 35
credit
    access to, 180
    commercial, 56
    consumption, 56
    moral economy of, 7
    new rules for, 165
    non-bank, 6
    positive connotations of, 7, 13
Credit Bureau, 18, 180, 184, 190
    and the Black List, 206–211
credit card companies, 171, 177
credit cards, 5, 136, 156, 167, 170, 179–180, 189, 215
credit economy, 1, 18, 100, 176–177, 184, 215
    blacklisting from, 180
    capitalist, 8, 13
    changes in, 5
    decline in availability, 180
    exclusion from, 4, 18, 100, 189, 214
    expansion of, 2, 4, 179, 215
    financial institutions and, 181
    growth of, 12
    inclusion in, 215–216
    lending at interest and, 12
    urban small-scale, 13
credit institutions, 101, 189
credit instruments, 33, 35, 136, 167, 176
    cheques as, 135, 137, 139, 143
    disputes involving, 32, 36
    negotiability of, 162
    new types of, 3
    regulation of, 136
credit market
    capitalist, 2–3, 12, 177, 215
    exclusion from, 182
    institutional lenders and, 133
    malfunctions of, 4
    participation in, 66
    privatised banks and, 178
    tightening of, 180
credit ratings, 84, 106
credit reports, 2, 4, 8, 11, 14, 18, 84, 100, 102–104, 107, 153, 172, 214
    as stories, 191
    gender disparity in, 154
    trust and, 100–107, 133
    used by Banamex, 107
credit scores, 7–8, 180, 189, 207
credit transactions, 8, 33, 99
creditors
    advantages for, 214
    as villains, 200
    committing fraud, 93
    conflicts with debtors, 13, 17, 41, 52, 89
    debtors as, 34
    disputes with debtors, 84
    exploitation of debtors by, 170
    gender of, 9
    institutional, 176
    landlords, 37
    laws favoring, 157
    liberalism and, 213
    power balance with debtors, 6, 56, 169, 214
    power of, 137, 215

power struggle with debtors, 10, 12,
    16–17, 54, 82, 164, 177, 180, 213,
    216–218
property rights of, 29
protection of, 92
protecton of debtors from, 171
rapacious, 96
relationships with debtors, 9, 13, 18, 33,
    54–55, 70, 82, 102, 135, 137, 139,
    155, 165, 176, 215, 218
religious institutions, 3, 5, 100
rights of, 6, 81
risks of, 71
rules for, 96
vulnerability of, 82–83, 96
worries about debtors, 91
credit-rating agencies, 63, 98–99, 102, 104,
    138, 183, 214, 216
    American, 184
creditworthiness
    assessment of, 18, 100, 107, 109, 184
    calculation of, 103
    criteria for, 100
    deterrents to, 124
    evaluation of, 111–120, 123
    influence on behaviour, 104
    rumour and, 132
crimes, *See also* bad cheques
    debt, 48
    deceit, 93
    economic, 164
    against honour, 41
    of falsehood, 94
    minor, 200
    property, 5–6, 12, 94, 138, 200
    violent, 47
    slander or mistreatment,
        20, 23, 40–41
    social history of, 164
    white-collar, 139, 158, 164
Cuellar, Josefa, 35, 37

Darbells, Apolinario, 42
data analysis, 184
data doubles, 104
Dávalos, Federico G., 123
de la Torre, José Pablo, 68
debt conflicts, 6, 47, 214, *See also juicios
    verbales*
debt imprisonment, 81, 89–91, 96–97, 139,
    164–165, 213, 215

debt litigation
    causes of, 214
    evidence in, 66
    increase in, 55–61, 71, 97, 213
    in *juicios verbales*, 97
    legal options, 75, 90
debtors
    absentee, 96
    accused of fraud, 215
    advantages for, 214
    as creditors, 34
    as victims, 211–212
    avoiding obligations, 83
    committing fraud, 93
    conflicts with creditors, 13, 17, 41, 52, 89
    creditors' worries about, 91
    delinquent, 96
    disappearance of, 92
    disputes with creditors, 84
    exploitation by creditors, 170
    gender of, 9
    liberalism and, 213
    power balance with creditors, 6, 56, 169,
        214
    power struggle with creditors, 10, 12, 16–17,
        54, 82, 164, 177, 180, 213, 216–218
    property of, 76–82
    protection of, 95, 170, 174
    relationships with creditors, 9, 13, 18, 33,
        54–55, 70, 82, 102, 135, 137, 139,
        155, 165, 176, 215, 218
    rights of, 6, 81
    risks of, 71
    rules for, 96
    tenants, 37
    vanishing, 71
    vulnerability of, 82–83, 96, 215, 217
    women as, 15
debts, *See also* indebtedness; unpaid debts
    amounts owed, 9
    attitudes toward, 99, 111
    civil, 5, 13, 56, 91
    conversion of, 174
    failure to pay, 190–191, 200
    household, 180
    moral economy of, 7
    negative aspects of, 180
    negative connotations of, 7
    of ordinary people, 216
    profit from, 133
    reasons for, 9

debts, (cont.)
  social life of, 155
  sovereign, 180
  unpaid, 11, 13
  value of, 137
debt-to-income ratio, 176
dehumanisation, 183–184
Delmotte, Florencia, 86–87
depósito irregular, 3
Díaz, Donoso, 162
Díaz, Estevan, 38
Díaz, Porfirio, 81, 101, 164–165, 174
diplomatic reports, 14
domestic servants, 24, 55
Donoso, Eloy, 162
Dun & Bradstreet Company, 103
Dun, Robert Graham, 103
Duviard, Emiliano, 86

ecclesiastic institutions, 81
ecclesiastic jurisdictions, 90
ecclesiastic law, 20
ecclesiastic property, 5, 41, 80, 100
Echeverría, Luis, 170–171
economic freedom, 4, 81, 91, 95–97
economic information, 8, 214, *See also* credit reports
  content and form of, 9
  gossip as, 131–133
economic justice
  access to, 10
  Cádiz liberalism and, 17, 20–21
  changes in, 12, 19, 218
  in contracts and disputes, 217
  for creditors, 214
  efficiency of, 17, 59, 214
  everyday, 23, 38, 49, 52
  for everyday people, 12, 27, 30, 51–52, 214
  failure of, 46
  for foreigners, 43
  gender dynamics in, 39, 154
  guilt in, 205
  and Hispanic liberalism, 50
  importance of, 170, 217
  and the law, 217
  moralism and, 205
  new ideas about, 167
  parameters of, 39–46
  understanding of, 200
  and unpaid debts, 7
  variables in, 72
  versus redistributive justice, 7
elections, 142
  municipal, 21
Elektra, 17, 170, 195
Elisalde, Manuel, 35, 37
embargo de bienes, 90
embargos, 36, 58, 86
Emerson, Ralph Waldo, 50
Enlightenment ideology, 22
entitlement payments, 177, 215
entity plaintiffs, 41
escribano, 23
Esnaurrizar, Miguel, 69
Espinosa, Juan, 53
Espinosa, Ventura, 20, 27, 32–33, 47, 52
eviction, 37–39, 46
exchange rates, 173, 179
exploitation, 7, 81–82, 96, 137, 141, 165, 169–170, 202, 212, 215–217
Exposición del Código Civil, 92

Facebook profiles, 184
fairness, 2–3, 7, 21, 42, 44, 46, 52, 55, 59, 93–94, 96–97, 164, 180, 189, 196, 200–201, 212–213, 217–218
  economic, 19, 95
  gender, 4, 24, 32, 41
  justice and, 9
  procedural, 39
  substantive, 39
Fajardo Cabo y Compañía, 69
Ferdinand VII, 21
Ferguson, James, 189
Fernandes, Felipe, 34
Fernández, Bertha, 159–160
Ferrary, Florimundo, 86
feudalism, 3, 97, 218
FICO scores, 184
film industry, 143, 145
financial exclusion
  Banamex and, 107–111
  of women, 101
financial inclusion and economic citizenship, 141–149
financial institutions, 136
  capitalist, 216
financial instruments, 5, 169, 176, 215
  misuse of, 12, 217, *See also* bad cheques; cheques; credit reports

modern, 153
new types of, 18
financialisation, 18, 138, 141, 157, 169, 215
  of bank accounts, 215
  coercion of, 153–165
  of everyday life, 136
  shift to, 136
Fisher, Alfredo, 160
Flores Flores, Graciela, 30–31, 44, 46
Fobaproa, 178–179
forced labour systems, 47
foreclosures, 175, 187
Fovissste, 175
Fox, Vicente, 168, 173, 184, 194
  letters to, 2, 12, 14, 19, 168–169, 172–173, 175, 184, 187–188, 190, 192–197, 200, 202, 204–205, 209–212
Francois, Marie, 6
fraud, 18, 82, 89, 91, 93, 96, 151, 164
  bad cheques as, 138, 165–166
  blaming for economic woes, 196
  contract, 93
  defined, 93–94
  financial, 158
  penalties for, 94, 138
  property, 94

García, Esther, 168–169, 175
García, Isaías, 152
García, Nicolás, 192
García Cubas, Antonio, 59
García Ramírez, Sergio, 166
Gayosso, Antonio, 85
Gayosso, Luz Salamanca de, 85
Gaytán, Alejandro, 85
gender bias, 39, 41
gender fairness, 4, 24, 32, 41
gender variables, 9, 25–26, 39–41, 44, 47, 65, 72, 76, 79, 83, 87, 106, 108, 111, 136, 140, 149, 154, 160, 186, 188
Gilly, Adolfo, 172
Girard, Tomas, 35
global commodity chains, 47
globalisation, 174
Gómez, León, 65
Gómez, Pedro, 193–194
Gómez Bolaños, Roberto, 135
Gómez Gordoa, José, 137
González Cosío, Arturo, 147
González, Ángel, 68

González, Eusebio, 117
González, Gregorio, 53
González, Jorge, 195
Gonzalez, Luis, 85
gossip, 53, 55, 61–63, 65–66, 77, 88, 103, 119, 125, 131
  as economic information, 2, 8, 131–133
  as financial information, 100, 132
Granados, Luis, 24
Groebner, Valentin, 84
guarantors, 46, 68–70, 90
  vanishing, 71
Guerra, François-Xavier, 4, 22
Guzmán, Joaquin, 38

Haber, Stephen, 178–179
Habsburgs, 48, 51
Hansen, Per, 136
Heeser, Agustín, 77–78
hegemony, 12, 49, 142, 216
Hermana trinquete, La (film), 134–135, 167
Hernández, Diego Castillo, 29
Hernández, Florencio, 68
hombres buenos, 23
honour
  bad checks and, 137
  crimes against, 41
  in debt and credit relationships, 124
  determination of, 130
  economic, 7, 63, 101, 124–131, 135, 206
  fairness and, 2, 7
  intellectual and legal understandings of, 63
  justice and, 7, 209
  political legitimacy and, 7
  reputation and, 55, 63
Huerta, Silvia Escanilla, 21
human rights, 173
Husz, Orsi, 157
Huve, Federico, 42
hyperinflation, 120

Iberia, 4
  mediaeval, 4, 10, 52, 54, 56, 81–82, 97, 146, 213, 218
identification technologies, 84
import substitution, 138, 142, 171
imprisonment, *See also* debt imprisonment
  for broken contracts, 54
  of artisans, 13, 56, 91
Inco, 175
indebtedness, 180–189

indigenous people
  dispossession of, 22
  historical analysis, 81
  as litigants, 49
  property of, 5, 80
indigenous property, 5
individual rights, 4, 21, 50
individualism, 4, 22
industrialisation, 59–60, 138, 142, 171
  in Britain, 164
inflation, 147, 174, 177–178
  hyperinflation, 120
information technologies, 8, 98, 100, 102, 104
injurias leves, 23, 40
instalment payments, 36, 204
institutional revolution, 29, 81
insurance, 103, 118, 120, 193–194
interest rates, 95, 171, 178–180, 200,
    See also usury
  in the USA, 179
International Monetary Fund (IMF), 178–179
Inverlat Finance Group, 175
investors
  domestic, 136
  foreign, 101, 136, 179
  property rights of, 29, 82, 122
  rights of, 6
IOUs, 32–33, 36, 139

J. M. Bradstreet & Son Company, 103
James, Timothy, 45
Jiménez, Hilario, 53–54, 56, 59–61, 77, 80, 89, 97
Juárez, Benito, 96–97
juicios conciliatorios, 30
juicios diversos, 50
juicios verbales
  analysis of, 30, 155
  compared to *providencias precautorias*, 72
  decreasing amounts of, 25
  economic justice in, 30, 38, 43, 52
  examples of, 20, 38, 43, 62
  fairness in, 41–42, 46
  gender differences, 48, 108, 160
  gender dynamics in, 39
  mediating debt disputes in, 18, 21–22, 30, 32–39, 46–47, 50–52, 59, 97
  in Mexico City, 25, 33
  numbers of, 56, 97
  numbers of litigants, 24, 49
  property rights and, 27, 31–32

records of, 22, 25, 43, 50, 71, 140, 154
role of magistrates, 17, 23, 34, 36, 40, 52, 57, 71
salary disputes, 42–44
tradition of, 46, 51, 71
just prices, 8, 89, 94
just profits, 8, 94–95
justice, *See also* economic justice
  civil, 22, 47
  fairness and, 9
  ground-level, 20, 48, 52
  Habsburg notions of, 48
  history of, 10, 19
  honour and, 7, 209
  legal, 135
  for Mexicans, 209
  in the modern world, 213
  narrow definition of, 44
  Platonic, 7
  procedural, 12
  redistributive, 7
  social, 172
  spiritual, 7
  struggle for, 120
  substantive, 12
  temporalities of, 218
  variables in, 160
  vulgar, 7

Kafka, Franz, 190
Kuntz Ficker, Sandra, 59–60

Labasque, Juan, 77
labour protection, 5
labour rights, 120
land ownership, 81, *See also* property rights
  corporate, 80
land reform, 5
land rights, *See* property rights
landlords
  avoiding, 37, 181
  as creditors, 37
  with delinquent tenants, 160
  duplicitous, 160
  institutional, 37, 41
  money owed to, 68, 158
  relationship with tenants, 38
  responsibility of, 38
  sued by tenants, 38–39, 83
  suing tenants, 39
Lanon, Pedro, 77

Lauer, Josh, 103–104, 184
Lavinas, Lena, 176
Lazzarato, Maurizio, 183
legal codes, 14, 17, 51, 55, 98, 139, 165, 203, 217
  early modern, 54
  Iberian, 10, 56
  liberal, 215
  mediaeval, 54
  Mexican, 202
  republican, 54
  usury in, 201
legal conflicts, 17, 51, 55, 59, 89, 218
legal history, 10, 80–81, 88, 97, 140
legal pluralism, 91
lenders, *See* creditors
lending
  federal, 101
  institutional, 120–124
lending at interest, 12
León de la Barra, Francisco, 123
León, Gil Mariano, 115
León, Manuel, 114
Le Roy Ladurie, Emmanuel, 11
letras de cambio, 139
Levy, Juliette, 6, 96
Ley General de Títulos y Operaciones de Crédito, 138, 160, 166
Ley Juárez, 80
Ley Lerdo, 80
liberal reform, 80
liberalism, 13, 213
  Cádiz, 17, 21–22, 24, 30, 32, 47, 52,
  colonial, 10
  Hispanic, 50
  modern, 4
  nineteenth-century, 51
libranza, 78
Libros de Juicios Verbales, 23, 50
Libros de Reos (Books of Criminals), 47
Lira, Andrés, 22
loan restructuring, 180
longue durée, 10–12, 52, 81, 155, 216, 218
López Portillo, José, 178
Lozano, Javier, 195
Lozano, Juan, 78
Luna, Carlota, 78–79

macroeconomic crisis, 175, 177, 179, 181, 189–190
macroeconomic freedom, 96

macroeconomic shocks, 169–170
Madero family, 114
Madero, Evaristo, 114–115
Madero, Francisco I., 114
Madrid, Miguel de la, 178
magistrates
  annual books of, 23
  appointed, 21, 49
  and economic justice, 50, 59
  elected, 2, 17, 20–22, 24–25, 27, 46, 49–50, 52, 62
  enforcing rulings, 46
  fairness of, 48
  favoring creditors, 32, 214
  favoring debtors, 38, 214
  geographical distribution of, 30
  hearing conflicts between people, 2, 17, 20, 22–25, 27, 31–32, 37, 39–40, 42, 44, 51–52, 62, 99, 214, 218
  hearing *juicios verbales*, 32, 34, 40, 57, 71, 97
  postponing cases, 33, 36
  role of, 21, 23, 40, 48, 52
  selection of, 44
  unfavorable views of, 45, 50
market economy, 39, 165, 211
Marx, Karl, 183–184
Marxism, 6
Masio, Serena, 177
mass consumption, 141
Maurer, Noel, 101, 120, 136
Maximilian, 96
McCaa, Robert, 120
medium enterprises, 18, 55–56, 66, 68–69, 76, 97, 102, 104, 111, 117, 131, 133, 144, 146, 174, 184, 214–215
Mejía Dávalos, Carlos Felipe, 166
Mendiola, Rafael, 35
Mercantile Agency, 102–104, 183
mercantilism, 3, 10, 97, 216, 218
Mexican miracle, 142–144, 167
Mexican Revolution, 5, 120, 165
Mexico
  1857 Constitution, 60, 80
  1917 Constitution, 5, 120, 165
  civil war, 5
  economic downturn in, 177
  elections in, 142
  financialisation in, 136, 138, 141, 157, 169–170, 215
  and the global economy, 3

Mexico (cont.)
  instability in, 179
  modernisation of, 101
  one-party rule of, 142
  recession in, 179
  transition to democracy, 173
Mexico City
  debt litigation in, 59
  demographic history of, 24
  economic life in, 30
  judicial structure of, 57
  low currency supply in, 33
  macroeconomic crisis, 25
  municipal elections in, 49
  municipal reforms, 48
  population growth, 61
  small claims cases, 29
  transition from traditional to modern economy, 59
  urban economy of, 24
Mexico City Archive, 139
Mexico City Poor House, 75
micro businesses, 174
middle classes, 143, 146, 177
  and consumer credit, 180
  credit ratings and, 216
  income range, 147
  indebtedness of, 181–182
  using financial products, 215
  writing bad cheques, 148
military law, 20
Milton, Nadia, 166
Mining Code, 29, 81
Miranda, José María, 35
modernisation
  economic, 60, 101
  financial, 136, 142, 156, 158, 164, 167
modernity financial, 18, 105, 149–153, 157
Montes de Oca, Francisco, 130–131
Montes de Oca, José Nicolás, 53–54, 56–57, 59–60, 76–77, 80, 87, 89, 97
Montes, Soledad, 69, 89, 97
moral economy, 39, 212
  changes in, 135, 141, 164, 166
  of credit and debt, 7
  debtor–creditor relationship, 217
  of peasant movements, 7
Morali, José Luis, 78
mortgages, 168–171, 175, 179, 187, 189, 191–192, 215

motionless history, 11
Muldrew, Craig, 66
Multibanco Comermex, 175
mutual aid societies, 118

narrative economics, 189–191
national debt, 178
nationalisation
  of banks, 178
  of capital, 100
  of ecclesiastic property, 100
Navarro, Ángel, 63, 66
Negrín, José Luis, 180
neoliberalism, 13, 178
New Institutional Economics, 29
New Spain, 3–4, 8, 12, 33, 43, 47, 49, 52–53, 75, 90, 95, 164, 201, 213
  early modern, 97
Niño-Zarazúa, Miguel, 177
Novísima Recopilación, 89–90, 95

O'Hara, Matthew, 3, 22, 47
obligaciónes, 34–35
oil boom, 178
Olivér, Paulino, 34
opportunity, 3, 7, 82, 96, 206, 212, 214, 216
Ordenanza de 1782, 30
Oropeza, Ignacio, 35

pagarés, 23, 139, 151, See also IOUs
Palomino, Diego, 145–146, 151
Palti, Elías, 45
Pando, Andrés, 36
Partido Revolucionario Institucional (PRI), 142
pawnshops, 6
Payno, Manuel, 45
Paz, Octavio, 143
Peraire y Compañía, 77–78
Pérez, Rodrigo, 162
Pérez, Rosa, 107–108
Pérez de Castro, Mariano, 20
Peru, 3
Picazo, Antonio, 63, 65–66
Piccato, Pablo, 63
Pinal, Silvia, 135
Plato, 7, 218
political history, 4, 10, 13, 62, 79
political rights, 51
popular sovereignty, 50
populism, 141

Index

positivism, 63
Poulet y Mier, Cristóbal, 53, 80
poverty
  combatting, 177
  feminisation of, 39
precautionary principle, 75
private enterprises, 29, 171
private property, 60, 164, See also property rights
  incorporeal, 63
privatisation, 169, 178
  of banks, 169, 178, 209
  of community lands, 80, 164
  neoliberal model of, 171
procedural justice, 12
Procuraduría Federal del Consumidor, 170
Profeco, 170–171, 175, 178, 193
Progresa, 177
promissory notes, 32
property crimes, 5–6, 12, 94, 138, 200
property fraud, 94
property law, 89
property rights, 2, 5–6, 9, 21, 29, 59–60, 86, 97, 120, 138, 164, 190, 200, See also land ownership
  archaic, 27
  colonial-era, 5
  of creditors and investors, 82
  defence of, 27
  history of, 5
  of investors, 122
  and land reform, 5
  politics of, 76–82
  protection of, 17, 32
  violations of, 122
property seizure, 76–82, 90, 96
property sequestration, 4, 53–54, 80, 89, 214
  fraudulent, 86
  pre-emptive, 91
  protection from, 92
prosopography, 11
providencias precautorias
  as advantage to creditors, 17, 79, 82, 87, 90–91, 100
  analysis of, 58, 62, 66–67, 72, 75, 80, 155
  compared to *juicios verbales*, 72
  creditors' use of, 55
  debtors and, 18, 82, 104
  deception and fraud in, 82
  examples of, 63, 66–70, 78, 80, 83, 86–87

  filing of, 53
  financial value of disputes, 72
  gender differences, 108, 154
  in New Spain, 75
  need for, 65
  procedure for, 57
  and property rights, 81
  records of, 54, 57–58, 71, 140, 154
  resolution of, 76–77
  risk and uncertainty in, 71–76
  rumour and gossip in, 63
  withdrawal of, 79

qualitative analysis, 15–16, 155
quantitative analysis, 15–17, 23, 58, 72, 82, 105, 140, 155, 190, 196
Querétaro lawyers' association, 166

R.G. Dun, 18, 100, 102–104, 180
  evaluations of creditworthiness, 111, 124
  instruction manual, 112, 117–118, 124, 132
  post-revolution changes, 122
Ramírez, Agustín, 70
Ramos, Marco Antonio, 191–192
red books, 102, 105
redistributive justice, 7
Reform War, 60
Reijmolen, Gustavo, 86
rent-seeking, 47
repayment plans, 32, 35, 38, 46, 90
representative government, 22
reputations
  of creditors, 3
  and credit scores, 8
  credit report influence, 118
  damage to, 69–70, 103
  as economic advantage, 124
  economic function of, 61–63, 66, 69
  evaluation of, 100
  fake, 88
  gossip and, 62–63
  honour and, 55, 63, 124
  risk to, 1
  trust based on, 61
Restored Republic, 81
Reyes, Rufina, 67
Rhetoric (Aristotle), 54
Ricardi, Juan Arturo, 36
Río de la Loza, Maximino, 86
risk
  analysis of, 120

risk (cont.)
    appraisal of, 122
    of bad cheques, 160–162
    calculation of, 71
    commodification of, 103
    of creditors and debtors, 71
    evaluation of, 100
    expropriation, 178
    failure to gauge, 10
    mitigation of, 9
    navigation of, 8
    in *providencias precautorias*, 71–76
    quantification of, 103
    technology of, 103
    trust and, 17
Rivera, Felipe, 152, 163
Rivera, José, 163
Rivera, Óscar, 162
Rizo Becerra, Salvador, 151
Roa, Victoriano, 2, 4–5, 17
Robledo, Raquel, 158–160
Romano, Efrén, 2, 4–5, 10, 12, 14, 17, 175, 194
Romano, Irma, 195
Romero, Ernestina, 187, 189–190, 199
Romero, Simón, 162
Romero Gil, José Hilarión, 91
Rotograbados, 145–146
royal decree (1590), 90
Rubli, Fridolin, 86
Rufino Azuceno, José, 77
rumour, 55, 62–63, 65, 77, 88, 100, 131

salary disputes, 42–44
Salazar Benavides, Rosario, 163
Salinas, Carlos, 174, 178
Sánchez, Mónica, 66–67
Sánchez Marmol, Manuel, 119
Sánchez Santiró, Ernest, 60
Scardaville, Michael, 30, 47–48
Scotiabank, 168–169, 175
Scott, Louis H., 99
Seguros Aba, 193
Senicreb, 206
Siete Partidas, 54, 56, 89–90, 92, 94–95, 159, 165
    Seventh, 93
    Third, 91
Silva, Gladys Lizama, 105
slavery systems, 29, 47
Slowitz, Morris, 147, 150–151, 157

small businesses, 18, 24, 29, 55–56, 66, 68–69, 76, 102, 104, 111, 117, 131, 133, 136, 144, 146, 174, 184, 194, 214
small claims, 2, 4–5, 12–14, 21, 214, See also *juicios verbales*
    gender fairness in, 16
    gender and, 40
    in Mexico City, 29, 32
    rent disputes, 37–39, 41
    salary disputes, 42–44
small claims records, 11
social inertia, 10–11, 153–164
social justice, 172
Solís, León, 152, 163
Spallanzani, Marco, 144
Spiekermann, Uwe, 164
spiritual justice, 7
stagecoach travel, 75
statistical analysis, 6, 14–16, 58, 125, 141, 154–155, 190
Stein, Emilia, 149, 151, 155
Strother, David H., 99, 124
structural readjustment programme, 178
structuralism, 190
substantive justice, 12
surveillance, 100, 104
    financial, 88, 104, 180, 184, 206
    new structures of, 84
Szmrecsanyi, Tamás, 27

Tappan, Lewis, 102, 104, 183
Taylor, James, 164
Taylor, William, 8
Teitelbaum, Vanesa, 29, 45
tequila effect, 179
tequilazo, 179, 191
tercerías, 54, 58–59, 84–86, 88
tertulias, 22
Thompson, E.P., 137
Tönnies, Ferdinand, 61
Topik, Steven, 27
trade liberalisation, 171, 176
Trejo, Francisco E., 78–79
Trevi, Gloria, 181–184
Tribunal Superior de Justicia del Distrito Federal, 57
trust
    based on personal relations, 59
    based on reputation, 61
    and the commoditisation of personal information, 8

and the credit report, 133
credit reports and, 100–107, 214
between debtors and creditors, 66, 79
determination of worthiness, 14
economic and, 214
establishment of, 71
and financial institutions, 100
litigation of, 55, 82–88
mechanisms of, 13
need for information, 62
risk and, 17
in small businesses, 68
structures of, 8
trustworthiness
  appraisal of, 66
  gauging, 59
  rating of, 63

underdevelopment, 27, 29–30
unjust profits, 97
unpaid debts, See also debts
  amounts owed, 9
  associated with personal failure, 184
  causes of, 54, 96
  conflicts over, 7, 12–13, 58, 155
  decriminalisation of, 91
  large, 10
  laws concerning, 88–96, 213
  letters about, 11–12, 168
  in the modern world, 1–2
  moral tensions about, 12
  penalties for, 90, 92, 97, 139, 164, 176
  property rights and, 5
  research on, 13–14, 16, 58–59, 66
  resolution of, 97
  rules for, 52, 55, 87–96
  small, 10, 12
  social life of, 157
unskilled laborers, 27
unwritten agreements, 33
urban economy, 24
urbanisation, 59–60
Urodani, Zendor, 42–43

usury, 4, 12, 81, 89, 95, 97
  and the new purgatory, 200–206

Vallejo, Alvina, 38
Vicente, Carmen, 84
Vicente, Francisca, 84
Vicente, Manuel de, 84
Vicente de Eguia, Agustín, 36
viceroyalty of Peru, 21
Vickers, Daniel, 69
Violante, Francisco, 68
Violante, José María, 68
violence
  of capitalist expansion, 165
  against citizens, 142
  domestic, 41
  gender, 44
  modernisation of, 158, 164
  in small claims cases, 152, 163–164
voluntary associations, 22
Vonnegut, Kurt, 190
vulgar justice, 7

Weinstein, Barbara, 189
Welch, E. B., 116–117
welfare state, 171
White, Hayden, 191
White, Luise, 62
Williams, Heather, 173
Winslow, Charles, 111
witness testimony, 53, 57, 63, 65, 67–69, 72, 77–78, 87–88, 140, 152, 159, 163
Wobeser, Gisela von, 3
Wood, Natalie, 166
Wyatt-Brown, Bertram, 102

Yahns, Johanna Wilhelmiene Margarita, 42–43
Yaqui Delta Land & Water Company, 122

Zambian Copperbelt, 189
Zapatistas, 174, 179
Zedillo, Ernesto, 168, 170, 177–178, 193
Zemon Davis, Natalie, 190

CAMBRIDGE LATIN AMERICAN STUDIES
(continued from page ii)

123. *Journey to Indo-América: APRA and the Transnational Politics of Exile, Persecution, and Solidarity, 1918–1945*, Geneviève Dorais
122. *Nationalizing Nature: Iguaza Falls and National Parks at the Brazil–Argentina Border*, Frederico Freitas
121. *Islanders and Empire: Smuggling and Political Defiance in Hispaniola, 1580–1690*, Juan José Ponce-Vázquez
120. *Our Time Is Now: Race and Modernity in Postcolonial Guatemala*, Julie Gibbings
119. *The Sexual Question: A History of Prostitution in Peru, 1850s–1950s*, Paulo Drinot
118. *A Silver River in a Silver World: Dutch Trade in the Rio de la Plata, 1648–1678*, David Freeman
117. *Laboring for the State: Women, Family, and Work in Revolutionary Cuba, 1959–1971*, Rachel Hynson
116. *Violence and the Caste War of Yucatán*, Wolfgang Gabbert
115. *For Christ and Country: Militant Catholic Youth in Post-Revolutionary Mexico*, Robert Weis
114. *The Mexican Mission: Indigenous Reconstruction and Mendicant Enterprise in New Spain, 1521–1600*, Ryan Dominic Crewe
113. *Corruption and Justice in Colonial Mexico, 1650–1755*, Christoph Rosenmüller
112. *Blacks of the Land: Indian Slavery, Settler Society, and the Portuguese Colonial Enterprise in South America*, John M. Monteiro, James Woodward, and Barbara Weinstein
111. *The Street Is Ours: Community, the Car, and the Nature of Public Space in Rio de Janeiro*, Shawn William Miller
110. *Laywomen and the Making of Colonial Catholicism in New Spain, 1630–1790*, Jessica L. Delgado
109. *Urban Slavery in Colonial Mexico: Puebla de los Ángeles, 1531–1706*, Pablo Miguel Sierra Silva
108. *The Mexican Revolution's Wake: The Making of a Political System, 1920–1929*, Sarah Osten
107. *Latin America's Radical Left: Rebellion and Cold War in the Global 1960s*, Aldo Marchesi
106. *Liberalism as Utopia: The Rise and Fall of Legal Rule in Post-Colonial Mexico, 1820–1900*, Timo H. Schaefer
105. *Before Mestizaje: The Frontiers of Race and Caste in Colonial Mexico*, Ben Vinson III
104. *The Lords of Tetzcoco: The Transformation of Indigenous Rule in Postconquest Central Mexico*, Bradley Benton
103. *Theater of a Thousand Wonders: A History of Miraculous Images and Shrines in New Spain*, William B. Taylor
102. *Indian and Slave Royalists in the Age of Revolution*, Marcela Echeverri

101. *Indigenous Elites and Creole Identity in Colonial Mexico, 1500–1800*, Peter Villella
100. *Asian Slaves in Colonial Mexico: From Chinos to Indians*, Tatiana Seijas
99. *Black Saint of the Americas: The Life and Afterlife of Martín de Porres*, Celia Cussen
98. *The Economic History of Latin America since Independence, third edition*, Victor Bulmer-Thomas
97. *The British Textile Trade in South American in the Nineteenth Century*, Manuel Llorca-Jaña
96. *Warfare and Shamanism in Amazonia*, Carlos Fausto
95. *Rebellion on the Amazon: The Cabanagem, Race, and Popular Culture in the North of Brazil, 1798–1840*, Mark Harris
94. *A History of the Khipu*, Galen Brokaw
93. *Politics, Markets, and Mexico's 'London Debt', 1823–1887*, Richard J. Salvucci
92. *The Political Economy of Argentina in the Twentieth Century*, Roberto Cortés Conde
91. *Bankruptcy of Empire: Mexican Silver and the Wars Between Spain, Britain, and France, 1760–1810*, Carlos Marichal
90. *Shadows of Empire: The Indian Nobility of Cusco, 1750–1825*, David T. Garrett
89. *Chile: The Making of a Republic, 1830–1865: Politics and Ideas*, Simon Collier
88. *Deference and Defiance in Monterrey: Workers, Paternalism, and Revolution in Mexico, 1890–1950*, Michael Snodgrass
87. *Andrés Bello: Scholarship and Nation-Building in Nineteenth-Century Latin America*, Ivan Jaksic
86. *Between Revolution and the Ballot Box: The Origins of the Argentine Radical Party in the 1890s*, Paula Alonso
85. *Slavery and the Demographic and Economic History of Minas Gerais, Brazil, 1720–1888*, Laird W. Bergad
84. *The Independence of Spanish America*, Jaime E. Rodríguez
83. *The Rise of Capitalism on the Pampas: The Estancias of Buenos Aires, 1785–1870*, Samuel Amaral
82. *A History of Chile, 1808–2002*, second edition, Simon Collier and William F. Sater
81. *The Revolutionary Mission: American Enterprise in Latin America, 1900–1945*, Thomas F. O'Brien
80. *The Kingdom of Quito, 1690–1830: The State and Regional Development*, Kenneth J. Andrien
79. *The Cuban Slave Market, 1790–1880*, Laird W. Bergad, Fe Iglesias García, and María del Carmen Barcia
78. *Business Interest Groups in Nineteenth-Century Brazil*, Eugene Ridings
77. *The Economic History of Latin America Since Independence*, second edition, Victor Bulmer-Thomas
76. *Power and Violence in the Colonial City: Oruro from the Mining Renaissance to the Rebellion of Tupac Amaru (1740–1782)*, Oscar Cornblit

75. *Colombia Before Independence: Economy, Society and Politics under Bourbon Rule*, Anthony McFarlane
74. *Politics and Urban Growth in Buenos Aires, 1910–1942*, Richard J. Walter
73. *The Central Republic in Mexico, 1835–1846, 'Hombres de Bien' in the Age of Santa Anna*, Michael P. Costeloe
72. *Negotiating Democracy: Politicians and Generals in Uruguay*, Charles Guy Gillespie
71. *Native Society and Disease in Colonial Ecuador*, Suzanne Austin Alchon
70. *The Politics of Memory: Native Historical Interpretation in the Colombian Andes*, Joanne Rappaport
69. *Power and the Ruling Classes in Northeast Brazil, Juazeiro and Petrolina in Transition*, Ronald H. Chilcote
68. *House and Street: The Domestic World of Servants and Masters in Nineteenth-Century Rio de Janeiro*, Sandra Lauderdale Graham
67. *The Demography of Inequality in Brazil*, Charles H. Wood and José Alberto Magno de Carvalho
66. *The Politics of Coalition Rule in Colombia*, Jonathan Hartlyn
65. *South America and the First World War: The Impact of the War on Brazil, Argentina, Peru and Chile*, Bill Albert
64. *Resistance and Integration: Peronism and the Argentine Working Class, 1946–1976*, Daniel James
63. *The Political Economy of Central America Since 1920*, Victor Bulmer-Thomas
62. *A Tropical Belle Epoque: Elite Culture and Society in Turn-of-the-Century Rio de Janeiro*, Jeffrey D. Needell
61. *Ambivalent Conquests: Maya and Spaniard in Yucatan, 1517–1570*, second edition, Inga Clendinnen
60. *Latin America and the Comintern, 1919–1943*, Manuel Caballero
59. *Roots of Insurgency: Mexican Regions, 1750–1824*, Brian R. Hamnett
58. *The Agrarian Question and the Peasant Movement in Colombia: Struggles of the National Peasant Association, 1967–1981*, Leon Zamosc
57. *Catholic Colonialism: A Parish History of Guatemala, 1524–1821*, Adriaan C. van Oss
56. *Pre-Revolutionary Caracas: Politics, Economy, and Society 1777–1811*, P. Michael McKinley
55. *The Mexican Revolution. Volume 2: Counter-Revolution and Reconstruction*, Alan Knight
54. *The Mexican Revolution. Volume 1: Porfirians, Liberals, and Peasants*, Alan Knight
53. *The Province of Buenos Aires and Argentine Politics, 1912–1943*, Richard J. Walter
52. *Sugar Plantations in the Formation of Brazilian Society: Bahia, 1550–1835*, Stuart B. Schwartz
51. *Tobacco on the Periphery: A Case Study in Cuban Labour History, 1860–1958*, Jean Stubbs
50. *Housing, the State, and the Poor: Policy and Practice in Three Latin American Cities*, Alan Gilbert and Peter M. Ward

49. *Unions and Politics in Mexico: The Case of the Automobile Industry*, Ian Roxborough
48. *Miners, Peasants and Entrepreneurs: Regional Development in the Central Highlands of Peru*, Norman Long and Bryan Roberts
47. *Capitalist Development and the Peasant Economy in Peru*, Adolfo Figueroa
46. *Early Latin America: A History of Colonial Spanish America and Brazil*, James Lockhart and Stuart B. Schwartz
45. *Brazil's State-Owned Enterprises: A Case Study of the State as Entrepreneur*, Thomas J. Trebat
44. *Law and Politics in Aztec Texcoco*, Jerome A. Offner
43. *Juan Vicente Gómez and the Oil Companies in Venezuela, 1908–1935*, B. S. McBeth
42. *Revolution from Without: Yucatán, Mexico, and the United States, 1880–1924*, Gilbert M. Joseph
41. *Demographic Collapse: Indian Peru, 1520–1620*, Noble David Cook
40. *Oil and Politics in Latin America: Nationalist Movements and State Companies*, George Philip
39. *The Struggle for Land: A Political Economy of the Pioneer Frontier in Brazil from 1930 to the Present Day*, J. Foweraker
38. *Caudillo and Peasant in the Mexican Revolution*, D. A. Brading, ed.
37. *Odious Commerce: Britain, Spain and the Abolition of the Cuban Slave Trade*, David Murray
36. *Coffee in Colombia, 1850–1970: An Economic, Social and Political History*, Marco Palacios
35. *A Socioeconomic History of Argentina, 1776–1860*, Jonathan C. Brown
34. *From Dessalines to Duvalier: Race, Colour and National Independence in Haiti*, David Nicholls
33. *Modernization in a Mexican Ejido: A Study in Economic Adaptation*, Billie R. DeWalt.
32. *Haciendas and Ranchos in the Mexican Bajío, Léon, 1700–1860*, D. A. Brading
31. *Foreign Immigrants in Early Bourbon Mexico, 1700–1760*, Charles F. Nunn
30. *The Merchants of Buenos Aires, 1778–1810: Family and Commerce*, Susan Migden Socolow
29. *Drought and Irrigation in North-east Brazil*, Anthony L. Hall
28. *Coronelismo: The Municipality and Representative Government in Brazil*, Victor Nunes Leal
27. *A History of the Bolivian Labour Movement, 1848–1971*, Guillermo Lora
26. *Land and Labour in Latin America: Essays on the Development of Agrarian Capitalism in the Nineteenth and Twentieth Centuries*, Kenneth Duncan and Ian Rutledge, eds
25. *Allende's Chile: The Political Economy of the Rise and Fall of the Unidad Popular*, Stefan de Vylder
24. *The Cristero Rebellion: The Mexican People Between Church and State, 1926–1929*, Jean A. Meyer
23. *The African Experience in Spanish America, 1502 to the Present Day*, Leslie B. Rout, Jr.

22. *Letters and People of the Spanish Indies: Sixteenth Century*, James Lockhart and Enrique Otte, eds
21. *Chilean Rural Society from the Spanish Conquest to 1930*, Arnold J. Bauer
20. *Studies in the Colonial History of Spanish America*, Mario Góngora
19. *Politics in Argentina, 1890–1930: The Rise and Fall of Radicalism*, David Rock
18. *Politics, Economics and Society in Argentina in the Revolutionary Period*, Tulio Halperín Donghi
17. *Marriage, Class and Colour in Nineteenth-Century Cuba: A Study of Racial Attitudes and Sexual Values in a Slave Society*, Verena Stolcke
16. *Conflicts and Conspiracies: Brazil and Portugal, 1750–1808*, Kenneth Maxwell
15. *Silver Mining and Society in Colonial Mexico: Zacatecas, 1546–1700*, P. J. Bakewell
14. *A Guide to the Historical Geography of New Spain*, Peter Gerhard
13. *Bolivia: Land, Location and Politics Since 1825*, J. Valerie Fifer, Malcolm Deas, Clifford Smith, and John Street
12. *Politics and Trade in Southern Mexico, 1750–1821*, Brian R. Hamnett
11. *Alienation of Church Wealth in Mexico: Social and Economic Aspects of the Liberal Revolution, 1856–1875*, Jan Bazant
10. *Miners and Merchants in Bourbon Mexico, 1763–1810*, D. A. Brading
9. *An Economic History of Colombia, 1845–1930*, by W. P. McGreevey
8. *Economic Development of Latin America: Historical Background and Contemporary Problems*, Celso Furtado and Suzette Macedo
7. *Regional Economic Development: The River Basin Approach in Mexico*, David Barkin and Timothy King
6. *The Abolition of the Brazilian Slave Trade: Britain, Brazil and the Slave Trade Question, 1807–1869*, Leslie Bethell
5. *Parties and Political Change in Bolivia, 1880–1952*, Herbert S. Klein
4. *Britain and the Onset of Modernization in Brazil, 1850–1914*, Richard Graham
3. *The Mexican Revolution, 1910–1914: The Diplomacy of Anglo-American Conflict*, P. A. R. Calvert
2. *Church Wealth in Mexico: A Study of the 'Juzgado de Capellanias' in the Archbishopric of Mexico 1800–1856*, Michael P. Costeloe
1. *Ideas and Politics of Chilean Independence, 1808–1833*, Simon Collier

For EU product safety concerns, contact us at Calle de José Abascal, 56–1°, 28003 Madrid, Spain or eugpsr@cambridge.org.

www.ingramcontent.com/pod-product-compliance
Ingram Content Group UK Ltd.
Pitfield, Milton Keynes, MK11 3LW, UK
UKHW040736121125
464990UK00013B/394